# Urban Girls

# URBAN Girls

## Resisting Stereotypes, Creating Identities

EDITED BY
Bonnie J. Ross Leadbeater and
Niobe Way

New York University Press
*New York and London*

NEW YORK UNIVERSITY PRESS
New York and London

Copyright © 1996 by New York University

Manufactured in the United States of America

Library of Congress Cataloging-in-Publication Data
Urban girls : resisting stereotypes, creating identities / edited by
Bonnie J. Ross Leadbeater and Niobe Way.
p.   cm.
Includes bibliographical references.
ISBN 0-8147-5107-5 (alk. paper).—ISBN 0-8147-5108-3 (pbk. :
alk. paper)
1. Poor teenagers—United States.   2. Teenage girls—United
States.   3. Urban poor—United States.   4. Minority teenagers—
United States.   I. Leadbeater, Bonnie J. Ross, 1950–      . II. Way,
Niobe, 1963–      .
HV1431.U73   1996
305.23'5'082—dc20              95-50185
                                      CIP

New York University Press books are printed on acid-free paper,
and their binding materials are chosen for strength and durability.

To Monisha and her mother, Tanacia

# Contents

Contents

Contents

# Acknowledgments

Niobe Way's idea that we edit a book about urban adolescent girls was greeted positively by all whom we approached. Some authors who inspired this work were already committed to other efforts to enhance our understanding of adolescent girls and could not participate directly in the current volume. They include Margaret Beale Spencer, Carol Gilligan, Betty Hamburg, and Linda Burton. However, their support of this project encouraged us to keep it alive. The authors who were able to contribute did so generously, and we thank them all.

The project was supported in part by a Junior Faculty Fellowship in the Social Sciences from Yale University and a Faculty Scholars Award from William T. Grant Foundation to Bonnie Leadbeater. We also thank Virginia Knight, Melissa Kuperminc, Sara Buchdahl, Tricia Harmon, and Wendy R. McCusker for help in editing and organizing the manuscript.

# Contributors

J. Lawrence Aber, Ph.D., School of Public Health, Columbia University and The National Center for Children in Poverty, New York, NY.

LaRue Allen, Ph.D., Department of Applied Psychology, School of Education, New York University, New York, NY.

Nancy Apfel, Ph.D., Department of Psychology, Yale University, New Haven, CT.

Ana Mari Cauce, Ph.D., Department of Psychology, University of Washington, Seattle, WA.

Anita B. Davis, M.A., Department of Psychology, University of Illinois at Urbana-Champaign.

Brunilda De León, Ed.D., School and Counseling Psychology Program, University of Massachusetts, Amherst, MA.

Jill Denner, Ph.D., Department of Developmental Psychology, Teachers' College, Columbia University, New York, NY.

Steve Dopkins, Ph.D., Department of Psychiatry, George Washington University, Washington, D.C.

Sumru Erkut, Ph.D., Center for Research on Women, Wellesley College, Wellesley, MA.

Jacqueline P. Fields, Ph.D., Center for Research on Women, Wellesley College, Wellesley, MA.

Michelle Fine, Ph.D., Department of Social/Personality Psychology, Graduate School and University Center, City University of New York.

Jewelle Taylor Gibbs, Ph.D., School of Social Welfare, University of California at Berkeley.

Nancy Gonzales, Ph.D., Department of Psychology, Arizona State University, Tempe, AZ.

Diane Graves, B.A., Department of Psychology, University of Washington, Seattle, WA.

Kwai Grove, B.A., Department of Psychology, University of Washington, Seattle, WA.

Yumi Hiraga, B.A., Department of Psychology, University of Washington, Seattle, WA.

Robin L. Jarrett, Ph.D., Department of Sociology, Loyola University, Chicago, IL.

Debra M. Hernandez Jozefowicz, M.S.W., Department of Social Work and Psychology, University of Michigan, Ann Arbor, MI.

Bonnie J. Ross Leadbeater, Ph.D., Department of Psychology, Yale University, New Haven, CT.

Marguerita Lightfoot, M.A., Department of Education, University of California, Los Angeles.

Fern Marx, M.P.H., Center for Research on Women, Wellesley College, Wellesley, MA.

Jennifer McCormick, M.A., Department of Teaching and Learning, School of Education, New York University, New York, NY.

Wendy R. McCusker, B.A., Department of Psychology, University of Connecticut, Storrs, CT.

Vonnie C. McLoyd, Ph.D., Center for Human Growth and Development, University of Michigan, Ann Arbor, MI.

Velma McBride Murry, Ph.D., Department of Child and Family Development, University of Georgia, Athens, GA.

Roberta L. Paikoff, Ph.D., Institute for Juvenile Research, Department of Psychiatry, University of Illinois at Chicago.

Jennifer Pastor, M.A., Department of Social and Personality Psychology, Graduate Center, City University of New York.

Anthony Raden, M.A., Department of Psychology, Yale University, New Haven, CT.

Le'Roy E. Reese, Ph.D., Department of Psychology, Chicago State University, Chicago, IL.

Jean E. Rhodes, Ph.D., Department of Psychology, University of Illinois at Urbana-Champaign.

Mary Jane Rotheram-Borus, Ph.D., Division of Social and Community Psychiatry, Department of Psychiatry, University of California, Los Angeles.

Kimberly Ryan-Finn, B.A., University of Washington, Seattle, WA.

Nuria Sabate, M.D., Department of Psychiatry, George Washington University, Washington, D.C.

Carlos Salguero, M.D., Child Study Center, Yale University, and Hill Health Center, New Haven, CT.

Edward Seidman, Ph.D., Department of Psychology, New York University, New York, NY.

Victoria Seitz, Ph.D., Department of Psychology, Yale University, New Haven, CT.

Rachel Sing, M.Ed., Graduate School of Education, Harvard University, Cambridge, MA.

Helena Stauber, Ed.D., L.U.K. Crisis Center, Inc., Fitchburg, MA.

Amy M. Sullivan, M.A., Department of Human Development and Psychology, Graduate School of Education, Harvard University, Cambridge, MA.

Jill McLean Taylor, Ed.D., Department of Education and Human Services, Simmons College, Boston, MA.

Deborah L. Tolman, Ed.D., Center for Research on Women, Wellesley College, Wellesley, MA.

Elizabeth M. Vera, Ph.D., Department of Counseling and Educational Psychology, Loyola University, Chicago, IL.

Janie Victoria Ward, Ed.D., Department of Education and Human Services, Simmons College, Boston, MA.

Mary C. Waters, Ph.D., Department of Sociology, Harvard University, Cambridge, MA.

Niobe Way, Ed.D., Department of Applied Psychology, School of Education, New York University, New York, NY.

Hirokazu Yoshikawa, M.A., Department of Psychology, New York University, New York, NY.

# Introduction

> People think of them as a girl who gets pregnant easy. And
> who doesn't care or anything, who's just a loser, so they say.
> But then there's one thing they have to watch is not to let
> people think they're like that. . . . It depends on how you
> present yourself. If you present yourself like what people think
> of you, well then they're not going to know who you are.
> —Pilar, a Hispanic urban adolescent girl quoted by Taylor,
> chapter 7 this volume

Urban adolescent girls—what do people think of them?
How do they present themselves? At a time when the rates of single-
parent (generally female-headed) families and of out-of-wedlock adolescent births continue to be higher in the United States than in most other
developed countries (Burns 1992; Alan Guttmacher Institute 1994), the
public eye is focused on single mothers. Current popular images see
inner-city neighborhoods as ghettos of despair where female-headed families with low aspirations have out-of-wedlock children who in turn
perpetuate intergenerational cycles of poverty. While the rate of poverty
is as high in rural areas as it is in urban settings, disadvantaged urban
families plagued by unemployment and crime are disproportionally visible as they have become concentrated and isolated in inner-city neighborhoods (Wilson 1995). The apparent deviance of urban adolescent girls
who eschew marriage and work for welfare benefits is emphasized by
many politicians of the 1990s. Demands abound that unmarried poor
adolescents "just say no" to pregnancy and that they move from welfare
to work. Although extensive research by economists has failed to support
the prevalent belief that welfare benefits provide an incentive for having
out-of-wedlock children (Danziger and Weinberg 1986), images of urban
poor adolescent girls as immoral and unmotivated persist. These stereotypes filter into urban adolescents' everyday experiences, as Pilar in the
opening quotation both recognizes and resists.

In the last two decades many social scientists have decried the absence
of high-quality research that addresses the psychological health and development of adolescent girls. Girls are "seldom seen and rarely heard"
(Bohan 1992); their voices are missing in the psychological research litera-

ture (Gilligan 1982); they appear defective in research comparing them to boys (Sherif 1992); and they are commonly marginalized by conventional research methods (Hare-Mustin and Marecek 1990). Authors, including Jewelle Taylor Gibbs, Joyce Ladner, and Margaret Beale Spencer, have also denounced the persistent identification of poor adolescents of ethnic and racial minority groups as "deprived, disadvantaged, deviant, disturbed, or dumb" (Gibbs 1985, 28). The need to recognize differences within ethnic and racial minority groups and within and across socioeconomic status has been emphasized repeatedly in the last decade (Sarigiani, Camarena, and Petersen 1993; Spencer and Dornbusch 1990; Way 1995).

This book presents several researchers' efforts to better understand the development of diverse groups of adolescent girls. In particular, it focuses on the experiences of low-income urban adolescent girls on their own terms and, often, in their own voices. In some chapters, girls are the sole focus of discussion, and in other chapters boys and girls are discussed in order to highlight gender similarities and differences in development. It is our hope that this book will be read in undergraduate and graduate courses in psychology, sociology, economics, and women's studies. We also hope that it will be read by policy analysts searching for new approaches to the prevention of poverty, approaches that reach beyond traditional stereotypes for more effective policies that will assist adolescent girls in their efforts to develop into healthy adults.

Like many texts on adolescence, this book emphasizes what is normative about this transitional period of life. The separate sections deal with central issues of adolescence: identity development; changing family, peer, and mentor relationships; sexuality; health risks; and career choices. These chapters can be read together or independently, as there is some overlap that permits this latter kind of reading. However, this is not just another book of readings to accompany existing textbooks on adolescence. These chapters illuminate pathways of adolescent development that are created by a cultural context of urban poverty and violence by asking such questions as: What are the pathways to healthy adaptation for urban adolescent girls? How does family poverty figure into girls' future career aspirations? How does violence and sexual harassment in inner-city schools affect girls' perceptions of their competence and futures? How do stereotypes, racism, sexism, and societal demands for acculturation create unique conflicts for identity development? How can either girls' sense of confidence or their low self-esteem be understood in the context of these conflicts? How can families, peers, and nonparental adults help to foster positive identity choices for girls? How does what is offered by our society create the foundations of development for urban adolescent girls?

## Developing an Identity and Being Identified

Adolescence is a pivotal period for establishing future life trajectories: an individual's life course can indeed be influenced by decisions made as an adolescent about education, childbearing, drugs, delinquent acts, and so forth. The process of committing oneself to an identity has been understood by American social scientists as central to this phase of life. Identity development has been understood as an intrapsychic search. Adolescents resolve the question "Who am I?" by actively exploring alternatives and making personal commitments in the domains of occupations, values, beliefs, and sexual activities and orientation (e.g., Marcia 1980). But Pilar, in the opening quotation, poses different questions about her identity: How should she present herself, given who we think she is? How can *we* know who she really is? This aspect of personal identity, one's meaning for others, is essential to Erikson's (1968) original definition of identity. In his words (which noticeably reflect the selective emphasis on males' development that characterized his time) identity formation was described as a two-way process of mutual affirmation:

Identity formation employs a process of simultaneous reflection and observation, a process taking place on all levels of mental functioning, by which the individual judges himself in the light of what he perceives to be the way in which others judge him in comparison to themselves and to a typology significant to them; while he judges their way of judging him in the light of how he perceives himself in comparison to them and to types that have become relevant to him. (1968, 22–23)

Identity development is for all adolescents a process of self-evaluation that involves weighing one's own goals, ideals, beliefs, strengths, and talents against future visions of what one could be. It also includes comparison of oneself with the standards and ideals of others in one's community. Rather than merely a search for self-coherence or commitment to self-chosen values, beliefs, and occupations, identity formation is, as Pilar recognizes, a social process of judging others and of being judged by them. It is about being accepted into or excluded from educational programs, being hired or refused employment, being chosen for the team or sidelined. Identity development involves reciprocal recognition, in which an individual's commitments to a career or a set of values are sustained by her family's and community's willingness to affirm these choices. An individual's talents and aspirations must be greeted with social opportunities for their actualization.

Adolescence is a developmental phase that confronts a continuously changing social context. The evolving economic, political, cultural, environmental, school, neighborhood, and family conditions in which adolescents develop create a context of risk and protective factors to which each developing individual must adapt (Jessor 1993). As Wilson (1987) has argued, for example, rapid changes from a production to a service economy in inner cities have created contexts of limited employment and opportunity for poor urban families.

## Roles for Women in the 1990s

Young women who grow up today in urban poor and working-class communities occupy a unique social position. The transition in women's roles from guardians of home and children to jugglers of work, home, and family must be considered in our conceptions of adolescent development. What has been prescribed by our society as ideal roles for women has long been tied to changing economic conditions. Only 11.3% of married women with small children worked in 1950, and 30.3% worked in 1970 (Children's Defense Fund 1994). Economic realities now make it probable that most women will financially contribute to the support of their children. Indeed, the majority (59.6%) of married women with children under six were a part of the labor force in 1993, reflecting, in part, the rise in divorce rates and male unemployment as well as the drop in welfare benefits.

One might think of the working mother as an ideal role aspiration for poor and working-class girls who have typically grown up in single-parent, mother-headed households. Poor and working class women in many ethnic and cultural groups, in fact, have long been wage earners (Collins 1994). But tensions and contradictions abound in this role for women. Children and childbearing are often seen as impediments to women's full-time availability to the work world, but child care remains expensive and hard to find (Schwartz 1989). Demands that young, poor and working-class women be economically independent are not supported by the institutional changes that would make this possible (e.g., access to high-paying careers, college educations, and work-based or school-based day care). Urban poverty is blamed on early childbearing and young mothers' lack of commitment to education, careers, or marriage, rather than on the educational institutions that fail to retain or inspire them and the employers who refuse to hire them. While middle- and upper-class women may be able to buffer some of the conflicts of being a working mother with child care and college educations, poor and working-class women commonly lack the financial foothold that make such steps possible.

## Stereotypes of Despair

The school dropout, the teenage welfare mother, the drug addict, and the victim of domestic violence or of AIDS are among the most prevalent public images of poor and working-class urban adolescent girls. The success stories of urban girls are seen as the exceptional struggles of heroic or resilient individuals rather than as the normative development of the majority of these girls (Jessor 1993). They are seen as beating the odds, rather than as resisting prevailing stereotypes. Musick (1993) presents this argument with a chilling cogency,

In order to avoid teenage motherhood girls growing up in poverty need to possess not just average but above-average psychological resources and strengths, self-concepts, and competencies. Considering the many forces drawing poor females toward early unprotected sex and early parenthood, the scarcity of viable alternatives steering them toward school and work, and the responses of family and peers, which validate pregnancies once they have occurred, it is remarkable that rates of adolescent childbearing are not even higher. (13)

Yet, despite the risks inherent in economic disadvantage, the majority of poor urban adolescent girls do not fit the stereotypes that are made about them. Nationwide surveys compiled by the Children's Defense Fund (1991) indicate that in 1988, 18% of white, 13.5% of black, and 17% of Latino adolescents under the age of eighteen reported ever using marijuana (white females had the highest and black females had the lowest percentage); 3.6% of white, 2.1% of black, and 4.6% of Latino youth reported using cocaine; 27.3% of white, 15.9% of black, and 25.4% of Latinos reported currently using alcohol (only 12% of black females); and less than 3% of white, black or Latino adolescents reported "serious" alcohol use (five or more drinks per occasion on five or more days in the past month). These surveys also indicated that in 1987, 71.1% of twenty- and twenty-year-olds from poor families (black and white) graduated from high school. The percentage of those who are poor and who drop out of school is almost exactly the same as the percentage of those who are poor and who go on to college (27.7% and 27.6%, respectively; see Children's Defense Fund 1991). This leads us to wonder why we have heard so much about those who are poor and drop out of school and so little about those who go on to college. Furthermore, the 1990 national birth rate statistics for fifteen- to seventeen-year-old girls indicated that 23 in 1,000 Whites, 84 in 1,000 Blacks, and 65 in 1,000 Hispanics gave birth (Alan Guttmacher Institute, 1994). In other words, for every 1,000 girls in this age group, 977 Whites, 916 Blacks, and 935

Hispanics did *not* become adolescent mothers. (Births per 1,000 increase for girls ages eighteen and nineteen to 72 for Whites, 163 for Blacks, and 148 for Hispanics, but the same point can be made.) While not specific to urban adolescent girls, these statistics show that the overwhelming majority of adolescent girls (many of whom are from poor urban families) are not school dropouts, teenage mothers, or drug addicts. Yet we know little about the lives of these girls.

Moreover, the outcomes for those who choose to have children during adolescence are not uniformly negative. Recent research indicates considerable within-group diversity in outcomes for adolescent mothers (Furstenberg, Brooks-Gunn, and Morgan 1987; Leadbeater and Linares 1992; Leadbeater and Bishop 1994). For some adolescent mothers, bearing a child signifies a commitment to life and encourages them, for their children's sake, to strive for and attain their educational and occupational goals. Factors that are most salient in creating negative outcomes for adolescent mothers, such as poor educational achievement, often existed prior to the first pregnancy (Way and Leadbeater 1995).

The widely cited results of the 1992 American Association of University Women's report entitled *How Schools Shortchange Girls* emphasized the difficulties many adolescent girls have maintaining a sense of competence in schools. They note ethnic and racial differences showing that African American girls hold on to their overall self-esteem more than white or Latina girls during the transition to adolescence. Latina girls showed the greatest drop in self-esteem, compared to white and African American girls. Puerto Rican and Cuban American girls have the highest rates of school dropout and are more likely than African American or white girls to have low-paying jobs and to live in poverty (Wetzel 1987). But it is not enough to note these ethnic differences. How can we understand them? How do African American families and communities raise daughters who feel good about themselves? How does racial or ethnic identity influence healthy adjustment? How do parents raise their daughters to resist stereotypes of failure? How do career aspirations influence self-esteem for urban adolescent girls? How does sexuality figure into their self-evaluations of competence?

## The Pathways toward Healthy Development

The collection of research presented here concerns how young low-income urban adolescent girls define the goals that shape who they are becoming and the steps they make toward claiming adult identities. It is about their struggles to succeed, the obstacles they face, their experiences of success and defeat, and their resistance to failure. It is also about racism, sexism, and the stereotypes that urban adolescent girls struggle with in this culture. It is about girls' relationships with their families, their friends, and sometimes with their children. It is about their views of themselves as women and their experiences of sexuality at a time when sexual activity is both condoned and held out to have untold risks for adolescent girls. It is about *not* getting pregnant and about the desires and fears that accompany sexual maturity. It is about growing up in poverty and in spite of poverty.

These articles offer concrete answers to questions of how culture and limited resources influence adolescent development. They point to steps that need to be taken to begin to know who these girls are and who they can become. The results of these studies demonstrate qualitative differences in the experiences of adolescent girls from diverse social class, ethnic, and racial groups.

The idea of this collective work was greeted with great enthusiasm by all who were asked to participate. The psychologists, sociologists, ethnographers, and demographers who have contributed to this volume, themselves, come from diverse backgrounds and intellectual disciplines. Several different methodological approaches are represented in these chapters, including the quantitative analyses of questionnaire and survey data, as well as qualitative analyses of ethnographic, interview, and focus group data. Individually, criticisms have been launched against each of these methodologies (see Guba and Lincoln 1994; Denzin and Lincoln 1994). Quantitative studies that rely on questionnaire data and statistical analyses are charged with generalizing findings at the cost of accurately representing the individual's experience. On the other hand, qualitative approaches to data are criticized for their selective focus on the individual's experience and their apparent lack of generalizability (see Denzin and Lincoln 1994; Maxwell 1992). However, juxtaposed as they are in this text, these different methodologies strengthen each other. While the more quantitative approaches present broad pictures and test hypotheses, the more qualitative approaches detail the specifics of girls' experiences and challenge us to generate new research to better represent the complexity of their lives. For example, Jean E. Rhodes and Anita B. Davis's quantitative study of the role of nonparent adult mentors for adolescent mothers (see chapter 12) is enriched by Amy M. Sullivan's theoretical questioning of the specific nature of the mentor relationship for girls and her qualitative analysis of interviews with urban adolescent girls (see chapter 13).

Some of the authors and the adolescents who talk about their efforts to resist the racism and sexism of our stereotypical visions are angry and are not easy to hear. Some of the theories discussed here have been the subject of great controversy and debate within the field of social sciences. For example, a few of the authors use methods and theories inspired by the work of Carol Gilligan. These authors, some of whom have worked with Gilligan on the Harvard Project on Women's Psychology and Girls' Development, attempt to respond to and expand her developmental theories. All of the chapters in this book raise questions and point to directions for future inquiry. Like Pilar, they challenge us to look beyond traditional stereotypes of urban adolescent girls, to get to know them better, to see how they present themselves, and to push outward the boundaries of how we are willing to see and understand these girls.

The research presented in this volume focuses on many racial and ethnic groups, including Caribbean and African Americans, Puerto Ricans, Mexican Americans, Portuguese Americans, Asian Pacific Americans, and European Americans. Yet, many voices and topics remain missing from this book. There is little in this collection of research from Native American, Asian American, or lesbian/bisexual adolescent girls. Certain topics such as the impact of AIDS and the role of employment opportunities and welfare in urban girls' lives are not covered. Further research in these topics as they relate specifically to girls is badly needed. Many of the studies presented focus intensively on small samples of ethnically diverse adolescent girls and successfully generate possible understandings of these girls' lives. However, larger-scale studies of urban adolescent girls' development must be undertaken to assess the generalizability of the findings. As researchers and as teachers in sociology, psychology, public health, women's studies, and ethnic and race studies, the authors of this volume jointly recognize the need to educate and inspire educators, counselors, policymakers, and our own students to understand and expand our visions of the possibilities that exist for urban adolescent girls.

## Research and Policy Implications

Frustrations with the apparent intractability of intergenerational poverty fuel a wish to simplify and localize causes of this problem. Control of sexual activity and teenage childbearing among inner-city girls may appear more possible than dealing with the complex economic and social structures and attitudes that contribute to a widening gap between rich and poor in this country. Clearly, initiatives that effectively deal with neighborhood and school violence, lack of employment opportunities, substandard inner-city education, gender and racial bias in schools, limited access to secondary education, lack of child care support from fathers, and poor quality day care would go a long way toward providing poor and working-class adolescent girls with a social context in which they could acquire the means to support themselves and to make their children's lives better. Recent policy initiatives also continue to be gender-biased in their focus on "deadbeat dads" and on efforts to resolve out-of-wedlock births by a return to marriage and family values. These initiatives fail to acknowledge that living in a two-parent family does not ensure relief from poverty. They also fail to explore how women's opportunities and earning capacities outside of marriage are affected by economic transformations like the recession of the 1980s, or how pay equity, universal day care, and initiatives to improve their career opportunities would buttress women's capacity for financial independence (Baca Zinn 1990). Broad policy statements directed at the prevention of teenage pregnancy have repeatedly emphasized the need to promote alternative life options for urban girls to encourage them to invest in their own future (Hayes 1987; Lawson and Rhodes 1993). Their identity "choices" *are* largely determined by what is offered. If school and community violence, sexual abuse and harassment, sexually transmitted diseases, substandard education, poverty, and low-paying job opportunities comprise the total menu, it is difficult to know how they will become aware of enhanced life options. Having children is seen to compete with opportunities for economic advancement, yet for many poor girls, having children represents a commitment to life and to the future. Beyond the acquisition of goods, making life better for their present or future children is a social value that motivates many urban low-income girls to struggle against the obstacles they encounter as they grow up.

The research presented in this book contributes to expanding our understanding of urban adolescent girls' lives. It also points out the need to search for a more accurate and more detailed picture of their experiences than current stereotypes and risk statistics offer. To date, very little research has focused on illuminating the actual contexts of these girls' lives or the real obstacles that impede their investments in the future. There is clearly a need to investigate what factors lead to different outcomes within groups of girls who represent varying ethnic or racial and socioeconomic backgrounds. Homogeneity of outcomes for individuals living in poor urban communities cannot be assumed. Indeed, such an assumption obscures the strength and resiliency evident among the majority of girls from these environments. There is also a need for research that assesses the effects of community and neighborhood resources and liabilities (in terms of education, work opportunities, schools, and so forth) in the lives of urban adolescent girls.

The research here makes specific many of the problems that need to be addressed to advance the life options of urban girls. The authors also leave us with concrete policy recommendations:

1. Start early! Poor and working-class urban adolescent girls (and boys) are often forced by their circumstances to make decisions about their identities as adults very early. While many middle- and upper-class girls postpone identity decisions through a college moratorium, low-income adolescent girls often make career and motherhood decisions as young teenagers.

2. Improve school retention. The best predictor of overall school performance is early school performance. Continuing gender and racial biases in education and in occupations contributes to the discouragement girls often feel in continuing their education. Fostering parents' commitments to daughters' educational aspirations will also increase the likelihood that girls will stay in school.

3. Expose urban girls to increased career options in middle school; include information about potential earnings, educational requirements for entry, and means of access. Establishing direct links between schools and work seems central to the success of this early exposure.

4. Demand respect for women's right to live safely within their own bodies. Sex education classes need to address the continued media presentation of women as victims of their sexuality and objects of others' pleasure, as well as the conflicts that this depersonalization creates for both girls and boys.

5. Promote mentoring or muse relationships and discussion groups, in which adult women join with adolescent girls to listen, support, guide, inspire, and learn from each other.

6. Help ethnic and racial minority youth and their parents comprehend and cope with the clashes that may occur between family, peer, and mainstream cultural values during the course of adolescence.

Policy decisions based on stereotypes can only serve to perpetuate them. If we believe that girls' irresponsible sexuality and lack of career or marital commitments *cause* the intergenerational transfer of poverty, policy efforts to alleviate poverty will be misdirected. We must reach for knowledge beyond these stereotypes and join these girls in resisting them.

REFERENCES

Alan Guttmacher Institute. 1994. *Sex and America's teenagers*. New York: Alan Guttmacher Institute.
American Association of University Women. 1992. *The AAUW report: How schools*

*shortchange girls.* Washington, D.C.: American Association of University Women Educational Foundation and National Educational Association.

Baca Zinn, M. 1990. Family, race, and poverty in the eighties. In *Black women in America,* edited by M. R. Malson, E. Mudimbe-Boyi, J. F. O'Barr, and M. Wyer. 245–63. Chicago: University of Chicago Press.

Bohan, J. S., ed. 1992. *Seldom seen, rarely heard: Women's place in psychology.* Boulder, Colo.: Westview Press.

Burns, A. 1992. Mother-headed families: An international perspective and the case of Australia. *Social Policy Report, Society for Research in Child Development* 4:1–22.

Children's Defense Fund. 1991. *The adolescent and young adult fact book.* Washington, D.C.: Children's Defense Fund.

———. 1994. *The state of America's children.* Washington, D.C.: Children's Defense Fund.

Collins, P. H. 1994. Shifting the center: Race, class, and feminist theorizing about motherhood. In *Representations of motherhood,* edited by D. Bassin, M. Honey, and M. M. Kaplan. New Haven: Yale University Press.

Danziger, S. H., and D. H. Weinberg. 1986. *Fighting poverty.* Cambridge: Harvard University Press.

Denzin, N., and Y. Lincoln, eds. 1994. *Handbook of qualitative research.* London: Sage Publications.

Erikson, E. 1968. *Identity: Youth and crisis.* New York: W. W. Norton.

Frye, M. 1983. On being white: Thinking toward a feminist understanding of race and race supremacy. In *The politics of reality: Essays in feminist theory freedom,* edited by M. Frye. Oakland: Crossing Press.

Furstenberg, F., J. Brooks-Gunn, and S. P. Morgan. 1987. *Adolescent mothers in later life.* Cambridge: Cambridge University Press.

Gibbs, J. T. 1985. City girls: Psychosocial adjustment of urban black adolescent females. *Sage* 2 (2): 28–36.

Gilligan, C. 1982. *In a different voice.* Cambridge: Harvard University Press.

Guba, E. G., and Y. S. Lincoln. 1994. Competing paradigms in qualitative research. In *Handbook of qualitative research,* edited by N. Denzin and Y. Lincoln. London: Sage Publications.

Hare-Mustin, R. T., and J. Marecek. 1990. *Making a difference: Psychology and the construction of gender.* New Haven: Yale University Press.

Hayes, C. D., ed. 1987. *Risking the future: Adolescent sexuality, pregnancy, and childbearing.* Washington, D.C.: National Academy Press.

Jessor, R. 1993. Successful adolescent development among youth in high-risk settings. *American Psychologist* 48:117–26.

Lawson, A., and D. L. Rhodes. 1993. *The politics of pregnancy: Adolescent sexuality and public policy.* New Haven: Yale University Press.

Leadbeater, B. J., and S. J. Bishop. 1994. Predictors of behavior problems in pre-school children of inner-city Afro-American and Puerto Rican adolescent mothers. *Child Development* 65:638–48.

Leadbeater, B. J., and O. Linares. 1992. Depressive symptoms in black and Puerto Rican adolescent mothers in the first 3 years postpartum. *Development and Psychopathology* 4:451–68.

Marcia, J. 1980. Identity in adolescence. In *Handbook of adolescent psychology,* edited by J. Adelson, 159–87. New York: Wiley.

Maxwell, J. 1992. Understanding and validity in qualitative research. *Harvard Educational Review* 62 (3):279–300.

Musick, J. 1993. *Young, poor, and pregnant: The psychology of teenage motherhood.* New Haven: Yale University Press.

Ortiz Cofer, J. 1991. *Silent dancing: A partial remembrance of a Puerto Rican childhood.* Houston, Tex.: Arte Publico Press.

Presser, H. B. 1989. Can we make time for children? The economy, work schedules, and child care. *Demography* 26:523–43.

Rutter, M., and M. Rutter. 1993. *Developing minds: Challenge and continuity across the life span.* New York: Basic Books.

Sarigiani, P. A., P. M. Camarena, and A. C. Petersen. 1993. Cultural factors in adolescent girls' development: The role of ethnic minority group status. In *Female Adolescent Development,* edited by M. Sugar, 138–56. New York: Brunner Mazel.

Schwartz, F. N. 1989. Management women and the facts of life. *Harvard Business Review* 67:65–76.

Sherif, C. W. 1992. Bias in psychology. In *Seldom seen, rarely heard: Women's place in psychology,* edited by J. S. Bohan, 107–46. Boulder, Colo.: Westview Press.

Spencer, M. B., and S. M. Dornbusch. 1990. Challenges in studying minority youth. In *At the threshold: The developing adolescent,* edited by S. S. Feldman and G. R. Elliot. Cambridge: Harvard University Press.

Way, N. 1995. "Can't you see the courage, the strength that I have?": Listening to urban adolescent girls speak about their relationships. *Psychology of Women Quarterly* 19:107–28.

Way, N., and B. J. Leadbeater. 1995. Pathways towards educational achievement among adolescent mothers: Reconsidering the role of family support. Manuscript submitted for publication.

Wetzel, J. R. 1987. *American youth: A statistical snapshot.* Washington, D.C.: W. T. Grant Foundation Commission on Youth and America's Future.

Wilson, W. J. 1987. *The truly disadvantaged.* Chicago: University of Chicago Press.

———. 1995. Jobless ghettos: *The disappearance of work and its effect on urban life.* New York: Knopf.

# I

# Identity Development

The influence of close relationships, especially with parents and peers, on who we become as individuals has been the focus of a great deal of research on adolescent identity development (Kroger 1993). Investigations of how social contexts (e.g., area of residence, schools, and neighborhoods) figure into adolescent identity development, however, have only begun to appear in the research literature (see Petersen 1993). Schools are perhaps the most salient institutions that shape adolescent experiences. Yet, neighborhoods as well as the structure of the communities that surround them (e.g., rural versus urban, wealthy versus poor) also have a hand in determining what adolescents do and with whom and how they feel about these interactions (Petersen 1993).

The influence of context on urban adolescent girls' identity development is demonstrated in these first four chapters. Attending urban schools, adolescent girls receive strong messages about being powerless in the face of racism and sexual harassment. The ethnic and racial composition of school environments and urban communities defines in-group and out-group identities that are incorporated into adolescents' personal and ethnic identities. Differences in social class translate into differences in what activities and experiences are available to and chosen by girls. Evidence for gender-linked differences in the pathways and processes of identity development suggests that societal experiences are also differently structured for boys and girls.

In chapter 1, Pastor, McCormick, and Fine, with their adolescent coauthors Andolsen, Friedman, Richardson, Roach, and Taverez, describe the girls' experiences in inner-city schools. Their study is informed by interviews and focus groups with urban adolescent girls, by field notes of observations made by the adult authors in their roles as participant observers, and by the voices and poetry of the adolescent authors. They render stark descriptions of school surveillance practices that criminalize all students, of weapons searches that humiliate, of peer sexual harassment and assault that intimidate, and of sexism and racism that undermine girls' sense of agency. The authors appeal to adult women to create "safe spaces" with adolescent girls for girls and women to preserve their cultural connectedness, resist prevailing racism and sexism, and collectively transform the obstacles to their growth.

In chapter 2, Rotheram-Borus, Dopkins, Sabate, and Lightfoot also ask how school contexts influence adolescents' identity, ethnic identity, values, and self-esteem. They contrast the traditional *intrapsychic* focus of theories of adolescent identity development with the group-oriented focus of the mixed ethnic and racial groups of adolescents whom they studied. The authors demonstrate how adolescents' identity searches must be understood as linked to gender and to ethnicity and race.

In chapter 3, Erkut, Fields, Sing, and Marx ask about the sources of competence in African American, Hispanic, Native American, European American, and Asian Pacific American girls of upper, middle, and lower socioeconomic status. These authors take the unusual course of asking girls about what *activities* make them feel good about who they are. Their findings point to the self-enhancing advantages for girls of mastering sports or arts-related activities. They also reveal clear ethnic, race, and social class differences in which activities are available to and chosen by adolescent girls.

The intersection of gender, race, and ethnicity is further elaborated in Waters's study of the identity development of the adolescent sons and daughters of black Caribbean immigrants in New York City. In chapter 4 Waters presents evidence from extensive interviews with a socioeconomically diverse group of Caribbean American adolescents to suggest that their pathways to identity development are shaped by gender-linked differences in their responses to American race relations. While Caribbean American girls experienced more parental restrictions than their male peers, they were also afforded more leeway in adopting a bicultural identity that allows for a flexible merging of both Caribbean and mainstream African American identities.

REFERENCES

Kroger, J. 1993. *Discussions on ego identity*. Hillsdale, N.J.: Lawrence Erlbaum Associates.
Petersen, A. C. 1993. Presidential address: Creating adolescents: The role of context and process in developmental trajectories. *Journal of Research on Adolescence* 3:1–18.

# 1

# Makin' Homes: An Urban Girl Thing

Jennifer Pastor, Jennifer McCormick, and Michelle Fine
*with Ruth Andolsen, Nora Friedman,
Nikki Richardson, Tanzania Roach,
and Marina Tavarez*

This chapter grows out of our collective work, which crosses the boundaries typically constructed by researchers. We actively cross generations, colors, classes, and ideologies by writing this chapter with the young women listed above.[1] This work is driven by the belief that we and they are the best narrators of our lives. The title draws from the fact that home is a theme that constantly surfaces in the lives of adolescent girls, and throughout this chapter we rely upon an old-fashioned and rich metaphor—that of homemaking. If we stay loyal to the nostalgic notion of home (Martin and Mohanty 1986) as a safe space, where one can weave whole cloth from the fragments of social critique and sweet dreams—a home few have known but most still search for— we can say that these young women are searching for such a place.

We do not limit home to traditional definitions, because homeplaces can be defined broadly to include comforting, safe spaces in institutions such as schools or in social groups such as clubs, social movements, or gangs. Listening to young women's critiques of schooling, domestic spaces, gender relations, racial hierarchies, and social violence, we have learned that homeplaces, so broadly defined, can also become constricting places from which they often try to break free. This can have profound and ironic consequences in young women's lives and for their emerging identities as women.

All of us write together toward a four-part, shared argument: First, urban girls of many colors cannot simply pursue autonomy, freedom, and independence as Erikson (1968) theorizes. The challenges of racism, sexism, classism, and cultural hegemony profoundly interfere. Second, this interference does not necessarily result in deficits for many urban girls, as for the African American women bell hooks (1990) writes about, because these challenges help girls learn how to develop critical consciousness. We theorize that this development becomes part of a successful coping strategy. Third, this critical consciousness allows urban girls ③ of color to know that there is much that is wrong with the world and that they cannot hide or "go underground" within white-dominated, class-based institutions as Gilligan (1991) has so aptly demonstrated white middle-class girls can do. Urban girls of color must learn how to assert themselves within white, often male-dominated institutions, because they know that these institutions are often not designed to protect them or promote their interests. We maintain as our fourth and last belief that this ④ critical consciousness can manifest itself in various individual behaviors and styles, but within these behaviors a troubling theme emerges. Unfortunately, urban girls of many colors do not seek each other out for collective action, which might address the inequities of which they are so critically conscious. There are <u>few experiences in their lives to prepare them to work collectively</u>, especially given their legacy of growing up in the Reagan-Bush years, marked as they were by an affirmation of socialization through gender and traditional notions of feminine behavior, which do not include collective action.

Yet urban girls are unstoppable in their desires to preserve and develop their personal integrity. We have found that <u>they construct individualistic strategies</u> for accommodating to the contradictory needs and desires of family, friends, and school, while resisting the offensive boundaries that are constructed against them because of their race, gender, class, or culture. We write with deep respect for the work that they do as they pursue their own identities.

## Methods

Our collective work draws from the young women's narratives, from girl's and women's group discussions, and from ethnographic observations of sites where the young women attended school. The work derives from two qualitative research projects, an ethnographic documentation project at an alternative public middle school (Jennifer Pastor), and a poetry workshop conducted within a traditional comprehensive high school (Jennifer McCormick). The young women who took part in the girl's and women's discussion groups, and with whom we write this chapter, were recruited from these two sites.

*Description of Ethnographic Sites*

The middle school is located in a working-class neighborhood of New York City that has a large Latino immigrant population. It is a small school with about 120 students and is committed to creating a safe, nurturing, and intellectually stimulating environment for its students.

The high school is also located in a working-class neighborhood of New York City and has a large Afro-Caribbean population. It is a comprehensive high school with roughly two thousand students.

*Participants*

Three adolescent girls from the middle school (Ruth, Nora, and Marina), two adolescent girls from the high school (Nikki and Tanzania), and three adult women (Jennifer, Jennifer, and Michelle) participated in the discussion groups. The girls were approached by the researchers at each site and invited to participate in the discussion groups taking place during the summer of 1993. The ethnic-racial composition of the girls included one Jewish American, one European–Latina American, one Dominican Latina, one African American, and one Caribbean–African American. The ethnic-racial composition of the adult women were Puerto Rican American, European American, and Jewish American.

*Procedures*

For two years Jennifer Pastor made weekly visits to the middle school in order to observe and talk to students, staff, and parents. She recorded field notes, conducted interviews and focus group discussions, and was a participant-observer in other activities. Jennifer McCormick tutored students and conducted poetry workshops over a two-year period. Conversations with numerous students were recorded or reconstructed from field notes.

The summer discussions were held at the City University of New York Graduate Center, a central location that was easily reached by all participants using public transportation. A total of seven discussions took place. Discussions tended to last about two hours and were taped and transcribed. The content of the discussions varied at each session, but focused on issues of gender and race politics in the lives of girls and women. The researchers often introduced current newspaper articles, videotapes, and published essays to the group in order to stimulate conversations, but conversations were not limited to these materials.

In this paper we focus primarily on the five girls who participated in the summer discussion groups. We also draw from field notes taken at the school sites, from interviews and conversations with other girls at each school, and from poetry written by the two high school girls.

## Social Individuality, Collective Identity, and Home-Making

As other feminist researchers of identity have done, we question the Eriksonian (1968) model, which states that successful identity achievers are those who have weathered an identity crisis and have resolved such a crisis by acquiring independence and autonomy. Previous work has argued that the Eriksonian model is problematic because girls and women develop "in relationship" (Miller 1976; Rotheram-Borus et al., chap. 2 of this volume). However, Lykes (1989) expands the notion of self-in-relation by calling attention to cross-cultural and cross-contextual variations in adult–child attachment processes. Lykes (1985) presents "social individuality" as a contrasting notion to autonomous individualism. According to Lykes, despite the fact that women's lives are nested inside power inequities, women have developed a keen ability to find spaces for resistance. Recognizing and making sense of social injustice and oppression is a fundamental part of social individuality.

Social individuality can arise from an awareness of racism. Robinson and Ward (1991) studied how a small group of African American adolescent girls attending an exclusive private school resist an individualism that views the self as disconnected from others. Similar processes within communities of color help individuals to preserve their cultural connectedness as a buffer against the isolation that could result from an overreliance on individualism, especially given the legacy of racism that dominates American culture (Phinney 1989). bell hooks, an African American writer, provides a historical example of social individuality. In "Homeplace: A site of resistance," hooks (1990) describes how African American women in the pre–civil rights era became resisters of white racist supremacy within the contexts of their own homes. By nurturing their own families in the belly of white racist oppression, by creating spaces where family members could connect with each other and reaffirm their sense of collective pride and spirit, African American women helped build a revolution within their communities. According to hooks, the stable homeplaces that these women nurtured gave African Americans a strong base from which to organize politically during the 1960s.

Social individuality is also informed by experiences of sexism. Both mainstream culture and "native sub-cultures" (Torres 1991) keep girls and women controlled and dependent throughout adolescence and often into adulthood (Klein 1992). Peers, family, school, religion, and social services work in concert to keep girls bound, presumably "protected" from boys and men who would abuse patriarchal privilege if girls were "free" (Fine et al. 1994). Yet, girls and women do resist oppressive gender structures and have done so for decades. Women often begin a lifetime of resistance as social individuals working to influence the interactions that take place in their homes, schools, and communities. The sense of agency that results from resisting oppressive structures influences who we are as women—our identity—and this identity formation process begins in our youth. The adolescent coauthors of this chapter illuminate how their identities are shaped by resistance at home, at school, and beyond. This developing sense of agency is the beginning of a process of building their own homeplaces, places where they can be connected with others in ways that they desire.

Oppression in the 1990s has many forms. In urban landscapes dotted with drugs, violence, and deteriorating schools, both public and private spaces can be particularly dangerous for young women. The young women of this chapter demonstrate how they engage in social individuality within this landscape and how they attempt to create their own homeplaces. However, because social individuality is an individual-based resistance process, it may not be an optimal way to address injustice within schools and communities. In those cases where major reforms are needed, more collective action may be necessary to bring about change. Later in the chapter we demonstrate how collective identity can be achieved in the lives of urban girls and how this affects their ability to create their own homeplaces.

## In Search of Safe Spaces

### Resistance and Accommodation

We introduce a young feminist in the making. Marina is a lively fourteen-year-old Dominican from New York City who has been in New York since about the age of five. Marina would not agree that the identity crisis of adolescent girls is resolved by independence and autonomy. In Marina's words, the trajectory for women is clear: "First you are owned by your father, and then you are owned by your husband." Yet her homeplace has been a site of resistance, but not against the forces of racism "out there." Instead, her homeplace has been a site for resisting the sexism "in here"; within her home, where boys and men are privileged in the family. When Jennifer Pastor asked Marina about the space between her present home and her future home, Marina explained:

Well I'm already engaged. I want to finish school and prepare for a career, but I'm going to marry my fiancé and hopefully things will work out. If it doesn't work out, I guess we'll have to get divorced, but you can make a difference in your own home and the way you are with your children.

Marina's early engagement is not surprising in Dominican culture, where such engagements are taken as a sign of a young man's serious intentions and respect for the girl and her family. In this sense, Marina is accommodating to the demands of her culture. Yet there are tones of resistance in her answer. She wants to have a career, and she wants to raise her children differently from the way she is currently being raised. Marina began to recognize her own process of resistance when she wrote six months later:

I know that by saying this [getting married] I am going against my strong beliefs about feminist liberation. Eventually I'll probably change my mind about marrying so young. I guess at this point my greatest goal is going to a good university and becoming a psychiatrist. I would like to be able to help young women struggling against the grain of society like I am.

Marina's dramatic change of heart seemed surprising until she explained how she had been exposed to feminist ideals through a teacher whom she admired in her new high school. Marina had also begun to reevaluate some of the relationships in her life.

Anyon (1982) introduced "resistance and accommodation" to describe how girls and women find themselves accommodating to even those gendered, raced, and classed structures that they may abhor. Many girls and women find themselves caught in cycles of resistance and accommodation where they learn that *options for resistance more often than not reproduce the very oppressive cultures they think they are resisting* (Bordo 1993; Fine and Zane 1989; Thorne 1993).

*Homesteading*

Stories narrated by young women display powerfully how they make sense of the worlds they have inherited. In each of these cases you will hear critique, resistance, and accommodation, a yearning for a safe homespace, and yet little sense that life could be very different.

Ana (pseudonym) was a quiet, reserved sixth-grade Latina. She was being repeatedly harassed by an eighth-grade African American boy known for abusing students and undermining teachers. Jennifer Pastor learned of Ana's situation during a visit to the middle school and recorded in her field notes:

A small group of girls surrounded Ana as she walked along crying. The girls attempted to comfort her. I asked one of them what happened. "Thomas hit her again" was the reply. I followed the group until I was able to get near Ana and talk to her privately about her dilemma. She told me that Thomas kept beating her and described how, on different occasions, her arms had been yanked up behind her back, and how her head had been knocked against a school locker. Feeling enraged, I asked Ana if she wanted me to talk to Thomas. She emphatically said no. I asked her if she wanted me to talk to the director. Shaking her head sadly, she said, "No, it won't do any good."

Jennifer Pastor decided to handle this situation by confiding in a teacher who she felt was strong enough to help her solve Ana's problem. The teacher, an African American woman, listened intently and said, "I will speak with Thomas and tell him that his behavior must stop immediately or else he'll have to deal with me." The teacher then went on to describe how Thomas had terrorized another girl until she (the teacher) forced him to stop.

What was striking about these events was that girls and women in the school found themselves solving the problem of male violence quietly, covertly, and without making any public fuss. Ana believed that if she "told," Thomas's behavior would only worsen. Ana's friends felt helpless to provide anything but comfort after the fact. As a participant-observer, Jennifer Pastor tried to respect Ana's wishes regarding the handling of the problem, but as she went underground with another woman of color to solve Ana's dilemma, she realized that this was another example of women and girls creating havens for one another without rocking the boat or changing the status quo. By not attempting to change the school, we had accommodated a structure where violence could take place, leaving potential violators wide latitude for abuse—and for getting away with it.

But not all girls or women are easily subject to continued abuse. Marina, the fourteen-year-old participant, is not a quiet, shy Latina. She is assertive, opinionated, and loves to wear her "tight little jeans." She can receive compliments on her appearance with cool poise and charm. She can also defend her space on the street from aggressive men who dare to get "too personal" by ridiculing their sexist behavior and reframing it as "stupidity." Marina does not live in fear of being victimized. Yet, by wearing the confidence of her sexuality publicly, Marina is also struggling with a culturally prescribed contradiction for Latinas—encouraging young women to be sexually appealing, and yet expecting them to remain sexually "pure." Thus, Marina's resistance to the gendered control of her sexuality displays an ironic accommodation to her culture.

Like Marina, many young women invent homes that cross the boundaries of culture, generation, and immigrant status. They not only cross borders, but they *knit bridges* for self and others (Moraga and Anzaldua 1981; Torres 1991). But these bridges can be woven with conflicting desires and the sense of being pulled in two.

Ruth, a participant in our discussion groups, is a thirteen-year-old who understands and embodies this pull. Born to white, middle-class parents in New York City and raised by a Puerto Rican babysitter, Ruth has grown up knitting more bridges with the Latin American community than she has with white, Anglo culture. In an interview with Jennifer Pastor, she explained: "I grew up in the same building I'm living in now, but across the street is not the same neighborhood. It turns into a whole different attitude and everything. That's where my babysitter lived and she used to let us stay on the street in the summer." This street, and all of the people connected with it, were Ruth's gateway into a different culture. The conflict for Ruth is that Latin culture becomes her home-place, while she resists the Anglo culture of her parents. To do otherwise, she would "lose" language, values, friends, activities, and her sense of identity, which is Latina. Yet she cannot escape that which is Anglo. Her home doesn't "feel like" the homes of her friends: "It's hard because my friends' parents do things differently than mine do. So sometimes I wish that my parents were different so that I can be *myself* and accept what they're saying." Ruth hovers at the margins, but feels pressure from all sides.

Girlfriends are fine. But like, with boys and stuff—they're scared of my parents! They don't even want to meet my parents, and I feel pressure from my parents. They want to meet my boyfriends, or anybody I'm with. They say I don't want to introduce them, but the reality is my friends think that most white people don't like their daughters going out with black guys or Spanish guys. I don't know. They just think my parents will flip or something, and in that sense it's hard for me.

Unable to imagine transforming European American culture, Ruth attaches to the culture she believes defines her childhood. Connections to biological family are sometimes tense, but so are her connections to boys who view her as different. Knitting bridges across treacherous waters, young women can swim in ways that feel quite alone.

A different kind of home-space is carved by Nikki, an African American sixteen-year-old who attends the comprehensive high school. Nikki chose to become involved in a poetry workshop at her school. Good-humored and passionately poetic, Nikki attends a high school that is systematically failing to provide her with opportunities for intellectual engagement or academic advancement. Poetry gives her a voice in this academic darkness. She reflects on, and writes about, a search for a home:[2]

> There is no place left to go
> There was no place left to go.
> She ran away from home,
> She went everywhere.
> She went to her boyfriend's house,
> He told her to leave.
> He couldn't keep her.
> She went to family members' houses,
> But there was no one home.
> She's walking up and down the street.
> She was scared and nervous.
> A man came to her, he was talking to her
>     and trying to rub up against her.
> She ran away from him.
> there was no place to go.
> She heard voices,
> there was no place to go.
> She walked to the nearest park,
> She saw a bench.
> She laid down,
> and went to sleep,
> and when she awakened,
> she was home,
> because there was no place left to go.

Nikki brings to life the pain, alienation, and loss that a girl can feel when she loses her connection to home without having found a new home-place. Whether home is thought of as a geographic, concrete structure or as an emotional space inside self, adolescent girls search for a home. As sites where homeplaces can be developed, what do urban secondary schools have to offer them in their life work?

## On Surveillance

Typically, public schools, especially large, comprehensive high schools of the sort where Nikki and Tanzania are assigned, have been most unlikely sites for makin' homes. Trying to imagine this institution as a cozy site for making sense of social critique, for trying on ways of being gendered and raced, for imagining "what could be" becomes difficult when surveillance begins the school day. Jennifer McCormick observed: "Lines stretch in two directions outside of a side entrance. Students hide their faces inside hooded jackets. Sleeves cover their fists. I ask one solemn faced girl why she waits. 'We are allowed in at the beginning of second period.' Metal detectors are positioned like sentinels directly inside the doorway."

Surveillance induces students to wait in the cold until they are allowed into school. It causes them to tolerate public humiliation. It criminalizes them.

> *McCormick:* Were you ever scanned?
> *Tanzania:* Yeah, I hate it.
> *McCormick:* Why did you hate it?
> *Tanzania:* I have to put myself down. I have to put my hands out (she places her hands on the table in front of us, fingers are stretched apart.) I don't feel right. I feel out of my element.
> *McCormick:* What do you have to do?
> *Tanzania:* I have to stand straight for a few minutes, legs apart, my hands out stretched in front of me. I have to take my bracelets off, take everything out of my pockets. It's very uncomfortable. I feel embarrassed amongst everybody else. It's not a productive way to start off school.

As subjects in an institution of subjugation, young women and men are both "subject to someone else by control and dependence, and tied to [their] own identity by a conscience or self-knowledge" (Foucault 1982, 212). Jennifer McCormick watched this self-knowledge emerge in a group of young women as they explored their own complexities through poetry and wondered how public school space enabled or impeded these explorations. She wondered how girls could negotiate identities that are richly cultural and personally safe inside an institution that, as Foucault writes, brands adolescents as violent. McCormick observed:

Once inside, electronic surveillance, hall passes and police radios fix movement. To enter the cafeteria, teens slide coded identification cards into a machine. A white man surrounded by African American guards oversees the operation. He yells orders. "You need a card . . . Can't come in." Newly arrived students stare in bewildered confusion. Inside the cafeteria, doors are bolted shut. Boys play ping pong in an area of the room not cluttered with lunch tables and food. They are ringed by uniformed guards.

Rudolph Giuliani, New York's current mayor, says he wants to create "safety zones" by assigning police officers inside schools where "security is inadequate" and funding is atrocious and inequitable (*New York Times,* November 11, 1993). This mix of concern and control is not new (Donald 1992). School hallways have long been viewed as "out of control"; but now they are spaces that must be patrolled by police. Rather than seeking educational responses to this trouble, we witness what Vergara (1994) calls the "bunkering of the poor."

This bunkering of the poor profoundly impacts how public policy becomes implemented, with effects that often undermine poor and working-class youth even further. For example, Michelle Fine (1991) and the American Association of University Women (1992) argue that placing the private lives of children and adolescents beyond school walls compromises a young person's education. When schools integrate young women's "public" and "private" lives, they may help young women commit to their education. However, we have seen these "solutions" pervert when implemented in schools serving poor children. When the private lives of poor adolescents become spectacles, public institutions may further brand those they "serve" and their families as deviant or immoral.

Adolescent girls are aware of this institutional surveillance and branding. Their desire to discuss personal issues diminishes radically when they believe that their "personal" stories will be turned against them, when their lives feel invaded but not engaged. If a poor or working-class student of color finds her way to a counselor's office, she may feel pried open, with little respect for her privacy: "Do you like your baby's father? . . . How long have you been without lights? Where does your child sleep?" One young mother complained that on numerous occasions her social worker "comes up too fast" (becomes personal too quickly). Her response was to remain silent. Within this context, silence is not an indication of passivity; it is a form of resistance and a means of protection. In a conversation with a young writer from the poetry workshop, Tanya (a pseudonym), describes an experience of intended help as one of surveillance:

I think counselors should ask what you want. Sometimes you don't want something to happen in a certain way but they do what they have to do. My friend . . . had an incident with her mother. Her mother has a lot of kids. She is single. She has eight kids. My friend felt neglected. She was not getting attention or nothing like that, so she went to her guidance counselor thinking maybe her guidance counselor could talk to her mother and tell her how she feels because sometimes you don't feel right to tell your mother this, but the guidance counselors reported it to B.C.W. (Bureau of Child Welfare). That was the last thing my friend wanted.

When this girl's search for a safe place to talk met the institution's desire and responsibility to report and protect, both desires were undermined. Many of the girls of color in our discussion groups live ever ready to question and resist such help, which they experience, rightly or not, as prying, overdetermined conclusions that await them at school, silencing or appropriating their narratives to fit what the state has allocated "for" them. In such contexts, occasions where young women should be able to talk freely are subverted by "helpful" intrusion.

Surveillance comes in many guises; yet, in its face many young urban women resist. Tanzania presents a strong example of this. Even when we first broached the notion of writing a collaborative essay, about her school and her community, Tanzania bristled: "I don't understand why we black teenagers are constantly being questioned about our neighborhood and the school we attend. What do they think is happening? Why are we constantly badgered? What do you want to find out? Do you want to confirm your own agenda? What information are you trying to get from me?" The voices of the young women in our group reflect an awareness of individual and group needs. Tanzania, for example, speaks of the differences between her community and the images that the white world projects in the media about her community. "I find it amusing that when one talks about city adolescents, we often see black or Spanish children. . . . If I were from another country, I would think that for some reason only black children in American schools are sexually abusive to one another. Should I be getting this message from the media?" Tanzania's awareness is unique, however, because it translates into the belief that she can protect others:

I was afraid something might happen at school, and you'd hear about it on the five o'clock news. I didn't see anyone standing up to any teacher, any corrupt teacher, any corrupt person in that school. I didn't see any one making a nuisance of themselves like I was. I was making a nuisance of myself to get the greater good out of these teachers. It wasn't fair to us that we have to get the second best. Why can't we get the best? Why?

Tanzania's tireless protection of herself and her peers leaves little room for vulnerability or sweet dreams. Her school is a place where she has learned to cultivate resistance against surveillance and oppression. This resistance extends into an understanding of gender politics as well. During a group discussion about a newspaper article on a series of gang rapes in New York City pools, Tanzania acknowledges that tensions of gender fracture her peers:

These rituals, as they are now called, sugar coat the fact that these damn boys think sexual harassment is something that only "adults" have to deal with. They've committed a sexual assault against someone and it's time they were penalized rather than praised, as they often are. They have to stop hiding behind the belief that boys will be boys. And I would like to ask this much: When the hell can girls be girls? No matter what "girl thing" that may be?

As female adolescents living in New York City, Tanzania and the other young women of our discussion group are highly aware of the sexual violence that pervades women's lives. They were able to critique and connect the oppression in both racism and sexism. Tanzania writes:

> Don't Hurt Me Anymore
>
> Don't follow me
> like a rapist stalks his prey
> Don't quiet the words I have to say
> like a rapist covers the mouth of his victim
> to hold back what she must say
> Don't rip savagely apart my dreams
> as a rapist rips the clothes off his victim
> don't throw me down when I try to get up
> like a rapist throws his victim down
> when she tries to escape
> Don't beat me when I struggle to learn and survive
> Don't pin my thoughts down
> like a rapist pins the arms of his victim
> on the cold concrete
> Don't heave your hateful thoughts down on me
> like a rapist heaves his body down on his victim
> Don't thrust anymore of your sick ideas into my head
> like a rapist thrusts his body into his screaming victim
> don't force me to say what you want
> like a rapist forces his victim
> to perform debasing sexual acts
> Don't leave me crying without a shred of confidence
>     to go on
> without a shred of dignity to continue living
> Don't make me second guess myself
> when I know I have the right to speak
> You've left me with the hate I never asked for
> Rapist. Racist. They look almost the same.
> Rapist. Racist. They are the same.

Tanzania's poetry displays an uncanny ability to *deconstruct*, critically, the messages floating in the culture about gender, race, sexuality, and class.

In our discussions with our young coauthors, we have found that they often engage in deconstructing what they see and feel around them. They question the meanings of people's actions; maneuver creatively within spaces they create (and the crevices that society allows them); and resist, while accommodating to, social prescriptions for girls. These deconstructions—*seeing and analyzing the discrepancies between what they are told they can achieve and what they witness as possible in their social contexts*—can be very unsettling, particularly so because they critique elegantly but often alone—without trust in social institutions, without a shared identity with other women, and without any sense that individual analysis could incite broad-based social transformation.

Nikki worries about tensions within her community that fracture relationships among peers—tensions such as those fostered by an individualistic focus on designer clothes and jewelry: "I would love to remove all the name brands that kids wear. They cause too much competition." She realizes the ironies of her community feeding the designer industry: "Look at the Ralph Lauren ad. You don't see a lot of black people playing polo. You see white people playing polo." Yet Nikki and her peers defend their individual spaces in the hallways of school, which have become unsafe territories due to unmitigated competition and escalating violence. They resist with talk; they refuse the role of passive victim. According to Nikki: "Girls talk more of their business in the hallway than they do at home. They speak loudly in the hallway." And some girls, eager agents within these unsafe territories, carry razors and knives, sometimes for protection and sometimes to "disfigure" other girls. In random school raids for weapons, young women are as likely as young men to be found "holding." But these individualistic strategies cannot change the ongoing oppression of surveillance sanctioned by police and the state, nor can it transcend harassment from young men, misogyny from (and toward) other young women, or low expectations from teachers. These young women, like the rest of us, yearn to know—is there possibility for transformation? Will young women ever be allowed the chance to create their own homeplaces that are respected and valued?

## Schools, Surveillance, and Possibilities for Young Women of Many Colors

We now ask how contemporary public schools could be designed to nurture a sense of homeplace that allows for growth, critique, and possibility for young women of many colors. Many large anonymous high schools are an unmitigated educational disaster that should be laid to rest (Fine 1994). Is it oxymoronic to expect these institutions of inequity and surveillance to melt their borders and barbed wire long enough to allow young women to nestle inside, to roll around with their critical contradictions and their confusions and breed a sense of "what could be?"

As we see it, there are several problems with the ways schools are currently designed, with respect to the kinds of concerns young women are narrating. These schools provoke and then pathologize critique, thus making an independent negative contribution to the intellectual, emotional, and cultural curtailment of young urban women. First, as described above, the schools most likely to be attended by urban girls of color are designed as sites of intrusive surveillance or "fortification" (Vergara 1994). These schools, costumed as prisons, educate young women and men to distrust and to understand that they are not to be trusted. Second, these schools (and sometimes families and peers) are organized in ways that discourage young women's pursuit of academically rigorous work and sanction male harassment of women's bodies and minds (Stein 1993). This happens across race, class, and ethnicity. Third, we have growing evidence to suggest that, notwithstanding Fine's early writings on silencing and Freire's writings (1985) on liberatory education, simply learning about social oppression can be problematic for young women (and men) of poverty or color, if they cannot imagine that their oppressive conditions can be interrupted and transformed. If young people see pervasive social inequity and its adverse consequences, but they cannot imagine transformation, such information may simply fold into a heap of hopelessness, cynicism, or alienation (Miller in press). Critical insights without opportunities for students to reconstruct a world rich in the wonders of race, culture, gender, and social justice may wound a sense of possibility. Indeed, we may be witnessing a generation of young women and men who know well, in heads and hearts, the horrors of race, class, and gender subordination, without being able to organize, or make it better. Collective protests and activism seem like a nostalgic memory of parents and grandparents.

Evidence for the latter point comes from a study conducted by Jennifer Pastor (1993) of "possible selves" (Markus and Nurius 1989) envisioned by African American, Caribbean American, and Latino eighth-graders in an inner-city junior high school in New York. A group of 136 students were asked to project themselves forward and list their "possible" occupational selves. Pastor correlated these responses with measures of their perceptions of racism and of limited economic opportunities. Greater awareness of racism and limited economic opportunities were significantly correlated with lower-prestige-level occupational aspirations. As with Fine's data on high school dropouts, it appears to be the case that students of color with sophisticated social consciousness of race and class relations may also have the most depressed sense of what is possible for themselves (see also McLoyd and Jozefowicz, chap. 20 of this volume).

Although the direction of causality could not be established in either

Pastor's (1993) or Fine's (1991) study, the results serve as a caution to educators who have embraced the ideals of multicultural and feminist curricula and are enthusiastic about teaching students of color about race and gender relations historically and currently. *While we are distressed by these findings, we should not be understood as retreating from multicultural and feminist educational ideals.* To the contrary, we are deepening our commitments to such education with the understanding that activism must also be learned. Without engaging an activist pedagogy that educates students of color in the history and politics of *successfully fighting conditions of injustice,* well-meaning educators may risk exposing students to a sense of disempowerment.

Girl's and women's groups can provide insular homeplaces where young women can begin to learn how to transform their isolated analyses and make the "personal political" with profound opportunities for development. Our experience, matched by that of a growing number of feminist educators of many colors who are bringing groups of girls together, is that the young women of the next generation are "hungry for an us" (Fine and Macpherson 1995). They are searching for ways to trust and connect with other girls and women. They are at the same time thrilled to carve out spaces for "girl talk" and frightened by the prospect. They become hopeful and excited when they realize they can create their own homeplaces.

We might try to imagine, then, what could (and does) happen inside schools and communities that engage young women (separately and with young men) in social critique and in activist experiences of social transformation? There are a growing number of feminist spaces, created between adult and adolescent women of many colors, from which we can breathe some sense of hope.

Recent writings by Linda Powell (1994) may help us picture such classrooms and schools. In an essay on Family Group, Powell describes how an urban high school is designed so that every student enjoys an adult confidant for all her years in high school; and every willing adult in the building has a critical mass of ten to fifteen students for whom she or he is responsible over time. Family Group, according to Powell, challenges the social defenses that constrict but also construct typical urban school culture. This process allows for community building and the possibility of erecting homeplaces for both teachers and students.

A variation on Family Group was crafted by Diane Waff (1994), an African American teacher-researcher in Philadelphia who set up a mentor group for her students. The creation of this group was an attempt to reinvent schooling as a safe homeplace for the poor and working-class Latina and African American young women in her class. Marked with the label "special education" for too many years, these young women carry stories and scars of racism, sexism, and classism in their bodies and minds. Waff created a mentor group and witnessed a remarkable shift: "As soon as the girls realized that someone was really listening to them, they were empowered to see themselves as people who mattered. They knew they had the chance to have a direct impact on their lives. They became more vocal about everything" (201). The space Waff created became the home that bell hooks talked about—the place where young women shared secrets, connected stories, made political sense out of personal misery, and organized in resistance.

If Family Group and Waff's girls' group represent emotional, intellectual, and political interventions within school life, there is also evidence that empowering education can also come from outside school. An example of this is Youth Force, an organization designed for, by, and about urban youth. Youth Force works to organize groups of young activists in New York City and testifies to the strength of democratic, activist education from the streets.

In an interview conducted by Nikki, Tanzania, and Jennifer McCormick with members of Youth Force, we hear a coalition of youth activists who critique and organize for collective change resulting in their own empowerment.

> *Wubnesh:* Youth Force was started five years ago by a woman and about twelve young people who were living in different welfare hotels in the midtown Manhattan area.
>
> *Cindia:* [The purpose of the organization] is to school young people to the fact that they are not powerless, that they should be heard and seen, and to also remind them, or even let them know, that young people were always on the front lines when it came to organizing . . . so to encourage them that they can make a difference.
>
> *Wubnesh:* And to give them resources that are not usually accessible and also to help them access public officials and policymakers who set policy around youth issues. *So we try to act as a group of young people who represent the masses of young people who, quote unquote, fall between the cracks or who society has dismissed as underprivileged, disadvantaged, high risk. . . .*
>
> *McCormick:* How do you maintain cohesion?
>
> *Cindia:* I think that a lot comes from maybe the struggles we face here. *Either we stay together and we move forward, or we decide to separate and everybody goes down.* To keep us moving forward we have to tolerate and learn how to deal with one another.

Critique and possibility braid in the biography of Youth Force, Family Group, Waff's classroom, the collective of activist adolescent women of color in the South Bronx who call themselves "Sistahs!" and groups of young women proliferating across the country. Young women of many colors are hungry for spaces in which to talk and dressing rooms for trying on (and discarding) ways to be women: white, African American, Latina, Asian American, straight, lesbian, bisexual, celibate . . .

Within contexts of plain talk and conversation, trust and solidarity, among peers and even a few adults, with a sense of connection and a democracy of shared differences, the one-time "deficits" of young women shine as strengths; their histories of oppression and victimization are reread as struggles and victories; their biographies of loss are reconstructed as archives of collective resilience. Peers link arms to create safe spaces/homeplaces. Fragile individualities can grow into stronger collectivities. Critique within community can be voiced and worked through. Knowing all too well Nikki's poetic plea for a place to go, these young women (and men) are creating such places. Do we not, as adult women and men, have an obligation to help them reinvent and create their own homeplaces?

NOTES

1. Our collaborative work with the girls includes reading, questioning, and editing earlier versions of this paper. We did not print anything that they did not approve of.

2. This poem was written in the context of a project done in Nikki Richardson's high school that was a collaborative program between the Poetry Exchange and the School Partnership Program of New York University.

REFERENCES

Jennifer Pastor and Michelle Fine are grateful to the Bruner Foundation for its support of portions of this research.

American Association of University Women. 1992. *The AAUW report: How schools shortchange girls*. Washington, D.C.: American Association of University Women Educational Foundation and National Educational Association.

Anyon, J. 1982. Intersections of gender and class: Accommodation and resistance by working-class and affluent females to contradictory sex-role ideologies. In *Gender, class, and education*, edited by L. Barton and S. Walker. London: Falmer Press.

Bordo, S. 1993. "Material girl": The effacements of postmodern culture. In *Negotiating at the margins: The gendered discourses of power and resistance*, edited by S. Fisher and K. Davis. New Brunswick, N.J.: Rutgers University Press.

Donald, J. 1992. *Sentimental education: Schooling, popular culture, and the regulation of liberty*. London: Verso.

Erikson, E. H. 1968. *Identity: Youth and crisis*. New York: W. W. Norton.

Fine, M. 1994. Chartering urban reform. In *Chartering Urban Reform: Reflections on urban high schools in the midst of change*, edited by M. Fine. New York: Teachers College Press.

————. 1991. *Framing Dropouts: Notes on the politics of an urban high school.* Albany: State University of New York Press.

Fine, M., T. Genovese, S. Ingersoll, P. Macpherson, and R. Roberts. 1994. White li(v)es: Looking for a discourse of male accountability. In *Unmasking social inequalities: Victims and resistance,* edited by M. Lykes, A. Banuazizi, and R. Liem. Philadelphia: Temple University Press.

Fine, M., and P. Macpherson. 1995. Hungry for an us. *Feminism and Psychology* 5(2):181–200.

Fine, M., and N. Zane, N. 1989. Bein' wrapped too tight: When low-income women drop out of high school. In *Dropouts from school: Issues, dilemmas, and solutions,* edited by L. Weis, E. Farrar, and H. G. Petrie. Albany: State University of New York Press.

Foucault, M. 1979. *Discipline and punish: The birth of the prison.* New York: Vintage.

————. 1982. The subject and power. In *Michel Foucault: Beyond structuralism and hermeneutics,* edited by H. Dreyfus and P. Rabinow. Chicago: University of Chicago Press.

Freire, P. 1978. *Pedagogy of the Oppressed.* New York: Continuum.

————. *The politics of education.* South Hadley, Mass.: Bergin and Garvey Press.

Gilligan, C. 1991. Women's psychological development: Implications for psychotherapy. In *Women, girls, and psychotherapy: Reframing resistance,* edited by C. Gilligan, A. Rogers, and D. Tolman. New York: Haworth.

hooks, b. 1990. *Yearning: Race, gender, and cultural politics.* Boston: South End Press.

Klein, S. S. 1992. Sex equity and sexuality in education: breaking the barriers. In *Sex equity and sexuality in education,* edited by S. S. Klein. New York: SUNY Press.

Lykes, M. B. 1985. Gender and individualistic versus collectivistic bases for notions about the self. *Journal of Personality* 53:356–83.

————. 1989. The caring self: Social experiences of power and powerlessness. In *Who cares? Theory, research, and educational implications of the ethic of care,* edited by M. Brabeck. New York: Praeger.

Markus, H., and P. Nurius. 1989. Possible selves. *American Psychologist* 41:954–69.

Martin, B., and C. T. Mohanty. 1986. Feminist politics: What's home got to do with it? In *Feminist studies, critical studies,* edited by T. de Lauretis. Bloomington: Indiana University Press.

Miller, F. S. In press. Living in chaos: Social adaption responses of African American adolescents. In *Psychosocial and physiological dimensions of black child development,* edited by J. C. S. Fray and J. King. Boston: Erlbaum Press.

Miller, J. B. 1976. *Toward a new psychology of women.* Boston: Beacon.

Moraga, C., and G. Anzaldua, eds. 1981. *This bridge called my back: Writings by radical women of color.* Watertown, Mass.: Persephone Press.

Pastor, J. 1993. *Possible selves and academic achievement among inner-city students of color.* Master's thesis, City University of New York.

Phinney, J. S. 1989. Stages of ethnic identity development in minority group adolescents. *Journal of Early Adolescence* 9 (1–2):34–49.

Powell, L. 1994. Family group and social defenses. In *Chartering urban school reform: Reflections on urban public high schools in the midst of change,* edited by M. Fine. New York: Teachers College Press.

Robinson, T., and J. Ward. 1991. "A belief in self far greater than anyone's disbelief". Cultivating healthy resistance among African American female adolescents. In *Women, girls, and psychotherapy: Reframing resistance,* edited by C. Gilligan, A. G. Rogers, and D. L. Tolman. Binghamton, N.Y.: Harrington Park Press.

Stein, N. 1993. It happens here too: Sexual harassment and child sexual abuse in elementary and secondary schools. In *Gender and Education,* edited by S. Biklin and D. Pollard. Chicago: University of Chicago Press.

Thorne, B. 1993. *Gender play: Girls and boys in school.* New Brunswick, N.J.: Rutgers University Press.

Torres, L. 1991. The construction of the self in U.S. Latina autobiographies. In *Third world women and the politics of feminism,* edited by C. Mohanty, A. Russo, and L. Torres. Bloomington: Indiana University Press.

Vergara, C. J. 1994. The bunkering of the poor. *Nation,* January 31, 1994, 121.

Waff, D. R. 1994. Girl talk: Creating community through social exchange. In *Chartering urban school reform: Reflections on urban public high schools in the midst of change,* edited by M. Fine. New York: Teachers College Press.

# 2 Personal and Ethnic Identity, Values, and Self-Esteem among Black and Latino Adolescent Girls

Mary Jane Rotheram-Borus,
Steve Dopkins, Nuria Sabate,
and Marguerita Lightfoot

Theories of adolescent identity development have traditionally focused on *individuals' intrapsychic* processes (Waterman 1993). The emphasis has been on individuation and an active, goal-focused search for roles, values, and meaning (Salett and Koslow 1994). Whether identity development is an epigenetic unfolding of an inevitable developmental pathway or whether identity evolves from an individual's self-perceptions and behavioral routines in social settings has been hotly debated (Berzonsky 1993; Kroeger 1993; Waterman 1993). In this chapter we will present data on how school contexts influence adolescents' identity, ethnic identity, values, and self-esteem and the implication of these findings for our fundamental assumptions about the nature of identity development.

Few would dispute that school environments influence adolescents' identity and self-concept (Bryk and Driscoll 1988; Coleman and Hoffer 1987). Most adolescents in the United States spend six to eight hours a day in high school. The size of the school (Rutter et al. 1979), the degree of ethnic tension in the school (Schofield 1981), and the violence experienced in school (Armsworth and Holady 1993) have the potential of shaping the adolescent's identity search (Erikson 1968), adjustment (Bennett 1991; Rotheram-Borus 1989), and achievement (Chubb and Moe 1990; Fordham and Ogbu 1986). Even in a highly "caring" interracial school environment, Van Galen (1993) found that African American students were socialized into roles associated with lower levels of achievement, despite the positive intentions of staff, parents, and peers. Everyday school encounters shape the salience and value of one's ethnic identity (Rosenthal, Whittle, and Bell 1989). An adolescent's language use, religion, social activities, maintenance of cultural tradition, family relationships, and physical characteristics are also influenced by everyday interactions at school (Rosenthal and Hrynevich 1985). In this chapter we describe differences in identity development, values, and self-esteem found among African American, Latino American, and white American adolescent girls who live in the same neighborhood but attend different schools. Qualitative data collected during this project led us to reexamine fundamental assumptions about how to define and assess identity development for adolescent girls.

Primary to the search for a personal identity is the exploration and commitment to roles and social identities that direct religious, political, and vocational choices and gender and ethnic reference-group orientations. Over the past forty years identity development has been hypothesized to be the central developmental task of adolescence (Erikson 1950, 1968). To facilitate empirical investigations of the process of identity development, Marcia (1966) identified four identity statuses: (1) diffuse: the status of adolescents who have not considered or explored their roles or reference groups; (2) foreclosed: those who have chosen and committed themselves to a role without exploring any alternative other than the role selected by their parents; (3) moratorium: those in the midst of exploring alternative roles and reference groups, but who have not made commitments; and (4) achieved: those who have explored and committed to roles and a reference group. Adolescents engage in this search in at least six domains: vocational plans, religious beliefs, values and preferences, political affiliations and beliefs, gender roles, and ethnic identities. Therefore, they can be at a different status with respect to their political beliefs in contrast to their religious beliefs or vocational plans.

Historically, women and African American males have been reported to more frequently delay their search for a personal identity until midlife and were seen as more likely to have a foreclosed identity (Douvan and Adelson 1966; Hauser 1972). In more recent examinations, however, gender differences in identity development among adolescents were not dramatic and were limited to specific domains. For example, although adolescent boys have been found to be more foreclosed in their exploration of gender roles than girls, girls and boys have been found to be equally achieved in their gender status (Archer 1989). The identity search has been assessed more often among college students and young adults than among adolescents, and therefore the data for adolescents are more limited.

In contrast to relative similarity between girls and boys in their search for a personal identity, there appear to be gender differences in the processes of identifying and committing to one's ethnic identity (Phinney and Tarver 1988; Waters, chap. 4 of this volume). Ethnic identity refers *ethnic identity definition –* to one's sense of belonging to an ethnic group and to the thoughts, feelings, and behaviors that are a result of this perceived affiliation. It is composed of factors such as ethnic awareness, ethnic self-identification, ethnic attitudes, and choice of reference group (e.g., Black Panther vs. Hip Hop) and ethnic behaviors (Rotheram-Borus and Phinney 1985). Recent research has provided evidence of the importance of social influences on the development of adolescents' ethnic identities (Salett and Koslow 1994).

Three ethnic social identities often identified by African Americans and Latino Americans have been identification with the mainstream, strong ethnic identification, and bicultural identification. *Identification with the mainstream* refers to identification with white, non-Latino, Anglo-Saxon Protestant cultural norms and identifications. *Strong ethnic identification* refers to those who align themselves with their country of family origin and retain traditional values, norms, and behavior patterns. *Bicultural identification,* or *biculturalism,* refers to identification with two distinct cultures within one society and has been hypothesized to reflect the stress of being caught between two cultures (Stonequist 1964). However, it can also imply the acquisition or acceptance of the cultural norms, attitudes, and behaviors of both one's own ethnic group and another ethnic group. Biculturalism in this definition suggests a cognitive and behavioral flexibility (Ramirez 1974)—a strength that can benefit an adolescent. Data have been found both to support and disaffirm the benefits and costs of biculturalism. For example, Rotheram-Borus (1989) found that biculturalism in adolescents was related to aspects of ethnic identity but not to self-esteem and adjustment in an integrated school setting.

Based on previous research, we anticipated that girls and boys would differ in the ways that school settings, ethnicity, and grade level influence personal and ethnic identity, as well as values and self-esteem. Hogg, Abrams, and Patel (1987) found clear gender differences in ethnic sentiment, and Grossman, Beinashowitz, Anderson, and Sakurai (1992), in their study of Anglo and Chicano adolescents, concluded that gender and ethnicity are important influences on individual identity.

To examine how school context, ethnicity, and grade level influence the personal and ethnic identity search, values, and self-esteem of male and female adolescents who are African Americans, Latino Americans, and white Americans, we sampled youths at two high schools in a working-class neighborhood in the northeastern segment of the United States (the rates of parental consent in each school varied). Within this ethnically diverse community, the socioeconomic status of youths was similar across ethnic groups. The two schools differed in size, staffing patterns, attractiveness of the physical plant, and ethnic tensions. This chapter summarizes the differences in identity, values, and self-esteem that were found among students at the two schools.

## Description of School Contexts and Students

### Schools

Table 2.1 summarizes differences observed among the setting and students at each school; table 2.2 identifies significant ($p < .05$) school, gender, ethnic, and grade-level differences on each dependent variable. The schools were located within a mile of each other and recruited youths from the same neighborhood. School 1 was designed to be a "traditional" school. The school was relatively small, ethnically balanced, and emphasized academic achievement and success. School 1 also had a dress code: boys wore ties and girls wore skirts. The school was housed in a relatively old building that appeared clean but overcrowded. The inner-city neighborhood of the school was integrated, and there was risk for crime and violence. Security guards controlled access at each entrance to the school. Teachers met formally and informally with the research team. The administration had cooperated in other research projects and was particularly interested in attracting college recruiters to the school. Although all students at the school were college bound, their aspirations

TABLE 2.1
*Summary of Differences between School 1 and School 2*

| Variable | School 1 | School 2 |
|---|---|---|
| Descriptive features | | |
| Emphasis | Academic | Typical |
| Number of students | $N = 325$ | $N = 1,500$ |
| Parental consent | 97% | 68% |
| Dress code | yes | no |
| Ethnicity | | |
| African American | 30% | 36% |
| Latino | 28% | 16% |
| Asian (primarily Filipino) | 19% | 0% |
| White | 23% | 48% |
| % Born in U.S. | 71% | 68% |
| Student % with weekly cross-ethnic contact | | |
| Hanging out | 40% | 43% |
| Attending parties | 27% | 27% |
| Studying | 26% | 21% |
| Parental background | | |
| Employed | 66% | 53% |
| H.S. graduate | 40% | 44% |
| English language | | |
| Home | 76% | 72% |
| Friends | 70% | 63% |

TABLE 2.2
*Summary of F Scores and Significance Levels Found for an Analysis
of Variance Conducted to Assess School, Gender, Ethnicity, and Grade Level
Effects on Student Characteristics*

| Variable | School | Grade | Ethnicity | Gender |
|---|---|---|---|---|
| % Born in U.S. | | $7.9^a$ | | |
| Cross-ethnic contact | | | | |
|   Hanging out | $6.1^a$ | $13.0^a$ | | $4.1^a$ |
|   Studying | $21.7^c$ | | $4.1^a$ | $15.1^c$ |
| Religious beliefs | | | $6.5^a$ | $7.9^a$ |
| Parental education | $17.8^c$ | | $23.4^c$ | |
| English language | | | | |
|   At home | | | $175.8^c$ | |
|   At school | $5.3^a$ | | $50.1^c$ | $7.1^a$ |
|   With friends | | | $78.5^c$ | $5.9^b$ |
| Grade point average | $8.1^a$ | $4.4^a$ | | $5.0^a$ |
| Personal identity | | | | |
|   Achieved | $3.6^a$ | $4.3^a$ | | |
|   Moratorium | $16.8^b$ | $31.8^a$ | | |
|   Diffuse | $8.8^b$ | | $3.9^a$ | |
|   Foreclosed | $14.9^b$ | | | |
| Ethnic identity | | | | |
|   Achieved | $5.3^c$ | | $4.9^a$ | |
|   Moratorium | | | | $6.1^a$ |
|   Diffuse | $8.3^b$ | | | |
|   Foreclosed | $32.3^b$ | | | |
| Ethnic reference group | $30.0^b$ | | $76.2^c$ | $8.0^a$ |
| Self-esteem | $7.0^a$ | $17.4^c$ | $2.9^a$ | $11.4^c$ |
| Traditional values | | | | |
|   Overall | $22.5^c$ | $4.3^a$ | $3.8^b$ | $6.0^a$ |
|   Group oriented | | | $3.9^a$ | |
|   Cooperativeness | $9.9^a$ | | | $8.5^a$ |
|   Respect for authority | $16.3^c$ | | $6.2^a$ | |
|   Emotional expressiveness | $11.4^c$ | | | |
|   Family expressiveness | | | $6.3^b$ | $7.8^b$ |

$^a p < .05$
$^b p < .01$
$^c p < .001$

focused on local colleges (no student at the school had been admitted to an Ivy League college). There were many scheduled after-school activities, and students occasionally remained at the school until 5 P.M. Although the building was overcrowded, the students were motivated to succeed, and the teachers aimed to ensure their students' success.

School 2 was about four to five times the size of school 1. It was difficult to assess the size of the school because it appeared that about 25% of the youths enrolled at the school had not attended in the previous two months. The building and grounds were about four times as large as those of school 1. The building had four floors of 8,000 square feet each. Situated on the top of a hill and surrounded by greenery, the school initially appeared palatial. However, the actual physical setting was more dilapidated and in greater disrepair than school 1. The smell of urine could be detected on the path to the cafeteria in the basement. The large grounds were bare and scattered with litter. The classrooms were overcrowded, and teachers had to move from room to room to conduct class. Teachers at school 2 were angry and bitter about the problems with the physical plant. The staff at both schools reflected the ethnic mix of the student body.

As shown in table 2.1, in school 1 about 25% of the student body was Asian, primarily Filipino; in school 2 there were few Asian students. Therefore, we have focused our analyses on students from African American, Latino American, and white American groups. After excluding the Filipino students from the analyses, there were fairly equal numbers of African American, Latino, and white students at school 1. In school 2, 520 of the 779 observed students signed informed consent. Of these students, most were white non-Latino, followed by African Americans. Latinos constituted the smallest population. In both schools the white non-Latinos were predominantly from immigrant Portuguese, Irish, or Italian families. Most students at both schools were born in this country. Latino students in both schools were less likely than their peers to be born in the continental United States.

Cross-ethnic contact was frequent at both schools. About 40% of the student body at each school reported hanging out with peers of other ethnic groups five times or more in the last semester. Students in grades nine and ten were more likely to have cross-ethnic contact, and boys were more likely than girls to have this contact. More than one-quarter had gone to parties with students from other ethnic groups more than five times in the last semester. Students of different ethnic groups studied with each other, as shown in table 2.1. African American and Latino American students, females, and students from school 1 were more likely to study together. Ten percent of the students at each school attended ethnically integrated churches. Latino students and girls were more likely to be religious and attend church in integrated settings.

While these data may lead one to conclude that the schools were similar in their high levels of cross-ethnic contacts, the quality of the contacts appeared quite different to the research team. Visiting the schools repeatedly over several months, the researchers observed that the tone of cross-ethnic contacts and cross-ethnic tension varied dramatically between the schools. Fights at school were not recorded by the administration; however, fights appeared common at school 2. Students gathered in same-ethnic cliques in school 2, but not in school 1. Ethnic dress (e.g., dreadlocks, tattoos) was more common at school 2 than at school 1. School 2 reported high cross-ethnic tension.

*Adolescents*

All students at each school were approached to participate. At school 1 a very high rate of active parental consent was received, and all students agreed to participate. At school 2 the rates of parental consent and adherence were calculated based on the number of students in the classes assessed who attended school at least 25% of the time. The absentee rate was about one-third on any given day. Informed parental and student consent was obtained from more than two-thirds of the student body approached.

Assessments were conducted in the school over three days within forty-five-minute class periods. The first day focused on responses to videotaped scenes; the second day focused on questionnaire assessments; and the third day, all ninth- and twelfth-grade girls were interviewed regarding their personal and ethnic identities. Assessments were conducted in gym classes in school 1 and in English classes in school 2, both of which were required classes. Each classroom had at least two monitors to ensure integrity in the data collection approach.

All students were from families of working-class backgrounds, and more than half of the students from both schools lived with both parents. Over half the students at each school had parents who both worked. Almost half of the parents of students in each school had attained a high school diploma or more. Parents of African American students had higher educational levels than parents of non-Latino white or Latino American students. Also, parents of students in school 1 were more educated than parents of students in school 2.

Language use is often an indicator of ethnic identity (Allen et al., chap. 19 of this volume; Heller 1984). As would be expected, Latinos were less likely to use English at home than African Americans or whites, in both schools. About three-quarters of the students at both schools reported speaking English at home. Latino students, girls, and students from school 2 were less likely to speak English at school. The patterns of language use at home were similar to those used with friends, with more than two-thirds reporting using English, and were similar at the two schools. Again, Latinos and females reported less use of English with friends.

Grade point average (GPA), as reported by students, was higher in school 1 and with older students and female students. While there were no significant ethnic group differences in GPA in school 1, there were significant ethnic group differences in GPA in school 2. White non-Latino students had significantly higher self-reported GPAs compared to their African American peers. Students in grades eleven and twelve had higher grades than those in grades nine and ten, which may be because many with low grades are likely to drop out or not attend in this community. In both schools girls had higher grades than boys.

### Contrasts in Personal Identity, Ethnic Identity, Self-Esteem, and Values

Table 2.3 presents the mean scores for personal identity, ethnic identity, self-esteem, and values across schools and by gender. For each psychosocial variable, significant gender, school, ethnicity, and grade differences were found, with few interaction effects. When analysis of variance revealed significant differences among the groups, post hoc analysis indicated which groups accounted for the significant differences. For complete copies of all mean differences, please contact the authors.

#### Personal Identity

Personal identity was assessed both on questionnaire (Adams, Shea, and Fitch 1979) and qualitative (Rotheram-Borus 1989) measures. For each student, four quantitative scores were generated, reflecting the four identity statuses (diffuse, foreclosed, moratorium, and achieved) within the domains of gender roles, vocational plans, religious beliefs, and political ideologies. For each category of identity status and within each domain, students endorsed statements on a scale of 1 to 6 (e.g., 1 = "not at all," 6 = "very much like me"). For example, within the domain of vocational plans, students endorsed statements on a scale of 1 to 6 for each of the identity statuses. Within the domain of religious beliefs, the students endorsed two statements related to the achieved-identity status and one statement for each of the remaining identity statuses. The endorsed statement ratings were summed to generate four (diffuse, foreclosed, moratorium, and achieved) scale scores. There were no significant differences by gender on measures of personal identity. This was an unexpected finding, given earlier work that finds that boys are more likely to be identity-achieved than girls (Douvan and Adelson 1966). Students at school 2 reported significantly higher scores on each of the identity statuses than students in school 1. Because each of the domains in each scale was strongly endorsed by students at school 2, questions were raised about the validity of the assessment measure at school 2. An alternative strategy would be to examine the relative endorsement of each scale within each school setting.

Grade differences were as expected, with students in grades eleven and twelve being more likely to report higher scores on achieved and

TABLE 2.3
*Mean Scores by School and Gender for Personal Identity, Ethnic Identity, Self-Esteem, and Values*

SCHOOL 1

| | Girls | | | Boys | | |
|---|---|---|---|---|---|---|
| | African American | Latino | White | African American | Latino | White |
| Variable | (N = 45) | (N = 73) | (N = 56) | (N = 24) | (N = 23) | (N = 38) |
| Personal identity | | | | | | |
| Achieved | 23.4 | 23.2 | 23.5 | 25.4 | 21.2 | 22.8 |
| Moratorium | 15.1 | 14.0 | 14.5 | 17.1 | 15.1 | 15.2 |
| Diffuse | 20.2 | 20.4 | 19.9 | 18.8 | 20.0 | 20.5 |
| Foreclosed | 14.9 | 14.3 | 16.4 | 12.8 | 16.1 | 16.4 |
| Developmental rank | 3.6 | 3.3 | 3.3 | 4.0 | 3.1 | 3.1 |
| Ethnic identity | | | | | | |
| Bicultural | 7.8 | 8.6 | 8.9 | 8.1 | 8.9 | 8.6 |
| Ethnic achieved | 4.6 | 3.7 | 4.3 | 4.5 | 3.4 | 3.6 |
| Ethnic moratorium | 1.4 | 1.9 | 1.6 | 2.8 | 1.8 | 1.9 |
| Ethnic diffuse | 4.9 | 4.6 | 4.2 | 3.3 | 4.0 | 3.4 |
| Ethnic foreclosed | 2.3 | 2.8 | 2.6 | 1.6 | 3.2 | 2.9 |
| Mainstream | 3.8 | 2.8 | 2.3 | 4.0 | 2.8 | 2.8 |
| Self-esteem | 31.8 | 33.1 | 31.8 | 32.3 | 33.4 | 34.2 |
| Values | | | | | | |
| Cooperativeness | 2.2 | 2.9 | 2.7 | 3.1 | 2.7 | 3.6 |
| Group oriented | 2.5 | 2.4 | 2.7 | 2.3 | 2.4 | 2.9 |
| Emotional expressiveness | 2.7 | 2.5 | 2.5 | 2.4 | 2.3 | 2.7 |
| Respect for authority | 2.1 | 2.1 | 2.4 | 2.4 | 2.6 | 2.6 |
| Overall traditional | 7.4 | 6.9 | 7.5 | 7.3 | 7.2 | 7.8 |

SCHOOL 2

| | Girls | | | Boys | | |
|---|---|---|---|---|---|---|
| | African American | Latino | White | African American | Latino | White |
| Variable | (N = 96) | (N = 46) | (N = 137) | (N = 91) | (N = 37) | (N = 113) |
| Personal identity | | | | | | |
| Achieved | 25.2 | 25.4 | 23.2 | 23.9 | 24.1 | 25.3 |
| Moratorium | 18.2 | 17.4 | 16.2 | 16.5 | 17.5 | 17.5 |
| Diffuse | 23.2 | 20.5 | 21.3 | 24.3 | 20.7 | 21.8 |
| Foreclosed | 16.6 | 17.0 | 17.4 | 18.7 | 20.0 | 17.4 |
| Developmental rank | 3.1 | 3.6 | 3.1 | 2.9 | 3.5 | 3.5 |
| Ethnic identity | | | | | | |
| Bicultural | 1.5 | 1.8 | 2.3 | 1.6 | 1.6 | 2.1 |
| Ethnic diffuse | 5.0 | 4.3 | 4.7 | 4.9 | 4.5 | 4.4 |
| Ethnic foreclosed | 3.2 | 3.7 | 3.7 | 4.1 | 3.9 | 3.8 |
| Ethnic moratorium | 2.1 | 1.6 | 2.0 | 1.6 | 1.8 | 2.0 |
| Ethnic achieved | 4.4 | 3.8 | 3.3 | 3.8 | 3.6 | 3.8 |
| Mainstream | 4.2 | 3.9 | 3.0 | 4.3 | 3.9 | 3.2 |
| Self-esteem | 30.4 | 31.9 | 30.4 | 31.4 | 31.8 | 31.8 |
| Values | | | | | | |
| Cooperativeness | 3.1 | 2.5 | 2.6 | 3.9 | 3.3 | 3.1 |
| Group oriented | 2.6 | 2.9 | 2.8 | 2.4 | 2.6 | 2.8 |
| Emotional expressiveness | 2.8 | 3.2 | 2.8 | 2.5 | 2.9 | 2.7 |
| Respect for authority | 2.5 | 2.7 | 2.8 | 2.4 | 2.6 | 2.6 |
| Overall traditional | 8.0 | 8.7 | 8.5 | 7.3 | 8.2 | 7.9 |

moratorium status. Ethnic differences in identity status also emerged, which is consistent with previous research (Hauser 1972). African American students reported significantly higher scores on the diffuse status in both schools.

## Ethnic Identity

Ethnic identity was assessed by self-report on two separate measures: (1) two items assessed the degree of exploration of and commitment to feelings, roles, and attitudes toward one's ethnicity (i.e., achieved, moratorium, diffuse, or foreclosed) in a manner that parallels personal identity, and (2) self-labeling as *strongly ethnically identified, bicultural,* or *mainstream* was elicited. Students rated themselves on a five-point scale based on how close they felt their identity was mainstream, or White Anglo-Saxon identified, bicultural, or strongly ethnically identified (Adams, Shea, and Fitch 1979; Rotheram-Borus 1990).

Ethnic identity status did not vary significantly by gender, except for the ethnic-diffuse status. Girls reported significantly higher scores on the diffuse scale compared to boys. School setting and ethnicity significantly influenced students' reports of exploration and commitment to their ethnic identity. Students at school 1 were significantly more likely to report higher scores on the ethnic-achieved status. The ethnic-moratorium scale indicated that boys at school 1 were significantly more likely to be in moratorium in contrast to their peers at school 2 ($F = 3.9$, $p < .05$). Students at school 2 reported significantly higher scores on both the ethnic-foreclosed scale and the ethnic-diffuse scale than did students at school 1. Overall, African American students reported significantly higher scores on the ethnic-achieved status; however, there were no other significant differences in other ethnic-status scales. White students reported significantly lower ethnic-achieved scores compared to Latino and African American students.

Labeling oneself as mainstream, bicultural, or strongly ethnically identified varied significantly by gender. Girls were more likely to identify as strongly ethnically identified and to be less mainstream in orientation. Both school and ethnicity also influenced students' chosen ethnic reference groups. Students from school 2 labeled themselves more mainstream than those from school 1. Whites considered themselves more mainstream than Blacks, and Blacks considered themselves more mainstream than Latinos. Reference groups also varied by the interaction of school and ethnicity ($F = 9.66$, $p < .001$). Black and Latino students at school 1 were similar in their reference groups. White and black students were more similar in their self-reports at school 2. Reference groups did not change with grade level, supporting Ogbu's assertions (1983) that ethnic roles are selected by early adolescence and remain relatively stable throughout adolescence.

## Self-Esteem

Consistent with previous research (Osborne and LeGete 1982), girls had significantly lower self-esteem than did boys, and self-esteem was significantly lower at the younger grades. Self-esteem also varied by ethnic group, with Latinos and Whites reporting lower self-esteem than Blacks. Students from school 1 (academically oriented) had higher self-esteem scores than those from school 2. Interestingly, there was a significant difference when self-esteem was analyzed by biculturalism. Students who rated themselves as strongly ethnically identified had higher scores for self-esteem than those who self-identified as mainstream or bicultural ($F = 6.05$, $p < .05$).

## Values

Traditional values include an orientation along four dimensions (Rotheram-Borus and Phinney 1985). Students who rated themselves as more traditional possessed the following characteristics: (1) a group and family orientation in contrast to an individual orientation, (2) cooperativeness in contrast to competitiveness, (3) respect for authority in contrast to egalitarianism, and (4) emotional expressiveness in contrast to emotional restraint. Students rated themselves on each of these dimensions on a scale of 1 to 6. A summary measure was constructed, with higher scores indicating more traditional values. On the index of traditional values, scores varied significantly by gender, school, ethnicity, and grade level. Girls were significantly more traditional in their values than boys; students at school 2 held more traditional values than those at school 1; African American and Latino American students held more traditional values than Whites; and students in grades nine and ten held more traditional values than students in grades eleven and twelve. Therefore, we conclude that these students were reporting a pattern in which traditional values were related to a variety of contextual factors.

There were also significant differences in the students' ratings of each dimension. Latino and black students reported significantly more group orientation, while white students tended to be more individually oriented. A two-way interaction of grade and school showed that students in grades nine and ten at school 2 were more group oriented than ninth and tenth graders at school 1 ($F = 4.22$, $p < .05$). Girls rated themselves as significantly more cooperative, compared to the boys' more competitive ratings. Students from school 2 rated themselves as more cooperative and less competitive than did students in school 1.

Latinos reported significantly more respect for authority than Blacks, and Blacks reported more than Whites. Another significant difference found was by school, with students from school 2 reporting more respect for authority than students from school 1. A two-way interaction of gender by school was found to be significantly different, with female students from school 2 reporting more respect for authority than boys from both schools and girls from school 1.

Students in school 2 reported more emotional expressiveness than students in school 1. Students in school 2 also rated their families as more expressive than students in school 1. There were also significant differences in the students' views of their families' expressiveness by sex and ethnicity. Girls reported their families as more expressive than boys did, and Latino students rated their families more expressive than did black or white students. A two-way interaction of grade and ethnicity revealed that younger Latino, older white, and older black students rated their families as more expressive than older Latino, younger white, or younger black students.

Table 2.3 also presents the differences that were found between girls at the two high schools. Differences were greater among students in the upper grades than among those in the lower grades. Choices made about which high school to attend were magnified and reinforced on a daily basis, so that by twelfth grade, girls who lived next door to each other but went to different schools were dramatically different. Recall that school 1 was academically oriented and had a much lower dropout rate than school 2.

*Qualitative Interviews*

Ninth- and twelfth-grade girls in the high school were interviewed regarding their personal and ethnic identities and also asked to describe their values and anticipated reactions to a variety of social settings to elicit identifying social norms and expectations. Boys were not interviewed because of our interest in girls' identity development. In this preliminary analysis of the girls' reports, we used the summary observations of trained interviewers. The interviewers ranged in educational background from college graduates to Ph.D. level psychologists. The interviews focused on only three domains of identity development: gender role, ethnicity, and vocational pursuits. The girls' responses to the qualitative interviews by identity domain are outlined in table 2.4. On the basis of

TABLE 2.4
*Qualitative Interview Responses by Identity Domain*

| Category | Vocational Plans | Ethnic Identity | Gender Roles |
|---|---|---|---|
| Identity process | | | |
| Explored alternatives | 54% | 36% | 28% |
| Experienced crisis | 18% | 13% | 0% |
| Made a commitment | 65% | 42% | 50% |
| Influences in identity development (rank ordered) | | | |
| Parents | 2 | 1 | 2 |
| Other family | 1 | 2 | 2 |
| Adult model | 4 | 0 | 0 |
| Counselor/teacher | 5 | 5 | 3 |
| Friends | 0 | 0 | 1 |
| Church | 0 | 4 | 3 |
| Experience | 3 | 3 | 0 |
| Media | 5 | 0 | 0 |
| Role model (percent) | | | |
| Parent | 7% | 33% | 43% |
| Book hero | 1% | 1% | 2% |
| Media hero | 7% | 5% | 7% |
| Historical figure | 2% | 4% | 4% |
| Other | 48% | 17% | 29% |

the qualitative interview questions, research assistants classified the girls' reports of three processes: (1) exploration, that is, having explored their beliefs and choices or not having considered alternative beliefs or behavior patterns; (2) crisis, that is, having experienced conflict between alternative choices or with significant others in their social support network over considering alternative choices; and (3) making a commitment to a set of beliefs and behavior patterns. These three processes were examined for the girls in the areas of their vocational plans, ethnic identity, and gender roles. In addition, within each domain the girls were asked to rank influences and role models from prepared cards and given the option to add other alternatives.

As noted in table 2.4, the occurrence of identity exploration, crises, and commitment varied significantly in each domain. The girls were most clear about their career goals and vocational plans. Girls at school 1 wanted to go to college, and they also strongly wanted to be mothers and wives. Most intended to attend the local community college, even though these were the brightest and the best academic students in their city. No student from school 1 had ever attended an Ivy League university, even though the school counselors had repeatedly attempted to place students in these settings. The aspirations of the girls were relatively low at school 2. Many of the high school seniors reported that they wanted to be beauticians; trade schools were often the best alternative these girls anticipated. Their ambitions reflected the alternatives available for working-class adolescents in an inner-city environment, as well as individual variations in achievement. The interviewers were struck, however, by the relatively limited aspirations of the adolescents at both schools.

At both schools, many students reported that they had never experienced racism. When queried regarding specific ways that prejudice may have occurred, students identified more experiences that could be identified as racial or ethnic prejudice. This was particularly surprising, given the high cross-ethnic tension in school 2. The interviewers rated the adolescents as having made a commitment to their ethnic group without having explored their feelings, beliefs, and behavioral patterns associated with their ethnic identity. Focus groups with the interviewers led us to hypothesize that perhaps the exploration of ethnic identity occurs at a slightly older age, consistent with the model proposed by Cross (1987).

Finally, girls reported fairly traditional beliefs regarding their gender roles. Girls had rarely experienced a crisis around their gender role. As noted above, girls at school 1 wore dresses or skirts on a daily basis as part of the school's dress code, which is unusual for a high school today. Only about one in four had explored alternative behavior patterns and beliefs regarding their relationships with men, but half perceived themselves as having clear and committed roles regarding their relationships with men. Because these data were collected in a social context prior to the gay rights movement for adolescents, no queries were made regarding sexual orientation or same-gender beliefs, actions, or behavior patterns. Therefore, our hypotheses are limited to heterosexual roles.

Consistent with data on adolescents in other issues (Damon 1983), adolescents perceived their parents as exercising the greatest control on their identity development; other family members were also strong influences. Adolescents' church affiliations, the media, and teachers ranked relatively low with respect to their influence on adolescents. Thus, parents offer a potential vehicle for shaping adolescents' identity search.

The source of the adolescent girls' role models varied as a function of the domain being examined. Parents were the primary role models for ethnic identity and gender roles; occupational choices were rarely influenced by media, books, historical figures, or parents. We do not have good reports on how adolescents' vocational ideas emerged; however, there is substantial literature on this from other sources (see De León, chap. 21 of this volume).

## Implications for Theories of Girls' Identity Development

Examining the influence of school contexts on identity development for these ethnic minority adolescent girls, as voiced in these interviews, led us to question current popularization of the dominant theories of adolescent identity development. The process of active, instrumental seeking out and committing to a personal identity is a gender- and ethnic-linked concept. Erikson's theories (1968) describe identity as a "process located in the core of the individual and yet also in the core of his communal culture, a process which establishes, in fact, the identity of those two identities." However, in American culture there has been an overemphasis on the individual in understanding Erikson's theories and promoting identity formation among adolescents (Phinney 1993). Most theorists and those attempting to promote adolescent identity achievement (e.g., Carlson 1971; Chodorow 1978; Gilligan 1982; Lykes 1985; Marcia 1966; Sampson 1985; Waterman 1993) implicitly assume the European, North American cultural norms of individualism (Roland 1994). This concept is at odds with most of the world's cultures (Geertz 1973). Self-direction, autonomy, high activity, differentiation, and self-reliance are valued norms and behavior patterns only within specific cultures, and for men. Yet these have been the critical characteristics of identity development, typically framed in terms of conflict and individual choices (Phinney 1993). These beliefs are in direct contrast to the values of group-oriented cultures (e.g., Japanese, Latino, and Hawaiian cultures) and those that value an unfolding and natural harmony with the universe (e.g., Native American) (Roland 1994).

Not only are there ethnic differences in these values, but even within North American cultures, girls are socialized to adopt a more group- and family-oriented focus. Archer (1993) has noted that the identity search for girls is often embedded within a framework of interpersonal relationships. Rather than asking themselves, "Who am I?" girls focus on, "Who am I in relation to others?" (Archer 1993; Gilligan 1982; Josselson 1988). However, beyond mere gender differences in the domains of the identity search, it is possible that the processes themselves are also quite different.

Rather than being socialized to actively and instrumentally seek their destinies, girls are more typically socialized to observe the natural unfolding or development of their identities and to intuit the feelings, goals, and ambitions of others. Waterman (1993) has reminded us that "honest" identity achievement is reflected in a state of "eudaimonia" (a subjective evaluation that one's identity search feels right) in contrast to states of being diffuse (not finding yourself) or disguised (choosing to be someone besides yourself). By focusing on eudaimonia, Waterman (1990, 1993) is calling for identity achievement to be defined as personal expressiveness, a state characterized by (1) intense involvement in an activity, (2) a special fit or meshing with an activity, (3) a feeling of intensely being alive, (4) a feeling that this is what one was meant to do, (5) a feeling that this is

49

who one really is, and (6) a feeling of being completely filled up when engaged in the activity. Ironically, while these definitions of achieving personal identity focus on subjective, internal peak experiences, the activities recommended to achieve this state (Waterman 1993) involve the assertive, instrumental seeking of a range of experiences, identification of role models, and intense self-analysis and critical problem-solving analysis. It is as if these experiences could occur outside an active interpersonal network of affirmation or rejection.

Rather than a process of active seeking and individuation, the girls' interviews suggest that the losing of oneself and one's boundaries in a group identity or passively waiting for an unfolding of one's "true" nature may be alternative routes to integrating one's personal identity. Uba (1994) has proposed a model of ethnic identity that focuses on recognition and acceptance of oneself. She outlines three stages: (1) consciousness of ethnicity, (2) adoption of ethnic identity or selection of a reference group, and (3) enactment of the ethnic identity and integration in everyday settings. This process of self-recognition and acceptance is not one that necessarily roots itself in conflict or in individuation. Recognizing contexts that make one highly comfortable and gaining recognition from the people who share similar values, norms, and styles awaken  one's identity. The contextual focus on identity must not be limited to the content of our investigations, but must extend to the process. As the background of the researchers studying and theorizing about identity development expands, the models of "successful achievement" must themselves expand. Our culturally bound notions of identity and the process of establishing an identity must be reexamined.

## REFERENCES

This work was completed with the support of Grant number 5R01HD20840-02 from the National Institute of Child Health and Human Development.

Adams, G., J. Shea, and S. Fitch, S. 1979. Toward the development of an objective measure of ego identity status. *Journal of Youth and Adolescence* 8:223–37.

Archer, S. 1989. Gender differences in identity development. *Journal of Adolescence* 12:117–38.

———. 1993. Identity in relational contexts: A methodological proposal. In *Discussions on ego identity,* edited by J. Kroeger, 75–100. Hillsdale, N.J.: Lawrence Erlbaum Associates.

Armsworth, M., and M. Holady. 1993. The effects of psychological trauma on children and adolescents. *Journal of Counseling and Development* 72:49–72.

Bennett, K. 1991. Doing school in an urban Appalachian first grade. In *Empowerment through multicultural education,* edited by C. Sleeter. Albany: State University of New York Press.

Berzonsky, M. 1993. A constructionist view of identity development: People as postpositivist self-theorists. In *Discussions on ego identity*, edited by J. Kroeger, 169–204. Hillsdale, N.J.: Lawrence Erlbaum Associates.

Bryk, A., and M. Driscoll. 1988. *The high school as community: Contextual influences, and consequences for students and teachers*. Madison, Wis.: National Center on Effective Secondary Schools.

Carlson, R. 1971. Sex differences in ego functioning: Exploratory studies of agency and communion. *Journal of Consulting and Clinical Psychology* 37:267–77.

Chodorow, N. 1978. *The reproduction of mothering: Psychoanalysis and the sociology of gender*. Berkeley: University of California Press.

Chubb, J., and T. Moe. 1990. *Politics, markets, and American schools*. Washington D.C.: Brookings Institution.

Coleman, J., and T. Hoffer. 1987. *Public and private high schools: The impact of communities*. New York: Basic Books.

Cross, W., Jr. 1987. A two-factor theory of black identity: Implications for the study of identity development in minority children. In *Children's ethnic socialization: Pluralism and development*, edited by J. Phinney and M. J. Rotheram, 117–32. Beverly Hills, Calif.: Sage.

Damon, W. 1983. *Social and personality development: Infancy through adolescence*. New York: W. W. Norton.

Douvan, E., and J. Adelson. 1966. *The adolescent experience*. New York: Wiley.

Erikson, E. 1950. *Childhood and society*. New York: W. W. Norton.

———. 1968. *Identity: Youth and crisis*. New York: W. W. Norton.

Fordham, S., and J. U. Ogbu. 1986. Black students' school success: Coping with the "burden of acting white." *Urban Review* 18(3):176–206.

Geertz, C. 1973. *The interpretation of cultures*. New York: Basic Books.

Gilligan, C. 1982. *In a different voice: Psychological theory and women's development*. Cambridge: Harvard University Press.

Grossman, F., J. Beinashowitz, L. Anderson, and M. Sakurai. 1992. Risk and resilience in young adolescents. *Journal of Youth and Adolescence* 21:529–50.

Hauser, S. 1972. Black and white identity development: Aspects and perspectives. *Journal of Youth and Adolescence* 1:113–30.

Heller, M. 1984. Language and ethnic identity in a Toronto French language school. *Canadian Ethnic Studies* 16:1–14.

Hogg, M., D. Abrams, D., and Y. Patel. 1987. Ethnic identity, self-esteem, and occupational aspirations of Indian and Anglo-Saxon British adolescents. *Genetic, Social, and General Psychology Monographs* 113:487–508.

Josselson, R. 1988. The embedded self: I and thou revisited. In *Studies in social identity: Integrative approaches*, edited by D. Lapsley and F. C. Power, 91–106. New York: Springer-Verlag.

Kroeger, J. 1993. Ego identity: An overview. In *Discussions on ego identity*, edited by J. Kroeger, 1–20. Hillsdale, N.J.: Lawrence Erlbaum Associates.

Lykes, M. 1985. Gender and individualistic versus collectivist bases for notions about the self. *Journal of Personality* 53:356–83.

Marcia, J. 1966. Development and validation of ego identity status. *Journal of Personality and Social Psychology* 3:551–58.

Ogbu, J. 1983. Crossing cultural boundaries: A comparative perspective on minority education. Paper presented at symposium, Race, Class, Socialization and the Life Cycle, in honor of Allison Davis, John Dewey Professor Emeritus, University of Chicago.

Osborne, W., and H. LeGete. 1982. Sex, race, grade level, and social class differences in self-concept. *Measurement and Evaluation in Guidance* 14:195–201.

Phinney, J. 1993. Multiple group identities: Differentiation, conflict, and integration. In *Discussions on ego identity,* edited by J. Kroeger, 47–74. Hillsdale, N.J.: Lawrence Erlbaum Associates.

Phinney, J., and S. Tarver. 1988. Ethnic identity search and commitment in black and white English graders. *Journal of Early Adolescence* 8:265–77.

Ramirez, M. 1974. Cognitive styles of children of three ethnic groups in the United States. *Journal of Cross Cultural Psychology* 5:212–19.

Roland, A. 1994. Identity, self, and individuation in a multicultural perspective. In *Race, ethnicity, and self: Identity in a multicultural perspective,* edited by E. Salett and D. Koslow, 11–23. Washington, D.C.: National Multicultural Institute Publications.

Rosenthal, D., and C. Hrynevich. 1985. Ethnicity and ethnic identity: A comparative study of Greek-, Italian-, and Anglo-Australian adolescents. *International Journal of Psychology* 20:723–42.

Rosenthal, D., J. Whittle, and R. Bell. 1989. The dynamic nature of ethnic identity among Greek-Australian adolescents. *Journal of Social Psychology* 129:249–58.

Rotheram-Borus, M. J. 1989. Ethnic differences in adolescents' identity status and associated behavior problems. *Journal of Adolescence* 12:361–74.

———. 1990. Adolescents' reference group choices: Self-esteem and adjustment. *Journal of Personality and Social Psychology* 59:1075–81.

Rotheram-Borus, M. J., and J. Phinney. 1985. Ethnic behavior patterns as an aspect of identity. Paper presented at a meeting of the Society for Research in Child Development, April, Toronto, Canada.

Rutter, M., B. Maughan, P. Mortimore, and J. Ouston. 1979. *Fifteen thousand hours: Secondary schools and the effects on children.* Cambridge: Harvard University Press.

Salett, E., and D. Koslow, eds. 1994. *Race, ethnicity, and self: Identity in a multicultural perspective.* Washington, D.C.: National Multicultural Institute Publications.

Sampson, E. 1985. The decentralization of identity: Toward a revised concept of personal and social order. *American Psychologist* 40:1203–11.

Schofield, J. W. 1981. Complementary and conflicting identities: Images and interactions in an interracial school. In *The development of children's friendships,* edited by S. R. Asher and J. M. Gottman. Cambridge: Cambridge University Press.

Stonequist, E. V. 1964. The marginal man: A study in personality and culture conflict. In *Contribution to urban sociology,* edited by E. Burgess and D. J. Bogue. Chicago: University of Chicago Press.

Uba, L. 1994. *Asian Americans: Personality patterns, identity, and mental health.* New York: Hillsdale Press.

Van Galen, J. 1993. Caring in the community: The limitations of compassion in facilitating diversity. *Urban Review* 25(1):5–24.

Waterman, A. 1990. Personal expressiveness: Philosophical and psychological foundations. *Journal of Mind and Behavior* 11:47–74.

———. 1993. Finding something to do or someone to be: A eudaimonist perspective on identity formation. In *Discussions on ego identity,* edited by J. Kroeger, 147–68. Hillsdale, N.J.: Lawrence Erlbaum Associates.

# 3 Diversity in Girls' Experiences: Feeling Good about Who You Are

Sumru Erkut, Jacqueline P. Fields, Rachel Sing, and Fern Marx

The evolving demographic profile of the young female population in the United States today poses a critical challenge to a growing body of research on adolescent girls, a challenge that is not solely theoretical. It also has profound practical implications for policies and programs to promote gender equity for girls and young women.

Research on women and girls until relatively recently focused primarily on white middle-class females. There is growing recognition, long overdue, in mainstream gender research circles that the absence or underrepresentation of girls from certain communities and contexts calls into question the generalizability of findings. Participation in mainstream academic knowledge building by different kinds of women, not only as study subjects but also as researchers, will require a reevaluation of the assumptions, approaches, and purposes that have shaped research on women and girls to date.

Inclusion of diverse experiences and perspectives undoubtedly will also challenge mainstream views in unforeseeable ways. We contend that race or ethnicity, social class, and urbanization of residence do not merely account for variations on a universal or essential experience of being female. Instead, these factors mediate gender in ways that produce qualitatively different "female" experiences for girls and young women.

In this chapter we briefly summarize some central concerns that have framed our own research on girls' sense of themselves and their world in different communities. We then report the results of a study of girls from five racial and ethnic backgrounds and their answers to the question "What activities make you feel good about yourself?" Self-regard is a construct that provides a lens for exploring girls' development in a social context in which race, ethnicity, class, and gender are inseparable defining features. We use the term *self-regard* to include a range of terms and concepts that refer to the feelings one has about oneself, such as self-esteem, self-perceived competence, self-concept, efficacy, and so forth.

## Are Adolescent Girls at Peril for Not Having Positive Views of Themselves?

In popular forums in the United States in recent years, from television talk shows to best-selling books, conventional wisdom about the connection between a person's psychological outlook and her or his success (e.g., academic attainment, career and income level, and social status) has proliferated. The notion that feeling good about yourself is a prerequisite for success has been prevalent. Similarly, in academic research, a prominent view is that positive self-perceptions of ability are more important in determining an individual's level of achievement than actual ability or competence (Bandura 1990; Seligman 1991). A positive personal outlook yields positive results. Conversely, low self-esteem and low self-appraisals of competence have been linked with low motivation and achievement. At the same time, some proponents of self-esteem have observed that success does not ensure high self-regard (Steinem 1992). It has been noted that particularly among females, who tend to attribute their achievement to external factors or good fortune rather than to innate ability, success does not guarantee high self-esteem (Clance 1985).

Concern about young women's self-regard converged with concerns about gender equity in such landmark reports as *Reflections of Risk: Growing Up Female in Minnesota, A Report on the Health and Well-being of Adolescent Girls in Minnesota* (Minnesota Women's Fund 1990) and the AAUW poll conducted by Greenberg-Lake, *Shortchanging Girls, Shortchanging America* (American Association of University Women 1991). Girls' high self-regard has been associated with motivation to achieve (academically and in a career) and confidence in their ability to achieve (AAUW 1991; Baruch 1975; Phillips and Zimmerman 1990). While some research indicates that an adolescent's self-concept generally remains positive (Marsh and Gouvernet 1989), other research notes a low point in many girls' self-regard beginning in early adolescence (AAUW 1991).

Longitudinal studies have found that a decline in positive self-regard among adolescent girls contrasts not only with males' experiences, but with younger girls' self-confidence, self-concepts, and optimism about their lives (Brown and Gilligan 1992; Phillips and Zimmerman 1990). Low self-regard has been associated with low personal aspirations (both academic and in career goals) and, in some cases, with low academic achievement (AAUW 1991). Other studies have reported that dissatisfaction with one's body, eating disorders, depression, and suicide attempts all occur at much higher rates for adolescent girls than for adolescent boys (Gans and Blyth 1990; Reinherz, Frost, and Pakiz 1990).

Increasingly, being female is being defined as a factor that puts a young person "at risk" (Earle, Roach, and Fraser 1987), and early adolescence is regarded as a critical time in girls' lives (AAUW 1991; Brown and Gilligan 1992). Indeed, in their recent work, Gilligan and her colleagues view adolescence as a "crossroads" for girls. They describe it as a time of crisis when girls become uncertain of what they know and can speak, a time when girls confront new prescriptions about their responsibility to themselves and to others and rules about knowledge and understanding that may be publicly expressed but may not be knowledge based on their own experience and intuition (Brown and Gilligan 1992; Debold, Wilson, and Malave 1993; Gilligan, Rogers, and Noel 1992). However, because this construction of girls' adolescence is based largely on research with white, privileged girls, it leaves open the possibility that these findings may be a product of that particular context.

## Limitations of Existing Notions of Risk and Resilience

An assumed correlation between self regard, motivation, and success has informed most theories and interventions around "at risk" youth (see Luthar and Zigler 1991). However, risk, to a large extent, is a matter of perspective. The risks that Michelle Fine (1991), Signithia Fordham (1988), or Maxine Baca Zinn and Bonnie Thornton Dill (1994) associate with systemic and institutionalized racism, cultural corrosion, and disconnection from the supportive ties of family and community contrast with the antisocial outcomes that Gary Wehlage (Wehlage, Rutter, and Turnbaugh 1987) associates with risk (e.g., repeating a grade, school tardiness, pregnancy.)

Notions of "resilience" and "protective factors" (e.g., Bernard 1991) often reflect white, middle-class cultural models of child rearing, interpersonal relationships, and lifestyles (e.g., Baumrind 1989; Luthar and Zigler 1991) that are not necessarily practiced or valued in every community. The sociocultural specificity of such concepts as "at risk" and "resilience" speak to the degree to which self-regard itself is a cultural construct. For example, the notion that the more an individual believes in her own capability, the more persistent she will be in the face of obstacles or adversity (Bandura 1990) is a cultural model that is not necessarily meaningful in all social contexts. One can argue that a girl's ability to rely on others, to access knowledge and resources in her community, and to cultivate a support network are just as important in enabling her to be persistent in the face of obstacles and adversity. In our exploration of "feeling good about who you are" among different girls in different communities, we have asked what "feeling good" means, what it entails, and how it manifests itself for different girls.

## Intersections of Gender, Race or Ethnicity, and Social Class

Critiques of feminist research on girls, such as the work of Carol Gilligan and her colleagues, have been directed at the tendency to universalize or essentialize characteristics and experiences observed among certain girls as the characteristics and experiences of all girls (for a summary, see J. M. Taylor 1994). Developmental models that may be appropriate in certain white, middle- and upper-middle-class settings cannot be generalized to all girls in all contexts (Robinson and Ward 1991; Stack 1994). One study has found that girls in different racial or ethnic groups exhibit different patterns of self-esteem (AAUW 1991). Indeed, self-regard among African Americans has been found to match or exceed that of their white peers (Powell 1985; Rosenberg and Simmons 1971; R. L. Taylor 1976).

A recent study on racial and ethnic differences in academic achievement (Steinberg, Dornbusch, and Brown 1992) demonstrated that, in addition to important differences between white adolescents and adolescents of color, there were notable differences among students of color that defy simple categorization. The researchers found that parenting styles, peer values and support, and historic social status in the United States interacted in such different ways for young people in different racial and ethnic groups that there was no simple formula—no single key factor—for students' academic success or failure. Their study points to the need for research on young people that explores not only between-group differences but also differences within groups, including gender differences. For example, Diaz-Guerrero (1987, cited in Rotheram-Borus 1989) notes a shift in cultural expectations of Latino males' behavior and attitudes during adolescence (i.e., to be assertive and to question authority) that is not paralleled in cultural expectations of Latinas, which, instead, continue to emphasize cooperation and respect for authority.

Research indicates that for adolescents of color, developmental processes may differ from those of white youth (Tatum 1992). Race and ethnicity generally are salient for adolescents of color, particularly in their identity formation, in ways that they are not salient for white adolescents (Phinney 1989; Rotheram-Borus 1989). "Racism," Tatum notes, "defined as a system of advantage based on race, is a pervasive aspect of U.S. socialization" (1992, 3). For white girls, gender may indeed be the principal site for struggle and negotiation in terms of personal identity and social place. For girls of color, culturally and linguistically different girls, working-class girls, and girls living in poverty, gender is not the only site for struggle and negotiation, nor is it necessarily the most salient site. There is also a need for exploring the implications of white identity in development, rather than viewing whiteness as neutral or as a norm.

There is significant social and cultural diversity within major racial and ethnic groups based on language, nationality, religion, socioeconomic status, immigration or migration history, and even skin color. This diversity suggests the need for exploring the "diversity within diversity." The research described below is based on responses of a racially, ethnically, and socioeconomically diverse group of girls. We present findings on their descriptions of what activities make them feel good about themselves.

## Diversity in Girls' Views of What Activities Make Them Feel Good

The data for this study were collected as part of a larger project on racial and ethnic diversity in Girl Scouting, which was carried out in twelve states.[1]

### Sample

The sample was recruited from the five broad ethnic classifications: Native American, African American, Anglo-European American, Asian Pacific Islander, and Latino. The field sites were three states in the East, three in the South, three in the Midwest, and three in the West. The field sites included a mix of urban areas, suburbs, small cities and towns, rural areas, and Native American reservations. We collected information from 77 Native American, 94 African American, 41 Anglo-European, 76 Asian Pacific, and 74 Latina girls. In total, we obtained data from 362 girls, 175 of whom were current Girl Scouts, 65 of whom were ex-Girl Scouts, and 122 of whom had never been associated with Girl Scouts in any way. The ages of the girls ranged from 6 to 18 with a mean of 12.4 ($SD = 2.6$).

### Procedures

The data collection occurred in small groups of three to five girls who met with an interviewer of the same race or ethnicity as that of the girls. The focus group interview included a question on activities that made the girls feel good about who they were and a follow-up question asking what about the activity made them feel good.

*Results*

Because there were no statistically significant differences among current Girl Scouts, former Girl Scouts, and girls who had never joined Girl Scouting, we combined the data on all girls for further analyses. Close to half of all girls (46%) gave answers that mentioned an *athletic* activity, such as playing basketball or baseball, swimming, or gymnastics. The next most frequently mentioned activity dealt with the *arts,* such as music, painting, ballet, drama, and arts and crafts activities, mentioned by 19%. Responses indicative of *service to others* were given by 14% of the girls, and *playing* was mentioned by 13%.

When asked what about the activity makes them feel good about themselves, 28% of the girls gave responses that were coded as indicative of *mastery or competence*—for example, "I can do it," "I'm good at it." Twenty-five percent indicated that they *enjoyed the activity,* 14% said it *helped people,* 10% said it was an opportunity to *be with friends,* and 6% said it was a way of *"expressing who I am."*

There were a number of patterns related to race or ethnicity, socioeconomic status (SES),[2] and urbanization of residence and interactions among these variables. Native American and Asian Pacific American girls were most likely to mention athletics as an activity that made them feel good about themselves (52 and 50%, respectively). In general, high SES girls were less likely to mention athletics (chi square = 23.3, $df = 8$, $p$ =. 003) but much more likely to mention an arts-related activity (chi square = 15.7, $df = 8$, $p = .05$). The tendency to find athletics self-enhancing was most pronounced for low SES Native American girls.

The arts appear to be an option most frequently available to middle and high SES girls who live in urban areas. Of all the girls who said an arts-related activity made them feel good about who they were, fully one-third were high SES girls who lived in big cities. The pattern of SES and urbanization interaction was even stronger for community service, whereby girls who lived in big cities and high SES girls were more likely to mention that being of service to others made them feel good (chi square = 17.0, $df = 6$, $p = .009$). This pattern of high SES and urban residence interaction was most pronounced for Asian Pacific American and European American girls (chi square = 31.4, $df = 8$, $p = .001$). Over 90% of the girls who reported service to others made them feel good said the reason was that they liked helping people.

The finding that mastery of the activity ("I can do it") was one of the main reasons it made one feel good is particularly relevant to a discussion of positive self-regard. Here again, we found race, ethnicity, and SES differences (chi square = 28.9, $df = 8$, $p = .0003$). Overall, Asian Pacific

American and Latina girls were more likely to say that mastering an activity made them feel good about who they were than were Native American, African American, or European American girls. However, SES interacted with racial and ethnic group. Among Asian Pacific Americans and European American girls, SES was positively related to mastery: high SES girls were most likely to report mastery, followed by middle SES girls, and then low SES girls. Among Latinas and Native Americans, however, it was negatively related to mastery: low SES girls from these groups were more likely to report mastery than high SES girls. Among African Americans, SES had no effect on reporting mastery.

African American and Asian Pacific American girls were more likely than the other groups of girls to say their enjoyment of the activity was the reason it make them feel good (30 and 28%, respectively) (chi square = 26.4, $df = 8$, $p = .009$). Residence in a rural area or reservation was associated with saying that the opportunity to be with friends while doing an activity was the reason the activity made them feel good (chi square = 12.1, $df = 6$, $p = .059$). Indeed, low SES Native American girls were the group most likely to give this response, accounting for 21% of girls who said being with friends was the reason the activity made them feel good. Opportunity for self expression (through art, music, or drama) was given as a reason by a small number of girls (6%). The majority of them were middle SES, African American girls who lived in big cities. They accounted for nearly a third of all who gave this reason.

*Discussion*

An unexpected finding was the frequent mention of athletics as an activity that made girls feel good about themselves. This finding was unexpected for two reasons. First, for a large number of girls, involvement in sports is a relatively new phenomenon in the United States, dating to the passage of Title IX in 1972. One of the provisions of the Title IX Education amendments of 1972 is that schools must provide equal athletic opportunity for both sexes. Although it is true that some girls have participated and excelled in school sports for a long time, before Title IX the range was limited, and cheerleading was the only "athletic" outlet available to girls in many public schools, and often even that was not an option for nonwhite girls in integrated schools. Since then public schools have attempted to provide more opportunities and support to girls' athletic activities. Title IX has by no means eliminated unequal access to sports for girls, but it has made sports programs more widely available to girls in institutions that receive federal financial assistance (see National Advisory Council on Women's Educational Programs 1986). In twenty years sports have become sufficiently available to girls to be a source of self-enhancement. This finding underscores the importance of historical time as a social context.

In addition, deriving self-enhancement from participating in a physical activity, and reporting mastery as the primary reason for such enhancement, has not been generally recognized in traditional or even modern female roles in the United States. Women (and girls) have been described as deriving their worth from relationships (see Brown and Gilligan 1992; Miller 1976). Yet only 10% of the girls in our study stated that a certain activity made them feel good about themselves because it gave them an opportunity to be with friends. The findings about sports and mastery suggest that the availability of opportunities, which may be context specific, plays a major part in defining gender roles.

It appears that sports are a relatively inexpensive, widely available source of self-enhancement, whereas the pursuit of arts-related activities requires a financial outlay for lessons or supplies and is more readily available to high SES girls. However, socioeconomic level appears to have the opposite impact on Asian Pacific American girls. In this group, high SES girls most frequently reported athletics as an activity that made them feel good, followed by middle SES girls, and then low SES girls. The finding that low SES Native American girls and high SES Asian Pacific American girls were most likely to find self-enhancement in athletics again underscores the importance of social context—in this case, the intersection of race or ethnicity, SES, and urbanization. Among low SES Native American girls, many of whom lived on reservations and in rural areas, more than three-quarters reported that sports made them feel good because it was a way to be with their friends. On the other hand, for high SES Asian Pacific American girls, sports is an activity that gives them a sense of mastery and enjoyment. Moreover, the finding that these girls discovered self-enhancement in sports, which has not been part of the traditional definition of Asian Pacific female identity, suggests the possibility of the high SES Asian Pacific American girls' greater resistance to the stereotype of the demure Asian female.

Overall, our results show a relationship between high SES and the desire to be of service to others; an association between living in rural areas, feeling good about oneself, and being with friends; and a correlation between high SES, urban residence, and finding arts-related activities to be a source of feeling good. These findings suggest that the presence or lack of opportunities and resources plays a major role in determining what makes girls feel good about who they are.

## Conclusion

Our research on activities that make a girl feel good about who she is and the reason why that activity makes her feel good is but one approach to the larger question of girls' self-regard. These data illustrate the diversity of girls' experiences and the importance of social context for understanding their development. Our data point to SES and rural/urban residence differences among girls from diverse racial and ethnic groups. These three broad categories (race or ethnicity, SES, and urbanization of residence) merely scratch the surface of relevant contexts of girls' lives. An important factor left out of our analysis because of sample size constraints is the diversity within racial and ethnic groups. Racial and ethnic groups can encompass diversity with respect to language, national origin, recency of immigration, religion, and skin color. Our data did not take into consideration the implications of differing abilities or of sexual orientation. Both are major determinants of one's identity and self-regard. Nor did it take into consideration perceived discrimination, which is another important social context for how one feels about oneself.

There is a need for explorations of girls' life experiences in multiple and diverse contexts in order to (a) illuminate gender as one kind of socially constructed difference among other kinds of difference that are equally significant (e.g., race or ethnicity and class), (b) detail how gender is configured and plays out differently in diverse communities and contexts, and (c) examine how gender as a configuration of power relations interacts with other asymmetries of power, including asymmetry based on race or ethnicity and class.

A girl's self-regard does not develop in a social or cultural vacuum. The gender roles, expectations, and relations that prevail in one community do not necessarily map well onto roles, expectations, and relations in another community. Qualities associated with "female" in one community may not translate to "female" in another community. The meaning of puberty and values around female sexuality can vary considerably. Attitudes, values, and behaviors that lead to survival and success for females in one context do not necessarily serve a girl's interests in another. The challenges that many girls face in constructing meaning, negotiating different environments, and finding affirmation of "who they are" are considerable. Orenstein (1994) depicts detailed examples of how similar and how different risks and opportunities can be for girls, depending on race or ethnicity, class, and urbanization of residence.

Similarly, as Fine and Zane (1989) note, the social context of girls' lives fundamentally shapes the choices girls have. Schooling for many girls of color, as well as immigrant and working-class or economically poor girls, may be experienced not as an enhancing process but instead, as Fordham and Ogbu (1986) state, as a "subtractive" process that involves denying, abandoning, or repressing important pieces of oneself. Fine (1991) echoes this perspective in her study on young African Americans who left high school before graduating. Fine observed that many students who left school departed as "feisty social critics." Their short-term strategy for self-preservation, however, did not serve them well in the long run. Four years later, Fine found many of them no longer feisty and critical, but depressed and struggling economically.

Robinson and Ward (1991) similarly find that girls' strategies to survive do not always serve them well. In their study of young African American girls' resistance to oppression, Robinson and Ward distinguish between "resistance for survival" and "resistance for liberation." Resistance for survival, which is short-term and often short-sighted, can include food addictions, substance abuse, school failure, and early pregnancy. Robinson and Ward associate it with internalized negative images, excessive individualism, and disconnection from community. Resistance for liberation, by contrast, involves girls' naming and addressing the oppressions in their lives (see also Ward, chap. 5 of this volume).

In conclusion, the major point we raise is that the questions that have guided most research on adolescent girls have not been informed by the wisdom of women and girls who are different from the white, middle-class mainstream. Nor have there been sufficient investigations of the diverse experiences of *all* girls. Just as studying women's and girls' experiences in the world opened many minds to seeing female development in a new, nonpathologizing, nondeviant perspective, so studying girls' experiences in the full social context of their lives will bring forth more valid and accurate understandings of female development.

NOTES

1. For greater detail on the methods employed in the Girl Scouts study see S. Erkut, J. P. Fields, D. Almeida, B. De León, and R. Sing, *Strength in diversity* (New York: Girl Scouts of the U.S.A., 1994).

2. Socioeconomic status is estimated using a composite index based on parent reports of parent(s)' education and total family income. The sample was divided into thirds—low, middle, and high SES groups—on the basis of their scores on the SES index.

REFERENCES

The research reported here was funded by a contract from Girl Scouts of the U.S.A for a study on racial and ethnic diversity. The literature review is based in part on Rachel Sing's qualifying paper submitted to Harvard Graduate School of Education. The collaboration of Deirdre Almeida, Brunilda De León, and Stephanie Geller in the research is gratefully acknowledged, along with the support provided by Sylvia Barsion, national director for research and evaluation for Girl Scouts of the U.S.A. We also thank the forty-five interviewers who participated in the collection of the data.

American Association of University Women. 1991. *Shortchanging girls, shortchanging America.* Washington, D.C.: AAUW, Analysis Group, Greenberg-Lake.

Baca Zinn, M., and B. T. Dill. 1994. Difference and domination. In *Women of color in U.S. society,* edited by M. Baca Zinn and B. T. Dill. Philadelphia: Temple University Press.

Bandura, A. 1990. Conclusions: Reflections on nonability determinants of competence. In *Competence considered,* edited by R. J. Sternberg and J. Kolligan, Jr. New Haven: Yale University Press.

Baruch, G. K. 1975. Girls who perceive themselves as competent: Some antecedents and correlates. Unpublished paper, Worcester Foundation for Experimental Biology, Shrewsbury, Mass.

Baumrind, D. 1989. Rearing competent children. In *Child development today and tomorrow,* edited by W. Damon. San Francisco: Jossey Bass.

Bernard, B. 1991. *Fostering resiliency in kids: Protective factors in the family, school, and community.* Portland, Oreg.: Western Regional Center for Drug-Free Schools and Communities, Far West Laboratory.

Brown, L. M., and C. Gilligan. 1992. *Meeting at the crossroads: Women's psychology and girls' development.* New York: Random House.

Center for Research on Women, Wellesley College. 1992. *How schools shortchange girls: A study of major findings on girls and education.* Washington, D.C.: American Association of University Women.

Clance, P. R. 1985. *The imposter phenomenon.* Atlanta, Ga.: Peachtree.

Debold, E., M. Wilson, and I. Malave. 1993. *Mother daughter revolution: From betrayal to power.* Reading, Mass.: Addison Wesley.

Diaz-Guerrero, R. 1987. Historical sociocultural premises and ethnic socialization. Cited in *Children's ethnic socialization: Pluralism and development,* edited by J. Phinney and M. Rotheram. Beverly Hills, Calif.: Sage Publications, 1989.

Earle, J., V. Roach, and K. Fraser. 1987. *Female dropouts: A new perspective.* Alexandria, Va.: National Association of State Boards of Education.

Fine, M. 1991. *Framing dropouts: Notes on the politics of an urban public high school.* Albany: State University of New York Press.

Fine, M., and N. Zane. 1989. Bein' wrapped too tight: When low-income women drop out of high school. In *Dropouts from school: Issues, dilemmas, and solutions,* edited by L. Weis, E. Farrar, and H. G. Petrie. Albany: State University of New York Press.

Fordham, S. 1988. Racelessness as a factor in black students' school success: Pragmatic strategy or Pyrrhic victory? In *Facing Racism in Education,* edited by N. M. Hidalgo, C. L. McDowell, and E. V. Siddle. Reprint Series no. 21. Cambridge: Harvard Education Review.

Fordham, S., and J. U. Ogbu. 1986. Black students' school success: Coping with the "burden of acting white." *Urban Review* 18 (3):176–206.

Gans, J., and D. Blyth. 1990. *America's adolescents: How healthy are they?* Chicago: American Medical Association.

Gilligan, C., A. G. Rogers, and N. Noel. 1992. Cartography of a lost time: Women, girls, and relationships. Paper presented at the Lilly Endowment Conference on Youth and Caring, February, Miami, Florida.

Luthar, S. S., and E. Zigler. 1991. Vulnerability and competence: A review of research on resilience in childhood. *American Journal of Orthopsychiatry* 61 (1):6–22.

Marsh, H., and P. Gouvernet. 1989. Multidimensional self-concepts and perceptions of control: Construct validation of responses by children. *Journal of Educational Psychology* 81 (1):57–69.

Miller, J. B. 1976. *Toward a new psychology of women.* Boston: Beacon Press.

Minnesota Women's Fund. 1990. *Reflections of risk: Growing up female in Minnesota, a report on the health and well-being of adolescent girls in Minnesota.* Minneapolis: Minnesota Women's Fund.

National Advisory Council on Women's Educational Programs. 1986. *Title IX: The Half Full, Half Empty Glass.* Washington, D.C.: U.S. Government Printing Office.

Orenstein, P. 1994. *Schoolgirls: Young women, self-esteem, and the confidence gap.* New York: Doubleday, in association with the American Association of University Women.

Phillips, D. A., and M. Zimmerman. 1990. The developmental course of perceived competence and incompetence among competent children. In *Competence considered,* edited by R. J. Sternberg and J. Kolligan, Jr. New Haven: Yale University Press.

Phinney, J. 1989. Stages of ethnic identity development in minority group adolescents. *Journal of Early Adolescence* 9 (1–2):34–49.

Powell, G. J. 1985. Self-concepts among Afro-American students in racially isolated minority schools: Some regional differences. *Journal of the American Academy of Child Psychiatry* 24:142–49.

Reinherz, R., A. Frost, and B. Pakiz. 1990. *Changing faces: Correlates of depressive symptoms in late adolescence.* Boston: Simmons College School of Social Work.

Robinson, T., and J. V. Ward. 1991. "A belief in self far greater than anyone's disbelief": Cultivating resistance among African American female adolescents. In *Women, girls, and psychotherapy: Reframing resistance,* edited by C. Gilligan, A. G. Rogers, and D. L. Tolman. Binghamton, N.Y.: Harrington Park Press.

Rosenberg, M., and R. Simmons. 1971. *Black and white self-esteem: The urban school child.* Rose Monograph Series. Washington, D.C.: American Sociological Association.

Rotheram-Borus, M. J. 1989. Ethnic differences in adolescents' identity status and associated behavior problems. *Journal of Adolescence* 12:361–74.

Seligman, M. 1991. *Learned optimism.* New York: Random House.

Stack, C. B. 1994. Different voices, different visions: Gender, culture, and moral reasoning. In *Women of color in U.S. society,* edited by M. Baca Zinn and B. T. Dill. Philadelphia: Temple University Press.

Steinberg, L., S. Dornbusch, and B. Brown. 1992. Ethnic differences in adolescent achievement: An ecological perspective. *American Psychologist* 47 (6):723–29.

Steinem, G. 1992. *Revolution from within: A book of self-esteem.* Boston: Little, Brown.

Tatum, B. D. 1992. Talking about race, learning about racism: The application of racial identity development theory in the classroom. *Harvard Educational Review* 62 (1):1–24.

Taylor, J. M. 1994. Adolescent development: Whose perspective? In *Sexual cultures and the construction of adolescent identities,* edited by J. M. Irvine. Philadelphia: Temple University Press.

Taylor, R. L. 1976. Psychosocial development among black children and youth: A reexamination. *American Journal of Orthopsychiatry* 46:4–19.

Wehlage, G., R. Rutter, and A. Turnbaugh. 1987. A program model for at-risk high school students. *Educational Leadership* (March): 70–73.

# 4 The Intersection of Gender, Race, and Ethnicity in Identity Development of Caribbean American Teens

Mary C. Waters

Adolescence is a time when young people explore and make decisions about their ethnic identities—coming to terms with the ethnic and racial identities of their parents and societal perceptions of their ethnicity and race and making decisions about how they will self-identify. For minority group members this often means developing a bicultural identity or awareness as they learn to function in both the culture of their own group and the culture of the mainstream. Rotheram-Borus (1993) describes this process as choosing a "desired self" or reference group orientation and notes that minority adolescents can choose a "desired self that is closely identified with the mainstream, one that is strongly ethnically identified, or one that is bicultural" (86). Adolescent children of immigrants face an even more complex task because, along with dealing with cross-cutting pressures of minority and mainstream identities, they also have to negotiate an identity between the culture of the society in which they live and the culture of the society in which their parents were raised. In addition, black immigrants and their children face the reality that race imposes an identity on them, despite the choices they might individually make.

In this chapter I examine the complexities of ethnic and racial identities for the children of Caribbean immigrants. Specifically, I examine the racial and ethnic identities developed by a sample of black adolescents who were either born in the United States of immigrant parents or who immigrated themselves to the United States at a young age. I discuss the ways American race relations shape and change the immigrant experience for those who are classified as minorities in the United States. I explore also the types of identities adopted by teens and the unique factors that affect inner-city girls as opposed to boys in these communities. Although I find that gender does not determine the type of identity chosen by the adolescents in my sample, it does shape the meanings attached to these identities. In effect, the task of developing a racial and ethnic identity is bound up with issues of gender identity as well. Choosing an American identity means something different to girls than to boys because the boundaries between different types of identities are more fluid and permeable for girls than for boys.

## The Study

Immigration from the English-speaking islands of the Caribbean has been substantial throughout the twentieth century, but the numbers of immigrants coming from the West Indies and Haiti increased dramatically after immigration laws were changed in 1965 (Bryce-Laporte 1972; Kasinitz 1992). According to the 1990 census, there were 1,455,294 foreign-born blacks in the United States, who comprised 4.8% of blacks nationwide. The vast majority of these are from the Caribbean. Miami and New York City, the chief destination cities for these immigrants, have a much higher concentration of foreign-born blacks and their children than other cities do. Currently about 25% of the black population in New York is foreign born, with a substantial and growing second generation. Because the census does not ask for the birthplace of parents, it is impossible to know exactly how many second-generation West Indians are living in the United States.

In 1990–92 I conducted a study in New York City of black immigrants to the United States from the Caribbean. The overall study was designed to explore the processes of immigrant adaptation and accommodation to the United States, to trace generational changes in adaptation and identification, and to explore the reactions of immigrants and their children to American race relations. The 212 interviews conducted included 72 first-generation immigrants from the English-speaking islands of the Caribbean, 27 native-born Whites, and 30 native-born Blacks, as well as 83 adolescents who were the children of black immigrants from Haiti and the English-speaking islands of the Caribbean. These adolescents, who are the focus of this chapter, were drawn from four sources designed to tap a range of class backgrounds and class trajectories. They include:

1. The public school sample: teenagers attending two public inner-city high schools in Brooklyn, New York, where I did extensive interviewing and participant observation (45 interviews).

2. The church school sample: teenagers attending Catholic parochial schools in the same inner-city neighborhood as the public high school

(although most of these students were not themselves Catholic) (14 interviews).

3. The street-based snowball sample: teenagers living in the same inner-city neighborhood in Brooklyn who could not be reached through the school—either because they had dropped out or because they would not have responded to interviews conducted in a formal setting (15 interviews).

4. The middle-class snowball sample: teenagers who had ties to this neighborhood, who were now living there and attending magnet schools or colleges outside of the district, or whose families had since moved to other areas of the city or to suburbs (9 interviews).

Overall, 16% of the 83 teens were from very poor families on public assistance, 49% were from families with at least one parent working at a low-wage job, and 35% were from middle-class families, with at least one parent in a job requiring a college degree. They included 34 (41%) who comprise the classic second generation—born in the United States of immigrant parents. Another 14 (17%) had immigrated to the United States before age 7. The rest of the sample included 35 young people who had immigrated after age 7 and had spent at least three years in the United States. The actual age at immigration for these more recent immigrants varied from 7 to 15. I use the term second generation broadly here to refer to adolescents who were either born in the United States or came to the United States before age 7, and I refer to the other adolescents as child immigrants.[1]

Of the adolescents interviewed for this study, 52% were female and 44% were from single-headed households. They ranged in age from 14 to 21, with an average age of 17. Twenty-two students were age 14–16, 37 were age 17–18, and 24 were age 19–21. The families of the students were from twelve different countries, including Jamaica (31%), Trinidad (21%), Guyana (16%), Barbados (10%), Haiti (10%), and Grenada (5%); a few came from each of the smaller islands of Montserrat, Saint Thomas, Anguilla, St. Lucia, Dominica, and Nevis. There were some differences, of course, in the experiences and cultures of people whose families came from different islands. However, the island of origin of the respondent's family did not affect the outcomes discussed here, so I will not focus on it in depth.[2]

I draw on the material from the first-generation interviews for the opinions held by individuals who resemble the parents of these teens.[3] The interviews of the adolescents were conducted by me (a white female) and three research assistants: a female second-generation Barbadian

American, a male black American, and a male second-generation Haitian American. The interviews were tape recorded and ranged in length from one to three hours. The questions elicited open-ended life histories and included a number of questions about racial and ethnic identity and attitudes, experiences of discrimination and prejudice, and relations with family, school, and peers. The interviews were transcribed and analyzed both holistically in terms of each individual's life history and story and thematically across interviews.

The two public schools were among the five most dangerous schools in New York City: they had inadequate facilities with crumbling physical buildings, high dropout rates, and serious problems of violence. I had thought initially that it would be necessary to match the race, ethnicity, and gender of interviewer and respondent, but after spending time in the schools I found that it was not necessary. We developed a rapport and a reputation among the respondents that allowed me to conduct cross-racial interviews and to obtain what I believe to be candid and valid results.[4]

One strategy that worked exceptionally well in the inner-city high schools was as follows: I asked a research assistant, a black male football player from Harvard University who had grown up in New York City, to spend time just hanging out in the school. He visited the cafeteria and the rooms where students spent their free time. His status as a college student who played football, as well as his outgoing personality, made him popular among the students. He answered all of their questions about me—the gray-haired lady who carried a tape recorder—reassuring the students that I was not associated with the high school and that it was OK to talk to me. This allowed the students to feel at home with me and contributed to the frankness and openness with which the teens in the two inner-city high schools answered the interview questions.

## The Problem of Identity Construction

First-generation black immigrants to the United States have generally been either classified with or contrasted to black Americans. In general the research shows that these immigrants tend to distance themselves from American Blacks—stressing their national origins and ethnic identities as Jamaican, Haitian, or Trinidadian. However, they also face overwhelming pressures in the United States to identify only as Blacks (Foner 1987; Kasinitz 1992; Stafford 1987; Sutton and Makiesky 1975; Woldemikael 1989).

Long-standing tensions between newly arrived West Indians and American Blacks have left a legacy of mutual stereotyping, with West

Indians holding many negative opinions of black Americans and vice versa.[5] The first-generation immigrants believe that their status as foreign-born blacks is higher than that of black Americans, and they tend to accentuate their identities as immigrants. Their accent is usually a clear and unambiguous signal to other Americans that they are foreign born.

The dilemma facing the children of the immigrants is that they grow up exposed to the negative opinions voiced by their parents about American Blacks and to the belief that Whites respond more favorably to foreign-born blacks. But they also realize that because they lack their parents' accent and other identifying characteristics, other people, including their peers, are likely to identify them as American Blacks (Bryce-Laporte 1972). How does the second generation handle this dilemma? Do they follow their parents' lead and identify with being Jamaican, Haitian, or West Indian? Or do they try to become American and reject their parents' ethnic immigrant identities?

Theories derived from the experiences of European immigrants and their children in the early twentieth century predict that the longer the time spent in the United States, the more exposure to American culture, the more likely youth are to adopt an "American identity" and to reduce ties to the immigrant or ethnic identities and culture of their parents. This "straight line" assimilation model assumes that with each succeeding generation ethnic groups become more similar to the mainstream Americans and more economically successful (Gans 1992).

However, the situation for recent immigrants and their children in the United States differs in many of the background assumptions of the straight line model. Because these recent immigrants come from Latin America, Asia, and the Caribbean, they are often subject to racial exclusion and discrimination to a much greater extent than are European immigrants. In addition, they do not enter a society that assumes a monolithic "American culture," but rather a consciously pluralistic society in which a variety of subcultures and racial and ethnic identities coexist. The current economy that immigrants enter is also different. The unskilled jobs in manufacturing that gave opportunities for job mobility for immigrants' children at the turn of the century have been lost as the economic structure of the United States has shifted to a service economy.

New theories describing the experiences of becoming American for recent immigrants and their children (Gans 1992; Portes and Zhou 1993) stress the multiple and contradictory paths that can be followed by second-generation children. Some achieve socioeconomic success while retaining strong ethnic attachments and identities, and others assimilate to American subcultures with limited socioeconomic mobility.

Portes and Zhou (1993) describe the various outcomes of groups of second-generation youth as "segmented assimilation." They argue that the mode of incorporation of the first generation leads to different opportunities in jobs, networks, and values, which, in turn, create different pulls on the allegiances of the second generation. For immigrants who come with strong ethnic networks, access to capital, and fewer ties to minorities in the United States, the second generation is more likely to resist acculturation and maintain strong ethnic ties to the parental generation. But for immigrants who face extreme discrimination in the United States and who reside in proximity to American minorities, the second generation is likely to develop an "adversarial stance" toward the dominant white society. This adversarial stance stresses that discrimination in the United States is very strong and devalues education as a vehicle of advancement. Portes and Zhou (1993) argue that the adversarial outlook directly contradicts the immigrant parents' expectations of upward mobility and educational success for their offspring and could prove "a ticket to permanent subordination and disadvantage for the youngsters who adopt it" (96).

John Ogbu (1990) describes a similar minority outlook as an oppositional frame of reference. Ogbu argues that involuntary minorities such as Blacks and American Indians in the United States respond to the derogatory images held by the dominant group and to blocked mobility by cultural inversion. Cultural inversion is defined as "the tendency for members of one population . . . to regard certain forms of behavior, events, symbols, and meanings as inappropriate, precisely because they are characteristic of members of another population, for example, white Americans" (Ogbu 1990, 148). Involuntary minorities may interpret behaviors that are opposed to the dominant society as intrinsic to "a sense of collective or social identity, a sense of self worth" (148). Behaviors such as speaking standard English or conforming to school requirements, associated with Whites, may threaten group solidarity or identity. Ogbu (1990) contrasts immigrants with involuntary minorities and distinguishes between an immigrant identity, which does not have this oppositional or adversarial stance, and an involuntary minority, which does. Second-generation West Indians may develop either an immigrant or ethnic identity like that of their parents or an oppositional identity like that of their black American peers.

Research with West Indians suggests that the second generation may hold onto their ethnicity and emphasize their distinction from American Blacks. This serves to remove them from the negative stereotypes of Blacks in the United States, and it allows them to maintain some sense of superiority over American Blacks (Justus 1976; Sutton 1973). Constance Sutton (1973, 142) proposes that assimilation holds opposite meanings for black and white immigrants. For Whites the move from being an immigrant to being an American represents upward social mobility. For Blacks the move from being an immigrant to "merely being American black" represents downward social mobility. Other researchers argue that the second generation will develop a strong racial identity, reject their parents' ethnicity, and identify themselves as black Americans out of a strong sense of racial identity (Michael 1990; Stafford 1987; Woldemikael 1989).

## Three Paths of Identity Development

My interviews suggest that, although there is a great deal of individual variation in the identities, perceptions, and opinions of these teens, their racial and ethnic identities can be classified into three general types: identifying as Americans, identifying as ethnic Americans with some distancing from black Americans, or maintaining an immigrant identity that does not reckon with American racial and ethnic categories. Gender affects these identity choices in subtle ways. Overall, boys and girls chose to identify themselves in about equal numbers across the three categories, but there were differences in the meanings attached to an American identity by boys and by girls. After an overview of the three types of identities I detected, I will focus on these different meanings.

### American Identity

An American identity characterized the responses of approximately 42% of the respondents. They tended to downplay their backgrounds as Jamaican or Trinidadian and described themselves as American. They did not see their ethnic identities as important to their self-image. Most included their ethnic identities as background, but none of them adopted the stance that they were not in a major sense American. This American-identified girl was asked to describe her ethnic background and how other people think of her:

*What is your ethnic background?*

I put down American[6] because I was born up here I feel that is what I should put down. . . .

*What do other people think you are?*

Black American because if I don't say . . . Like if they hear my parents talk or something they always think they are from Jamaica. . . . But they just think I am black American because I was born up here. [17-year-old female, born in U.S. of Jamaican parents, American-identified]

Some of these young people told us that they saw few if any differences between ethnic Blacks and American Blacks; their experiences were that whatever differences there were quickly went away. Many stressed the Caribbeanization of black New York and described how much the American kids were interested in adopting Caribbean styles of dress, talk, music, and food.

The American-identified teens reported that, overall, their parents held many negative opinions of American Blacks. However, these teens either disagreed with their parents' statements about American Blacks, reluctantly agreed with some of them but provided qualifications, or perhaps, most disturbingly, accepted the appraisals as true of American Blacks and of themselves. This young Trinidadian American hears her parents' stereotypes and directly applies them to herself:

*How close do you feel in your ideas about things to West Indians?*

Not very close. My feelings are more like blacks than theirs. I am lazy. I am really lazy and my parents are always making comments and things about how I am lazy. They are always like in Trinidad you could not be this lazy. In Trinidad you would have to keep on working. [16-year-old female, born in U.S. of Trinidadian parents, American-identified]

These youngsters are very aware of the generalized negative view of Blacks in the wider culture. In answer to the question "Do Whites have an image of Blacks?" all responded that Whites had a negative view of African Americans as criminals, lazy, violent, and uncaring about family. The American-identified teens saw this racial prejudice as a fact of their lives that occurred because they were black. Unlike the ethnically defined youngsters, they did not think that their parents' immigrant origins afforded them any protection from these prejudices.

Elements of an "oppositional identity" among the American-identified teens were also apparent. These teens were more likely than the ethnic or immigrant teens to describe racial prejudice as pervasive and as limiting their own individual chances. They more often described the school as representing white culture and white requirements. They were also more likely to report that they would describe someone as not "acting black" or as "acting white." The ethnic-identified and immigrant-identified teens were aware of these terms but were more likely to see them as problematic. They were less likely to use the terms to describe other people.

*Ethnic Identity*

Another 30% of the respondents adopted a very strong ethnic identity that involved a considerable amount of distancing from American Blacks. It was important for these respondents to stress their ethnic identities and for other people to recognize that they and their parents were not American. These respondents tended to agree with parental judgments that there were strong differences between Americans and West Indians and that West Indians were superior to American Blacks in their behaviors and attitudes. As one teen says:

The West Indians tend to go that extra step because they, Whites, don't usually consider them really black Americans which would be working class. They don't consider them I guess as black. They see them as a person. [17-year-old female, born in U.S. of Trinidadian parents, ethnic-identified]

Some of the ethnic-identified teens echo the feelings we heard from the first generation that American Blacks are too quick to use race as an explanation or an excuse for not doing well. Unlike the American-identified teens, who saw a great deal of racial discrimination directly affecting them, the ethnic-identified youngsters thought the role of race in American society was often overblown. The ethnic-identified teens who were doing well tried to understand how it was that they were so successful when black Americans were not. Often they attributed their socioeconomic position or their success in school, or both, to immigrant family values that stress education. Aware of, and sometimes sharing stereotypical negative images of black Americans, these teens also perceive that Whites treat them better when they realize they are not "just" black Americans.

However, these young people also know that unless they tell people of their ethnicity, most Whites have no idea that their families are not American. Many of these teens coped with this dilemma by devising ways to advertise their identities as second-generation West Indians or Haitians. One girl carried a Guyanese map as part of her key chain so that when people looked at her keys they would ask her about it and she could tell them that her parents were from Guyana. Another young woman described having her mother teach her an accent so that she could use it when she applied for a job or a place to live. Others just try to somehow work it into the conversation when they meet someone. This means that their self-identification is almost always at odds with the identifications others make of them in impersonal encounters in American society. Unlike the American-identified youngsters, who gave little thought to how to "manage" others' impressions of them, these youngsters were very aware that they needed to counteract assumptions of other people if their ethnic, and not their racial, identity was to be known.

### Immigrant Identity

A final 28% of respondents had what I call an immigrant identity. They did not feel as much pressure to choose between identifying with or distancing from black Americans as did either the American-identified or the ethnic-identified teens. Strong in their identities with their or their parents national origins, they were neutral toward American distinctions between ethnics and black Americans. While an ethnically identified Jamaican American is aware that she might be seen by others as American and thus actively chooses to present herself as Jamaican, an immigrant-identified Jamaican could not conceive of herself as having a choice, nor could she conceive of being perceived by others as American. An ethnic-identified teen might describe herself as Jamaican American, but for the immigrant-identified teen Jamaican would be all the label needed. Most teens in this category were recent immigrants themselves. The few U.S.-born teens classified as immigrant-identified had strong family roots on the islands, were frequent visitors to the islands, and had plans to return there to live as adults. A crucial factor that allowed these youngsters to maintain their identity was that their accents and styles of clothing and behavior clearly signaled to others that they were foreign born.

> *Do you identify more with being Guyanese or more with being black American?*
>
> Well, I'll be more a Guyanese person because certain things and traditions that I am accustomed to back home, it's still within the roots of me. And those things have not changed for a long period of time. Even though you have to adapt to the system over here in order to get ahead and cope with what is going on around you. [18-year-old Guyanese male, in U.S. 7 years, immigrant-identified]

Whereas the ethnic-identified tended to describe people treating them better when they were aware of their ethnic origins, and the American-identified tended to stress the anti-Black experiences they had had and the lack of difference between the foreign born and the American, the immigrant-identified teens spoke about seeing a lot of anti-immigrant feelings and discrimination and responded with pride in their national origins.

### Influences on Identity Development

Social class was an important influence on what type of social identity the teens adopted. Only 8% of the very poor youngsters in the sample had ethnic identifications, while 42% of them were American-identified and 50% of them were immigrant-identified. Of the working-class youth, only 20% were ethnic-identified, 49% were American-identified, and 31% were immigrant-identified. Of the middle-class youth, 57% were ethnic-identified, 32% were American-identified, and only 11% were immigrant-identified. Teens from a middle-class background apparently are more likely to identify ethnically, while those from a working-class or poor background seem more likely to identify as Americans.

Although there was no overall difference in the numbers of boys and girls in the choice of identity adopted, there were significant differences in the meanings they attached to being American. The two main differences were that girls were under greater restrictions and control from parents than boys and that racism appeared to have a different impact on boys than on girls. Boys discussed being black American in terms of racial solidarity in the face of societal exclusion and disapproval. Girls also faced exclusion based on race, but they discussed being American in terms of the freedom they desired from strict parental control. In the next section I describe the teens' own perceptions of these cross-cutting pressures, and I conclude with a discussion of their possible effects on the boundaries between different types of identities.

## Strictness of Parents

All respondents thought that West Indian parents were much stricter than American parents and that the former were even more strict with girls than with boys. The girls also reported far more restrictions placed on their activities and movements by their immigrant parents than did the boys. While the ethnic-identified adolescent girls tended to point to their parents strictness as a very positive factor in their lives and stated that they would bring their children up the same way, the American-identified girls responded to this differential treatment by criticizing their parents for being too strict and for not understanding American culture. This 16-year-old says:

My mother's strict, she don't give me that much privileges, and at some time I said to them, you know I wish I had an American parent because, you know they would be—I'm not saying they would let me on the loose but I would have some kind of freedom. That's not a word that should be in our vocabulary you know, because I am not allowed to go to parties. [16-year-old female, born in U.S. of Haitian parents, American-identified]

Many of the American-identified girls pointed to the freedom their brothers had to stay out late, date, talk on the phone, work at part-time jobs, and so forth, and were upset that they did not have the same privileges. They saw their American classmates having much more freedom. Frequently, this reinforced their American identity.

### Reactions to Racism

Ironically, although parents monitor girls' activities more than they do boys' activities, the boys face a more violent environment than do the girls because of the differential effects of American racism. The boys reported far more racial harassment from Whites and from police than did the girls, and they felt less at ease when they left their all-black neighborhoods than did the girls. The types of incidents reported by the boys included instances of gangs of Whites threatening them or starting fights with them when they ventured into white neighborhoods. Common situations faced by both girls and boys were being followed in stores because they were suspected of shoplifting and seeing people recoil in fear in public places—on the street, on the subway, in parks, and anywhere the youngsters encountered Whites. A girl from Guyana describes this situation:

When you're on the trains, and like white people start holding their pocketbooks because they think you're going to rob them or walking down the street, they'll cross the street and stuff like that. [17-year-old Guyanese female, in U.S. 11 years, American-identified]

She goes on to say that this type of thing, although it happens to girls, is much more likely to happen to her male friends. This was a common perception, and the boys described being hurt and very angry by white people's reactions to them.

The white ladies on the street, they see us coming and they stop and the women start looking in the window. And like quick, look in the window until you pass by and then they start walking again. Like one time I was going to summer school. And this old lady was at the bus stop and she turned around, and I was walking, and she started walking. And I walk pretty fast, and I was walking behind her. And I caught up to her and she stopped at the bus stop. And I was going there too, and so I stopped to see if the bus was coming. And the first thing I see the lady do, she was walking so fast. The first thing she took her bag off, and she put her arm through it and she had it on like this [across shoulder]. [18-year-old Jamaican male, in U.S. 15 years, ethnic-identified]

Some of the ethnic-identified boys and girls, like this one, blame their treatment on Whites who confuse them with black Americans. This young man told his interviewer that if this woman had known he was Jamaican, and not black American, she would not have been afraid of him. The ethnic-identified teens assume that Whites have valid reasons for being afraid of black Americans on the street, but not of Caribbean Americans. The American-identified teens did not describe these behaviors as understandable; rather, they saw racial prejudice by Whites as the cause, and racial solidarity among Blacks was important to them in the face of such pressures. Rather than looking to the police as a source of safety from being attacked by Whites in these neighborhoods, the American-identified males told many stories of being singled out by police in a threatening way for things they did not do. This 18-year-old male from Grenada was stopped at a train station and pushed against the wall by a police officer who yelled racial slurs at him and his friends when they were on their way to their summer jobs. He said he and his friends concluded:

Because what happen really with the cops nowadays, don't care what they do. They just want to manhandle you anyhow because the law is in their hands. They think they could do anything that they want to do to you.[18-year-old Grenada male, in U.S. 9 years, American-identified]

In the two high schools where we interviewed, it was far more likely for girls to graduate from high school than for boys. The girls also perceived having more job opportunities than did the boys. The message that boys get from the behavior of Whites, the police, and from these educational outcomes is that they are unwelcome in mainstream society. This appears to create a rigidity in their attitudes toward racial solidarity that is not present so much among the girls. Two pieces of evidence in our data that appear to suggest that boys pay acute attention to racial boundaries are that the boys were more likely to speak of social stigma if they spoke standard English among their friends, and that they were more likely to report that they accuse others of "acting white" than were the girls.

All of the youngsters interviewed described behaviors that were considered to be "acting white." These included speaking standard English, having white friends, listening to "white people's music," walking a particular way, and refusing to adopt particularly "black" ways of doing things. While the girls described these differences and could point to girls who "acted white," the boys tended to have more polarized opinions about it. For American-identified boys the phenomenon of "acting white" or speaking standard English was a very important way of describing others and determining with whom they could be friends. Ethnic-identified boys usually denied that "acting white" was a real phenomenon. They were proud of their ability to code-switch in speech, although many of them said some of their classmates would accuse them of "acting white" for behaving that way. "Acting white" and speaking standard English were not the same for the girls, and they were far less likely to say that they would describe others that way or that they would choose their friends on that basis. "Acting white" for the boys was also often associated with challenging masculinity. According to a few respondents, both boys and girls, a girl could use standard English and not be ostracized by her peer group for doing so, but a boy who used standard English could have his masculinity questioned. This 17-year-old describes someone who acts white as "like a faggot":

> *Do you know anyone who acts white?*
>
> Yeah
>
> *What did they do to make you think they are acting white?*
>
> Well it was a combination of acting white and being a faggot. It was a combination. He used to, like there are certain things he would do. He would be around us and we'd be talking in a certain tone of voice and he would just sound different. He wouldn't sound like us. And then, yeah another thing, he never had a girl. He never had no girl, And we were like, damn dude what's wrong? [17-year-old male, born in U.S. of Jamaican parents, American-identified]

## Conclusion

In this study an equal number of boys and girls chose to be ethnic or American or immigrant in their social identities. This choice appears to be a harsher and more all-encompassing one for the boys than it is for the girls. Girls appear to have more leeway. They are able to claim a racial identity, maintain a stance of racial solidarity, and also to be more bicultural. Signithia Fordham (1988) also found a gender difference in her study of black Americans in a Washington, D.C., elementary school. Although those students did not have an alternative ethnic identity to choose when accused of "acting white," some developed a "raceless" identity in order to conform to mainstream educational requirements. She says this appears to be much easier for the girls than the boys and that the girls also appear to be "much less victimized [than the boys] by the fact that they are required to live in two worlds concurrently" (Fordham 1988, 67).

Similarly, for the boys in the current sample, choosing not to conform to specific ideas of black racial identity appears to also challenge their gender identity. Girls, who are less violently stigmatized in the wider society for their race, seem to have more latitude for adopting a bicultural identity. However, stricter control of girls and the pressures toward less equality for girls in Caribbean households will push these girls toward desiring an American lifestyle, which includes more freedom to date, less discipline, and greater equality of sex roles.

An ironic element of our findings is that although the parents typically appeared to believe that teenage girls were more in need of protection by parents, the boys see fewer opportunities in their future, are under more peer pressure not to do well in school, and experience more overt racial hostility and violence than do the girls. It may be that because many black girls perceive less racial exclusion from mainstream society, they may feel less desire to develop oppositional or adversarial components of racial identities than do boys. Girls may be more flexible and fluid in their racial and ethnic identities and adopt an oppositional racial identity that does not completely forestall another type of identity. Concretely, this may mean that the boundaries between an ethnic-identified and an American-identified adolescent described in this study might be sharper for males than for females and more consistently maintained by males than by females. Males who identify with the mainstream or with their parents in opposition to their peer group may be less able to move in and out of an American black identity than are girls, for whom the oppositional component of that American identity may not be as important.

NOTES

1. Some researchers have suggested using the term "generation 1.5" for these young-sters born abroad but educated in whole or part in the United States (Rumbaut 1991; Rumbaut and Kenji 1988). Others have used "second generation" to include both children of immigrants and the immigrants who came as children (Jensen 1990; Portes and Zhou 1993).

2. The biggest difference that did affect the outcomes discussed here is the difference between teens whose families came from Haiti and the rest, whose parents came from English-speaking islands. The Haitian students had an even wider cultural difference from their parents, because the parents spoke Haitian creole. Most of the Haitian students we talked to who grew up in the United States could understand and speak Creole with their parents, but they spoke English as their first language, and they distanced themselves from their parents quite a bit by speaking English.

3. Note that the first-generation immigrants are not the parents of the second-generation respondents. The adolescents did report many of the same beliefs and experiences for their parents as we heard from our respondents.

4. This conclusion is based on comparing tapes of interviews conducted by myself (a white female) and the other interviewers who were black, especially looking at sensitive subjects such as race relations and antisocial behaviors. I conducted about 65% of the in-terviews.

5. The question of the origins of these stereotypes and the empirical question of the types of differences that do exist between foreign-born and native-born Blacks in the United States is a complex one that goes beyond the scope of this paper. See Kasinitz (1992) for a discussion of the origins of these stereotypes, and Model (1991) and Farley

and Allen (1987) for a discussion of the socioeconomic differences between foreign-born and native-born blacks.

6. Note that this respondent uses "American" and "black American" interchangeably in her response. Even though the question in this case did not ask her what she fills in on forms that ask about ethnicity, this young woman replied in that way. Obviously she has grown used to filling out forms that ask for race and ethnicity.

REFERENCES

Bryce-Laporte, R. 1972. Black immigrants: The experience of invisibility and inequality. *Journal of Black Studies* 3:29–56.

Farley, R., and W. R. Allen. 1987. *The color line and the quality of life in America.* New York: Russell Sage Foundation.

Foner, N. 1987. The Jamaicans: Race and ethnicity among migrants in New York City. In *New immigrants in New York,* edited by N. Foner, 195–218. New York: Columbia University Press.

Fordham, S. 1988. Racelessness as a factor in black students' school success: Pragmatic strategy or pyrrhic victory. *Harvard Education Review* 58 (1):54–84.

Gans, H. 1992. Second generation decline: Scenarios for the economic and ethnic futures of the post-1965 American immigrants. *Ethnic and Racial Studies* 15 (2): 173–92.

Jensen, L. 1990. Children of the New Immigration: A comparative analysis of today's second generation. Institute for Policy Research and Evaluation Working Paper no. 1990–32. Pennsylvania State University, University Park.

Justus, J. B. 1976. West Indians in L.A.: Community and identity. In *Caribbean immigration to the United States,* edited by R. S. Bryce-Laporte, and D. M. Mortimer. RIIES Occasional Papers no. 1. Washington, D.C.: Research Institute on Immigration and Ethnic Studies, Smithsonian Institution.

Kasinitz, P. 1992. *Caribbean New York: Black immigrants and the politics of race.* Ithaca, N.Y.: Cornell University Press.

Michael, S. 1990. Children of the New Wave Immigration. In *Emerging perspectives on the black diaspora,* edited by A. V. Bonnett and G. L. Watson. Lanham, Md.: University Press of America.

Model, S. 1991. Caribbean Immigrants: A black success story? *International Migration Review* 25 (2):248–57.

Ogbu, J. 1990. Minority status and literacy in comparative perspective. *Daedalus* 119 (2):141–68.

Portes, A., and M. Zhou. 1993. The New Second Generation: Segmented assimilation and its variants. *Annals of the American Academy of Political and Social Science* 530:74–97.

Rotheram-Borus, M. J. 1993. Biculturalism among adolescents. In *Ethnic identity: Formation and transmission among hispanics and other minorities,* edited by M. E. Bernal and G. P. Knight. New York: State University of New York Press.

Rumbaut, R. G. 1991. The agony of exile: A comparative study of Indochinese refugee adults and children. In *Refugee children: Theory, research, and services,* edited by F. L. Ahearn, Jr., and J. L. Athey, 53–91. Baltimore: Johns Hopkins University Press.

Rumbaut, R. G., and K. Ima. 1988. *The adaptation of Southeast Asian refugee youth: A comparative study.* Washington, D.C.: U.S. Office of Refugee Resettlement.

Stafford, S. B. 1987. The Haitians: The cultural meaning of race and ethnicity. In *New immigrants in New York,* edited by N. Foner, 131–58. New York: Columbia University Press.

Sutton, C. R. 1973. Caribbean migrants and group identity: Suggestions for comparative analysis. In *Migration: Report of the Research Conference on Migration and Ethnic Minority*

*Status and Social Adaption,* 133–48. Publication no. 5. Rome: United Nations Social Defense Research Institute.

Sutton, C. R., and S. R. Makiesky. 1975. Migration and West Indian Racial and ethnic consciousness. In *Migration and development: Implications for ethnic identity and political conflict,* edited by H. I. Safa and B. M. Dutoit, 113–44. The Hague: Mouton.

Woldemikael, T. M. 1989. *Becoming Black American: Haitians and American institutions in Evanston, Illinois.* New York: AMS Press.

# II

# Family Relationships

As adolescents become more like adults in physical characteristics, cognitive capacities, and assumed roles, previously established adult-child family relationships must be reworked to accommodate the emerging equity. Despite common rhetoric about a generation gap and the intrafamilial conflicts that are a product of this period, research has repeatedly demonstrated that adolescents typically remain emotionally close to their parents and rely on them for advice concerning decisions about career, residence, education, and marriage. As we hear in the chapters in this section, mother-daughter, father-daughter, and extended family relationships provide the relational context for development that can reinforce girls' strengths and buffer some of the adversities associated with racism or poverty.

In chapter 5, Ward addresses the question of how African American parents foster their daughters' inner strength and perseverance in a social context that is replete with negative images of African Americans. Using interview data, she distinguishes parents' "tongues-of-fire" truth telling, which criticizes and demoralizes children's efforts to resist racism, from parents' resistance-building truth telling, which socializes children to think critically about the realities of racism and to learn to cope with the negative emotions that accompany experiences of racism.

Cauce, Hiraga, Graves, Gonzales, Ryan-Finn, and Grove, in chapter 6, report on a study conducted with thirteen-year-old African American girls and their mothers. Using videotapes of mother-daughter interactions and self-report questionnaires, they describe the mothers' and daughters' efforts to balance the sometimes confusing expectations concerning autonomy and closeness that stem from the hope that daughters will grow up self-reliant and resourceful, yet remain attached and loyal to their family and community.

In chapter 7, Taylor elaborates how Hispanic mothers and daughters negotiate not only the daughters' growing autonomy as American adolescents but also the tensions that arise between the beliefs and values of Hispanic cultures and those of mainstream culture. Taylor argues that cultural taboos against women's expressions of anger and disagreement and against speaking about sexuality can create alienating impasses in these mother-daughter relationships.

The specific place of fathers in the lives of forty-five urban, ethnically diverse adolescent girls is addressed in chapter 8 by Way and Stauber. They argue that the demographics of family structure (single- versus two-parent families) fall short in representing the complex relationships of fathers with their daughters. Few of the girls interviewed had no contact with their fathers, and only one-quarter described emotionally distant relationships with them. The girls typically described having intricate, passionate, and occasionally conflicted attachments to their fathers. Far from absent, most of the fathers—even those fathers who did not live with their daughters—appeared actively involved in their daughters' lives.

Apfel and Seitz, in chapter 9, go beyond the stereotypes of failure associated with teenage parenting to examine how differences in family supports figure into outcomes for African American women who were adolescents when their first child was born. They construct longitudinal case studies from extensive interviews conducted at eighteen months, six years, and twelve years postpartum to describe the developmental trajectories of adolescent mothers and their firstborn daughters. The longitudinal perspective of this study illuminates some of the processes by which family supports foster positive outcomes for adolescent mothers, and some ways by which lack of support multiplies risks that often existed prior to the first birth.

# Raising Resisters: The Role of Truth Telling in the Psychological Development of African American Girls

Janie Victoria Ward

H-236
11.3.99

> When my daughter Patsy was four, I would sit her down between my legs and every morning as I combed and braided her hair I would have her reach up and run her hands through it. "Look," I'd say, "Look at how pretty your hair is. Feel how tight and curly it feels. Look at how pretty it can be when you style it up with ribbons, beads and bows, or when you just let it be. Look at how different it is from your little white friends and how special that is."

Lillian's story, offered in response to questions about raising black children, illustrates how black mothers directly and indirectly incorporate into the daily routine of parenting powerful lessons of resistance. Like countless African American mothers before her, Lillian fashions a unique psychological script for parenting that is shaped by the socialization experiences that African Americans have accumulated as marginalized members of American society. Lillian has a foreboding sense of what her young daughter will soon encounter—the attacks upon her self-esteem by those who measure her beauty against a white standard and devalue her blackness and self-worth. In teaching Patsy to feel, play with, and cherish her naturally kinky hair, Lillian believes she will arm her young daughter with the tools necessary to resist the relentless assault of American beauty myths on the black woman's sense of self. Lillian has had a lifetime to learn about and set in place the psychological fortification that her daughter will need in order to develop into a competent and confident African American woman. In the safety of a homespace of care, nurturance, refuge, and truth, black mothers have learned to skillfully weave lessons of critical consciousness into moments of intimacy between a parent and child and to cultivate resistance against beliefs, attitudes, and practices that can erode a black child's self-confidence and impair her positive identity development.

As agents of socialization, black families play an essential role in orienting their children to the existing social environment, teaching them what they need to know about the world and their place in it. African American parents socialize their children based on cultural and political interpretations and assumptions derived from their lived experience of being black in white America. The parenting of a black child is a political act. The psychological survival of a black child largely depends on the black family's ability to endure racial and economic discrimination and to negotiate conflicting and multiple role demands.

In this chapter I explore the intergenerational transmission of race-related resistance strategies passed down from black parent to adolescent child. My analysis of this issue is empirically informed by the interview responses of African American adolescent girls and boys and the mothers and fathers of black adolescents. These adolescents and parents of adolescents voluntarily participated in private, open-ended, semistructured interviews in which they were asked to interpret the nature of the socialization process in their own voices and on their own terms. Nearly sixty African American individuals from four geographical regions of the nation (Boston, Massachusetts; Philadelphia, Pennsylvania; Raleigh, North Carolina; and Albuquerque, New Mexico) were represented in this study. The mothers and fathers were thirty-five years and older; the adolescents ranged between thirteen and twenty years old. In general, the parents and teens were not related to one another. Respondents were from a variety of socioeconomic groups and family configurations, including members of the middle or working classes and those of low income status. Some were single, separated, or divorced. Levels of education ranged from respondents with doctoral degrees to those with less than a high school diploma.

The study attempted to uncover indigenous, implicit, and explicit assumptions about race that serve as guidelines for how black parents and adolescents make sense of the world. The interview was organized by three primary themes that encompass essential elements of the experiences of African Americans: racial identity, race relations, and racial discrimination.

In investigating the intergenerational transmission of resistance as it is both constructed and transformed within black families, I was particularly interested in the process of racial socialization during adolescence. The teenage years are often described as a period of idealism, conflict, and uncertainty. Adolescents are engaged in forming an identity, renegotiating social relations and power dynamics, and redefining the self. As the balance of parent-child power shifts in adolescence, teens frequently question their parents' values, pronouncements, and authority. In my research I inquired into what the African American adolescents had learned as children about racism and racial matters and whether they would, in this period of experimentation and individual emancipation, reject what they had learned. Would they, in the effort to separate and individuate from their parents' knowledge of the past, renounce what they had learned and construct in its place new truths that they felt more accurately affirmed their emerging sense of identity, values, and meaning in life? The adolescents were also asked to discuss whether or not they spoke to their parents about racial matters, the content of these discussions, and how they were making sense of the information they received.

Homespace is an important socializing setting where black children initially learn to deal with racism and prejudice and where they develop attitudes toward their own ethnicity and toward the larger social system. Parents provide their children with ways of thinking, seeing, and doing. Racial socialization includes the acquisition of the attitudes, values, and behavior appropriate to the social and political environments in which black children are raised. Homespace is the primary site of resistance. Through relational ties African Americans pass on the knowledge needed to resist internalizing the prevailing negative images and evaluations of Blacks and to construct an identity that includes blackness as positive and valued. This process of "self-creation" depends upon the Blacks' ability to invoke an "oppositional gaze" (hooks 1992), to observe the social world critically, and to oppose ideas and ways of being that are disempowering to the self. Resistance is seen as the development of a unique cultural and political perspective—a perspective that stands against that which is perceived as unjust and oppressive. Lessons of resistance are those that instruct the black child to determine when, where, and how to resist oppression, as well as to know when, where, and how to accommodate to it.

## The Role of Resistance in the Development of Girls' Self-Esteem

Current research (primarily with white girls) on girls' psychological development suggests that prior to early adolescence, girls have a confidence and a clear sense of their own identity that declines as they reach the brink of adolescence. They receive powerful messages from adults and from the culture that undermine their self-confidence, suppress their self-identity, and force them to conform to limiting gender roles (Brown and Gilligan 1992). Brown and Gilligan identify self-silencing and taking one's knowledge underground as among the costly strategies girls employ to remain accepted by others. This silence provides a frightening illustration of women's response to and capitulation in the face of a patriarchal culture that demands compliance to conventions of femininity. Self-silencing, however, may have different motives and consequences for black adolescent girls.

Fordham (1990) complicates our understanding of girls' silence in her exploration of the use of this strategy among a group of academically successful African American girls. In her study silence was used not as a form of acquiescence but rather as an act of defiance. These black girls invoked silence as a critical rejection of the low expectations of black students held by many school officials. Fordham's study is an example of the growing literature addressing the unique strengths of black girls, highlighting their ability to be assertive, powerful, resilient, and resistant (Gibbs, chap. 17 of this volume; Way 1995).

The American Association of University Women's 1990 report entitled *Shortchanging Girls, Shortchanging America* provides evidence in support of black girls' strong sense of self. This study of self-esteem and the educational climate polled nearly 3,000 children and adolescents enrolled in elementary, middle, and high schools across the country and identified a gender gap in self-esteem that increases as girls get older, with boys consistently having higher self-esteem than girls. Important interactions between race and gender in self-esteem were also present in the cross-sectional data. Black girls in the study began with and were better able to retain higher levels of self-esteem through adolescence than their white and Latina counterparts. A sense of individual and personal self-worth was important in the structure of self-esteem for black girls.[1] Closeness to family was also central to overall self-esteem, and family and black community reinforcement appeared to sustain high levels of self-esteem (AAUW 1991, 1992).

This research finding was met with surprise in some circles, as it runs counter to the stereotype that black girls are victims of low self-esteem. Skeptics point to the large numbers of black girls growing up in less than optimal conditions—single parent, low income families situated in urban communities frequently beset by violence and crime. Although such characterizations do indeed describe the living conditions of far too many African American children today, it is inaccurate to conclude that all black children succumb to a fate of chronic self-doubt and low self-esteem. Scholars of the African American family have long observed that African American children, both male and female, are instilled with similar traits of assertiveness, willfulness, and independence (Lewis 1975). Strong values are placed on inner strength and perseverance. Moreover,

African Americans have particularly high expectations for their daughters. Historically, black daughters have been socialized toward both traditional (care and nurturing wife and mother) and nontraditional roles (worker or employee). Parents recognize that their daughters will be at least partially, if not totally, responsible for the financial survival of their families. This orientation to the dual roles of mother and worker and the values placed on black women's strength and perseverance are important elements of their healthy self-esteem.

Finally, it is during the process of racial socialization that black children are taught to resist internalizing the notion that the enemy resides within the psyche of the black individual, that is, that it is the black individual's lack of motivation, unsuccessful identity formation, internalized self-hatred, or learned helplessness that explains his or her lack of success. Undoubtedly, most black parents acknowledge the importance of personal effort and responsibility and do not wish to devalue their effect. However, many also recognize that a vital part of their child's socialization is to learn when to attribute lack of success to individual effort and when to attribute it to social forces. The refusal to allow oneself to become stifled by victimization or to accept an ideology of victim-blame entails the development of a critical perspective on the world—one that is informed by the particular knowledge gained from one's social and political position. Such knowledge, in mitigating self-abnegation while fostering self-esteem, enables Blacks' resistance to oppression. It is one of the most powerful weapons African American families have had throughout our history in the United States.

The AAUW data suggest that there is something positive and very powerful occurring among African American families. In shaping their daughters' understanding of racial and gender oppression, parents help them develop a healthy resistance to cultural pressures that call for maladaptive changes. Sandra Bem (1983) makes a similar argument as she encourages white parents to strengthen their daughters' resistance to traditional gender socialization and gender inequality. Parents of other ethnic and cultural groups who hope to raise strong and resistant daughters might learn from the socialization practices of African American families.

## Raising Resisters

Despite advances in civil rights legislation and enforcement, racial inequalities in American social, political, and economic structures continue to impact negatively the lives of African American people. Moreover, there is a widening gulf between white and black Americans' perceptions of the effect of racism. National polls of black and white Americans suggest that compared to Blacks, Whites see more racial progress and continue to downplay the extent of racial discrimination and the significance of race for economic success (Sigelman and Welch 1991). Black children raised in the United States are barraged with messages proclaiming fairness and racial equality for all. According to these messages, this is a color-blind meritocracy where upward mobility is open to all those who put forth the effort. Yet the experiences of black parents run counter to these prevailing messages. Although the most overt signs of racism have all but disappeared, African American parents know that racism today may be more pernicious, since it is disguised in our daily course of conduct. Parents fear what can happen to a naive and unsuspecting black child if she unquestioningly accepts the dominant culture's interpretation of her reality.

Black parents are deeply aware that "lying is done with words, but also with silence" (Rich 1975, 186). They know that one does not have to look far to find black people's lives misrepresented and distorted in the larger society, whether through overt lies perpetuated to serve the interests of others or through lies concealed by silence that marginalizes African Americans. In either case black parents see the misrepresentation and distortion as undermining the efforts of Blacks to gain self-determination and achieve personal and racial affirmation. Furthermore, black parents know that silence is often the voice of complicity. The black child who is unwilling to stand up in her own defense is vulnerable to cultural and psychological alienation. In my study black parents break the silence with political knowledge and self-knowledge. One parent says: "I don't teach it's an even playing field, all men are created equal, do what's right and you will be received fairly." Another puts it as follows: "If you want your children to be able to survive in this society, they'd better understand what reality is, you know, and you can never forget who you are."

These quotations from two African American fathers from New Mexico and North Carolina comment on the purposeful intent behind the child-rearing strategies they employ to prepare their offspring for the realities of racism and frequent economic discrimination that they and their children must face.

In her study of racial socialization in black families, Peters (1985) found that black mothers were acutely aware of the reality of racism in their own lives and that they shared their personal experiences of discrimination with their children. These parents felt it was their responsibility to tell their children the truth about the sociopolitical environment, teaching them that they would probably face discrimination in their lifetime and that they must be prepared. This preparation included the presentation of alternatives and instilling racial pride, self-respect, and the assurance of love as a protective buffer against the negative images a black child might encounter (Peters 1985).

In the current study I asked African American adolescent girls if they talked to their parents about race, and if so, why? April responds:

> Maybe somewhere down the line they've seen some of the same things and, of course, they got over them. Once you get out into the world, or even before you get out into the world, you're gonna hear things that you have to have the pride to back you up . . . so I won't be out there blind-folded. So many [Blacks] are fooling themselves. They say racism doesn't exist, then when it happens—shock. It's too much to handle if not fore-warned.
>
> *Interviewer:* Is it helpful to talk about it?
>
> I don't want to say I accept it, but I don't have the hostility that might be there if I hadn't been taught about it before. I can't say I get rid of the hostility and the frustration all completely, but that always helps—to be able to talk about it.

According to April, the racial pride and self-respect that repudiates nega-tive images and evaluations about black folk also helps her control the range of affective reactions to frustrations associated with racial oppres-sion. Arising from a sense of vulnerability and powerlessness, anger and rage can cause black children to experience heightened stress. As Mrs. Grant cautions her children, "If [hate] affects you, it can bring you down, defeat and demoralize you." Black parents believe it is their task to help their children "sublimate the enduring rage and hostility in prosocial ways" (Powell 1983, 67).

Lori concurs with April, when asked "Do you talk to your parents about race?" She says: "Definitely. Because they know what it was like to be black in the last generation and they know what it's like to be black now." Both April and Lori find strength in the intergenerational perspectives offered by their parents to make sense of the sociopolitical world. As adolescents they do not reject what they have learned as children from their parents, but rather hold tight to their parents' experi-ence and beliefs. In this study mothers and fathers reported that they recounted with their children stories of prejudice and institutional racism in their past and in their present. In sharing their own personal, often painful experiences, African American parents transmit to their children the knowledge that they have been there too and they can see what their children see, feel their pain, and share their frustration. Through this process black parents communicate to their children what psychologist James Vander Zanden (1989) calls " a psychological sense of oneness," an understanding that speaks to the child's assumption that her or his own inner experiences and emotional reactions are shared by others. More-over, in the service of racial identity, communicating this sense of psy-chological oneness helps children to develop the awareness that they are not merely in the group but of the group (Vander Zanden 1989, 336). In acknowledging the unfairness of racism, as well as its capricious nature and its lack of care, black parents create the conditions in which black children feel safe in placing their confidence in parental authority. The forthright acknowledgement of racism also helps children to trust that the adults may know the way out of the pain.

Yvonne says that her Dad tells her stories of what he had to go through growing up: "My father has been through a lot because he just had to work extra hard to get where he is. Maybe . . . if he was a white man, I'm sure he would have gone up there much faster. Because of his race, he was not given the same opportunity." She further explains that her parents don't say, "You're black, you need to watch out. I learn more from their actions and just the things they do." Adolescents such as Yvonne revealed in their interviews that information about racism can be transmitted from parents in a number of ways. In *observing* the obstacles her father has had to overcome, Yvonne has learned much about blocked opportunities. Her story provides an example of how, through both direct and indirect methods of instruction, black parents teach their chil-dren the racial realities they must endure.

The political socialization inherent in racial socialization requires devel-opment of the ability to identity and analyze issues of power and author-ity embedded in relationships between Blacks and non-Blacks (Ward 1990). Mrs. Jones, a mother in Boston, explains: "We have to be very intentional about preparing our children for this society." Both black parents and black adolescents earmarked films, television, newspapers, and magazines as deserving particular critique. According to her mother, says sixteen-year-old Marie, most of what white people know about black people is learned through observation and acceptance of what they see on TV. Marie's mother teaches her children specific skills, including taking a critical perspective, the ability to detect racial stereotypes, and the understanding of how images shape perceptions and often obscure the truth. Most importantly, Marie's mother instills in her daughter a desire to resist both internalizing and emulating the media's negative images and stereotypical characterizations of African American people, values, and cultural beliefs. Erika summarizes the political socialization of black girls, saying in her response to my question, "Why talk to your parents about race?" "because I learn self-knowledge, purpose, resistance and how to overcome obstacles."

In this study I heard African American mothers and fathers stating that they believe they have an obligation to tell the truth about racism, an obligation made morally significant by the recognition of negative consequences that could result from their silence. Black children who are not well prepared to confront racism may fall victim to self-deception and self-hatred. Moral attitudes are mediated by social context, and undoubtedly for some black parents there are considerable obstacles to speaking about discrimination and prejudice. Fear, embarrassment, and anger may cause some to avoid it. But many black parents have learned that racism can be neither ignored nor denied. Some black parents take a hard line, believing in the importance of exposing the moral and inherent contradictions of a society that professes freedom yet maintains racial and gender subjugation. Moreover, many parents fear that if children grow up in an atmosphere shrouded with deceit and illusion, not only will they be unprepared for racism, but the world may suddenly be seen as chaotic, unpredictable, hostile, and rejecting when it is unveiled. Children in such a situation, feeling vulnerable and insecure, will find their perceptions about the safety and security of human relationship shaken, and they may approach larger systems with greater fear and suspicion than if they had been prepared for racism.

Black parents who successfully instill healthy psychological resistance in their children help them to cope with rather than to repress these feelings. Addressing racism and sexism in an open and forthright manner is essential to building psychological health in African American children. In explicitly acknowledging the vulnerability of their children to discrimination and oppression, black parents hope that rather than being overwhelmed and disabled, their children will instead become empowered in the face of their condition and resist negative images. But parents' truth telling can also carry the seeds of betrayal and discouragement in some families.

## "Tongues-of-Fire" Truth Telling

The poignant memoir of the late Audre Lorde (1982) provides a powerful example of the truth telling that some black women use to prepare their children for racism. Lorde attended a small Catholic elementary school where the racism was "unadorned, unexcused and particularly painful because I wasn't prepared for it" (1982, 250). When she complained about the treatment she had to endure in school, she received no help from home. Her mother bitterly complained, "What do you care what they say about you anyway? Do they put bread on your plate? You go to school to learn, so learn and leave the rest alone. You don't need friends." In her story Lorde tells us that elections for the sixth grade class president

93

were scheduled. According to the teacher, winning would be based on a number of criteria; however, grades would be the most important factor. Since Audre was the smartest girl in her class, she thought she had a fair shot at winning the office. Lorde's mother was furious at the idea that she would run in the election: "What in hell are you doing getting yourself involved with so much foolishness? . . . We send you to school to work, not to prance about with president this, election-that." Audre felt destroyed and betrayed when she learned she had lost. She was the smartest in the class, yet the teacher chose another student as class president. Heartbroken, Audre wondered: Was this what her mother was always talking about, that I should have won but they wouldn't let me? In the midst of her daughter's disappointment and distress, Audre's mother let loose her frustration. Slapping Audre's face she cried, "See— the bird forgets but the trap doesn't! I warned you. . . . Child why you worry your head so much over fair or not fair? Just do what is for you to do and let the rest take care of themselves" (1982, 251).

Recoiling at her daughter's naive innocence, Lorde's mother raged back with "tongues of fire," a form of truth telling that bell hooks (1993, 32) describes as a characteristic of some black mother and daughter relationships. The intent of the harsh critique is "to tell it like it is," to dismantle futile idealism, unmask illusions, and ultimately strengthen character. Audre's mother offers, embedded in the admonishment, "The bird forgets but the trap doesn't," a striking image of power relations and a compelling lesson about justice and fairness. Hooks argues that when black women tell their daughters, "I would be less than a mother if I didn't tell you the truth" (1993, 34), it sets in motion a survival strategy for coping with the unfairness of sexism and racism. Lorde's mother clearly did not mask her own anger, yet she refused to allow or join her daughter's feelings of disappointment and rejection. The message to young Audre was to toughen up, mask your feelings, disguise your thoughts, and whatever you do, never let them see you sweat.

This bold, unreserved, "in-your-face" truth telling in the service of racial socialization can become a point of tension. As bell hooks argues, it may be partially responsible for the high rates of emotional distress experienced by many African American women. Rather than strengthening the character of the young black child, the harsh negative critique of the world illustrated by Mrs. Lorde may have a demoralizing effect. Uncertainty and helplessness can become ingrained in the psyche, and race-related anger can lead to self-hatred and racial resentment. Truth telling with "tongues of fire" may serve to prevent the development of a secure identity, impair a child's ability to form and sustain satisfying relationships with others, and discourage her belief in her own ability to effect change.

In raising resisters, I believe that there is a relationship between the resistance strategies that girls choose to employ (short-term or long-term) and the messages they receive about who they are in the world. Previously Tracy Robinson and I (Robinson and Ward 1991) argued that not all resistance strategies are healthy. We identified two major strategies that black adolescent females adopt in their resistance to the realities of an oppressive, demeaning, and judgmental sociopolitical environment: "resistance for survival" and "resistance for liberation." The first strategy, "resistance for survival" is oriented toward quick fixes that offer short-term solutions. They might make you feel better for a while, but in the long run they are counterproductive to the development of self-confidence and positive identity formation. "Tongues-of-fire" truth telling can lead black girls to adopt short-term and often short-sighted resistance strategies. For example, sixteen-year-old Barbara says that she believes many lower income Blacks have become disillusioned and resentful while struggling just to stay afloat. They have adopted jaded and ill-fated attitudes toward personal and collective advancement. She suggests that these black folk should channel their energy into hard work in order to achieve their goals. Seventeen-year-old Toni says too often black adolescents blame everything on racism and use it as an excuse for their own inadequacies. Both of these are examples of evading personal responsibility by letting strong race-related emotions cloud one's judgment. These "quick fixes" represent adaptations to racism and will, in the long run, usually prove to be strategies that advance neither individual nor group goals.

## Resistance-Building Truth Telling

The second strategy outlined by my colleague and me (Robinson and Ward 1991) is "resistance for liberation." This type of resistance offers solutions that serve to empower African American females through confirmation of positive self-conceptions, as well as strengthening connections to the broader African American community. Truth telling that is liberating replaces negative critique with positive recognition. It helps a girl to experience constructive, critical affirmation of the individual and the collective by encouraging her to think critically about herself and her place in the world around her. Sharon provides a striking illustration of a black woman's resistance strategy undertaken in the service of self-determination.

The setting is a university sports arena. This is the first time a soloist has been invited to sing the national anthem at the largest sports event of the season. Seventeen-year-old Sharon was initially auditioned by the athletic director, who was pleased with her rendition. About ten minutes before Sharon was scheduled to sing, the director came down into the pit and said, "You'll do great—have fun, but just try not to sing it too . . . you know." Sharon responded:

No. I don't know. What are you talking about? And he said, "Just don't make it a jazz piece." And then he gets this very condescending tone of voice and continues. "See a couple of years ago a black girl sang the National Anthem, and she sang it to the point where no one could even understand it. It was just a bunch of frills and groans and grunts." I just looked at him. I couldn't believe he was saying this. So he walks off, and then in a few minutes he returns and asks, "Are you ready? Remember, you're going to sing it *right*, aren't you?" I said, I'm going to sing it my way. So he says, "well we don't need you to sing it if you're going to sing it (that) way." Now here I am stressing—I have 30 seconds before I have to get out there and sing in front of a stadium full of people and I don't know . . . if I sing this "black" is he gonna come and take the mike away from me?

I asked Sharon what was going through her mind during what she had described as the longest thirty seconds in her life. She explained that she prayed and then she asked herself:

Should I be black or should I be white? Not that I could be physically, but in terms of the song. So I got up there and I (sang) the first two bars very white and then . . . then something just came over me. It was worse than what I was going to do! I wasn't going to be that black . . . and if he hadn't said that to me, it would have been fine. But he did, and I . . .

I asked her if she thought she had done the right thing, and she explained, "I know I did, because it felt so good. Not only do I have the right to sing my own way, but if that happens to be in the Afro-American heritage that I've acquired, I'm just going to do it that way." And then Sharon lowered her voice and sat up straight in her chair and declared, "and I believe that was a stand for being black."

Just about the same time that Sharon shared her story with me, this nation was savoring the newly won victory of Desert Storm and was welcoming back the returning troops with the emotional rendition of the national anthem that was sung by Whitney Houston, with Miss Whitney's African American heritage all over it! In Sharon's narrative of racial conflict there remains, for some people, a right—read "white"—way to be. Sharon felt her artistry and her sense of herself as a black woman was being made unwelcome. For Sharon, taking a stand against this was a transformative act of self-conscious agency.

Throughout her interview Sharon provided evidence of stories told and lessons learned in her family about racism, race relations, and racial identity. Her parents, who themselves were strong and defiant role models of resistance, appear to have successfully nurtured Sharon's psychological growth, emotional maturity, and strong self-esteem. According to their daughter, they achieved this task by neither sugar-coating nor avoiding the truth about racism. African American parents such as Sharon's are exemplars of a parenting style that integrates a liberating truth telling into their repertoire of racial socialization strategies. They provide, over the course of a child's lifetime, plenty of opportunities within the family for meaningful discussions in a safe and supportive environment. In addition, these parents help their children to confront racism in ways that are both age and individually appropriate. Children develop different capacities at different points in their lives, and the information parents give about race to their children begins modestly and grows more complex over time. Most importantly, black parents who engage in truth telling that is liberating allow for strong, often painful, race-related emotions to surface. Parents, by teaching their children to cope with these emotions, refuse to allow them to equate their disappointments with psychological destruction.

In this study black parents and adolescents provided many examples of how a liberating truth telling can be used to strengthen character and encourage healthy psychological development in black children. This truth telling is effective in filling in the silences. As we saw in Lillian's attempt to instill in her young daughter positive messages about her beauty, it is often invoked as a corrective to those who would diminish the black child's self-worth. Healthy psychological resistance fostered through a liberating truth telling has a transformative quality. It helps children to grow strong as a resister on the individual level and empowered by their sense of belonging to a group whose very survival has been dependent upon the collective ability to resist. African American families, building upon their long tradition of raising resisters, continue a process of racial socialization that invites black children into the community of resisters, transmitting to the next generation the truths they will need to know, as they come to trust themselves as sources of knowledge.

NOTES

1. It is important to note that the AAUW (1991) study asked students to assess themselves in a number of different domains deemed important in children's lives, and black girls showed evidence of a significant decline in their academic self-esteem over the course of their years in the school system. Many of the black girls appear not to be relying on school to give them a positive sense of self. Their academic confidence was judged as "not as important." The girls showed a drop in their positive feelings about their teachers and their school work. They were not feeling good about their academic performance nor about the evaluations and validations received from school personnel. Such a decline in academic self-esteem has serious implications for academic achievement and may engender apathy in school, resulting in low grades and poor academic performance.

REFERENCES

American Association of University Women. 1991. *Shortchanging girls, shortchanging America: A call to action.* Washington, D.C.: American Association of University Women.

——. 1992. *The AAUW report: How schools shortchange girls.* Washington, D.C.: American Association of University Women Educational Foundation and National Educational Association.

Bem, S. L. 1983. Gender schema theory and its implications for child development: Raising gender-aschematic children in a gender schematic society. *Signs* 8 (4):598–616.

Brown, L. M., and C. Gilligan. 1992. *Meeting at the crossroads: Women's psychology and girls' development.* Cambridge: Harvard University Press.

Fordham, S. 1990. Phantoms in the opera: Black girls' academic achievement at Capital High. Paper presented at symposium, New American Women. Annual meeting of the American Anthropological Association, November, New Orleans.

——. 1993. "Those loud black girls": (Black) women, silence, and gender "passing" in the academy. *Anthropology and Education Quarterly* 24 (1):3–32.

hooks, b. 1992. *Black looks: Race and representation.* Boston, Mass.: South End Press.

——. 1993. *Sisters of the yam: Black women and self recovery.* Boston, Mass.: South End Press.

Lewis, D. 1975. The black family: Socialization and sex roles. *Phylon* 36:221–37.

Lorde, A. 1982. *Zami: A new spelling of my name.* Freedom, Calif.: Crossing Press.

Peters, M. F. 1985. Racial socialization in young black children. In *Black Children,* edited by H. P. McAdoo and J. McAdoo, 159–73. Beverly Hills, Calif.: Sage Press.

Powell, G. F. 1983. Coping with adversity: The psychosocial development of African American children. In *The Psychosocial development of minority children,* edited by G. Powell, 49–76. New York: Bruner-Mazel.

Rich, A. 1975. Women and honor: Some notes on lying. In *On lies, secrets, and silence,* edited by A. Rich. New York: W. W. Norton.

Robinson, T., and J. V. Ward. 1991. "A belief in self far greater than anyone's disbelief": Cultivating healthy resistance among african american female adolescents. In *Women, girls, and psychotherapy: Reframing resistance,* edited by C. Gilligan, A. G. Rogers, and D. Tolman, 87–103. Binghamton, New York: Harrington Park Press.

Sigelman, L., and S. Welch. 1991. *Black Americans' view of racial inequality: The dream deferred.* Cambridge: Cambridge University Press.

Steele, S. 1990. *The content of our character.* New York: St. Martin's Press.

Taylor, R. L. 1991. Childrearing in African American families. In *Childwelfare: An Afrocentric perspective,* edited by J. Everett, S. J. Chipungu, and B. R. Leashore. Brunswick, N.J.: Rutgers University Press.

Vander Zanden, J. W. 1989. *Human Development.* 4th ed. New York: Knopf.

Ward, J. V. 1990. Racial identity formation and transformation." In *Making connections: The relational worlds of adolescent girls at Emma Willard School,* edited by C. Gilligan, N. Lyons, and T. Hanmer, 215–32. Cambridge: Harvard University Press.

Way, N. 1995. "Can't you hear the courage, the strength that I have": Listening to urban adolescent girls speak about their relationships. *Psychology of Women Quarterly* 19:107–28.

White, J. L., and T. A. Parham. 1990. *The psychology of Blacks: An African American perspective.* 2d ed. Englewood Cliffs, N.J.: Prentice Hall.

# 6

# African American Mothers and Their Adolescent Daughters: Closeness, Conflict, and Control

Ana Mari Cauce, Yumi Hiraga,
Diane Graves, Nancy Gonzales,
Kimberly Ryan-Finn, and
Kwai Grove

I see her clearest when I stand in the mirror, the jagged reflection of us both. Hers is the color of unground pepper; mine the brown of old honey. No matter where I might go, she has made sure to remind me that I too, am a woman from Sparta.
—Fabienne McPhail

I am most passionate in my relationship with mama. It is with her that I feel loved and sometimes accepted. She is the one person who looks into my heart, sees its needs, and tries to satisfy them. She is also always trying to make me be what she thinks is best for me to be. . . . She wants to love and control at the same time. Her love is sustained and deep. Sometimes I feel like a drowning person, saved by the pulling and tugging, saved by the breath of air that is her caring.
—bell hooks

The African American community has always recognized and respected the unique relationship between its mothers and daughters. A common saying among African Americans is that "Mothers *raise* their daughters and *love* their sons." This is a simple yet powerful statement about the character of these relationships, a character based on the experiences that come with African American womanhood. This character unfolds as the African American mother teaches her daughter how to survive, cope, and succeed in a hostile environment, while fostering family and community loyalty.

Research that specifically examines African American mother-daughter relationships is virtually absent in the literature. Those studies that have focused on African American parenting at all typically consist of cross-cultural comparisons (Wyche 1993; Graham 1992, McLoyd and Randolph 1985). Yet, it is not enough to compare African American mother-daughter relationships with their white counterparts. This type of research seldom gives due respect and consideration to the distinct experience of African American women (Wyche 1993). Instead, de-contextualized examinations of African American mothering implicitly support the dominant groups' exploitation of African American women by blaming them for their characteristic reactions to their own subordination. Such studies also foster internalized oppression, which may be passed on from African American mother to daughter (Collins 1987). In designing research on African Americans, one should consider their unique historical and social context in this country.

Our research was designed to explicitly focus on a normative sample of African Americans in their own right, not in relation to any other cultural group (Cauce and Gonzales 1993). The specific study we present here focused exclusively on African American mothers and their adolescent daughters. In order to minimize distortions and incorrect inferences from any single measurement, the mother-daughter relationship was assessed through both mother and daughter self-reports and via a videotaped structured family interaction task that mothers and daughters participated in together.[1] This task was based on a revealed-differences paradigm in which mothers and daughters were first directed to choose their greatest source of conflict and then to discuss the topic in order to come to a mutually agreed upon solution. The entire task, which they were given fifteen minutes to complete, was videotaped. The interviews and videotaped interaction took place at the University of Washington campus and was supervised by an advanced graduate student working with trained undergraduate students. At least two researchers were present for every interview, and in every case at least one of them was African American.

In total, fifty-nine African American mothers and their daughters participated in the study. All of the daughters were in the seventh or eighth grade at the time of recruitment,[2] with an average age of thirteen years and three months. The vast majority (90%) were attending a public middle school at the time of the study. One-third were living with both biological parents, and about half (52%) were living in single parent households. Nearly all the mothers (93%) had at least a high school diploma or equivalency, a few (13%) had completed a college education, and most (86%) worked outside the home. Although a range of incomes was represented, this was primarily a working-class to lower-middle-class sample, with 40% earning less than $20,000 and 18% earning over $40,000 a year (in 1990–91 dollars).

What do African American mothers and daughters argue about? Must African American daughters pull away from their mothers in order to establish their unique identities? How do African American mothers protect their daughters from a hostile environment while allowing them to develop a healthy sense of autonomy and competence? In this chapter we present a qualitative examination of the study described above in order to answer these questions about closeness, conflict, and control within the relationships of African American mothers and daughters. However, first we provide an overview of what it means to be an African American woman and mother. The overview provides an important context from which to interpret the data we present.

## Race and Gender: Reference Points for African American Women

A key developmental task for all African Americans is learning how to live among White persons, while becoming black persons (Greene 1990). In order to do this, some have suggested that African Americans must find ways to incorporate two often diametrically opposed frames of reference: "Afrocentrism," an African perspective, and "Eurocentrism," a Euro-American perspective (Boykin 1986; Greene 1990). The ethos of Afrocentrism is the survival of the tribe, whereas the ethos of Euro-centrism is the survival of the fittest. The values and attitudes of Afrocentrism center on group sameness, rather than on the individual as in Eurocentrism.

How behavior is expressed also differs, with Afrocentrism centering on commonalities and similarities and Eurocentrism centering on individual differences. The African perspective emphasizes spiritualism and affect, whereas the Euro-American one emphasizes materialism and reason above all else. An even orientation toward time and an orally based culture in the African perspective contrasts with a clock orientation and a culture based on the printed word in the Euro-American perspective. Afrocentric thought is based on the spirit of the people, interdependence, and a collective consciousness (Boykin 1983, 1986). Its themes have served to unite and support African Americans, despite wide within-group diversity. For example, it is not uncommon for upwardly mobile African Americans to feel a sense of responsibility to the African American community where they grew up and which supported them in their struggle to "make it."

This dual socialization process occurs on many levels and is active throughout the lifetimes of African Americans, serving as a source of both opportunity and challenge. On the positive side, they are exposed to two cultural scripts and develop competence in both of them. Many African Americans routinely move between predominantly black and predominantly white settings with a skill much more uncommon among white European Americans. On the negative side, this "dual consciousness" or biculturality can become a source of tension, unease, and even shame when an essential aspect of one's self is put down, negated, and denigrated[3] in a society where subtle, and not so subtle, manifestations of racism are ever present (McCombs 1986).

The devastating tension that can result from the desire to maintain one's blackness within a white world is seen in the description that Lenita McClain, an African American woman and award-winning journalist, provided in a "My Turn" *Newsweek* column five years before she committed suicide (October 1980, 21, cited in McCombs 1986).

I am burdened daily with showing whites that blacks are people. I am, in the old vernacular, a credit to my race. I am my brother's keeper, and my sisters', though many of them have abandoned me because they think I have abandoned them. . . . Some of my "liberal" white acquaintances pat me on the head, hinting that I am a freak, that my success is less a matter of talent than of luck and affirmative action. I may live among them, but it is difficult to live with them. How can they be sincere about respecting me, yet hold my fellows in contempt? And, if I am silent when they attempt to sever me from my own how can I live with myself? (75–76)

For African American women gender is an additional struggle in the socialization process. They confront not only racism, but sexism as well. Negative images of her beauty, intellect, and potential are constant companions throughout an African American woman's development (Richie 1992). The "American" ideal feminine figure—petite proportions, slim hips, and small facial features—is not often seen among African American women. With a continuum of brown skin colors, voluptuous silhouettes, and large facial features, most African American women cannot achieve this ideal, and society's response to them is to define their appearance as ugly and undesirable.

African American women sit below white men and white women in the social hierarchy, and often they sit below African American men[4] as well. Being at the bottom of the hierarchy has meant that African American women have had to climb many levels just to be heard, and they have had to work with determined perseverance for change for themselves, their families, and their communities. While some of their needs are addressed in the civil rights movement, and some of their needs are addressed in the feminist movement, they have increasingly found their own political voice within the "women of color" movement (Hull, Bell Scott, and Smith 1982). Still, while many noteworthy African American women have served as trail blazers, many more are still climbing and working diligently just to keep from being invisible.

While confronting sexism and racism, the African American woman searches for her niche—her life's course. In the midst of her identification with multiple referent groups, she evaluates her options and decides which path to travel. These multiple referents, unique to African American women, play a major role in the relationships they have with their daughters. They strive to teach their daughters to become African American, to accurately assess their environments, and to gather information from a variety of sources to create positive self-concepts and identities. This process is described below:

When I see my daughter, I see a stronger healthier version of myself when I was young. It still scares me, though. Her first boyfriend seemed to be a real hooligan—all jive talk and flashy clothes. I told her that kinda boy would only get her in trouble, but I didn't want her to think I was putting down Black men or Black people . . . we spend so much time with White folk around here, I worry she'll grow up believing all that shit you always hear about Blacks. . . . You know, he turned out to be not so bad. He was . . er, just trying to be what he thought Black men were supposed to be like too . . . I'm glad she chose to go to a (historically) Black college where she can learn that there are lots of ways to be Black. I don't want her . . um . . thinking we're so . . . um special from other Blacks.

These comments, from a recent Ph.D. and mother of a daughter now in college, describe her struggle to help her daughter develop a positive identity while growing up in a predominantly white middle-class neighborhood. This struggle to overcome racist stereotypes is not limited to the African American underclass, but also occurs among the relatively privileged.

## African American Motherhood

The reality of motherhood for many African American women is often a struggle for survival, both for themselves and for their children. Historically, African American mothers have often functioned as supermothers, caring for their own families at home *and* for the children of white families on the job. Currently, they are repeatedly challenged to develop effective coping strategies for an increasing pool of problems ranging from finances to violence.

Despite these challenges, motherhood has also provided African American women a base for self-actualization. In the African American community, motherhood is a source of power and respect. Mothers are generally seen as key educators, responsible for continuing the cultural traditions of the past and supporting the community's future (Collins 1987). Often the community provides much needed assistance to new mothers: entire neighborhoods, churches, and informal networks will converge and pour their resources into support of the mother and child (McPhail 1987). Placing much less emphasis on biological relationships, African American women realize that the survival of the community's children depends on the people willing to raise them. Child care is viewed as a collective responsibility, and the women who care for children are often fluid and changing (Wilson and Tolson 1990). This is implicit in the African adage, "It takes a village to raise a child."

In this country the village is increasingly one made up of networks of women. According to the 1990 census, more than half (55%) of African American children lived in a single parent, mother-headed household, with 27% of these headed by women who had never married (O'Hare et al. 1991). These numbers are influenced by the availability of African-American men, who suffer from much higher youthful mortality rates than their white counterparts. Among African Americans 25 to 34, there are 89 men for every 100 women (132/100 for Whites) between 35 and 44, there are 67 African American men for every 100 African American women (97/100 for Whites) (Wyche 1993). Thus, it is not altogether surprising that in a recent study conducted in inner-city Atlanta, the adults in the social networks of both African American adolescent girls *and* boys were primarily female (Graves 1994).

## African American Mothers and Their Adolescent Daughters

Three constructs—closeness, conflict, and control—have been traditionally used to describe parent-child relationships during the adolescent transition between the dependency of childhood and the independence of adulthood. Although we use those constructs here, it is important to keep in mind that childhood as a protected developmental period during which children mature and explore the world is not the reality for many African American girls. From an early age many African American girls, especially those living in urban settings, face a world filled with "adult" decisions and danger.

*Closeness*

With some exceptions, children learn from a very young age that they can go to their mothers for love and comfort when they are in pain or feeling insecure. This knowledge does not disappear during the transition from childhood to adolescence. For girls in particular, it can be reassuring to know that their mothers are there to help make sense of all the changes—biological and social—that might be going on in their lives. In fact, the mother-daughter bond has been described as one of the strongest and most influential throughout life (Gold and Yanof 1985). Adult women, white and African American alike, have described their mothers' affection and love as one of the most rewarding of all their relationships (hooks 1984; Troll 1987).

Developmental examinations of mother-daughter relationships, albeit with primarily white samples, have found that mothers play an important nurturing role in their daughters' development. This literature suggests that adolescent girls relish a more intimate attachment[5] to their mothers than to their fathers. For instance, Youniss and Smollar (1985) found that girls described their interactions with their mothers "in terms of intimate exchanges." Girls confided more in their mothers, and their mothers gave them more advice on personal matters. In addition, adolescent girls chose their mothers as their confidant on personal topics such as family problems and feelings, school, career, and the future.

The African American adolescent daughters in our study characterized their relationships with their mothers in a very similar fashion. This was suggested by an item analysis of their responses to the "mother" scale of the Inventory of Parent and Peer Attachment (IPPA) (Armsden and Greenberg 1987). This adolescent self-report measure, conceptually informed by attachment theory, assesses adolescents' relationships with their mothers, fathers, and peers. Adolescents respond to items such as "My mother expects too much from me" and "My mother respects my feelings" on a 5-point scale ranging from 1 (almost never or never true) to 5 (almost always or always true)." The five items that were most highly rated by the daughters are presented in table 6.1. Mean ratings for

TABLE 6.1
*Five Most Endorsed Items on the IPPA-Mother*

1. I feel my mother does a good job as a mother.
2. My mother accepts me as I am.
3. I trust my mother.
4. My mother respects my feelings.
5. My mother can tell when I'm upset about something.

NOTE: $N = 59$

TABLE 6.2
*Mean Ratings of Emotional Support by Provider*

| Provider | Mean | SD |
|---|---|---|
| Mother | 4.6 | .67 |
| Best friend | 4.2 | .90 |
| Grandparent | 3.9 | 1.2 |
| Boyfriend/Romantic friend | 3.8 | 1.0 |
| Father | 3.5 | 1.3 |
| Sister/Brother | 3.3 | 1.2 |
| Teacher | 2.9 | 1.3 |

NOTE: These ratings are based on the complete sample of girls, not just those who participated in the videotaped interaction. N's range between 81 and 86, except for Father ($N = 62$) and Boyfriend ($N = 55$).

all these items were above 4.00, indicating a high level of endorsement across the sample. These items paint a portrait of close, loving relationships characterized by acceptance and respect, precisely those characteristics that lead individuals to feel supported and loved (Sarason et al. 1987).

It is not surprising, therefore, that daughters also rated their mothers highly on the Social Support Rating Scale—Revised (Cauce et al. 1994). This measure asks adolescents to rate potential providers, such as mothers, fathers, friends, and teachers, in terms of the amount of emotional support and help and guidance available in those relationships. Table 6.2 presents their mean ratings of support from various members of their social network. This table illustrates the key role that mothers play in the lives of their adolescent daughters. Not only was the overall rating of emotional support from mothers high—an average of 4.6 on a 5-point scale—but it is also the highest rating of any network member, including best friends. Thus, it is quite clear that in general the daughters in our sample viewed their mothers as a central source of support during the adolescent transition.

## Conflict and Control

Although the once common notion that adolescence is necessarily a time of extreme conflict, or "Sturm und Drang," has been discredited, conflict between parent and child is still viewed as a hallmark of this developmental period. Conflict between mothers and daughters appears to be particularly high. Female adolescents have been found to be in conflict with mothers approximately twice as often as were sons with either parent (Montemayor 1986).

Early family and developmental theorists, like families themselves, typically described this conflict as negative. In contrast, more recent theorists have noted that it often serves an adaptive function in the reorganization of the parent–child relationship necessary for individuation, identity formation, and psychological growth (Steinberg 1990; Hill and Holmbeck 1986). Furthermore, contrary to common stereotypes, adolescent–parent arguments are generally about matters of family routine. They are more likely to relate to cleaning and homework than to sex and drugs.

The African American mothers and daughters in our sample were not found to differ from this pattern. As part of our study they completed the Issues Checklist (Prinz and Kent, cited in Robin and Foster 1984), which lists forty-four issues that can result in conflict between adolescents and their parents. In completing the checklist, respondents indicated whether the issue had come up in the previous four weeks, how often it had come up, and the degree of anger that had accompanied a discussion of the issue. Table 6.3 presents a list of the conflicts mothers and daughters were most likely to have had. It also lists their five most intense conflicts.[6]

Perhaps most remarkable about these results is the degree to which mothers and daughters agreed about what they disagreed about. With forty-four issues to rate, the overlap between their top five conflicts is quite striking, both in terms of whether conflicts occurred and in terms of the intensity of the conflicts when they did occur. This agreement is even stronger in the category of what they argue least about. Consistent with previous studies using primarily white samples, most of the conflicts between our African American mothers and daughters were about relatively mundane issues, such as cleaning around the house and arguments with siblings. There is nothing obviously "adolescent" about the nature of these conflicts, based on the lists in table 6.3.

However, mothers and daughters do argue about issues that seem to be at the crux of adolescent development—going places without parents and wanting to be left alone. Of the conflicts chosen for discussion in the revealed-differences lab task, one-third (33%) centered around issues of autonomy-control (e.g., going places without parents, curfew, and the adolescent's choice of friends). Close to one-fourth (23%) were about household chores or cleanliness.

Moreover, upon closer inspection, the *way* in which even ordinary issues about cleaning came up or were elaborated in arguments also raises questions of whether and how parents exercise control over an adolescent's life. For example, in arguing about cleaning up the bedroom these adolescent girls told their mothers, "It's my bedroom, why can't I decide when to clean it . . . or if I clean it?" "You clean your room your way, I don't say anything," and "You're always telling me what to do." Mother responses to these conflicts often brought up issues of control-

TABLE 6.3
*Likelihood and Intensity of Mother-Daughter Conflicts
by Respondent*

| | Daughter<br>(Rank) | Mother<br>(Rank) |
|---|---|---|
| **Five Conflicts *Most* Likely to Occur** | | |
| 1 | Cleaning up bedroom | 2 |
| 2 | Bothering teen when she wants to be left alone | (14) |
| 3 | Helping out around the house | 1 |
| 4 | Fighting with brothers and sisters | (7) |
| 5 | Going places without parents | (17) |
| 6 | Putting away clothes | 3 |
| (13) | Telephone calls | 4 |
| (10) | Doing homework | 5 |
| **Five Conflicts *Least* Likely to Occur** | | |
| 1 | Smoking | 1 |
| 2 | What time to have meals | 3 |
| 3 | Cursing | 5 |
| 4 | Table Manners | (9) |
| 5 | Picking books or movies | (10) |
| (6) | Drinking beer or other liquor | 2 |
| (8) | Putting feet on furniture | 4 |
| **Five Most Intense Conflicts[a]** | | |
| 1 | Talking back to parents | 1 |
| 2 | Fighting with brothers and sisters | 2 |
| 3 | Lying | (15) |
| 4 | Getting in trouble at school | 4 |
| 5 | Messing up the house | 3 |
| (18) | Cleaning up the bedroom | 5 |

NOTES: $N = 59$; parentheses indicate rank for those not in top five for that respondent.
[a] Only included if at least 20% of mothers and daughters listed it as a conflict which had occurred.

autonomy as well—"If you're so grown up, you should help out more, not less," "It (the mess in the room) may be okay with you, but it's not okay with me," "What I do isn't the issue; I'm your mother."

The centrality of autonomy-control in these conflicts was apparent in both mother and daughter responses, but the way in which autonomy was conceptualized appeared to be different for each. For example, many daughters viewed their mothers' attempts to get them to clean their bedrooms as a violation of their privacy or an intrusion into what should be their zone of control. This is consistent with research indicating that adolescents often conceptualize conflicts with their parents in terms of personal jurisdiction (Smetana 1989; Smetana, Braeges and Yau 1991). However, unlike previous researchers, we did not observe that appeals to social conventions were common among the mothers. Instead, conflicts often escalated because mothers viewed the very behaviors that daughters felt interfered with their autonomy as an attempt to get them to exercise *more* autonomy and to take on more adult responsibilities. As one mother put it, "I want you to be grown-up. Adults vacuum, and wash dishes, and sweep floors, and fold clothes . . ."

Autonomy in its most general sense has been defined as "the ability to behave independently, to do things on one's own" (Newman and Newman 1984). As a child develops, his or her desire for autonomy increases and often conflicts with adults' desire for control. This parent-child struggle around autonomy and control changes dramatically as the child matures. For instance, forms of control that are used successfully during middle childhood may no longer be appropriate, nor appreciated, during the early adolescent years (Eccles et al. 1991). Indeed, the development of autonomy is regarded as one of the most critical psychosocial tasks of adolescence. During this period parents and children must negotiate the levels of autonomy and control afforded to each family member.

Issues of autonomy-control were quite salient in the mother-daughter conflicts we observed. Nonetheless, when responses by each to the Decision Making Questionnaire (DMQ) (Steinberg 1987) were examined, we found that they were in striking agreement about who decided what in their household. Those issues most apt to be decided by mothers alone or daughters alone, respectively, are listed in table 6.4. As this table indicates, mothers monitor their daughters' whereabouts, how late they stay out, and their sexuality (e.g., when they can begin dating or having friends over alone). On the other hand, they allow their daughters latitude to make their own decisions about personal issues, such as hairstyle and clothing. They also allow their daughters to make fairly major decisions about both their present course of action (e.g., who their friends are and what activities to take part in) and their futures (e.g., job or career). The mothers in our sample kept a close watch on their daughters, while allowing them freedom to develop their own identity. They didn't squander their time and resources regulating clothes and hairstyles, relatively minor issues that adolescents nevertheless view as central to their individuality of expression. In this sense the way these mothers exercised control was quite different from the "authoritarian" or "inconsistent" parenting style that has sometimes been attributed to minority parents.

Belying this apparently textbook-perfect parenting style, however, mothers in our sample were very confused about how to both support their daughters' desire for autonomy (and ability to handle it) and help keep them safe. We believe it is in large part because of their attempt to ensure their daughters' safety that African American parenting styles have at times been viewed as generally harsh. For example, when one of the adolescent girls in our sample called her mother "pal," her mother replied: "I'll give you pal in the mouth. I'm *not* your pal." Although at first

TABLE 6.4
*Who Makes Decisions in the Family*

| | Daughter (Rank) | Mother (Rank) |
|---|---|---|
| | **Top Five Areas in Which Mothers Decide** | |
| 1 | How late you stay out on weeknights | 3 |
| 2 | Whether you do chores around the house | (7) |
| 3 | When you can begin dating | 4 |
| 4 | What time you have to be home on weekend nights | (6) |
| 5 | Whether you can have friends over when your parents aren't home | 5 |
| (7) | Whether you tell your mother where you are when you go out | 1 |
| (6) | At what age you can leave school | 2 |
| | **Top Five Areas in Which Daughters Decide** | |
| 1 | What kind of job or career you[a] will have | 1 |
| 2 | What hairstyle you wear or haircut you get | 2 |
| 3 | Which friends you spend time with | (6) |
| 4 | What activities you take part in | 5 |
| 5 | What sorts of clothes you wear to school | 3 |
| (6) | How you spend your money | 4 |

NOTES: For each item, daughters indicated whether their parents (1) dictated exactly how they should behave, (2) asked their opinion but retained the final say on the matter, or (3) left the decision entirely up to them. Mothers answered these same questions in terms of themselves.

[a] Taken from the teen questionnaire; "you" refers to daughter.

glance this appears to be a rather harsh response, the interaction in its totality was characterized by a great deal of give and take, warmth, and good humor. Even in this instance, the mother's manner was an almost teasing one, and both were smiling and engaged. This is not to say that the mother was not deadly serious. Time and again in the course of the revealed-differences tasks we saw mothers clearly reminding their daughters that when push comes to shove, *they* (the mothers) were in charge.

In their conversations with interviewers, however, these same mothers were much more tentative about how much control they should be asserting. One mother told us that her family had moved to Seattle from East Los Angeles, hoping to find a place in which she could let her son and daughter play outside, walk to school, and go out with friends as she had as a youth. Instead, she found herself ever watchful, trying to keep them as close to the house as possible because of drug dealing and gang activity in her neighborhood. Another mother intimated that she wanted to give her daughter more freedom but was afraid that even one small slip could "ruin her life." Mothers often pointed out that not only were African American teens faced with an often hostile and dangerous environment, but they were also less likely to be given a break when they erred than were white teens. We heard many stories about how African American teenagers were arrested at the drop of a hat and punished more severely when they were caught doing wrong. In general, mothers

*111*

described their children as caught between a rock and a hard place, and their own attempts to exert the right amount of control as akin to threading a needle in the dark.

## The Fabric of African American Mother–Daughter Relationships

We have measured and described closeness, conflict, and control as separate entities, but it is in combination that they best describe mother–daughter relationships.

> *Mother:* Why do you get low grades in school?
>
> *Teen:* Why do I? Because I don't like the people.
>
> *Mother:* Really? You hang with them.
>
> *Teen:* Not when I go out at night.
>
> *Mother:* You're a smart girl, you can get A's—maybe B's—(laughter between the two)—at least C's. . . . You're good at French when you want to be. What's the deal? We have to resolve the conflict. . . .
>
> *Mother:* So how you [going to be] keeping up your grades—studying more?
>
> *Teen:* Yes—one hour every day.
>
> *Mother:* Cuz we'll have to get you a tutor if you don't. That's good though—I'm glad you're studying more. . . .
>
> *Mother:* Do we resolve conflicts pretty well?
>
> *Teen:* Yeah.
>
> *Mother:* Do you think we do?
>
> *Teen:* We sure do.

In this interaction, in which mother and daughter attempt to resolve their conflict about the importance of school grades, we can sense the closeness and warmth between them. The mother listens to her daughter, points out her strengths, and obviously cares about her daughter's opinions. The mother allows the daughter to come to her own solution, yet makes it clear she is prepared to take control (e.g., hire a tutor) if that solution doesn't work. Thus, this single interaction tells us much about closeness, conflict, *and* control in this dyad.

These three constructs, which have been used to describe parent-adolescent interactions in primarily white samples, have proved useful in guiding our qualitative examination of mother-daughter relationships. They have also proven useful in our quantitative analyses (Mason et al. 1994). However, in the interactions we observed, the way in which these separate threads are interwoven is as distinctly African American as is jazz, rap, or the blues. The notes are universal, but the style and verve echo the African American historical and cultural experience and have a signature integrity of their own (Boykin 1983, 1986).

African American girls enter the adolescent transition within a society that passively and actively condones the oppression of its members on the basis of race, gender, and socioeconomic status (Robinson and Ward 1991). They grow up in a world that views them with suspicion and fear. The books they read and the history they learn in school are generally devoid of African American women and their contributions to society. There are countless derogatory portrayals of African American women in the media, and large numbers of African American girls live in neighborhoods where violence, drugs, and other forms of environmental stress are the day-to-day reality. While the dangers for African American boys have received increasing attention, perhaps due to their elevated mortality rate, African American girls also receive a clear message that society places a low premium on their existence (McCombs 1986). The child-rearing practices and attitudes of their mothers reflect these realities.

These practices typically encourage the development of attachment and loyalty to parents and community, while supporting a great deal of personal independence as well (Fu 1984). In addition to more traditional manifestations of closeness and care, African American mothers may also demonstrate their love by working hard to provide for their children and by enforcing strict rules for the safety of their children. Nonetheless, the most consistent message that African American adolescent girls get from their mothers is to be self-reliant and resourceful (Collins 1987). Perhaps this is why a study of African American parenting found them to score highly on measures of both "authoritative" and "authoritarian" parenting (see Dornbusch et al. 1987). This straightforward classification system, which has been so useful in describing white parenting styles, may not do as good a job of capturing the dialectical nature of raising African American children. Indeed, this is something that Baumrind (1972), the creator of the classification system, concluded after carrying out her own observations of African American mothers and their children. In our own descriptions of African American parenting, we have coined the term "precision parenting" to describe the difficulty African American parents face in finding just the right amount of control to exert in order to encourage their children to stand on their own two feet while trying to make sure that they are not gunned down (Mason et al. 1994).

As we continue to examine the diversity of the adolescent experience, we are likely to continue to find simpler categorizations and schemas giving way to more complex and differentiated organizing structures. This will improve our descriptions of adolescent-parent relationships across cultures and genders. For example, observations of primarily white female development lead Chodorow (1978) and Gilligan (1982) to the notion of the "self-in-relation," which is still being developed by the

Stone Center group of theorists, researchers, and clinicians. From this perspective, a girl does not need to break her bond with her mother to establish an autonomous identity. Quite to the contrary, her ongoing relationship with her mother provides her with a sense of trust, security, and relatedness that enhances her sense of self. Rooted in Bowlby's attachment theory, the idea that adult functioning is not necessarily achieved by sacrificing familial bonds has been used by more current theorist-researchers to compellingly describe pathways to identity formation in white adolescents of both sexes (Allen et al. 1994). We believe that this notion of the self-in-relation or "autonomous-relatedness" can be used to describe parent-adolescent relationships in families of color as well.

We began this chapter by arguing that African American mother-daughter relationships could be understood only within the context of the unique cultural and ecological soil that they grow in. The composition of this soil has many common elements across mother-daughter pairs, most notably the peculiarities of race and gender as they are manifested in this country at this time. Nevertheless, there is as much diversity within a cultural group as there is between cultures, leading to a garden of immense variety. As we struggle to learn how each bud blossoms, the lessons we learn will enrich us all.

NOTES

1. By requiring the participation of both mother and daughter we eliminated families from our study in which there was no mother or in which the mother was unavailable. It is also unlikely that neglectful and abusive mothers, who can be found in all cultures, would have participated.

2. A few had graduated to the ninth grade by the time of study participation.

3. An examination of this very word reveals the racism of this society, in that to denigrate means to make like a Negro.

4. The literature is mixed on this point, with some researchers noting that male-female roles are more egalitarian among African Americans.

5. Unless otherwise stated, we use the word "attachment" according to its dictionary definition; no specific theoretical position is implied by our use of the word or concept.

6. A list of the frequency of arguments is available from the first author upon request. It was not included here because the variability of within-rater (e.g., within-daughter, within-mother) responses was so great. For example, the most frequent argument listed by daughters was "messing up the house," but while the average number of times it came up in the last four weeks was 22.7, the standard deviation was 26.8. The minimum number of times it came up was 1; the maximum was 99.

REFERENCES

The data presented in this chapter were collected in conjunction with Nancy Gonzales's dissertation, and she deserves the lion's share of the credit for many of the ideas elaborated here. Order of authorship reflects work on this chapter alone and not on the general study that it is drawn from. We thank Craig A. Mason for his help throughout this project. The full study was funded by a National Institute of Child Health and Human Development (HD24056) grant to Ana Mari Cauce.

Allen, J. P., S. T. Hauser, K. L. Bell, and T. G. O'Connor. 1994. Longitudinal assessment of autonomy and relatedness in adolescent-family interactions as predictors of adolescent ego development and self-esteem. *Child Development* 65:179–94.

Armsden, G. C., and M. T. Greenberg. 1987. The Inventory of Parent and Peer Attachment: Individual differences and their relationship to psychological well-being in adolescence. *Journal of Youth and Adolescence* 16:427–53.

Baumrind, D. 1972. An exploratory study of socialization effects on black children: Some black-white comparisons. *Child Development* 43:261–67.

Boykin, A. W. 1983. The academic performance of Afro-American children. In *Achievement and achievement motives,* edited by J. Spence. San Francisco: W. Freeman.

———. 1986. The triple quandary and the schooling of Afro-American children. In *The school achievement of minority children,* edited by U. Neisser. Hillsdale, N.J.: Erlbaum.

Cauce, A. M., and N. Gonzales. 1993. Slouching towards culturally competent research: Adolescents of color in context. *Focus: Psychological Study of Ethnic Minority Issues* 7:8–9.

Cauce, A. M., J. T. Ptacek, C. A. Mason, and R. E. Smith. 1994. *The social support rating scale—revised: Three studies on development an validation.* Manuscript.

Chodorow, N. 1978. *The reproduction of mothering.* Berkeley: University of California Press.

Collins, P. H. 1987. The meaning of motherhood in black culture and black mother/daughter relationships. *Sage* 4:3–10.

Dornbusch, S. M., P. L. Ritter, D. R. Liederman, and M. J. Fraleigh. 1987. The relation of parenting style to adolescent school performance. *Child Development* 58:1244–57.

Eccles, J. S., C. H. Buchanan, A. F. Flanagan, A. Fuligni, C. Midgley, and C. Yee. 1991. Control versus autonomy during early adolescence. *Journal of Social Issues* 47:53–68.

Fu, V. R. 1984. Maternal dependency and childrearing attitudes among mothers of adolescent females. *Adolescence* 19:795–804.

Gilligan, C. 1982. *In a different voice.* Cambridge: Harvard University Press.

Gold, M., and D. S. Yanof. 1985. Mothers, daughters, and girlfriends. *Journal of Personality and Social Psychology* 49:654–59.

Graham, S. 1992. "Most of the subjects were white and middle class": Trends in published research on African Americans in selected APA journals, 1970–1989. *American Psychologist* 47:629–39.

Graves, D. R. 1994. Developmental changes in the personal networks of inner-city African American adolescents: Comparisons between membership composition and incidence of drug and alcohol use. Manuscript, University of Washington.

Greene, B. A. 1990. What has gone before: The legacy of racism and sexism in the lives of Black mothers and daughters. *Women in Therapy* 9:28–29.

Hill, J. P., and G. N. Holmbeck. 1986. Attachment and autonomy during adolescence. In *Annals of Child Development,* vol. 3, edited by F. W. Whiteburst. Greenwich, Conn.: JAI Press.

hooks, b. 1984. Reflections of a "good" daughter: From black is a woman's color. *Sage* 1:28–29.

Hull, G. T., P. Bell Scott, and B. Smith. 1982. *But some of us are brave.* Old Westbury, N.Y.: The Feminist Press.

Mason, C. A., A. M. Cauce, N. Gonzales, and Y. Hiraga. 1994. An ecological model of externalizing behaviors in African-American adolescents: No family is an island. *Journal of Research on Adolescence* 4:639–55.

McCombs, H. G. 1986. The application of an individual/collective model to the psychology of black women. *Women in Therapy* 5:67–80.

McLoyd, V. C., and S. M. Randolph. 1985. Secular trends in the study of Afro-American children: A review of child development, 1936–1980. *Monographs of the Society for Research in Child Development* 50:78–92.

McPhail, G. 1987. Mothers and daughters talking together: An interview with filmmaker Cheryl Chisholm. *Sage* 4:53–56.

Montemayor, R. 1986. Family variation in parent-adolescent storm and stress. *Journal of Adolescent Research* 1:15–31.

Newman, B. M., and P. R. Newman. 1984. *Development through life: A psychological approach.* Homewood, Ill.: Dorsey Press.

O'Hare, W. P., K. M. Pollard, T. L. Mann, and M. M. Kent. 1991. African-Americans in the 1990's. Population Bulletin vol. 46, no. 11. Washington, D.C.: Population Reference Bureau.

Pardeck, J. A., and J. T. Pardeck. 1990. Family factors related to adolescent autonomy. *Family Therapy* 17:223–31.

Richie, B. S. 1992. Coping with work: Interventions with African American Women. *Women and Therapy* 12: 97–111.

Robin, A. L., and S. L. Foster. 1984. Problem-solving communication training: A behavioral-family systems approach to parent-adolescent conflict. In *Adolescent behavior disorders,* edited by P. Karoly and J. J. Steffen. Lexington, Mass.: Heath.

Robinson, T., and J. V. Ward. 1991. A belief in self far greater than anyone's disbelief: Cultivating resistance among African American female adolescents. *Women and Therapy* 11: 87–103.

Sarason, B. R., E. N. Shearin, G. R. Pierce, and I. G. Sarason. 1987. Interrelationships among social support measures: Theoretical and practical implications. *Journal of Personality and Social Psychology* 52:813–32.

Smetana, J. G. 1989. Adolescents' and parents' reasoning about actual family conflict. *Child Development* 60:1052–67.

Smetana, J. G., J. L. Braeges, and J. Yau. 1991. Doing what you say and saying what you do: Reasoning about adolescent-parent conflict in interviews and interactions. *Journal of Adolescent Research* 6:276–95.

Steinberg, L. 1987. Single parents, stepparents, and the susceptibility of adolescents to antisocial peer pressure. *Child Development* 58:269–75.

———. 1990. Autonomy, conflict, and harmony in the family relationship. In *At the threshold: The developing adolescent,* edited by S. Feldman and G. Elliott. Cambridge: Harvard University Press.

Troll, L. 1987. Mother-daughter relationships through the life span. *Applied Social Psychology Annual* 7:284–305.

Wilson, M. N., and T. F. J. Tolson. 1990. Familial support in the black community. *Journal of Child Clinical Psychology* 19:347–55.

Wyche, K. F. 1993. Psychology and African American women: Findings from applied research. *Applied and Preventive Psychology* 2:115–21.

Youniss, J., and J. Smollar. 1985. *Adolescent relations with mothers, fathers, and friends.* Chicago: University of Chicago Press.

# 7

# Cultural Stories: Latina and Portuguese Daughters and Mothers

Jill McLean Taylor

> Of course my daughter read when she was little, of course she
> spoke so well so soon. She spoke for me. She said what I
> never dared. She said "I won't," she said "I want," she said
> "You're a bad mami," she said "Give me that," she said
> "I will!"
>
> —A. L. Morales and R. Morales

Complicated and contradictory stories about mothers and about relationships between daughters and mothers—both biological and symbolic—are part of our lives. Whether mothers of daughters or not, women have in common the experience of being a daughter, an experience that is shaped by and infused with cultural values, beliefs, and traditions (Coles 1991). In the United States the understanding of mother-daughter relationships is most often drawn from the experiences of white middle-class women, as though race, ethnicity, and social class have little impact on how these relationships are shaped (Joseph and Lewis 1981; Spelman 1988). In the prevailing story, tied also to a traditional view of development, daughters are to separate from their mothers during adolescence. At the same time mothers are to socialize their daughters to fit into a world that is receptive to dependent, obedient, and passive women, a world that is hostile to girls and women who question, challenge, or disrupt.

To shift culture to the center of understanding mother-daughter relationships requires taking into account how the effects of race, ethnicity, and class shape the contexts of mothers' lives and the identities of their children (Collins 1994). Hispanic[1] and Portuguese mothers teach their daughters to negotiate the social worlds of home, school, and community, to become in effect bicultural (Garcia Coll 1992). The importance of being bicultural has been emphasized by many and was made famous by African American sociologist W. E. B. Du Bois in 1903 when he discussed the need for black people to develop "double consciousness" as part of their identity: "This sense of always looking at one's self through the eyes of others, of measuring one's soul by the tape of the world that looks on in amused contempt and pity" (Du Bois [1903], 1989, 5). Recent feminist work posits that all girls, as members of an oppressed group in this culture, need to be bicultural and have "double vision" and "double voice" (Gilligan 1990; Brown and Gilligan 1992; Rogers 1993; Waters, chap. 4 of this volume). Cynthia Garcia Coll (1992) stresses the importance of being bicultural for Hispanic people. The concept of "multiple consciousness" suggested for black women by Darlene Clark Hine in *Lure and Loathing* (1993) may be useful for understanding women and girls from oppressed racial or ethnic groups.

The mother-daughter relationships that are discussed here are drawn from a larger project, the Understanding Adolescence Study, a three-year longitudinal, qualitative study of adolescents "at risk" who were attending a large urban high school in the Northeast. Adolescents were selected for this study on the basis of standard variables used to define traditional notions of "at risk" for early parenthood and school dropout. We were interested in including at risk adolescents because their voices had traditionally been missing or inadequately represented in psychological inquiry of normal development and overrepresented in studies of deficit and deviance. Generally, "at risk" is used to describe children and adolescents who for a number of material and social reasons are not expected to become responsible adults and who are more likely to engage in deviant behaviors, such as alcohol and drug use, unprotected sex, and dropping out of school (Dryfoos 1990).

An expanded definition of risk has emerged from research with girls and women. In earlier work of the Harvard Project on Women's Psychology and Girls' Development, Carol Gilligan and colleagues heard a paradox that Jean Baker Miller also noted in psychotherapy with women— that to sustain relationships with others, adolescent girls and women may cover over their own thoughts, needs, and desires (Gilligan 1977, 1982; Gilligan, Ward, and Taylor 1988; Gilligan, Hanmer, and Lyons 1990; Miller 1976, 1988). A five-year longitudinal and cross-sectional study conducted by Lyn Mikel Brown, Carol Gilligan, and members of the Harvard Project at an independent day school allowed researchers to hear a shift that occurs as adolescent girls comply with the expectations and pressures of the dominant culture (Brown and Gilligan 1992). The majority of adolescent girls in this setting sought to conform to an image of the ideal girl—one who is always nice and never hurts other people's feelings, who can control her own feelings, particularly anger, and her desires, such as hunger and sexuality. The healthy resistance or opposition to disconnection that girls showed in childhood became at adolescence a resistance to knowing one's feelings, to knowing one's body, and to being in authentic relationship with others. This process of psychological dissociation has profound consequences for psychological health and development.

As girls from all cultural backgrounds become adolescents, changes occur with respect to how they feel about themselves and how other people respond to them, causing relationships to be redefined and renegotiated (Apter 1990; Espin 1984). Within Hispanic and Portuguese cultures, renegotiation is in the context of cultural conventions about femininity and womanhood—such as the goodness and suffering of women, the responsibility to look after others, and a double standard regarding sexuality—that may make it difficult for these adolescents to speak about their knowledge, feelings, and desires and to stay in relationship with their mothers.

Using a voice-centered, relational method of research developed by the Harvard Project on Women's Psychology and Girls' Development and extended by this study with a diverse population, I trace Hispanic and Portuguese daughters' relationships with their mothers during the three years during which this research took place. Focusing on three adolescents, I present examples of healthy resistance, of resignation to cultural conventions of femininity and womanhood, and of what Jean Anyon (1982) names "resistance within accommodation."

## The Study

Participants in the Understanding Adolescence Study were respondents in a Dropout Prevention Planning Survey[2] administered in the spring of 1987 to seventh and eighth graders in a large urban school system. The co-occurrence of racial and ethnic background or economic disadvantage with three of six additional variables—low self-esteem, being overage for grade, frequent tardiness or absence from school, the need for additional academic support, speaking English as a second language, and living in a single parent household—led us to consider students to be at risk for school dropout or early parenthood, or both. Teachers with whom these students had relationships helped trim a provisionary list of students, because the at risk predictors in themselves provide limited information about students' lives.[3] The final list included 48 adolescents, 33 girls and

15 boys, who were in the study for three years. In this chapter I draw on the interview data of the four Hispanic and eight Portuguese adolescent girls in the study.

The study followed students from eighth to tenth grade. Interviews were designed to give the participants opportunities to speak about a number of different relational domains in their lives, including their relationships with their mothers. In the first two years of the study the interviews lasted forty-five to ninety minutes. In the third year two separate interviews of sixty to ninety minutes were scheduled. Every effort was made to have each interviewer interview the same adolescent each year, as an ongoing relationship between interviewee and interviewer is understood to be an advantage of this relational method. The interviews were taped and transcribed for later analysis.

## Analysis

In the Understanding Adolescence Study, we used a voice-centered method of analysis. Developed by members of the Harvard Project and described in the "Listener's Guide" (Brown et al. 1988), this method is a systematic, clinical, and literary method of interpretation.

Generally, the method entails at least four separate readings of an interview. The first focuses on the overall outline and details of the stories being told. Researchers make notes on worksheets about their first impression of recurring themes, contradictions, and images, recording a girl's actual words and how the investigator interprets or makes sense of what was said. At the same time researchers record their emotional responses to the adolescent girl and her story. Both "voices" are explicitly included, codifying a practice of reflexivity that has been linked with feminist methods (Morawski 1990).[4]

The second time through the interview, researchers follow the voice of the narrator, the "I," listening to what a girl says, thinks, feels, does — and also notice what she does not say that might be expected, where she sounds sure of her words, and where she sounds tentative or confused. We noted phrases such as "I don't know" and "this may not be right, but . . ." The use of colored pencils — such as green for following the narrator, red for healthy resistance, blue for psychological distress — provides one way of organizing and gaining visual access to interpretations of a text and is congruent with the layered reading of this method.

In the third reading we listened for psychological health, taking as evidence girls' resistance to disconnection from their own thoughts and feelings. It could be resistance to the conventions of femininity and womanhood, both in the dominant culture and in the girl's own culture;

resistance to internalizing the negative messages about her value; or resistance to idealized messages about relationships. The nature of this resistance is political in that girls are standing up to, and refusing to accept, messages that attempt to define their thinking and feeling.

On the fourth and last round we listened for evidence of psychological distress, which we heard as girls' psychological dissociation from their knowledge, needs, and desires. Ana, for example, tells a story in which she first describes being hurt by her mother's lack of trust and feeling disappointed and angry when her parents curtailed her activities. Ana quickly reframes this situation, however, and names it as one that she feels good about, perhaps for the interviewer's sake and perhaps because she feels these conflicting emotions at the same time. She says she feels protected by her parents concern: "But I feel good, because of the fact that they make it sound so, how do I say it, they make it sound like, I don't know, it just proves to me they don't want anything to happen to me."

In this reading for psychological distress, researchers follow the tension between a girl's knowing and not knowing what is painful yet also, from a personal and political point of view, may be important for her to be aware of in the world in which she lives.

In research in which those involved are different in terms of race, ethnicity, and social class from the interviewees, who is listening as well as who is speaking becomes a central focus. In a patriarchal society differences in social location are played out through voice and linked to who is speaking and who is heard, not listened to, ignored, or devalued. Voices traditionally "missing" from psychology have been those marginalized by virtue of race, ethnicity, social class, religion, sexual orientation, and disability, except when studied from a social, educational, or health problem perspective. In this study the researchers analyzing the texts included one black and three white women. Although we were reading Latina and Portuguese literature and research from different disciplines, we were "outsiders." There is an ongoing and at times rancorous debate about the ability of "outsiders" to hear and understand the experiences of people different from themselves, but as Elliot Mishler (1992) believes, there "are a number of possible retellings of a story." Together, interviewer and interviewee produce narrative accounts, depending not only on the open-ended questions of the interviewer and the experiences of the narrator, but also on the "social location" of both. This applies also to interpretations of interviews and how meanings are made. It is from the standpoint of who I am—a middle class Pakeha New Zealander[5] who has lived in this country for many years, the mother of three adolescent sons, and a wife, to name but a few of the obvious markers—that I interpret these interviews. As I am reading, my interpretations are informed and guided by my affiliation with a particular interpretive community, central to which is our understanding of psychology as a relational practice with relational dimensions of listening, speaking, taking in, and interpreting the words, the silences, and the stories of other people.

## Socialization into Womanhood: Cultural Contexts

Although the languages of Hispanic and Portuguese people differ, they share many values and beliefs, particularly those relating to the primacy of the family unit and respect for parents and other family members (Ribeiro 1981). For children and adolescents in Hispanic (and Portuguese) families who are going to school in the United States and are inundated with messages about individualism from mainstream culture, growing up has many contradictions (see Salguero and McCusker, chap. 18 of this volume). Cultural values enforced and rewarded in family life are frequently different from those observed in school, in social groups, and in work life (Vazquez-Nuttall and Romero-Garcia 1989). Complex cultural values, such as "marianisimo/machismo" and "respeto," play specific roles in the context of family and in the context of assimilation and acculturation, making it difficult for children to reconcile with dominant cultural conventions (Vazquez-Nuttall, Romero-Garcia, and De León 1987; Stevens 1973).

The Hispanic and Portuguese girls speak of their efforts to conform to their cultures' beliefs and expectations, while simultaneously being part of mainstream culture in school. Some speak of unfairness that is based on gender difference; others have a well-developed, critical perspective on the images that others have of them. Maria, a serious and thoughtful adolescent who came to this country from Portugal at age eleven, explains her bicultural awareness of being part of a minority group and part of the mainstream in a brief story. In eighth grade, in response to the question "Can you tell me a time you felt good about yourself outside of school?" Maria says: "This Portuguese lady was trying to say to the man what she wanted, she didn't know how to speak English, and I helped her. My friend said, 'No, don't do that. They're going to find out you're Portuguese.' I don't care, I'm Portuguese and proud. I just want to help the people." Like Maria, Pilar, a Latina adolescent, acknowledges the view that she believes the dominant culture holds of Hispanic girls. When asked in the tenth grade, "What do you think Hispanic girls in this school need to know?" she says:

People think of them as a girl who gets pregnant easy. And who doesn't care or anything, who's just a loser, so they say, but then there's one thing they [Hispanic girls] have to watch is not to let people think they're like that. . . . It depends on how you present yourself. If you present yourself like what people think of you, well then they're not going to know who you are.

Pilar invokes an image of vigilance with her words "have to watch," which is a theme in several girls' explanations of what it would be good to know as Hispanic or Portuguese girls in their high school. What sociologist Patricia Hill Collins names "controlling images" (Collins 1990) or negative stereotypes will, according to Pilar, prevent people from knowing "who you are."

Bettina's mother, sounding like mothers everywhere, tells her to "put my hair down and everything. She doesn't like my hair when its out to here, you know, thick, so she'd like, 'Put it down,' and everything. It's for my own good, because she doesn't want people looking at me because people talk. It's like you always feel bad. She doesn't want me to feel bad or anything." Being part of an oppressed minority and "looking at one's self through the eyes of others" calls for Portuguese girls such as Bettina and other adolescent girls of color to be self-conscious and vigilant. Mothers not only teach their daughters conventions of femininity and womanhood, of their own culture and of the dominant culture, but also—because they are inextricably linked—conventions of masculinity (Anzaldua 1987; Moraga and Anzaldua 1981).

Daughters in Hispanic and Portuguese families are socialized to be dependent, obedient, responsible, and submissive; disagreement and conflict with parents and elders are often not tolerated (Pepler and Lessa 1993). Tensions and conflicts around being bicultural or multicultural are apparent in mother-daughter relationships, given the mother's roles as the bearer and guardian of culture and her possible ambivalence in educating daughters to "fit in" and simultaneously "be themselves." Psychologist James Zimmerman raises two central questions: "How can a Hispanic daughter be passive and compliant and at the same time fulfill her own unique potential; and how can she go beyond her mother and stay in relationship with her at the same time?" (Zimmerman 1991, 228–29). The second question is salient for many low income and working-class girls across different cultural groups.

Oliva and Ana, both Latina, and Isabel, who is Portuguese, describe complex and at times contradictory emotions in their relationships with their mothers, relationships that are shaped by cultural beliefs, values, and traditions and by mainstream white middle-class society. Oliva resists complying with cultural values and beliefs; Isabel seems to resign herself to her mother's cultural values and beliefs, and Ana describes her attempts to both accommodate to and resist cultural expectations in her relationship with her mother. Mothers, too, are caught between passing on cultural traditions and preparing their daughters for a very different world from the one in which they grew up.

## Resistance: Are the Costs Too High?

The tension between her mother's values and beliefs and her own is woven throughout interviews with Oliva, a Hispanic adolescent whose family came to the United States from Columbia. Passionately and with a well-developed critique of "falseness" in relationships, Oliva describes how her mother suffers through her "niceness." In tenth grade she says her mother is "like the nicest person in the world. . . . She's so nice to everybody and she does favors for everybody. Even though like when she asks them to do something, they'll say no. She'll do it for them anyway. She'll do a favor for them anyway." Oliva complains of this concern to her mother: "I'm like ma, but it's not right. It's not right. You're so nice to them and do everything for everybody, and it's like, you're not getting anything out of it." But when she speaks her mind to those who will not return her mother's favors, "My mother gets mad at me because like when I tell them I'm like why are you doing that to my mother. Don't talk about her. . . . And my mother gets mad. She doesn't say anything to them. She says, 'Don't say anything to them.'" Oliva indicates there is no easy way out: if she speaks out in defense of her mother, her mother gets angry: if she does what her mother wants, she silences herself and becomes an unwilling bystander while others take advantage of her mother.

Oliva points to the seeming unevenness of her mother's niceness: "All she does is complain to me, so there's no real relationship there. . . . And she's nice to everybody else, that's what gets me mad, she's nice to everybody else . . . and she's not nice to us." While Oliva's assertion that her mother is not nice to her daughters can be heard as part of an adolescent litany of complaints about mothers, her mother's niceness and helpfulness to others can also be understood as the selflessness and suffering ascribed to good women (Medrano 1994). When Oliva speaks of "no real relationship," she is tapping into the paradox that Gilligan and Miller found in women, which has been noted in other work with adolescent girls—namely, the impossibility of being in a "real" relationship when one person keeps her thoughts and feelings out of the relationship. In this instance, to stay in relationship with her mother means keeping her confusion, criticism, and anger out of the relationship. At the same time, according to Oliva, her mother is concealing her feelings from others. The anger that her mother has but does not express with those for whom she "does favors" reduces the range of available feelings for Oliva and her sister, leaving them wishing for more positive attention. For Oliva's mother to begin speaking of her feelings and break cultural prohibitions against expressing anger might be an act of political resistance that is too difficult to tolerate. Oliva recognizes both the toll on her mother that "being nice" extracts and the hypocrisy of others in taking her mother's help without reciprocating.

Oliva's own voice stands out in the group of twelve Hispanic and Portuguese girls, as she critiques and resists the demands of compliance to conventions of femininity in both her own and the dominant culture.

## Resignation: And Idealized Relationship?

Among the Portuguese adolescent girls in the study we heard evidence of girls not knowing or speaking about their thoughts, desires, and feelings. All of these girls were in school at the end of tenth grade and graduated from high school either two or three years later. All were living with both mother and father except for two, whose fathers died during the course of the study. The supremacy of the family unit ranks high among the protective aspects of Portuguese culture (Moitoza 1982). Isabel, who came from Portugal to this country as a young child, and whose mother understands but does not speak English, at first resists the restrictions imposed by her parents. In eighth grade, Isabel spoke of how she had elicited the help of her sister-in-law in persuading her parents to let her do more, go out with her cousin, and wear a hint of makeup. She was animated, excited, and eager to talk and wanted to find out the reasons for doing a study at her school. In ninth grade, despite having been home for several days with a severe cold, Isabel came to school to keep her interview appointment. This year, Isabel told a complicated story of a relationship with a boy whom her brothers did not want her to go out with and how she was worried that her parents would find out. She seemed glad to have someone in whom to confide. By the tenth grade, Isabel was concerned about the confidentiality of the interview. As I interviewed her I was aware of a loss of the "zest" so apparent in her in the eighth and ninth grades. She seemed to have accommodated to the "tyranny of femininity" in both the dominant culture and her own. Stating that the reason she continued to participate in the study is "because it is nice to help people," she suggests that her thinking and actions this year are organized around self-sacrifice. Isabel speaks of "feeling guilty" that she disobeyed her mother once about a year ago: "Because it's just the point that she puts us under her roof, feeds us and stuff, we have to be kind, like if she was our boss. You never really talk back to your boss." "Talking back" in Isabel's terms may mean saying what she thinks, but Isabel seems to have accepted the kind of relationship with her mother that conforms both with the ideal of no disagreement and anger and also with a Portuguese value of respect for parents and extended family members and commitment to the family.

In Portuguese families respect for parental authority as well as others outside the family, according to age, sex, and social class, is highly valued. Like "respeto" in Latino culture, this kind of respect

is more than the tone of social relations; it is the relation of one person to another, child to parent, student to teacher, citizen to police officer, worker to boss, and neighbor to neighbor. Ideally, respeto does not operate in only one direction; ideally respeto acts as a brake on the driving individualism of Anglo society and makes a person more familial, more communal in his orientation. (Shorris 1992, 106)

In ninth and tenth grades change was apparent in many Portuguese and Hispanic daughters. During these latter years, many appeared to embrace an idealized version of the relationship with their mothers, refusing to argue and accepting their mothers' views about what should be important in their lives (Pepler and Lessa 1993). Strict prohibitions about women expressing anger in Hispanic and Portuguese cultures mean that the stakes are high when girls get angry (Comas-Diaz 1987).

## Accommodation and Resistance

The mother-daughter relationships that these adolescent girls describe appeared bounded and defined by rules about gender roles and sexuality, rules that the girls both resist and find protective. In interviews girls describe their relationships with their mothers in the context of these rules and restrictions, how they come to negotiate conventions of femininity in Hispanic and Portuguese culture, including the expression of anger, and how their interests in and fears about sexuality are shaped by these relationships.

Ana is a Latina adolescent whose parents came from South America "for a better life." The presence and authority of Ana's own voice—her opinions, her feelings—may be at risk as she accommodates to the ideal of concern and protection in her relationship with her mother. In ninth grade Ana describes the unpredictable nature of her conversations with her mother about boys:

This is so weird, because if I go and talk to my mother about boys, sometimes she will go along with it . . . but if she feels all grouchy . . . she'll start saying "all you think about is boys" . . . and I'll be like, oh wow, one day she is like this, coming with, and she will talk about her kinds of boys and then she'll talk about this, and I'm like I don't know.

Ana's voice in this relationship takes on an additional dimension when she speaks of the difficulties she has communicating with her mother through barriers of language and culture: "My mother doesn't know about school things, she doesn't hardly even know English. . . . She doesn't know what pressures we're going through in school, what temptations. . . . We can't really talk to them about it because they don't understand." Ana keeps her concerns about school out of her relationship not only with her mother, but also with others. She responds when the interviewer asks who she talks to about these pressures and temptations, "I mostly don't talk to anybody."

The complexity of Ana's relationship with her mother and with their shared cultural context appears most dramatically in her account of the aftermath of her experience with a boy who attempted to force her to have sex with him. The importance of this incident for Ana is evident in Ana's retelling of it each year. In ninth grade, Ana tells us about the impact of this experience in her relationship with her mother. She tells this story both as an example of when she and her mother were close and as an example of when they were not close at all. Shortly after the incident with the boy, Ana told her mother about it, because she was afraid her mother might hear of it from someone else. It also provided a way for Ana to speak about how she felt. Ana said that her mother "stuck in every way with me and we did whatever we could to get him in trouble, to really punish him, you know." Ana said that she and her mother were brought closer together because of this, "and we really talked about it and I told her how I felt and everything and she stood there by me, she really understood, she believed me and that's all I wanted to hear." Yet Ana's mother made a doctor's appointment for Ana to have her "checked out." Ana responded by asking her mother, "Isn't my word enough?" Ana has named other instances of her mother's not believing her, but this time she downplays this aspect of the situation and offers the account as an example of a time when she felt especially close to her mother.

However, when she is asked to speak about a time when she and her mother were not close at all, she chooses this same situation and tells of how she later felt betrayed by her mother. She says, "She told somebody, a so-called best friend she calls. And that so-called best friend told somebody else, and they had like a spark all over." Ana says, "I felt like she betrayed me." The metaphor of fire, of being hurt as a consequence of speaking openly, is powerful both at home and in school, where Ana, in ninth grade and again in tenth describes her feelings in almost identical terms: "When I leave this school, I don't leave happy. I don't. I don't know, I just don't feel happy. I feel like, I know that somebody must have talked about me today. . . . But I always, I don't know, it must be the people, I don't know." Ana's frequent "I don't know's" signal perhaps her loss of confidence in what she knows and desires and her concern with reputation. Her unhappiness at school when held up against the high dropout rates for Hispanic adolescent girls seems to make her particularly vulnerable to becoming a dropout. Ana challenges these expectations, however, by graduating from high school.

## Discussion

As the Hispanic and Portuguese adolescent girls in this study speak about relationships with their mothers, they tell stories that are imbued with cultural beliefs and values, as well as stories that may be regarded as "typical" of white middle-class adolescents. They say their parents are too strict, treat their daughters differently from the way they treat their sons, and are "too concerned" about their safety. If high school graduation is taken as a measure of success, then aspects of their cultures that adolescent girls speak about as restrictive, such as denial of their emerging sexuality and their parents' close monitoring of their social life, may also be protective.[6] Not speaking about subjects that will lead to conflict may be a resistance that does not lead to psychological distress, remaining instead within the typical contours of mother-daughter relationships in Latina and Portuguese cultures. On the other hand, these same protective aspects may lead to psychological distress, so that girls lose their knowledge of what they think and feel, rely on others to tell them what is good for them, and give up "authorization" of their own experience.

Tension for adolescent girls resides between the expectations to respect and obey their mothers (and fathers) and to maintain a connection to their own thoughts, feelings, and desires. Similarly, a dilemma for educators and women working with girls is centered around how to support a girl's psychological development—her own voice—and at the same time be knowledgeable and respectful of her cultural context. Encouraging healthy resistance in the form of "speaking out" may lead to hurtful conflicts between mothers and daughters (see also Ward, chap. 5 of this volume). Schools may be able to encourage girls to both understand and critique conventions of femininity and womanhood both in the dominant culture and in their own cultures that limit opportunities for girls and women. Making it possible for girls to experience a range of emotions—often contradictory and confusing—that include anger, sadness, joy, pleasure, and love may require providing a safe place in which to do this and contact with women and girls from the same cultural background who may verify girls' perceptions of reality.

## NOTES

1. Although "Latina" is currently the preferred descriptor, I am using "Hispanic" in the text because it was the descriptor used when we asked the girls in our study about their racial or ethnic background.

2. The Dropout Prevention Planning Survey was developed by Dr. Anne Higgins, working with Dr. Elsa Wasserman. We were able to include the Rosenberg Self-Esteem Scale, a ten-point Likert scale used widely for adolescents and adults, and to use sections of the survey to generate a list of students who met our criteria for "at risk" that are based on standard variables of risk.

3. Teachers supplied information that enabled us to exclude some students who met standard criteria of "at risk," such as chronic tardiness or frequent absence combined with being a racial or ethnic minority and coming from a single parent family, by explaining, for example, that a student was doing well in school, but as his or her mother worked, the student was providing care for younger family members.

4. This reflexivity introduces into our interpretation what bell hooks calls "a politics of location," which necessarily "calls those of us who would participate in the formation of counter-hegemonic cultural practice to identify the spaces where we begin the process of revision." (hooks 1990, 145).

5. *Pakeha* is the Maori word for whites. White New Zealanders had traditionally referred to themselves as New Zealanders, but as Maori women and men pointed out, they too are New Zealanders and were so long before European settlers arrived. The Maoris ask that white New Zealanders refer to themselves as *Pakehas*.

6. Literature on at risk children and adolescents posits that intact families are "protective" in terms of promoting resilience and overcoming risks associated with low social class and race and ethnicity. Cultural values and beliefs are closely tied to values, both religious and cultural, about families, so that it is difficult to separate them.

## REFERENCES

Anyon, J. 1982. Intersections of gender and class. Occasional Paper no. 10. In *Issues in education: Schooling and the reproduction of class and gender inequalities,* edited by L. Weis. Buffalo: State University of New York Press.

Anzaldua, G. 1987. *Borderlands la frontera.* San Francisco: aunt lute books.

Apter, T. 1990. *Altered loves: Mothers and daughters during adolescence.* New York: St. Martin's Press.

Brown, L. 1991. Telling a girl's life: Self-authorization as a form of resistance. *Women and Therapy* 11(3/4): 71–86.

Brown, L., D. Argyris, J. Attanucci, B. Bardige, C. Gilligan, K. Johnston, B. Miller, D. Osborne, M. Tappan, J. Ward, G. Wiggins, and D. Wilcox. 1988. *A guide to reading narratives of conflict and choice for self and moral voice.* Monograph no. 1. Cambridge: Harvard Graduate School of Education, Project on Women's Psychology and Girls' Development.

Brown, L. M., and C. Gilligan. 1990. Listening for self and relational voices: A responsive/resisting reader's guide. Paper presented at symposium, Literary theory as a guide to psychological analysis, annual meeting of the American Psychological Association, August, Boston, Mass.

———. 1992. *Meeting at the crossroads: Women's psychology and girls' development.* Cambridge: Harvard University Press.

Coles, J. 1991. Preface to *Double stitch: Black women write about mothers and daughters,* edited by P. Bell-Scott. Boston: Beacon Press.

Collins, P. H. 1986. Learning from the outsider within. *Social Problems* 33 (6):14–32.

———. 1990. *Black feminist thought.* Boston: Beacon Press.

———. 1994. Shifting the center. In *Representations of Motherhood,* edited by D. Bassin, M. Honey, and M. Kaplan. New Haven: Yale University Press.

Comas-Diaz, L. 1987. Feminist therapy with mainland Puerto Rican women. *Psychology of Women Quarterly* 11:461–74.

Dryfoos, J. 1990. *Adolescents at risk.* New York: Oxford University Press.

Du Bois, W. E. B. [1903] 1989. *The souls of black folk.* Reprint, New York: Penguin Books.

Espin, O. 1984. Cultural and historical influences on sexuality in Hispanic-Latin women: Implication for psychotherapy. In *Pleasure and danger: Exploring female sexuality,* edited by C. S. Vance, 149–64. Boston: Routledge and Kegan Paul.

Garcia Coll, C. 1992. Cultural diversity: Implications for theory and practice. Works in Progress series, no. 59. Stone Center, Wellesley College, Wellesley, Mass.

Gilligan, C. 1977. In a different voice: Women's conceptions of self and of morality. *Harvard Educational Review* 47:481–517.

———. 1982. *In a different voice: Psychological theory and women's development.* Cambridge: Harvard University Press.

———. 1988. Remapping the moral domain: New images of self in relationship. In *Mapping the moral domain: A contribution of women's thinking to psychological theory and education,* edited by C. Gilligan, J. Ward, and J. Taylor, 3–19. Cambridge: Harvard University Press.

———. 1990. Teaching Shakespeare's sister: Notes from the underground of female adolescence. In *Making connections: The relational worlds of adolescent girls at Emma Willard School,* edited by C. Gilligan, N. Lyons, and T. Hanmer, 6–29. Cambridge: Harvard University Press.

Gilligan, C., T. Hanmer, and N. Lyons. 1990. *Making connections: The relational worlds of adolescent girls at Emma Willard School.* Cambridge: Harvard Univeristy Press.

Gilligan, C., J. Ward, and J. Taylor, eds. 1988. Mapping the moral domain: A contribution of women's thinking to psychological theory and education. Cambridge: Harvard University Press.

Hine, D. C. 1993. "In the kingdom of culture": Black women and the intersection of race, gender, and class. In *Lure and loathing: Essays on race, identity, and the ambivalence of assimilation,* edited by G. Early. New York: Allen Lane Penguin Press.

hooks, b. 1984. *From margin to center.* Boston: South End Press.

———. 1990. *Yearning: Race, gender, and cultural politics.* Boston: South End Press.

Joseph, G., and J. Lewis. 1981. *Common differences: Conflict in black and white perspectives.* Garden City, N.Y.: Anchor.

McGowan, O. T. P. 1976. Factors contributing to school leaving among immigrant children: The case of the Portuguese in Fall River, Massachusetts. Ph.D. diss., Catholic University of America, Washington, D.C.

Medrano, L. 1994. AIDS and Latino adolescents. In *Sexual cultures and the construction of adolescent identities,* edited by J. M. Irvine. Philadelphia: Temple University Press.

Miller, J. B. 1976. *Toward a new psychology of women.* Boston: Beacon Press.

————. 1988. Connections, disconnections, and violations. Works in Progress series. Stone Center, Wellesley College, Wellesley, Mass.

Mishler, E. 1992. Narrative accounts in clinical and research interviews. Paper presented at conference, Discourse and the Professions, Swedish Association for Applied Linguistics, August, Stockholm.

Moitoza, E. 1982. Portuguese families. In *Ethnicity and family therapy,* edited by M. McGoldrick, J. Pearce, and J. Giordano, 412–37. New York: Guilford Press.

Moraga, C., and G. Anzaldua, eds. 1981. *This bridge called my back: Writings by radical women of color.* Watertown, Mass.: Persephone Press.

Morales, A. L., and R. Morales. 1986. *Getting home alive.* Ithaca, N.Y.: Firebrand Books.

Morawski, J. 1990. Toward the unimagined: Feminism and epistemology in psychology. In *Making a difference: Psychology and the construction of gender,* edited by R. Hare-Mustin and J. Marccck. New Haven: Yale University Press.

Pepler, D., and I. Lessa. 1993. The mental health of Portuguese children. *Canadian Journal of Psychiatry* 38:46–50.

Ribeiro, J. 1981. Cultural, social, and psychlogical factors related to academic success of Portuguese youth. Ph.D. diss., Boston College, Boston, Mass.

Rogers, A. 1993. Voice, play, and practice of ordinary courage in girls' and women's lives. *Harvard Educational Review* 63 (3):265–95.

Shorris, E. 1992. *Latinos.* New York: W. W. Norton.

Spelman, E. 1988. *Inessential woman: Problems of exclusion in feminist thought.* Boston: Beacon Press.

Stevens, E. 1973. Machismo and marianismo. *Society* 10 (6): 57–63.

Vazquez-Nutall, E., and I. Romero-Garcia. 1989. From home to school: Puerto Rican girls learn to be students in the United States. In *The psychosocial development of Puerto Rican women,* edited by C. Garcia Coll and M. M. de Lourdes. New York: Praeger.

Vazquez-Nuttall, E., I. Romero-Garcia, and B. De León. 1987. Sex roles and perceptions of femininity and masculinity of Hispanic women: A review of the literature. *Psychology of Women Quarterly* 11:409–25.

Zimmerman, J. 1991. Crossing the desert alone: An etiological model of female adolescent suicidality. *Women and Therapy* 11 (3/4):223–40.

# 8

## Are "Absent Fathers" Really Absent? Urban Adolescent Girls Speak Out about Their Fathers

Niobe Way and Helena Stauber

In the midst of a lunch break during one of our writing sessions for this paper, we ran into a friend who asked us what we were writing about. When we told her that we were writing about urban girls' relationships with their fathers, she immediately inquired, "Do these girls even have fathers in their lives?" Her question reflected one of the most pervasive beliefs about the family relationships of low-income, inner-city children and adolescents, particularly those who are black or Hispanic. Quite in contrast to this stereotype of father absence in the inner city, however, our studies with low-income urban adolescent girls suggest that these fathers are typically very much present in their daughters' lives. Although many of the girls in our studies told us that their fathers did not live with them, the majority offered accounts of complex, multilayered relationships with their fathers. In this paper we describe the stories of father-daughter relationships told to us by a group of urban adolescent girls.

The literature on fathers, particularly low-income and ethnic minority fathers, has been replete with reports about the behavioral, cognitive, and socioemotional effects of father absence for children and adolescents (see Alston and Williams 1982; Crockett, Eggebeen, and Hawkins 1993; Hetherington 1972; Laiken 1981; for review see McAdoo 1988). Other areas of investigation have focused on the role of fathers in two-parent families (see Cowan and Cowan 1987; Jackson 1974; Willie 1976); child-rearing attitudes and behaviors of fathers (see Allen 1985; Bartz and Levine 1978; Roopnarine and Ahmeduzzaman 1993); and fathers' perceptions of their involvement in child rearing (see Jackson 1986; Connor 1982). In addition, there is a growing body of research on adolescent fathers (see Leadbeater, Way, and Raden, chap. 11 of this volume) and their experiences of fatherhood (see Achatz and MacAllum 1994; Furstenberg and Harris 1993).

There exist, however, many gaps in the research literature on fathers. One significant lacuna concerns adolescent girls' qualitative accounts of their relationships with their fathers. As Terri Apter has pointed out, the research has generally left "the daughters' subjective stories [of their fathers] untold. . . . Girls' own experience of their relationship with their fathers has barely been featured in the stories told in the social sciences about this bond" (1993, 165). Although some researchers have examined middle-class adolescent girls' perceptions of their fathers (see Youniss and Smollar 1985), there is a dearth of studies that examine how low-income or ethnic minority adolescent girls experience this relationship. Reasons for the shortage may lie with the seemingly implicit assumption in the research literature that those fathers who do not live with their daughters have no relationships with their daughters. Studies do exist, however, that show that fathers from low-income communities who do not live with their children often continue to play an active role in their children's lives (see Earl and Lohmann 1978; Liebow 1967; Rivara, Sweeney, and Henderson 1986; Stack 1974).

The purpose of our study is to address this void in the research literature by exploring urban adolescent girls' perceptions of their relationships with their fathers. The study is inspired by theory and research that has focused on the study of human lives and has stressed the interpretive nature of psychological inquiry (see Apter 1993; Fine 1991; Brown and Gilligan 1992; Ladner 1971). Our intent is not to produce findings that can be generalized to larger populations of adolescent girls, but rather to listen to the subtleties and nuances in the narratives of a small group of urban adolescent girls.

## The Study

### Method

*Sample.* The sample is comprised of 45 adolescent girls who attended an inner-city public high school in a large northeastern city. The girls ranged in age from fifteen to nineteen and identified themselves as African American (22), Puerto Rican (5), Dominican (4), Irish or Italian American (5), West Indian (7), Syrian (1), and Native American (1). The adolescents all came from poor or working-class families (social class was inferred from the parents' educational backgrounds and current occupations). The sample was drawn from classrooms with students who represent the range of academic abilities. All of the students who volunteered to participate in the study (95% of those who were told about the research project) were included.[1]

*Procedure.* The participants were interviewed when they were in the ninth ($N = 12$), tenth ($N = 8$), eleventh ($N = 14$), or twelfth ($N = 11$) grade. Twelve of the girls (randomly selected from the forty-five girls) were also involved in a three-year longitudinal study (see Way 1995; Way in press). The interviewers—psychology doctoral students at the time of the study—included an African American middle-class man, two white middle-class women (the authors), and one white man from a working-class family. The interview lasted from one and a half to two hours and included questions concerning the girls' relationships with their parents or with the people who raised them (e.g., How would you describe your relationship with your father/mother? What do you like/dislike about this relationship? What would you like to change about this relationship? How do you think it has changed over the years?).[2] Although each interview included a standard set of initial questions, follow-up questions were open-ended in order to capture the adolescents' own ways of describing their relationships. All interviews were tape recorded and transcribed by a professional transcriber.

Our interview analyses included detailed readings of each interview. Typical of many qualitative approaches, our method involved content analyses in which interview data were partitioned into content domains for the comparison of themes across individual cases (Strauss 1987). We, the authors of this paper, independently read for common themes in the adolescents' narratives of their fathers. Only those themes that were identified independently by both of us were considered common themes in the interviews. The following section describes these common themes.

### Themes

*Demographic Findings.* Forty-two percent ($N = 19$) of the girls lived with their fathers (two lived only with their fathers); 15% ($N = 7$) did not live with their fathers but had frequent contact (daily or weekly) with them; 22% ($N = 10$) did not live with their fathers but had occasional contact with them (e.g., anywhere from once or twice a month to two or three times a year); and the fathers of 20% ($N = 9$) were either dead ($N = 3$) or entirely absent ($N = 6$). In sum, 36 of the adolescent girls had daily, weekly, or occasional contact with their fathers, and only 9 had completely absent fathers. We detected ethnic/racial differences within the group of girls who lived with their fathers: 77% of the Latina, 80%

of the white, and only 24% of the black girls in the sample lived with their fathers (28% of these black girls were of West Indian origin, and the remainder were African American).[3]

Most of the 19 girls who lived with their fathers reported that they had lived with their fathers all of their lives and that their parents had been married or together for twenty years or longer. Among the 17 girls who did not live with their fathers but had occasional or regular contact, 11 reported that their fathers lived in their neighborhood or in close proximity (e.g., in nearby cities), while 6 girls reported that their fathers lived at a considerable distance (e.g., in another state or country). Of the 6 girls who had no contact with their fathers but whose fathers were still alive, 5 girls stated that their fathers lived in a distant location, and only 1 stated that her father lived close by.

*Qualitative Findings.* The girls in our sample who had contact with their biological fathers ($N = 36$) typically appeared to have one of three types of relationships with their fathers: conflicted and engaged (33%), warm and open (36%), or emotionally distant (25%). These three categories were created in response to our interview data—they are data-driven categories. They represent our attempts to capture the prevailing quality of the interpersonal contact between the girls and their fathers. Those girls who described conflictual and engaged relationships with their fathers were more likely to live with their fathers, whereas those who had distant relationships were more likely to live apart from their fathers. Girls who lived with their fathers were as likely to describe warm and open relationships with their fathers as were those who did not live with their fathers.

1. *Feeling Conflicted/Being Engaged.* When Melissa, an Irish American adolescent girl, is asked about her relationship with her father in her junior year, she reaches into her backpack and pulls out a poem she has recently written. She asks her interviewer if she may read it aloud. This poem provides a poignant illustration of the anger and attachment that may coincide within a father-daughter relationship and the tension and dialogue between these two conflicting emotions:

> Why do I hate you so much?
> It's not like we always argue and fuss.
> I shouldn't be this way to him,
> It's not like his name is Tim.
> He seems to never accomplish much,
> But he I would never trust.
> He has led me the wrong way,
> Why do I stay?

I shouldn't have let him influence me.
Stupidness is so hard to see.
I care, but he has not kept his promise.
No, his name isn't Thomas.
He seems to think he's the greatest,
In today's news, that's not the latest.
He seems always to finish last.
Everything he's done has been done in the past.
He's filled with knowledge,
even though he's never finished college.
I am always in second place
for only his son and him see face to face.
In the end he will regret his choice,
that's the day he'll never hear my voice.
I will leave him without a word,
I know that sounds absurd.
I hate being second in line,
That's how I get treated when I'm kind.
As I get older, life gets much harder.
I want you to know this poem is all about my father.

Melissa, who recently chose to leave her mother and move in with her father, expresses through her poetry an admiration for her father ("he's filled with knowledge . . . "), a desire for his attention ("I hate being second in line"), and an impassioned anger toward him ("Why do I hate you so much?"). Despite, or perhaps because of, the intensity of her feelings, Melissa is ambivalent about revealing them directly to her father. She tells her interviewer that her father discovered her poem when he opened her mail (she had submitted this poem to a youth newspaper), and consequently she felt bad because she knew the poem would "hurt his feelings." At the same time, her choice to leave the letter out in the open, knowing that her father has a tendency to read her mail (which did not appear to bother her), suggests a competing wish to reveal her feelings to her father.

After discussing her poem, Melissa says to her interviewer that she gets along with her father but only "talk[s] to him . . . like I don't really speak to him that much." "Speaking," she implies, means openly discussing her thoughts and feelings. In her decision to move in with her father, in "talking" but not "speaking" to him, in her concern about hurting his feelings, in her assessment that she "gets along" with her father, and in her statements of simultaneous admiration and hatred, Melissa suggests a relationship that is characterized by strong and sometimes opposing emotions of ire, frustration, affection, and love. Melissa exhibits conflicted feelings about her father, and also appears to be deeply emotionally engaged with him.

Similar themes were heard from eleven of Melissa's peers, seven of whom lived with their fathers and four of whom did not. These girls spoke at length and with great emphasis about their anger or frustration and their feelings of being hurt by their fathers. Concurrently, however, they also spoke about wanting to connect with, admiring, and/or identifying with their fathers. These twelve girls expressed emotional attachment with their fathers in tandem with feelings of pain and frustration.

Marie, a Dominican student who lives with both her parents, says in her freshman year:

Sometimes I feel like my father treats me like shit, you know . . . sometimes he treats me nice. . . . Ok, he gives me everything I want. He cares for me a lot and everything. It's not like he's a bad father . . . and . . . thing is, sometimes . . . he's not understanding. It's like he always—he always every time something happens he always thinks it's me, it was my fault that that happened. . . . He's nice and everything but he doesn't think when he does things. . . . So I'm always like trying to defend myself. Every time they blame me for something, I try to talk back and they're always "you ain't got no respect. You always talk back."

Marie's words reflect a theme that was heard repeatedly among the girls in the sample—especially among those who lived with their fathers and who had conflicted and engaged relationships with their fathers. Eight of the twelve girls who had conflicted and engaged relationships (as well as five of the thirteen girls who had warm and open relationships) stated that they were outspoken with their fathers. When they experienced frustration with or felt that they were being treated unfairly or unkindly by their fathers, these girls expressed their feelings directly to their fathers in protest.

Marie, interviewed again in her sophomore year, reiterates the complexity and variability of her feelings for her father. On the one hand, she says that her father gives her anything she wants and is "sweet" and "there" for her, while on the other hand, she says that he's a "pain" because he is not understanding of her. When asked to describe herself, she says:

I can't stay shush on anything. Like my oldest brother, he and my parents, like my father, he's always be like [to my brother], "you did this and you did that." My brother'll be just standing there like. And he don't answer, he don't say nothing, you know. And he'll back up. And I can't be like that, I can't keep it in myself. I gotta talk back, you know. Speak my mind. Tell him my side of the story even though you're gonna lose. My brother's like, "You gonna lose anyway. They ain't gonna listen to you so why talk back." You know like I don't know, I just can't, I try but I can't. It gets me into trouble.

Rather than silencing herself with or distancing herself from her father when she is angry, Marie speaks back to her father's accusations.

Christine, an African American student interviewed in her sophomore year, also seems to be irritated with, embittered by, and engaged with her father. Christine's engagement, like Marie's, is suggested when she discusses her ability to speak her mind with her father:

We always have discussions every once in a while. But then I don't agree with his view so. When he says something, you know, I try to challenge it. You know, find out why he thinks that way. And he'll get mad. 'Cause he doesn't like when people try to challenge him. He wants to think that he's always right. And when you do tell him he's wrong, he gets mad and tries to tell you you're just trying to act grown [up].

Christine does not retreat when she disagrees with her father but challenges him directly even when he disapproves of her challenges. In her desire and ability to speak out, Christine appears actively engaged with her father. At a later point in her interview, Christine tells her interviewer the reason for her behavior:

I'm really the only person that'll stand up to [my father]. Talk to him word for word. So he really doesn't argue with me or try to you know. I can't really explain. . . . I get it from him. . . . He doesn't bug down . . . to nobody and so neither do I. . . . He doesn't like to listen, he wants everything to go his way. He likes to be his own boss. And I'm the same way . . .'cause he always taught me never to let people take advantage of you, take control of you. You should always speak up, talk for yourself. And that's what I do. It just so happens I do it with him.

Stating her similarity to her father in their shared tendency to assert themselves, Christine suggests a bond and a sense of identification with her father. Five of the twelve girls who had conflicted and engaged relationships with their fathers and one of the thirteen girls who had warm and open relationships, identified with their fathers. These girls expressed feelings of frustration and anger toward their fathers—with whom they regularly fought—and also stated they were "just like" their fathers and appreciated the ways in which they were alike. These statements of identification and appreciation in the face of irritation and animosity contributed to our interpretation that an adolescent felt *conflicted* rather than exclusively angry or loving toward her father.

The coexistence of anger and identification is heard in the words of Tyiesha, an African American student, who says in her freshman year:

"[My father and I] argue. We're too much alike. That's why we don't get along too well. . . . We always arguing—too much alike." In her junior year, Verlinda, also African American, says that she does not like her father's "attitude" or temper. However, she says that she thinks she gets her "attitude" and temper from her father: "Me and my father are pretty much the same. . . . My mother always tells me 'You're just like your father.' " Verlinda says at the end of her interview that sometimes she likes her "attitude," implying that occasionally she appreciates her father's influence. A similar theme is heard in the words of Gabriela, an Irish American adolescent, who says that her father "expects me to keep my mouth shut [when he gets angry] but I don't I'm not gonna keep my mouth shut. . . . I ain't taking it from him. . . . Like he gets mad when I'm like this, but he gave me this." While Gabriela is angry at her father, she also realizes, much like Christine, that her father has taught her a skill she considers valuable—her ability to speak her mind.

In sum, twelve of the thirty-six adolescent girls in the sample (33%) who had contact with their fathers voiced conflicted feelings about their fathers in their expressions of outrage, hurt, appreciation, and attachment. They did not typically distance themselves from their fathers when they were angry or upset, but engaged with their father through arguments, disagreements, and confrontations—skills that they often said they had learned from their fathers. Their conflicted feelings were suggested by their statements of identification, their stories of speaking out, and their verbal shifts between expressions of appreciation, admiration, and warmth, on the one hand, and displeasure, frustration, and anger, on the other.

*2. Open and Warm Relationships.* Mary, an Irish American student, says in her freshman year that her father is her role model because he "has so much patience with me. . . . He can cope with, you know to have a teenage daughter and everything." Mary's mother died when she was ten, and since that time, she says that she and her father have been close. Interviewed again in her sophomore year, Mary says that she is getting along with her father even better than she did the previous year because she listens to him more "where before I was like, 'You don't know anything.' . . . He listens to me and understands that, you know, that he can't always treat me like a baby." She says she is open and honest with her father and considers him to be her role model because he has "patience . . . and he has the energy and he's just—I don't know, he's great." In her junior year, Mary says that she enjoys her relationship with her father because she can sit down and tell him "everything . . . frustrating problems like my boyfriend . . . and school. . . . Anything to do with that I'd go to my father." She says that out of all her relationships, she is closest to her father. Her perspectives on her father over the three years that she is interviewed suggest a consistent theme of warmth and openness.

Thirteen of the thirty-six girls (36%) who had contact with their fathers described their relationships with their fathers as being warm, open, and connected (six lived with their fathers and seven did not). Sonia, a Puerto Rican student who lives with both of her parents, says in her freshman year that she feels closer to her father than to her mother—a common feeling among those who appeared to have warm and open relationships with their fathers. Sonia says that she feels that she can more freely speak with her father and that he is more understanding of her than is her mother. She explains, "He shows that he cares more than my mother at times. . . . He's just always there for us, you know. He's like a good father. He never hit us, or, you know, or really argue with us. You know, we play around." In her sophomore year, Sonia's reflections about her relationship with her father suggest a continuity and a stability to her positive feelings as she says that her relationship is "wonderful. . . . We've always had a good relationship." She also reiterates in this interview that she would turn to her father more than to her mother if she wanted to discuss personal concerns and that she has become more open with him about her personal life over time. She repeats that he has "always been there for [me]."

Yolanda, a Puerto Rican senior who lives with both of her parents, also says that she feels closer to her father than to her mother:

*Like when you're concerned about anything, will you turn to your mother or will you turn to your friends first?*

I feel more comfortable talking to my father.

*Oh really?*

Yes 'cause he's just for some reason, he won't say—he'll just be like "um-hm." . . . And my mother, if I tell her, she'll give me like a whole hour speech about . . . and I'm like "Forget it. Thanks anyway." But I feel more comfortable talking with my father about things. . . . He's more easy to talk to.

Resisting the interviewer's assumption that she would choose between her mother and her friends, Yolanda states with emphasis that it is her father to whom she prefers to turn in times of need.

Souad, a Syrian adolescent, conveys a similar theme in her junior year:

My father has, you know, too much knowledge and he has an open mind, he's different from other parents, Arabic parents. Because Arabic people are very closed sometimes, especially with dealing with their children, like they are stubborn, when they say anything, you know the children should do it. My father is not like that. We can argue with each other. We can always, if I have any problems, I can speak with him . . . I can speak with him. . . . My mother is a little bit more, she's nervous and she sometimes, I can speak with her because she is like my friend, you know, but not like my father. My father can understand more than my mother why we do that, or I can argue with my father more than my mother. . . . My relationship with my father is easier.

Unlike some of her peers who have conflictual relationships with their fathers, Souad seems to experience her arguments with her father as one of the more positive aspects of their relationship: their disagreements seem to enhance, rather than compromise, their sense of connection. Souad, who also lives with both her parents, says that when she grows up, she would like to have her father's "open mind" and her mother's "patience."

Florence, an African American girl whose parents have been separated since she was six years old, says when interviewed in her freshman year that she sees her father "all the time . . . every week." She describes their relationship as communicative:

We get along good. He's like—I can talk to him about—I, I think I could talk to him more than I could talk to my mother. . . Since he's not with me all the time, he like wants to know everything I'm doing so he's always like "What are you doing?" and—so he gets to know more about what I do than my mother does. And my mother's there so she thinks she sees everything. Sometimes she asks. But my father asks all the time.

Interviewed again in her junior year, Florence brings more detail and insight to her reflections about her father's role in her development:

I think my father had a lot to do with [my maturity and independence] . . . because he would call me—even though we didn't live together—he would just preach to me every day. School this, school that. And [as I was growing up] we had a good relationship, me and my father. And like we—he didn't live with me but yet it was almost like he was there 'cause he kind of like raised me from a distance. You know, like things [my mother] didn't tell me, he told me. You know, he talks to me about sex, about boyfriends, about school. Things that she never sat down and told me. So it was almost as if he was like my mother and she was like the father.

Directly challenging the idea that a father who is not at home with his daughter has little influence, Florence describes the important role her father has played in her life. She also appreciates his absence:

I keep telling him "In a way I'm glad you didn't live with me,"—he probably could have taught me more things if he was there. But then again I wouldn't have got a chance to go out and have so much freedom. I don't know. In a way freedom made me kind of smart, you know. I can't explain it. . . . I know I'm glad he didn't [live with me] 'cause he might have held me back from a lot of things and you know like going to parties, being with my friends and stuff.

Florence suggests that she recognizes both the losses and gains of not living with her father during her childhood and adolescence. She implies that her mother's and father's different styles of parenting have complemented each other to promote her growth and her sense of responsibility. Her father's relative distance by virtue of living in a different home seems to have balanced rather than jeopardized their relationship and contributed to her appreciation of the relationship.

Chloe, interviewed in her sophomore year, also portrays a warm, involved relationship with her father, who lives near her and visits her daily. Unlike Florence, Chloe reports that her father lived in Trinidad when she was growing up, and that she had little contact with him until recently. Now, she says that "me and my father get along great." She goes on to describe how her father assumes the role of mediator in her often contentious relationship with her mother:

Like we talk about things, like you know, when I'm staying with my mother and we're having conflicts and you know, he always gets involved, because my mother makes him get involved. . . . When I talk to her, nothing gets through to her, you know, nothing gets through. So he tries to talk to me, and when he talks to me we have an open mind. I listen to his side, and he listens to mine and the reasons I did whatever I did, you know, and I like that.

For Chloe, as for Florence, not living with her father does not seem to endanger her perception of him as available and involved.

These thirteen girls whom we have described as having warm and open relationships with their fathers appeared consistently willing to discuss their thoughts and feelings with their fathers and commonly felt more willing to speak openly with their fathers than with their mothers. Some did not have to live with their fathers to maintain such warmth and openness and, in fact, for a few of the girls, the physical distance between themselves and their fathers seemed to enhance the warmth and openness in their relationships. Although these warm and open relationships involved conflicts or disagreements at times, the conflicts did not appear to stem from or lead to conflicted feelings about the relationships per se; these thirteen girls appeared unambivalent in their warm feelings for their fathers.

3. *Disengaged.* Nine of the thirty-six girls who had contact with their fathers (25%) portrayed emotionally distant relationships with them. At times these girls spoke about their fathers in a language that seemed as sparse and as disconnected affectively as the relationships they described. Denise, an African American senior, recently moved back with her

mother after living with her father and stepmother in another city. She says that while she is currently having "a little bit of trouble" with her father, she generally gets along with both her parents because "I can get along with anybody." Her descriptions of her relationships with both her father and her mother are notably reserved and are characterized neither by adversity nor by warmth. Emotional distance from both of her parents is captured in her statement that "my parents aren't important figures in my life really."

Affective distance is also heard in the words of Patrice, an African American junior whose father has been separated from her mother for seven years and lives in her community:

*What's your relationship like with your dad?*

I dunno.

*It sounds like it's mixed.*

We're not close.

*You're not close. Like how often will you see him about?*

Twice a month.

*Twice a month. And when you see each other, what will you guys do usually?*

Nothing.

*Nothing?*

No. Just talk.

*Just talk. So you won't share things with him that are personal at all.*

Nope.

*It sounds like you're somewhat angry at him. Is that a right reading or no?*

No. Not really.

*Not really? Do you feel like he makes any effort to be close to you?*

No.

*Do you think that you try to be close to him, or not really?*

No. Not any more.

*Not anymore. What happened that you started to not make the effort anymore?*

I didn't want to.

Patrice makes no attempt to communicate her feelings directly to her father. While anger might be discerned in her terse description of their relationship (she was more talkative in other parts of the interview), Patrice seems primarily resigned to her disconnected relationship with her father and communicates little interest in changing it.

In the narratives of Cerise, an African American sophomore whose father lives out of state, anger is clearly evident. Cerise's contact with her father is currently "like off and on. Now that I live with my aunt, he calls occasionally. Comes up here like Christmas and stuff." Her description of her history with her father suggests that disillusionment and emotional distance predated their current "off and on" contact. She explains, "When I lived with my mother, I never really talked to him. And like when he did come over, I'd get confused 'cause I didn't want to call him Daddy or whatever." Cerise expresses disappointment in her current relationships both with her mother, whom she describes as "inconsistent," and her father, who "makes a lot of empty promises." Cerise also reveals that although her relationship with her mother has shifted from a closer to a more distant one, she has never felt close to her father.

Delane is an African American freshman whose father moved out of the family home two years earlier. She estimates the frequency of her current contact with him as "a few times a month," and the quality of their contact as "all right." She claims that she does not like to be with her father because she does not like to "be with a man. I don't care if he is my father." She says she does not understand the origins of this discomfort and claims to have "always felt this way." When asked by her interviewer whether she can confide in him, she says:

> I can tell him. I won't talk to him. I'll tell him. . . . But I won't say it in a serious mood because he thinks—he's kind of old fashioned—he doesn't like a lot of stuff that I like so I'll tell him. I won't ask him or talk to him. I'll tell him.
>
> *So it's not a dialogue . . . it's just reporting.*
> Um-hm.

In her sophomore year Delane says she sees her father every week and their relationship is "fine . . . but I still wouldn't tell him a lot of things, like I would . . . [with] my mother." In her junior year Delane says she still sees her father every week. When asked if she will confide in her father, she says:

> I don't talk to males about any problem that I have. Rather keep it to myself. I feel that fathers aren't—some people can go to their fathers and talk to them about things and others don't. I just don't have that kind of relationship where I can—I don't like—I don't feel—I feel—feel that I should talk to my mother more so than my father. The only thing I talk about to him is like school . . . , car, jobs, something like that. The basics.

Although resignation, disappointment, discomfort, or anger appears to have contributed to and resulted from the distant relationships described by Patrice, Cerise, and Delane, other girls described distant relationships with their fathers that seemed to have less negative origins and consequences. These girls described their relationships with their fathers as "fine" but not close. Some claimed that the reason for their emotionally distant relationships with their fathers was that they rarely saw their fathers, because of their fathers' work schedules or because they lived far away. When asked about her relationship with her father, Bettina, an African-American senior, says: "Well, I don't talk to him all the time. But it's better than with my mother. I never argue with him. He gives me anything I want whenever I see him. But he has his own family now so I don't really go—I don't go down to see him. . . . I see him only when he comes up here." Bettina's relationship with her father does not seem particularly close, angry, or engaged; she seems at once appreciative of and emotionally distant from her father.

Whether or not these nine girls saw their fathers occasionally or regularly, the girls did not seem actively involved in these relationships. They did not confide in or argue with their fathers, and their response to anger and frustration with their fathers was typically to avoid direct confrontation. In contrast to their peers who had conflicted and engaged or warm and open relationships, these girls did not express admiration, connection, or identification with their fathers. These disengaged relationships were more common among those who did not live with their fathers ($N = 6$) than among those who did ($N = 3$).

## Discussion

Whereas nine of the girls in this sample had no contact with their fathers and had not had any contact for many years (three of the fathers had died), twenty-six had daily or weekly contact (nineteen lived with their fathers), and ten had occasional contact with their fathers. The father-daughter relationships described by those girls who had daily, weekly, or occasional contact were varied. Some involved simultaneous feelings of attachment and anger, and others primarily involved feelings of affection and understanding. A smaller percentage of girls who had contact with their fathers appeared to have emotionally distant relationships with them.[4]

Unexpectedly, this latter finding stands in contrast to previous findings of father-daughter relationships within different populations of adolescent girls (see Apter 1993; Steinberg 1987; Youniss and Smollar 1985). Youniss and Smollar found, in their studies of primarily white middle-class adolescent girls, that the majority of girls described relationships with their fathers that were "distant," "lacking emotional content," "uncomfortable and withdrawn" (1985, 91). The girls in their studies reported that conflicts or intimate communication with their fathers were rare.

Youniss and Smollar concluded that "the [girls'] relationship with their fathers may more aptly be described as 'nonrelation' than as a negative one" (1985, 51). Apter (1993) concluded in her qualitative study of white working- and middle-class adolescent girls that many of the girls in her sample had relationships with their fathers that involved little intimacy or direct engagement. In a review of the research literature on adolescent girls' relationships with their fathers—research that primarily focuses on white middle-class girls—Steinberg concluded that "fathers appear to have emotionally 'flat' relations with their teenagers. . . . The father-daughter relationship appears to be the outlier, distinguished by its affective blandness and relatively low level of interaction" (1990, 266). In the present study, however, only 25% of the girls' relationships with their fathers could be classified in Youniss and Smollar's category of "nonrelation" or be described as "emotionally flat." Sixty-nine percent of the adolescent girls who had contact with their fathers described relationships in which there was much affect and communication—either in the form of conflicts or in the sharing of thoughts and feelings, or in both. While many of the adolescent girls suggested feeling misunderstood by and angry with their fathers, just as many girls spoke about feeling closer to their fathers than to their mothers, being able to express themselves more to their fathers than to their mothers, and identifying with and admiring their fathers. Given the previous findings on primarily white middle-class populations, these current findings suggest that there may be important differences across social class, race, and ethnicity in the quality of relationships between adolescent girls and their fathers. It also suggests that girls' relationships with their fathers may be changing as we move into a era of more involved fathers. Future studies should explore these possibilities.

Our data suggest that fathers who do not live with their daughters, as well as those who do, often play critical roles in their daughters' lives. Far from being absent, most of the fathers appeared actively engaged with their daughters. Continued qualitative exploration of father-daughter relationships, particularly among the under-studied population of urban adolescent girls and focused especially on girls' own perspectives, is essential to a growing understanding of adolescent female development.

NOTES

1. This study is part of a larger, cross-sectional study of ninety urban adolescents (forty-five girls and forty-five boys), which focused on the socioemotional correlates of risk-taking behavior. This larger project was funded by the National Institute of Drug Abuse (principal investigator, Perry London). Since the purpose of the larger project was

not focused solely on girls' relationships with their fathers, we were able to recruit a diverse sample of adolescent girls—those who had and those who did not have relationships with their fathers. Twenty-four of the adolescents (twelve boys and twelve girls) from the larger cross-sectional study were also participating in a longitudinal study that focused on the ways urban adolescents speak about their worlds (see Way in press). The latter project was funded in part by a grant from the Henry Murray Research Center in Cambridge, Mass.

2. Questions were also asked about self-perspective, future goals and aspirations, and relationships with friends, siblings, and role models. These questions were asked as part of a larger study being conducted with these adolescents.

3. Previous studies of Hispanic and black adolescents have also found that Hispanic adolescents are more likely to live with both of their parents than black adolescents are (see Murry, chap. 15 of this volume).

4. There were two girls in the sample who did not fit into any of our three categories. One spoke only of her fears of her father, and another indicated that she had warm, affectionate feelings about her father, but she did not speak openly with him about her thoughts and feelings.

## REFERENCES

Achatz, M., and C. A. MacAllum. 1994. *Young unwed fathers: Report from the field*. Final report from Public/Private Ventures, Philadelphia.

Allen, W. R. 1985. Race, income, and family dynamics: A study of adolescent male socialization processes and outcomes. In *Beginnings: The social and affective development of black children*, edited by M. B. Spencer, G. K. Brookins, and W. R. Allen. Hillsdale, N.J.: Lawrence Erlbaum.

Alston, D., and N. Williams. 1982. Relationship between father absence and self-concept of black adolescent boys. *Journal of Negro Education* 51 (2):134–38.

Apter, T. 1993. Altered views: Fathers' closeness to teenage daughters. In *The narrative study of lives*, edited by R. Josselson and A. Lieblich. London: Sage Publications.

Bartz, K., and E. Levine. 1978. Childrearing by black parents: A description and comparison to Anglo and Chicano parents. *Journal of Marriage and the Family* 40 (4):709–19.

Brown, L. M., and C. Gilligan. 1992. *Meeting at the crossroads: Women's psychology and girls' development*. Cambridge: Harvard University Press.

Connor, M. E. 1982. A survey of the parenting attitudes of young black fathers. Paper presented at the annual meeting of the Western Psychological Association, April 7–11, Sacramento, Calif.

Cowan, C. P., and P. A. Cowan. 1987. Men's involvement in parenthood: Identifying the antecedents and understanding the barriers. In *Men's transition to parenthood*, edited by P. Berman and F. A. Pedersen. Hillsdale, N.J.: Lawrence Erlbaum.

Crockett, L., D. J. Eggebeen, and A. J. Hawkins. 1993. Father's presence and young children's behavioral and cognitive adjustment. *Journal of Family Issues* 14 (3):355–77.

Earl, L., and N. Lohmann. 1978. Absent fathers and black male children. *Social Work* 23 (5):413–15.

Fine, M. 1991. *Framing dropouts: Notes on the politics of an urban high school*. Albany: State University of New York Press.

Furstenberg, F., and K. M. Harris. 1993. When and why fathers matter: Impacts of father involvement on the children of adolescent mothers. In *Young unwed fathers: Changing roles and emerging policies*, edited by R. Lerman and T. Ooms, 117–38. Philadelphia: Temple University Press.

Hetherington, E. M. 1972. Effects of father-absence on personality development in adolescent daughters. *Developmental Psychology* 7:313–26.

Jackson, J. J. 1974. Ordinary black husband-fathers: The truly hidden men. *Journal of Social and Behavioral Sciences* 20 (2):19–27.

———. 1986. Black fathers of infants: Attitudes and values associated with being a father. Paper presented at the annual meeting of the Association of Black Psychologists, August 16, Oakland, Calif.

Ladner, J. 1971. *Tomorrow's tomorrow: The black woman.* Garden City, N.Y.: Doubleday.

Laiken, D. 1981. *Daughters of divorce.* New York: Morrow.

Liebow, E. 1967. *Tally's corner.* Boston: Little, Brown.

McAdoo, J. L. 1988. Changing perspectives on the role of the Black father. *In Fatherhood today: Men's changing role in the family,* edited by P. Bronstein and C. P. Cowan. New York: John Wiley.

Rivara, F., P. Sweeney, and B. Henderson. 1986. Black teenage fathers: What happens when the child is born? *Pediatrics* 78 (1):151–58.

Roopnarine, J., and M. Ahmeduzzaman. 1993. Puerto Rican fathers' involvement with their preschool-age children. *Hispanic Journal of Behavioral Sciences* 15(1):96–107.

Stack, C. 1974. *All our kin: Strategies for survival in a black community.* New York: Harper and Row.

Steinberg, L. 1987. The impact of puberty on family relations: Effects of pubertal status and pubertal timing. *Developmental Psychology* 23:451–60.

———. 1990. Autonomy, conflict, and harmony in the family relationship. In *At the threshold: The developing adolescent,* edited by S. Feldman and G. Elliot. Cambridge: Harvard University Press.

Strauss, A. 1987. *Qualitative analysis for social scientists.* New York: Cambridge University Press.

Youniss, J., and J. Smollar. 1985. *Adolescent relations with mothers, fathers, and friends.* Chicago: University of Chicago Press.

Way, N. 1995. "Can't you hear the courage, the strength that I have?": Listening to urban adolescent girls speak about their relationships. *Psychology of Women Quarterly* 19 (1):107–28.

———. In press. *In their own words: Listening to urban adolescents speak about their worlds.* New York: New York University Press.

Willie, C. V. 1976. *A new look at black families.* Bayside, N.Y.: General Hall.

# 9

# African American Adolescent Mothers, Their Families, and Their Daughters: A Longitudinal Perspective over Twelve Years

Nancy Apfel and Victoria Seitz

Deciding to bear and rear a child while still in adolescence is a life-altering choice. Developmental tasks of adolescence include acquiring the skills and sense of identity necessary to leave one's family to become an adult member of society. The responsibilities of parenthood conflict with an adolescent's ability to complete these tasks. Many young parents find it difficult to remain in school, to become self-supporting adults, and to establish secure households in which to raise their children (Hamburg and Dixon 1992).

There has been so much publicity about adolescent mothers that most people have set ideas about what the outcomes are for adolescents who have children. Yet often these beliefs are based on misconceptions that have arisen because most research has been limited to relatively short-term outcomes. To date only two studies have followed teenage mothers until their children became teenagers. One of these was conducted in Baltimore, Maryland (Furstenberg 1976; Furstenberg, Brooks-Gunn, and Morgan 1987), and the other in New Haven, Connecticut (Horwitz et al. 1991; Klerman and Jekel 1973). Both of these studies focused on urban adolescents who became mothers in the 1960s. More recently, we have been studying a birth cohort of New Haven school-age mothers who delivered firstborn children in 1979–80 (Apfel and Seitz 1991; Seitz, Apfel, and Rosenbaum 1991; Seitz and Apfel 1993, 1994). Our study has continued until the teenagers' children were twelve years old. In this chapter we will examine what our study and the two other longitudinal studies have revealed about life outcomes for adolescent mothers and the factors that lead to better versus poorer outcomes for them.

## Long-Term Outcomes and Factors Affecting Such Outcomes

A common misconception about adolescent parents is that they necessarily have negative life outcomes (e.g., dropping out of school, depending on welfare, and bearing many children with multiple problems). In fact, outcomes for teenage mothers are diverse. Researchers have found that many earn high school diplomas, pursue further education, and become self-supporting. Some limit their family size and raise children who are successful in school and community activities and who do not drop out of school, engage in delinquent behavior, or become teen parents themselves (Furstenberg 1976; Furstenberg, Brooks-Gunn, and Morgan 1987; Horwitz et al. 1991; Klerman and Jekel 1973; Seitz, Apfel, and Rosenbaum 1991; Seitz and Apfel 1993).

Why do some teenage mothers succeed in education, employment, and parenting, while others fall short of their goals? Why do some children of teenage mothers develop capably, while others have trouble at school, at home, and in the community? Many factors could contribute to this disparity, but in all three long-term studies, one factor—rapid repeated childbearing—has been found to overshadow others in its impact on the lives of adolescent mothers and their children.

In our own longitudinal work we have found that teenagers who waited at least two years before delivering a second child had much better educational outcomes than did those who delivered a second child more quickly. We defined a good educational outcome as remaining in school or a training program and earning passing grades, or, for older teens, having graduated from high school or having earned a GED certificate. Two years after they first gave birth, 69% of the teenagers who had not had a second child had good educational outcomes, but only 35% of the teens who had already delivered a second baby had good educational outcomes. These statistically significant results persisted at six years postpartum, when we found that of those who had not had a second child, 72% had completed a high school degree, compared to only 46% of those who had had a second child. In addition, at six years postpartum only 9% of the women who had not delivered a second child within two years, versus 30% of those who had, were completely dependent on welfare to support their families. Delaying subsequent childbearing for at least two years appears to lead to better outcomes for adolescent mothers for several years after their first birth (Seitz and Apfel 1993). Similarly, Furstenberg and his colleagues describe the impact of large family size on life outcomes of young mothers as follows: "Women who had two or more additional children by the 5-year follow-up were almost four times more likely to be on welfare and 72% less likely to be economically secure at the 17-year follow-up" (Furstenberg, Brooks-Gunn, and Morgan 1987, 138). Horwitz and her colleagues (1991) report that women who limited themselves to at most three children were fourteen times more likely to enjoy long-term educational and economic success.

Family support is a second factor that strongly affects how well adolescent mothers and their children adapt. The effects of this second factor are not nearly as well understood as are the effects of repeated childbearing. Support is difficult to measure because it can take so many different forms—emotional, financial, task-oriented, mentoring, provision of shelter, and so forth. Also, support can come from many different people—the adolescent's parents, grandparents, siblings, uncles, and aunts, the baby's father, his family, and others. In addition, support can be perceived by the recipient in quite different ways. If the teenager's family attempts to help, she may be grateful or she may resent the offer as an implication that she is an inadequate parent. Family support is not a simple, unitary concept, and the components to be studied should include source, type, and amount, as well as the degree of reciprocity between adolescent mothers and those who provide support (Nath et al. 1991).

Many researchers have assumed that a teenager's continuing to live with her family constitutes her receiving of family support. However, some mothers of teen mothers provide a roof over their heads but little else. Others provide minimal child care assistance but offer emotional and financial help. In research with older mothers, such support has been found to have positive indirect effects on an adult mother's parenting (Belsky 1984). Still other mothers of teenagers fully share child care responsibilities, or even become their grandchildren's primary caregivers. We have also seen that significant support can be provided to a young mother even if she and her mother live apart.

In spite of the difficulty that researchers have had conceptualizing and defining family support, research has shown that family support is a powerful variable in the lives of adolescent parents (Furstenberg and Crawford 1981; Kellam, Ensminger, and Turner 1977). Many researchers have found that an adolescent mother's parenting style can be enhanced by her mother's support and that, if her parenting is compromised by her youth, inexperience, or mental state, these negative factors can be buffered by support (Apfel and Seitz 1991; Colletta 1981; Crockenberg 1981; Leadbeater and Bishop 1994).

More recent longitudinal research has identified a third factor—maternal depression—as a potent influence on adolescent parents and their offspring. Leadbeater and her colleagues have found that a significant proportion of adolescent mothers in their New York City population experienced depressive symptoms (Leadbeater and Linares 1992). Leadbeater and Bishop (1994) have also found that the more support depressed teen mothers receive, the fewer difficult behaviors they report their children as having. Because this longitudinal work on depression is recent, the children of these teen mothers are still quite young, not yet in school, and the long-term effects of maternal depression on the teen mothers and their offspring are unknown.

In this chapter we will describe our study of an urban population of adolescent mothers and their firstborn children from infancy to early adolescence. We will examine, with illustrative case studies, how families adapt to adolescent childbearing. The support given by families to their fledgling teen mothers will be described. There are undoubtedly many factors at work in these lives, including depression, child abuse and neglect, and substance abuse. Adolescent mothers as a group tend to have higher rates of risk factors: they tend to have been unsuccessful academically, to have behavior problems, and to be from single-parent, low income households (Ensminger 1987; Horwitz et al. 1991). However, our primary focus in this chapter is on the process of family support—when it has been sufficient to keep a young mother on track and when it has not. We will also illustrate how the process of rapid repeated childbearing can put a young mother and her children at serious risk and overwhelm her family's ability to provide adequate support.

Our case studies will focus on two generations of urban adolescent females: the adolescent mothers and their firstborn daughters as they develop from toddlers to adolescents themselves.

## Overview of Our Study

### Subjects

As part of an ongoing study (Seitz, Apfel, and Rosenbaum 1991; Seitz and Apfel 1993, 1994), we searched New Haven hospital records to identify all residents of New Haven who were younger than eighteen years old when they delivered a firstborn child between March 1, 1979, and February 29, 1980. In this chapter we will present results for the African American adolescent mothers from this sample. There were 115 such adolescent mothers in the city during the twelve months examined. These mothers' ages ranged from thirteen to seventeen, with an average age of sixteen. Their average grade level was ninth grade. Six percent were married. At the time that these teens were making their transition into parenthood, 95% of them had their own mother or some other adult woman helping them, and 88% were not married or cohabiting with a male partner. The majority were from low income families. The participation rate of the subjects at eighteen months postpartum was 85%; at six years postpartum the rate grew to 91%, and at twelve years postpartum 92% of the subjects participated in the follow-up. In this study we thus are reporting results for a high percentage of an entire birth cohort of African American school-age mothers living in an impoverished urban area.

## Procedures

We have studied these adolescent mothers and their firstborns for twelve years, examining the course of their educational and occupational careers, the support given to them, their health, their parenting, and their children's development. We interviewed the teen mothers and their mothers (the infants' grandmothers) or the teens' surrogate mothers at eighteen months postpartum and then reinterviewed the young mothers at six and twelve years postpartum. Over the years our interviews were often conducted in the mothers' homes and sometimes, if they preferred, in our office or in a public school. Our semistructured interview included questions concerning parenting practices and beliefs, child care arrangements, daily routines, and household composition. We also asked about the teen mother's education and work history and her child's school, home, and community achievements and behavior. Part of the eighteen-month postpartum interview was drawn from an approach that Provence (1977) described for pediatricians to use in talking with parents about their children. It is called a "typical day" interview and includes details about what happens to a child in the course of a typical day. We elicited details about feeding, dressing, playing, and sleeping routines from the toddler's teen mother and grandmother. We administered standardized developmental, cognitive, and achievement measures to the firstborn children at the three follow-up times and interviewed the children at the twelve-year follow-up visit. We have also collected extensive medical and school record data on these young mothers and their firstborn children, including interviews with the children's teachers at ages six and twelve.

## Results: Family Support and Child Rearing

In the present chapter we will describe what we have learned about the style of family support that is provided to adolescent mothers by their mothers. We have described other findings elsewhere (Seitz and Apfel 1993, 1994; Seitz, Apfel, and Rosenbaum 1991).

At eighteen months we found four models of familial adaptation to adolescent parenthood (Apfel and Seitz 1991). These models appear to reflect the beliefs of the grandmothers about how to care for an adolescent mother and her baby. In the first model, the Replacement Model, the young mother was not acting as primary caregiver of her toddler. At this early stage of adolescent parenting we found that only 10% of the teen mothers had been replaced as their firstborn's primary parent, and it was usually the teens' mothers who had replaced them. In some cases the teen parent lived apart from her infant and mother, but replacement could also happen when the teen mother lived at home but pursued the lifestyle of her nonparenting peers. Some families raised the teen's child so that she could devote herself to school, as in the case of one teen parent who went away to college.

The most prevalent model, Parental Supplement, occurred in about 50% of the families. In this adaptation, child care was shared between the teen parent and her mother, and sometimes with other relatives as well. The child care could be divided by task or by time, and families were variable in how they organized responsibilities. In some families it was assumed that the young mother would care for her child when she was home; in others the grandmother would feed or bathe the baby even if the teen mother was present.

Twenty percent of the families fell into a third category, Supported Primary Parent, in which the teen mother was responsible for the full-time care of her own child with some degree of help from her family. These teen mothers could receive family support in the form of regular communication, visiting, financial help, child care, and household help. Although half of this group lived with their families, they were receiving a more limited style of support than were those young mothers in the Parental Supplement Model, where the child rearing was more fully shared.

We also discovered a small group of grandmothers, about 10%, who treated their daughters as "apprentice parents," attempting to educate them without supplanting them in this role. We labeled this the Apprentice Model. These mentoring grandmothers expressed a belief in teaching parenting skills to the fledgling mothers, whereas the other grandmothers seemed to assume their daughters would know how to parent a child because of past babysitting or because of inborn maternal instincts. Apprenticing grandmothers spoke of how they kept a watchful eye as their daughter performed child care tasks, offering praise and suggestions as she gained confidence and competence.

At six years postpartum we looked at the typology of parenting again

(Apfel and Seitz 1993). As would be expected, we found some changes in how these families were interacting with the young mothers around child-rearing issues. Sixteen percent of the teen mothers were not acting as their baby's primary parent. Although this maternal replacement is higher than the 10% level we found at eighteen months postpartum, it is not a statistically significant change. The most prevalent model, found in approximately half the families, was the Supported Primary Parent, in which the young mother was primarily responsible for rearing her child, but was still receiving some family support. Surprisingly, almost a third of the group continued to rely on the grandmothers for significant parenting assistance (Parental Supplement). This group of women were raising their own children, but the degree of grandmother help and involvement in child rearing was high. The Apprentice Model had faded away by this point, which is not a surprising development, given that it is probably an inappropriate style of interaction with the mother of a six-year-old.

At twelve years postpartum we made the startling discovery that 28% of the young mothers were not parenting their twelve-year-olds and, in fact, did not even live with them. We also found that almost half of the firstborn children had lived away from their own mothers for several months or more during their lives. The degree of early family support (at eighteen months postpartum) was predictive of whether the young mother was her child's primary parent in later years. We found that early adaptations by the grandmothers that were extreme—either completely taking over the care of the infant or leaving their adolescent daughters to provide most of their infants' care with little guidance or help—often led to the young mother's replacement as primary caregiver by six years postpartum (Apfel and Seitz 1993). It would appear that familial provision of a balanced, "good enough" style of early parenting support to teen mothers can be effective in helping them remain their child's primary parent for the duration of childhood.

In the following pages we will illustrate through case studies the processes by which family support and subsequent childbearing work to improve or worsen the outcomes for the teen mother and her firstborn. Names and some details have been changed to protect privacy. The first two cases illustrate how family support can take quite different configurations and yet be equally effective. The third case shows how insufficient family support and multiple childbearing can affect an adolescent mother and her children adversely. The fourth case is illustrative of difficulties experienced by a teen mother who has no parents and virtually no family support to guide her.

## Case Studies

### Case 1: A Fledgling Mother Matures in the Nest

*First Interview: Eighteen Months Postpartum.* At eighteen months postpartum we found Lorraine, age eighteen, and her daughter, Cantrice, living with Lorraine's mother and her fifteen-year-old brother. Lorraine, an eleventh grader, had dropped out of school after Cantrice's birth and was spending her days caring for her child while her mother worked at two jobs to support the family. Lorraine usually fed and dressed Cantrice. Lorraine's mother was often away from home, but it was she who went to Cantrice when she cried at night and who played with her on weekends. Lorraine said her mother helped her with child care and "spoiled" Cantrice. Lorraine seemed to be enjoying her firstborn and told us proudly how Cantrice learned something new every day.

Cantrice's father was uninvolved in her life. Although Lorraine's immediate family was small, there was a strong extended family available in times of need. When asked about the biggest emergency she had experienced, Lorraine told of when Cantrice had fallen and hit her mouth, causing a lot of bleeding. In response to this event, Cantrice's grandmother, aunt, and cousin accompanied her and Lorraine to the hospital's emergency room to provide emotional support.

*Second Interview: Six Years Postpartum.* By six years postpartum Lorraine had had no additional children. She and Cantrice still lived with Lorraine's mother and brother in the same house in which she had grown up. The grandmother still worked full time to support the family, returning at the end of her workday to cook dinner for the family. Lorraine and her mother shared the other housework and child care responsibilities. There was still a strong sense of family commitment to each other with daily contact also between Lorraine and her older sister, who did not live with them.

Cantrice's father paid erratic attention to her and made promises to her that he did not keep. The paternal grandmother was seen "once in a blue moon," but the paternal grandfather had a daily chat with his granddaughter by phone or in person. Cantrice was a first grader, and by this time Lorraine was enrolled in a GED program. Lorraine had been on welfare support since becoming a mother, except for one brief foray into employment, which had not gone well because she developed allergies to the materials used in her assembly line job. This experience prompted her to improve her employability by going back to school. Cantrice was doing well in school, and her mother reported that she was pleased with Cantrice's report card. Lorraine told of how she had a little joke with her daughter about the report card by pretending it was bad when she first looked at it. Lorraine said, "She knew it would be good. We laughed!" Lorraine appeared to take pleasure in her daughter's growth and school progress.

*Third Interview: Twelve Years Postpartum.* By twelve years postpartum, Lorraine had still limited her family to her one child. She said, in response to a question about how many children she would eventually like to have, "I have what I want." She still shared a household with her mother, whom she described as her main support. They shared the housework, and both were employed full time. Lorraine was fully self-supporting with a data management job at a national insurance company. She had taken job training in data entry skills after having successfully completed her GED. Lorraine still reported high extended family involvement: "They're still spoiling her! Why, she gets everything she wants!"

Cantrice's father had died of a heart attack when she was twelve, but her paternal grandfather still visited or called her daily, and she saw her paternal grandmother about once a month. Cantrice was doing very well in school, on the honor roll regularly, and had perfect attendance. Her teacher rated her as an enjoyable child to have in class. Lorraine said that she and Cantrice were close to each other and would "joke and play around" together. Lorraine proudly reported that Cantrice had taken her shopping on Mother's Day and had bought her a ring. She added, to demonstrate how caring Cantrice can be, "When you don't feel well, this child will stay right by you."

*Case Commentary.* At eighteen months postpartum, about 70% of the teens were coresiding with their families; however, by twelve years postpartum only about 10% of the teens were doing so. This maternal grandmother and mother had formed a stable parenting duo in which this first, and so far only, child of an adolescent thrived.

This case illustrates how a grandmother provided support to her daughter that allowed her to fulfill her multiple developmental tasks of becoming an adult and a parent. This grandmother did not attempt to take over the child-rearing tasks; instead, she backed up the young mother's efforts at mothering and filled in when she was needed. Other significant contributions of this grandmother were the creation of an economically secure environment and of a role model—a working mother—for her daughter and granddaughter.

Cantrice, with her perfect attendance, honor roll grades, and positive teacher comments, has a good prognosis for continuing to do well in school. Her mother had a slower start on her own education, but she achieved a GED degree and further job training. This led to a white collar job in a well-respected company with good benefits. The absence of Cantrice's father and then his death seemed to be counterbalanced by the presence of a paternal grandfather who was attentive and constant throughout the first twelve years of Cantrice's life.

*Case 2: A Motherless Teen Mother Finds Her Way*

*First Interview: Eighteen Months Postpartum.* At age sixteen Bonnie became pregnant with her first child. A few months before her pregnancy Bonnie had lost her mother, who died from complications of alcoholism. Bonnie was an only child, and after she delivered her daughter she continued to live with her father. Bonnie became a school dropout because she had trouble finding a trustworthy sitter to care for Tara. Bonnie commented, "It's hard to find someone you really trust because Tara is at an age when she's into everything. I don't mind [not being in school] too much. My first concern is my daughter and getting her into school."

Bonnie was Tara's primary caregiver; however, Bonnie's father played with Tara and knew about her habits and her daily routines. He commented in his interview that he would kiss Tara and "jump her on my knees" and sometimes help feed her and change her diaper. Bonnie's father was supportive and helpful with child care, but he would defer to Bonnie's ability to figure out Tara's needs. The baby's father, who was in jail, had seen her about a dozen times in all. He was minimally involved in Bonnie's and Tara's lives. Bonnie was affectionate with her toddler and had a gentle sense of humor about her, chuckling about Tara's funny way of babbling and shaking her finger at Bonnie.

*Second Interview: Six Years Postpartum.* At six years postpartum Bonnie reported that she had married Joseph, who was not Tara's biological father, when Tara was two years old. Joseph was employed full time in the mailroom of a large company. Bonnie worked as a receptionist. Her husband, her father, and her father's girlfriend helped by taking care of Tara while Bonnie worked. Tara was doing well at school and at home. Bonnie was involved in Tara's school life, going on field trips with her and proudly displaying her school work on the refrigerator.

When asked about whether she had a mother figure to help her, Bonnie commented that she had not since her mother had died. "My Dad has been supportive, but I had no female substitute for my Mom. I used to ask questions of my old boyfriends' Moms." Tara's paternal grandmother had been involved in their lives, seeing them regularly until her death, when Tara was five years old. Tara's father, who was still in jail, and her paternal grandfather had remained uninvolved.

*Third Interview: Twelve Years Postpartum.* By the time Tara was twelve years old, she was living with her mother and stepfather, Joseph, and two other children whom Bonnie had recently taken in to raise for friends who were "in trouble." (These women, who were drug addicted, had often left their children alone and unfed in the apartment below Bonnie's.) Bonnie had wanted to have another child of her own, but had experienced a miscarriage when Tara was seven. Bonnie seemed to accept with equanimity the task of rearing the two additional children she had taken in, one of whom was an adolescent.

At our twelve-year follow-up interview, Bonnie spoke of how she and Joseph both worked full time to support their growing responsibilities. Both Bonnie and Joseph had worked at their jobs for the past six years. She also had begun to study for her GED by going to school in the evenings. Bonnie's husband and her father provided emotional support and help with household tasks. Bonnie reported having no other close friends because she worked too many hours to see other people.

Twelve-year-old Tara's school attendance was excellent, and she performed at or above grade level in the nationally standardized school achievement tests we administered. While her grades in nonacademic subjects (art and cooking) were stellar, her grades in academic subjects were mediocre (Cs and Ds). She was not performing up to her ability, as indicated by her test results in math, English, and science.

Tara and Bonnie reported that they were close to each other and had fun together. A favorite activity was to go shopping together on weekends. Bonnie said, "She pleases me all the time." Bonnie commented about their relationship, "We grew up together."

*Case Commentary.* Unfortunately, it is not unusual for teen mothers to have their mothers uninvolved in their lives. In our study about one-fifth of the young mothers' own mothers were unavailable to them when these teens delivered their firstborn children. This was due to death, substance abuse, distance, or previous child abuse. Bonnie's mother's alcoholism must have influenced how Bonnie was parented, although Bonnie never complained or commented about her mother's condition. The prognosis for such cases typically would not be good. She could have found that having a demanding infant and increased responsibilities just after her mother's death was too difficult to manage. Bonnie was fortunate to have a father who gave her enough love and support at this risky time in her life to prevent her from falling apart. He spoke of his playful and helpful activities when his granddaughter was a toddler, but he also articulated his respect for his daughter's knowledge of her own baby.

Although Tara's father was in jail, his mother (Tara's paternal grand-mother) was a positive presence for the first formative preschool years of Tara's life. Bonnie found a steady helpmate in her husband, Joseph, early in her child-rearing, when Tara was only two years old. This marriage of over a decade's duration has proved to be a solid foundation for Tara's development. From a risky early start, Bonnie has created a strong family in which to nurture her daughter. Although Tara's maternal grandmother could not be part of this process, her grandfather apparently shored up the family and provided the backing that a motherless young mother needed.

### Factors Leading to Success

These two cases both demonstrate how vital family support is to the well-being of an adolescent mother and child, particularly during the transition to parenthood; the cases also show the different configurations such support can take—in one case a mother and in the second a father provided enough help, emotionally and practically, to keep their teen daughters' lives on course. In the first case the coresidence of grand-mother, mother, and granddaughter continued throughout the twelve years; in the second case the coresidence of grandfather, mother, and granddaughter lasted only for the first two years postpartum until the teen mother married and established her own two-parent household. In both cases the child has always lived in a household with at least two adults who provided parenting. Both of these adolescents were also able to limit their family size—the second factor related to positive outcomes for teen mothers. These firstborn daughters remained the only children their young mothers had to care for during their first decade of parenting.

### Case 3: A Teen Mother Becomes Overwhelmed

*First Interview: Eighteen Months Postpartum.* Dawn came from a family of seven children born to a mother who had started her family at the age of fifteen. Dawn had a history of conflict with her mother, and her early adolescence was punctuated by episodes of depression and even suicide attempts. She delivered her firstborn as a seventeen-year-old. When she first participated in our study, Dawn was living with her eighteen-month-old firstborn, Casey, and Casey's father. For the first few months of Casey's life, Dawn lived with her older sister, Ann, also a teen mother, and Ann's infant. Dawn indicated that she hardly ever saw her mother. When we interviewed Dawn's mother eighteen months after Casey's birth, she commented about adolescent mothers, "They don't know how to care for kids." Despite this opinion, she was almost entirely absent from Dawn's day-to-day experiences and did not help with caring for her grandchildren. Dawn and her sister Ann would spend their days together at each other's apartments, and it was clear that Ann was acting as a mother figure for Dawn. "She is just like a parent," Dawn said about Ann. The account of the days they spent together revealed a chaotic arrangement with little or no advance planning about meals, nap times for the toddlers, activities, and outings. A worrisome pattern, reported by both Dawn and Ann, was that Casey had eaten several potentially toxic substances, such as cigarette butts, paint chips, and make-up.

Casey's father was very involved in her life during her infancy. Dawn said, "He feeds her, gives her a bath, dresses her, takes her for walks, changes her diaper, and greases her hair. He thinks he knows more about her than I do." In a comment about the support she was receiving from Casey's father and paternal grandmother, Dawn said: "Believe me, I never could do it [care for her baby] by myself. I'm glad I had help from her [Casey's] father and his mother."

Dawn said she had plans to finish high school, to go to college, and to have no more children. She had become a high school dropout, explaining that she had experienced baby-sitter problems, so she could not attend school. Her past experiences with school had been negative, and the only subject that she had liked was gym. We interviewed Dawn in the spring of 1981. By August of that year, with the birth of her second child imminent, Dawn was considering giving this baby up for adoption because Casey's father (also the father of her second child) had become inattentive to her and Casey. In the end Dawn kept her new baby.

*Second Interview: Seven Years Postpartum.* By the time of the six-year follow-up, Dawn was very difficult to locate because she had been living in homeless shelters with some of her children. We did not find her until seven years postpartum, by which time she had delivered six children. She lived with her boyfriend (not the father of Casey) and three of her children. The other three were in foster care or adoptive homes. Records indicated that the children had been taken from Dawn because she had not cared for them appropriately. Casey's father had moved out of town. As a seven-year-old, Casey still lived with her mother, although as a two-year-old she had lived with her paternal grandmother for a period of time when Dawn brought home her second baby. Casey would stay regularly with her paternal grandmother on weekends. Dawn told us, "She [the paternal grandmother] picks up the slack their father is supposed to."

According to her mother, Casey liked school and did well as a first grader. She was expected to help her mother care for her siblings regularly, even if this meant that she would miss school. When asked what Casey did that was upsetting to her, Dawn replied, "A lot of things. When I ask her to go do something, like to get the baby's bottle, she'll say, 'What did you say?' and I go, 'I know you hear me.' She cries so easily. I can't yell at her because she'll cry." Later in the interview, Dawn indicated that she routinely left Casey, a seven-year-old, in charge of her two younger siblings when she went out. "I tell her to call me. I'll come home if the baby starts crying." Casey, not her mother, was the one who heard the youngest baby's crying at night and would go to comfort her baby brother. Dawn described an accident in which Casey fell and injured herself, bleeding copiously. Dawn explained that she could not stand the sight of blood and therefore asked her brother to take Casey to the hospital so that she would not have to go. Dawn seemed oblivious to any need that her injured firstborn child might have had for her attention and comfort.

On a standardized scale of social development, Casey demonstrated lagging social skills and was showing signs of stress such as bed-wetting, teeth grinding, impulsive behavior, and high emotionality. These and her many school absences could be seen as warning signs that her ability to cope with her many responsibilities was in jeopardy.

*Third Interview: Twelve Years Postpartum.* By twelve years postpartum Dawn had given birth to nine children. Three of these had been permanently taken from her by the state, and six, including Casey, were living with their mother. The state agency responsible for monitoring the well-being of children at risk had been involved over the years due to parental failure to provide adequate housing and clothing. Casey had lived apart from her mother for about three of her twelve years. At eight years of age she had lived with her paternal grandmother for about a year. As a nine- and ten-year-old, Casey had lived with her maternal grandmother and aunt for about a year and a half in an overcrowded two-room apartment. Even though she had lived with both grandmothers for long periods of time, Casey, as a twelve-year-old, still reported that her mother was the person who was "most like a mother" to her and that no one else filled that role except her mother.

At the time of the twelve-year interview, Casey's father was addicted to drugs and offered no support to Dawn and his children. On the other hand, his mother and sister provided help to Dawn with child care, taking Casey into their home at various times.

Dawn had remained a high school dropout and had not sought any job training. She once had had thoughts of training as a hairdresser or of going to an inner-city job training program, but the effort of doing so seemed overwhelming to her. She commented, "about the hairdressing . . . No I didn't want to," and about the job training, "I didn't want to get dressed up." Over the years, after the birth of her fourth child, Dawn had made repeated appointments to have a bilateral tubal ligation to prevent further pregnancies, but had never carried through with this plan.

Dawn described herself as very attached to Casey and said she considered her a friend. She did not want her to be away from home or from her, even to attend school. Casey had become the primary caregiver of her five siblings and often missed school to take care of them. Dawn had trouble getting up in the morning to prepare her children for school. "Casey missed a lot of school. I was lazy. I was oversleeping." The school record spoke of Casey's "pervasive attendance problems." Her attendance was worsening: she had missed about 28 days in each of her fourth and fifth grade years, 43 days in her sixth grade year, and 89 days in her seventh grade year (there are typically 180 school days in a year). She was retained a grade due to her attendance problems. Despite this high absenteeism, Casey was able to do astonishingly well on standardized academic achievement tests, performing at, and even above, her expected grade level. She was receiving grades of D in her academic subjects, probably due more to her absences than to her inability to perform the work. She would start extracurricular and after-school remedial programs at school and then become a nonattender. Casey at age twelve was described by her teacher as one of her most enjoyable students, but also as a sad child. Her mother described her as being very nervous and not having many friends.

*Case Commentary.* This teen mother started her adolescence with obvious signs of difficulty—her depression, suicide attempts, poor school performance, and absenteeism were classic indicators of trouble. She herself was the fifth child born to a former teenage mother. She experienced conflict and estrangement from her mother; her older sister attempted to parent her as best as she knew how, but she too was a teen mother. Dawn's repeated pregnancies and subsequent children overwhelmed the fragile supports that were there for her. Among these supports was a paternal grandmother who periodically would take Casey into her household and provide another parent figure for Casey.

Dawn, however, put the burden of child rearing onto her firstborn daughter at a very early age, depriving her of a childhood in which she could go to school freely and attend after-school programs. Casey showed the signs of stress from this "parentification" process in measures of social development and maladaptive behaviors, such as nail biting, high emotionality, and impulsivity. Her anxiety symptoms, lack of peer connections, poor school performance, and high absenteeism are trouble signs also seen in Dawn's early medical and school records.

Dawn's mother had been distant, offering little support to her own teenage daughters as they made the transition to motherhood. Dawn's sister, Ann, was perhaps the child in their family who tried to carry the burden of parenting her mother's children, as twelve-year-old Casey was struggling to do. Once Dawn began the cycle of repeated childbearing, she seemed to lose the will to do anything different from what she had experienced in her own childhood. Dawn lost her dreams of finishing school and of becoming a dancer in New York City; she lost even her more modest hope of having job training.

Dawn feels close to her daughter and sees her as a friend, but she has entrapped her, as she probably feels entrapped by the needs of the large family she has created. Casey, her preadolescent daughter, ridden with anxiety and expected to take care of her mother's many children, appears to be at serious risk of falling into the same pattern as her mother and her grandmother. Casey would seem to typify the child about whom Radke-Yarrow and Sherman (1990) were speaking when they wrote that some children seem resilient, but their past has created vulnerabilities in them that leave them susceptible to future problems.

### Case 4: A Teen Mother in the Shadow of Her Past

*First Interview: Eighteen Months Postpartum.* Lena had been a child of the foster care system for many years by the time she became part of our study. She had been a victim of neglect and abuse by her own mother and was placed in her first foster family in late childhood. The placements never seemed to work out well, because Lena was rebellious and refused to respond to rules and family expectations. She became pregnant and delivered her firstborn at the age of fourteen. Since the birth of her daughter, Toni, Lena had been in four different foster homes; Lena said, "I couldn't get along with four foster mothers." When we first met her she was a fifteen-year-old living with another adolescent mother and baby in a dark, disorderly, dirty apartment with many people coming and going, in one of the city's most dangerous neighborhoods. To involve Lena in our study, we had to visit her in her apartment, because there was no other way to reach her. When we first met her, it was difficult to talk with her; she quickly became angry and suspicious. A second try several months later went better. Lena's case worker had helped her move to a brighter, safer apartment. Lena was attending a modified shortened-day school program while Toni was in day care.

Lena expressed pleasure in Toni's development, saying that she had been happy when Toni had taken her first steps and when she had called her "Mommy." She liked to tell Toni the names of the things around her, "even though she don't understand."

*Second Interview: Eight Years Postpartum.* When we tried to relocate Lena and Toni at six years postpartum we had a good deal of difficulty; it took many months of searching before we found them. The child, Toni, was living with a foster family at that point, but her life with her mother before that had been transient, with many moves, homelessness, and some time spent living in motel shelters. Lena was in a women's prison for risk of injury to a minor, assault, larceny, and drug-related charges. Toni had been found by police alone in a hotel room the night that her mother was arrested. She was able to show the officers where drugs were in the room and describe to them how they were prepared.

Toni was doing well in her foster family. When she had first arrived she had had many behavior problems—lying, stealing, temper tantrums, aggressive acts toward other children—and she was extremely sensitive, crying "at the drop of a hat," according to her foster mother. After living with this family for a year, Toni had improved, and most of her maladaptive behavior had disappeared. She was doing very well in school. Her foster mother spoke sadly of the temporary nature of her connection to Toni. She expected Lena to reclaim her once she was released from prison. Therefore she was teaching Toni to be ready to take care of herself. She taught her "how to cook simply and to keep herself clean and presentable." Even in this family setting, this eight-year-old child's foster mother felt that she had to be taught survival skills so that she could manage in her uncertain future.

We interviewed Lena in prison; she was open and talkative about her troubles and her relationship to her daughter. The leg irons she wore were a stark contrast to her lacy socks and patent leather shoes. The prison officials were wary of Lena, commenting about her volatile temper. They said that Lena was in lock-up and wore leg irons because of a disturbance she had created.

In talking about Toni, however, Lena revealed a softness. She said that Toni made her happy, "She hugs me and says, 'I love you.'" Lena said of encounters with her daughter, "I get all emotional." Lena described how regretful she felt about the time she had been high on coke and had struck Toni when Toni had a tantrum. "It was my drug problem. . . . My own mother abused me and left scars. She was a drug addict." Lena was honest about her past misdeeds, blaming them on drugs. She claimed that her relationship with her daughter was different from her relationship with her mother. She did not forgive her mother; however, Toni, she believed, had forgiven her.

The social worker handling this case spoke of her troubles in trying to help Lena. She was trying to establish new connections for Lena through church programs and job training, but Lena's out-of-bounds behavior made her ineligible for many programs. Lena had exhausted her few past family and foster family connections by lying and stealing from them. This social worker, who had known her for many years, was her only support.

*Third Interview: Twelve Years Postpartum.* By the twelve-year postpartum follow-up, Lena was in jail again, this time for fighting with a man and destroying his apartment. She had not been able to remain off drugs. She earned a living, when not in jail, through prostitution and thievery. Her life was filled with violent encounters. Toni's father (who had never been involved in Toni's life) had died, and Lena's brother had been shot and killed in the past year. About her own mother, Lena said, "She's harmful, not helpful." The only person who was still a positive support to Lena was the same social worker who had been trying to help her over the years.

Lena softened once again in speaking of her twelve-year-old daughter, saying, "All the time I'm with her I'm happy. My daughter is my friend." Lena was proud of how Toni had developed. "She is beautiful, smart, and a virgin!" Lena exclaimed. Toni had not lived with her mother after her early years. Toni, at the age of twelve, continued to live in a stable home with the same warm and caring foster family. They were actively involved in her school life and in church and civic activities. Toni and her foster mother loved to go bowling together. Toni's grades were high and her attendance at school was good. She performed at, and even above, grade level on academic achievement tests. Toni said that she felt very close to both her biological and her foster mothers, but when she was asked to name the members of her family, she listed only Lena, her mother.

Toni's foster mother was worried about her. When she was out of jail, Lena would return to their neighborhood and wait around Toni's school to see her and talk with her. The foster mother said, "Toni does mind [obey] me now. My problem will come later when she's fifteen and I say [to her] 'You can't go out with that boy.' Will she crawl out the window to her mother and freedom?"

*Case Commentary.* An abused teenager floating from foster family to foster family became a parent. The social service system struggled unsuc-cessfully to keep Lena and her infant in a family setting so that she could mature before being on her own. Lena's records and her own stories revealed that past abuse and lack of adequate parenting had created a young mother whose behavior alienated all who attempted to help her. As she slipped into drug abuse and criminality, she took her young child into this corrosive environment with her. Toni was taken from this young neglectful mother who could not provide a safe, healthy home for her but who, nevertheless, felt an attachment and love for her. Fortunately, because of a strong foster family she was transformed from an aggressive, angry, fearful child to a well-adjusted, happy, and successful one. Perhaps all that this foster family has instilled in Toni will keep her from falling into the same trap that her mother fell into. Toni also has had much more nurturing, family support, and family connections than her mother ever had.

### Factors Predisposing Teen Mothers to Failure

In these last two cases, the grandmothers were nonsupportive or absent, and alternative family and community supports were insufficient to prevent the teen mothers from school, economic, and parenting failure. Overwhelmed by her many children, Dawn has not developed skills that would allow her to parent effectively or to earn a living. In the last case, Lena has not had other children only because her risky life style has left her infertile. The only parental modeling provided to her was one of abandonment and abuse. Unfortunately, because of the increased incidence of AIDS and drug addiction in urban communities, it is probably more common now than it was in the late 1970s for teen mothers not to have their mothers available to them. The outcomes by twelve years postpartum for the young mothers in these two cases are discouraging, and their life possibilities have been severely limited by the paths they have taken. However, their daughters' outcomes are not yet determined. In both cases there are alternative supports available to these young girls, on the verge of adolescence, that could lead them to better life outcomes than their mothers have experienced so far.

### The Ties That Bind

Family ties in our urban population of African American adolescent mothers were surprising for their diversity. The children in our study had kin from both their mother's and their father's side of the family, regardless of the marital status of their parents, and even from their siblings' fathers' kin, although there was no blood tie. The definition of a family can thus be expanded to include those to whom one has no genetic or legal connection. In her study of families in Chicago, Carol Stack described the expansive African American kinship network and its subsequent responsibilities to each of its members (Stack 1974). This phenomenon of an expanding definition of family is currently recognized, as we invent new terms like "blended family" to describe what is taking place in all ethnic groups and classes. This broader context of family connection helps us to understand how individuals cope with transitions and challenges, such as adolescent parenthood.

Family support leading to positive outcomes for an adolescent mother and her child can superficially appear to be quite variable, yet may have a common thread. Our case histories show that cooperative alliances of teen mothers with a mother, father, or husband, where there is a division of labor, shared recreation, mutual affection, and respect are potent processes of support. Even when living apart, young mothers often obtain substantial help from immediate and extended family (Apfel and Seitz 1991). When family support is too fragile or attenuated, and community support is unable to fill the gap, the young mother can multiply the risk factors for herself and her child by rapid repeated childbearing, low educational achievement, welfare dependency, substance abuse, and even criminality.

Whether an adolescent mother remains living with and parenting her child is one index of life success. However, we need to assess a broader constellation of outcomes that include child and maternal well-being to truly measure a successful outcome for teenage mothers. Significant indices of better versus poorer outcomes for the teen mothers are their own health, education, and avoidance of criminality and their ability to support themselves and their children and to parent them adequately. For the children they include their health, school performance, peer and adult relationships, and avoidance of delinquency and teen pregnancy.

In our study the outcomes are still undetermined. Even as the children of the teen mothers approach adolescence themselves, the story is ongoing and incomplete. As Rutter describes in his examination of psychosocial resilience and protective mechanisms, there are turning points in lives, where success in a new task such as school, marriage, work, or parenting can be protective and "may change the life course onto a more adaptive trajectory" (Rutter 1990, 208). The cases we described that appear to have a good prognosis still have risk factors. Will these daughters of teen mothers become teen mothers themselves? Will they become school dropouts? Will they lose their mothers at an early age? Nevertheless, those whose school and home adjustment look excellent now appear to have a much better chance than those who already exhibit the risk factors attributed to many teen mothers at their age—school absenteeism, grade retention, low grades, and a neglectful or abusive family situation. Family support, in all its variations, is critical to counterbalance the negative circumstances and events in the lives of an adolescent mother and her children.

## REFERENCES

This research was funded by grants from the William T. Grant Foundation, the Smith Richardson Foundation, and the National Institute of Child Health and Human Development. We deeply appreciate the participation of the grandmothers, young mothers, and children who have shared so much information about their lives over many years. We also gratefully acknowledge the dedicated work of our staff, Laurel Bidwell, Jean Davis, Reissa Michaels, Laurie Rosenbaum, Lynn Ugolik, Moira Whitley, and Kathryn Young.

Apfel, N., and V. Seitz. 1991. Four models of adolescent mother-grandmother relationships in black inner-city families. *Family Relations* 40:421–29.

———. 1993. African-American grandmothers, adolescent mothers, and their firstborns: Their relationship during the first six years. Paper presented at the conference, Translating Research into Practice: Implications for Serving Families with Young Children, sponsored by the Administration on Children, Youth, and Families, the Society for Research in Child Development, and the National Council of Jewish Women Center for the Child, November 4, Washington, D.C.

Belsky, J. 1984. The determinants of parenting: A process model. *Child Development* 55:83–96.

Colletta, N. D. 1981. Support and the risk of maternal rejection by adolescent mothers. *Journal of Psychology* 109:191–97.

Crockenberg, S. B. 1981. Infant irritability, mother responsiveness, and social support influences on the security of infant-mother attachment. *Child Development* 52: 857–65.

Ensminger, M. E. 1987. Adolescent sexual behavior as it relates to other transition behaviors in youth. In *Risking the future,* edited by S. L. Hofferth and C. D. Hayes. Vol. 2, 36–55. Washington, D.C.: National Academy Press.

Furstenberg, F. F., Jr. 1976. *Unplanned parenthood: The social consequences of teenage childbearing.* New York: Free Press.

Furstenberg, F. F., Jr., J. Brooks-Gunn, and S. P. Morgan. 1987. *Adolescent mothers in later life.* New York: Cambridge University Press.

Furstenberg, F. F., Jr., and A. G. Crawford. 1981. Family support: Helping teenage mothers to cope. In *Teenage sexuality, pregnancy, and childrearing,* edited by F. F. Furstenberg, R. Lincoln, and J. Menken, 280–300. Philadelphia: University of Pennsylvania Press.

Hamburg, B. A., and S. L. Dixon. 1992. Adolescent sexuality, pregnancy, and child rearing: Developmental perspectives. In *Early parenting and coming of age in the 1990s,* edited by M. K. Rosenheim and M. F. Testa, 17–33. New Brunswick, N.J.: Rutgers University Press.

Horwitz, S. M., L. V. Klerman, H. S. Kuo, and J. F. Jekel. 1991. School-age mothers: Predictors of long-term educational and economic outcomes. *Pediatrics* 87:862–68.

Kellam, S. G., M. E. Ensminger, and R. J. Turner. 1977. Family structure and the mental health of children. *Archives of General Psychiatry* 34:1012–22.

Klerman, L. V., and J. F. Jekel. 1973. *School-age mothers: Problems, programs, and policy.* New Haven, Conn.: Linnet.

Leadbeater, B. J., and S. J. Bishop. 1994. Predictors of behavior problems in preschool children of inner-city Afro-American and Puerto Rican adolescent mothers. *Child Development* 65:638–48.

Leadbeater, B. J., and O. Linares. 1992. Depressive symptoms in black and Puerto Rican adolescent mothers in the first 3 years postpartum. *Development and Psychopathology* 4:451–68.

Nath, P. S., J. G. Borkowski, T. L. Whitman, and C. J. Schellenbach. 1991. Understanding adolescent parenting: The dimensions and functions of social support. *Family Relations* 40:411–20.

Provence, S. 1977. An interview for one day. In *Ambulatory pediatrics,* edited by M. Green and R. J. Haggerty, 947–48. Philadelphia, Pa.: Saunders.

Radke-Yarrow, M., and T. Sherman. 1990. Hard growing: Children who survive. In *Risk and protective factors in the development of psychopathology,* edited by J. Rolf, A. S. Masten, D. Cicchetti, K. H. Nuechterlein, and S. Weintraub, 97–119. New York: Cambridge University Press.

Rutter, M. 1990. Psychosocial resilience and protective mechanisms. In *Risk and protective factors in the development of psychopathology,* edited by J. Rolf, A. S. Masten, D. Cicchetti, K. H. Nuechterlein, and S. Weintraub, 181–214. New York: Cambridge University Press.

Seitz, V., and N. H. Apfel. 1993. Adolescent mothers and repeated childbearing: Effects of a school-based intervention program. *American Journal of Orthopsychiatry* 63:572–81.

———. 1994. Effects of a school for pregnant students on the incidence of low-birthweight deliveries. *Child Development* 65: 666–76.

Seitz, V., N. H. Apfel, and L. K. Rosenbaum. 1991. Effects of an intervention program for pregnant adolescents: Educational outcomes at two years postpartum. *American Journal of Community Psychology* 19: 911–30.

Stack, C. B. 1974. *All our kin: Strategies for survival in a black community.* New York: Harper and Row.

# III

# Peer Relationships

Adolescent culture is in many ways predominantly a culture of peers. Age segregation has been created by societal pressures ranging from the historical enactment of compulsory education and child-labor laws to the modern diminishing presence of working parents in both single-parent and two-parent homes (Fasick 1994). The corollary of age segregation has been the development of a distinct adolescent culture of activities, clothes, entertainment, and employment opportunities (e.g., in retail and fast food restaurants). In this context peers come to hold a key role in adolescent development. The negative influence of peer pressure has been widely researched, but close friendships between peers can also provide the mutual affirmation and interpersonal respect that is believed to be the foundation of self-esteem and real concern for others. Disruptions in these relationships can leave adolescents painfully lonely. For teenage girls who also become single parents, disruptions in relationships with boyfriends can have more serious consequences. As the next two chapters show, urban environments create difficulties that may undermine adolescents' abilities to rely on same- and opposite-sex peer relationships for support.

In chapter 10, Way reports on the themes found in urban adolescent girls' and boys' descriptions of their friendships with peers. In-depth interviews were collected longitudinally over a three-year period. Most of the twenty-four ethnically diverse adolescents in the study reported difficulties in trusting their same-sex peers and often felt betrayed in these relationships. Striking gender differences and similarities were also evident in the adolescents' desires for intimacy with peers and in their responses to their fears or direct experiences of betrayal by their peers.

Using quantitative and qualitative data collected longitudinally from seventy-nine African American and Puerto Rican mothers over the first three years after the birth of their children, Leadbeater, Way, and Raden, in chapter 11, cite many reasons for the relational difficulties observed between adolescent mothers and their children's fathers. Some mothers said they had little or no contact with them due to their children's fathers' involvement with other women, excessively macho or abusive behaviors, involvement in selling or using drugs, or death. However, many of the adolescent mothers reported having frequent contact with their children's fathers and stated that their children's fathers were regularly involved with their children. Although the quality of this parental contact was conflictual for many, for some it was supportive and nurturing.

REFERENCE

Fasick, F. A. 1994. On the "invention" of adolescence. *Journal of Early Adolescence* 14:6–23.

# 10

# Between Experiences of Betrayal and Desire: Close Friendships among Urban Adolescents

## Niobe Way

Over the past two decades much research has been conducted on the qualities and benefits of friendships among adolescents (see Laursen 1993; Selman 1980; Shulman 1993; Youniss 1980; Youniss and Smollar 1985). Close friendships have been shown to satisfy adolescents' desires for intimacy; to enhance vastly their interpersonal skills, sensitivity, and understanding (Youniss 1980); and to contribute considerably to cognitive and social development and psychological adjustment (Hartup 1993; Savin-Williams and Berndt 1990). Close friendships, considered by many to be the "most rewarding and satisfying of all human relationships" (Savin-Williams and Berndt 1990, 277), are clearly important for adolescents of all ethnic, racial, and socioeconomic groups (Clark 1989). Our knowledge of friendships among adolescents is limited greatly, however, by the fact that few research projects have explored friendships among urban, poor, or working-class adolescents. Despite the reality that almost 40% of all adolescents are from poor or working-class families (Alan Guttmacher Institute 1994), 20% live below the poverty line (Sum and Fogg 1991), and many poor and working-class adolescents live in urban areas, few researchers of adolescent friendships have focused on this particular population. As is true of the majority of adolescent research in developmental psychology (Jessor 1993), research on adolescent friendships has focused primarily on white middle-class adolescents from suburban environments.[1]

Research that has investigated friendships across social class, race, ethnicity, or culture has typically found significant differences (Dubois and Hirsch 1990; Gallagher and Busch-Rossnagel 1991; Hamm 1994; Jones, Costin, and Ricard 1994). In their study of the quality of friendships among 240 Mexican American, African American, and European American sixth and ninth graders (SES was predominantly lower middle to middle class), Jones, Costin, and Ricard (1994) found that among the males in their sample, African American males were the most likely to reveal their personal thoughts and feelings with their male friends. Furthermore, sex differences were not evident in the levels of self-disclosure in African American same-sex friendships. European American adolescents were the only ones who revealed significant sex differences in their same-sex friendships: the European American girls were more likely to reveal their personal thoughts and feelings to their same-sex friends than were their European American male peers. These and other similar findings (see Dubois and Hirsh 1990; Gallagher and Busch-Rossnagel 1991) suggest that the quality of friendships may differ substantially depending on the social and cultural context. Given this possibility, it seems critical not only to explore the quality of friendships among populations other than white middle-class adolescents, but also to conduct within-group comparisons (e.g., gender or ethnic differences within groups of poor or working-class adolescents).

In this chapter, I report on a three-year longitudinal, qualitative study I conducted that explored the ways in which urban, poor, and working-class adolescent girls and boys perceive their close friendships over time. I chose to focus on girls and boys in my study because I believe that the uniqueness of a person's experience can be detected by comparing it to the experiences of others who are similar (e.g., within groups of girls) as well as to those who are different (e.g., across groups of boys and girls). Although much of the current qualitative research on adolescent girls focuses exclusively on girls' experiences, it is important to continue our investigations of gender differences and similarities. The perceptions of boys should not be used as a norm from which to compare girls' perceptions, but rather as a way to understand the various ways in which girls' experiences differ from or are similar to boys' experiences. Including boys and girls in the present study enhanced my understanding of the unique friendship experiences among boys and among girls.

The study was inspired by theory and research that has focused on the study of human lives and has stressed the interpretive and value-laden nature of psychological inquiry (Apter 1990; Brown and Gilligan 1992; Campbell 1984; Fine 1991; Ladner 1971). It is grounded in the following four assumptions. First, the depth and richness of a person's world can be understood only by listening closely to that person's story. Listening in this way allows one to hear the nuances and subtleties that form a central part of a person's worldview. Second, the words of individuals cannot be separated from the cultural and societal contexts in which these words are embedded. The culture in which people live is always already a part of their words. Third, studies of human development need to investigate how the individuals themselves perceive their environment (e.g., the interpersonal environment of friendships).[2] Among social science researchers there has been an overreliance on methods that impose predetermined definitions and categories on the experiences of research participants. The types of quantitative measures commonly used in studies of friendships are useful in determining how well the participants fit into the categories set up by the measures; they are of less use in exploring how the participants perceive their friendships in their own terms. My fourth and final assumption is that researchers, especially those focusing on populations that have been excluded from theory-building research, should seek to create data-driven theory rather than rely solely on theory testing (e.g., hypothesis testing). Exploratory research is essential for understanding those processes or populations about which we, as social scientists, have little knowledge.

The present study is an exploratory, qualitative project, one in which I intend to generate rather than test hypotheses, to create rather than test theory. My findings are not meant to be definitive but rather suggestive of patterns that may be found if larger samples were examined.

## Method

### Sample

The sample for this study was comprised of 24 adolescents (12 girls and 12 boys) who attended an inner-city public high school in a large northeastern city during the first year of the study. At the time of the first interview the adolescents were fifteen or sixteen years old. They identified themselves as African American (11), Puerto Rican (4), Dominican (3), El Salvadorian (1), Bolivian (1), Irish American (2), or West Indian (2). They all came from poor or working-class families and were all raised in the United States. Social class was inferred from the parents' educational backgrounds and their current occupations. The sample was drawn from classrooms with students who represent the range of academic abilities (a special education, a traditional, and a college bound classroom). Among those students who volunteered to participate (95% of those who were told about the project), 24 students were randomly selected for this longitudinal study.[3]

### Procedure

The participants were first interviewed when they were in the ninth or tenth grade, and a follow-up interview was then conducted each year for two more years. The participants were interviewed in English[4] by me (a white middle-class woman) or one of my colleagues (a white working-class man, an African American middle-class man, and a white middle-class woman). The interview was a one-to-one, in-depth, semistructured interview that typically lasted between one and a half to two hours. The interview protocol included questions about friendships (e.g., "Do you have close or best friend(s)?" "What is this relationship like?" "What do you like or dislike about this relationship?" "What would you like to change about this relationship?" "What qualities are important for you in a friend?" "If you do not have a best or close friend, why not?" "Would you like to have a close or best friend(s)?"). Each student was paid ten dollars after each interview. All interviews were audiotaped and transcribed by a professional transcriber.

### Data Analysis

The data analysis of the interview transcripts included two techniques: narrative summaries (Miller 1988) and a variation of a data analytic technique called the Listening Guide (Brown et al. 1988). The intent of narrative summaries is to condense the stories told by each participant, while quoting the participant as much as possible in order to maintain the flavor of the discussion (Miller 1988). In the present analysis I created narrative summaries for each friendship discussion in each interview. Following this step, I identified themes across and within the narrative summaries. In order to check reliability, a psychology doctoral student also independently identified themes in the narrative summaries (she was unaware of the themes that I had detected). Those themes that were detected independently by both myself and the doctoral student and found among at least 50% of the boys or girls in any one year were considered common themes in the data.

Each common theme was then read for in the interviews. Reading for themes entails highlighting each passage, sentence, or word in the text that suggests the particular theme for which one is reading. This process of highlighting helps to create a trail of evidence for the themes one is focusing upon. My technique of reading for themes is based on the Listening Guide technique developed by Lyn Mikel Brown and her colleagues (1988) to systematically analyze interview data (see Taylor, chap. 7 of this volume, for a more extensive description of this method). Unlike narrative summaries, the Listening Guide encourages the reader to pay close attention to both the form and the content of the interviews (i.e., how the story was told as well as what was said) and to follow one's own process of interpretation. Both data analytic techniques encourage the reader to listen closely to the nuances, contradictions, and continuities within each story, and to come into relationship with the person telling the story.

## Patterns

The doctoral student and I independently detected four common themes in the friendship data. Although my original intent was not focused on detecting gender differences per se, two of the four themes that we noted appeared to differ across gender lines. Two additional themes were evident among both the girls and boys. Although the interviewers never asked the adolescents to respond specifically about *same-sex* peers when discussing their friendships, all of the adolescents spoke primarily about same-sex peers when asked about close friendship (two boys, however, stated that their girlfriends were close friends, and one girl included her boyfriend in her network of best friends). In the following pages, I discuss each of these themes by providing narrative detail from the adolescents' interviews.

### Distrusting One's Peers

Malcolm, an African American adolescent, tells his interviewer in his freshman year that he used to have a best friend when he was in elementary school but that currently no such friend exists:

*Do you have a best friend or close friend?*

Oh no, nobody. Not even around my way. It's like everybody else is just associating, you know. No it's just like, it's like things like friendship take time. Just like a relationship. You can't really, you know, rush into that. You have to just take it slow and be able to know for true who's your friend, who's not.

Malcolm is cautious about whom he is willing to call a friend, choosing to call those he knows "associates" until he is more certain. Although Malcolm does not directly state that he is wary of trusting his peers, he seems to imply such a belief in his response.

In Malcolm's sophomore year, his interviewer asks him whether or not he has a close or best friend:

No, right now, I don't know, I don't like to be crowded too much. No . . . just my girlfriend really. I be chilling with her. . . . With my girlfriend, I could relax . . . we could do certain things that you can't—don't do with other guys. Well, you can do it, but it's just not the same feeling. Like when you're walking with a girl because with a girl you can express certain feelings and stuff you know. . . . You can talk about certain things and with boys it's just harder to like . . . some of the things you may want make you seem you're gay or something. . . . It's more relaxing when you're with a girl so you can just chill. Seems like you have more to talk about.

Although Malcolm may desire close, intimate male friendships ("where you can express certain things"), he seems to find it too risky ("make you seem like you're gay"), so he chooses instead to spend time with his girlfriend, with whom, perhaps, he does not fear breaking social norms.

In his junior year, Malcolm tells his interviewer why he finds it difficult to have close or best male friends:

> I might talk with people but it won't get real deep. . . . There is nobody there to talk to. . . .
>
> *Do you think you have a close or best friend in your life right now?*
>
> Right now, no.
>
> *No?*
>
> I had a couple like once when I was real young, around ten. . . . But right now, nobody really 'cause it seems that as I've grown, you know, everybody just talk behind your back and stuff. You know, so I just let it go because it seems like no people that I've been meeting can hold up to their actions. . . . Something might've happened like between me and a person where other people felt that we shouldn't even be friends no more. So they sit there and talk about me to that person while I'm not around or something and that person will just talk about me too, you know. Whatever, 'cause . . . you know all throughout my neighborhood, you know, I always hear "He talks about you, he says this or he says that." . . . So I just don't really bother with it trying to make you know best friends, you know.

Although there are suggestions in Malcolm's earlier interviews that he is having difficulty trusting his peers, it is not until his junior year interview that he makes these difficulties explicit. Malcolm has currently given up hope of having the kind of close friend he had when he was younger because people in his world do not "hold up to their actions." When he is asked whether he wishes that he had a close or best friend, he says:

Somewhat because then they [his "associates"] wonder why like I don't call them and stuff or you know. Because it's you know I really don't wanna be with them. . . . It's not somebody I could trust. Because like there's even times then I found stuff missing. Like I try to like hang out in my room and I find that things are gone, you know they're gone. Certain things like my tapes are missing and stuff . . .[5]

In Malcolm's world (the world he is willing to reveal to his interviewer), male peers betray him and steal from him, and he is therefore unwilling to consider any of his male peers his best friends.

By the time of their junior or senior year interviews, 21 of the 24 adolescents in the study spoke about having difficulties trusting their same-sex peers. Although the boys' expressions of distrust of their male peers were often more categorical (e.g., "I don't trust *any* of my [peers]") and frequent within their interviews, the boys and girls were almost equally likely to suggest, especially during their latter interviews, that they struggled to trust their same-sex peers (11 of the 12 boys and 10 of the 12 girls). Some of the students (7 of the 12 boys and 4 of the 12 girls) stated such beliefs each year they were interviewed, and others only began making such explicit statements during their junior and senior years in high school (4 of the 12 boys and 6 of the 12 girls).

When Tyiesha, a soft-spoken African American adolescent girl, is asked in her freshman year why she considers her best friend of three years to be her best friend, she says: "I could tell her something and she won't tell nobody else. Like if it's real important or something and she tells me things and I don't tell nobody." Tyiesha says that although she and her friend "sometimes argue" with each other, they "usually be friends again" shortly afterward. In her sophomore year, Tyiesha tells her interviewer once again about a best friend (different from the one mentioned in the previous year) whom she is able to trust and "tell her stuff and she doesn't tell nobody else."

> *Why is this best friend closer than the others?*
>
> She is more trustworthy. . . . I really don't trust anybody that lives around my way.
>
> *Why?*
>
> They're phoney.
>
> *What does phoney mean?*
>
> If you tell them something soon as you turn around somebody's coming back telling you what somebody told you. . . . when my friend tells me something I don't go around telling everybody.

By her junior year Tyiesha says she does not have any best friends because she cannot trust any of her peers: "You can't really trust people these days . . . 'cause they're supposed to be your best friend and you tell her not to say something and she go back and say something. There you go. . . . Right now, I don't call nobody nothing." While Tyiesha does not explain directly why her best friend from her sophomore year is no longer her best friend, she implies that her reasons lie with her experiences of betrayal.

When Albert, a Dominican student, is asked during his junior year whether there is anybody in his life he would call a close or best friend, he explains:

> My closest friend? My mother that's all. Even though I got a lot of friends you know my mother's my closest.
>
> *Besides your mother is there someone else who you would consider close?*
>
> Not now you know I got friends and everything but I don't consider them as close friends not now.
>
> *Why is that?*
>
> No 'cause it's like I haven't known them that good I know them this year and a part of last year you know so I don't know them good. . . . You know some friends they show they can be good friends. You could show it but you have to see it a few more months maybe a year you know to find out really good friends or something. . . . Some friends be your friend when you're not in trouble, when you have money or something. Once you don't have a lot of money or something they'll be like back off. But a real friend will stick right there with you. He won't back off.

By his senior year Albert tells his interviewer that he still does not have a close or best friend:

> Can't trust people no more, you know. Before you could, but now, you know when you got a girl, and they think that she's cute, you know, they still might go try to rap to her and everything you know. You can't trust 'em like before, you know, that they will be serious. Like that friend I had in New York, my best friend I could trust him with my girl, you know and he could trust me with his girl, you know. . . . People ain't like that no more, you know . . . back then[6] you could trust, you know.

The majority of the adolescent boys and girls in this study discussed, especially in their latter year interviews, their difficulties trusting their same-sex peers to "be there" for them, to keep their "secrets" confidential, not to "steal" their romantic partners, and not to take their material possessions.

*Variations in the Consequence of Distrust*

> *Do you have a close or best friend?*
>
> No.
>
> *No you don't?*
>
> I don't trust nobody.

*You don't trust nobody, How come?*

(Pause) Can't trust nobody these days.

*Um have you had bad experiences with people?*

Yeah especially this year.

*Can you tell me about one of them?*

Yeah okay. Me and my friend got, you know, in trouble at school 'cause we broke the elevator.

*Oh you did?*

Don't say nothing about it. And [my friend] he went and told Mr. Talcott [the school disciplinarian] that I was the one who did it. . . . nobody knew that we did it. So he just went and told him. He went ahead and told and I got in trouble. I got suspended for five days. (Joseph, El Salvadorian, junior year)

For Joseph and Malcolm (see "Distrusting One's Peers" above) the consequence of their lack of trust in their peers is that they have given up in their search for a best friend. The adolescent boys in the sample were more likely than the girls to report *not having* close or best friends because they did not trust their peers. Nine of the twelve boys and four of the twelve girls stated in at least one of their interviews that they had *no* best or close friend *because* they could not trust their peers. While this type of assertion was more common in the adolescents' junior and senior year interviews, four of the boys and none of the girls made such assertions during all three of their interviews.

In contrast to the boys, however, the girls were more likely to report that while they struggled to trust their same-sex peers, they maintained close or best friendships with at least one of their girlfriends. Eight of the twelve girls and three of the twelve boys suggested this pattern in their interviews; half of these girls and none of the boys stated this perspective during all three of their interviews. An apparent gender difference in the friendship data was not the theme of distrusting one's peers; rather, the difference lay in the girls' versus the boys' responses to their experiences of betrayal or their feelings of distrust. Violations of trust in close male friendships were frequently given as reasons for terminating all of their close friendships, whereas violations of trust did not appear to have such consequences among many of the girls. The boys typically appeared to avoid intimacy with their male peers as a result of their experiences of betrayal by and lack of trust in these male peers, while the girls typically continued to pursue intimacy with female friends despite betrayal by them (although not necessarily with the same friends who had betrayed them).

Albert says in his senior year when asked if he has a close or best friend:

Best friend? no, just friends . . . I don't trust 'em too much, you know
. . . I had a best friend . . . and he [tried to steal my tapes and my girl-
friend] and, you know, [I] can't trust nobody else.

*Uh huh.*

[I have] kind of friends, you know, but to have another best friend, that
would be pretty hard, now . . . can't trust nobody else no more.

Marie, a student from the Dominican Republic, says that she has had
the same best friend for six years. She also tells her interviewer: "I had
like a lot of friends but like either I had a big argument with them or they
like were two-faced or something, you know, and they were like good
friends to talk to but then they weren't like totally good." Her current
best friend, however, seems to stand apart from her other friendships. In
her description of this friendship in her freshman year, Marie says:

We haven't had the first argument yet and she's like she doesn't lie to me and
she's like—she's real—I dunno—it's like I could really, really trust her and
could be sure about her. Sometimes people be like your best friend could be
your worst friend because they know everything, you know. But I'd be telling
my mother "Oh, she's my best friend" and my mother's like, 'cause my mother
you know she had a lot of friends who did bad things to her—she'd be like
"Don't be telling everything to your best friend—'cause you don't know."
. . . "Can't really trust your best friends you know. . . ." But it's like I feel that
I can because we've been so long [together] already.

Warned by her mother about trusting her peers, Marie explains that bad
things can happen when a friend "knows everything." Marie, however,
has a best friend who is the exception among her peers.

Robyn, an African American student, conveys a similar view in her
sophomore year:

Sonia is my best friend. . . . I talk to her all the time because I know if I was
going through something [difficult] everybody would probably turn their back
on me and stuff, except for her. . . . Because she's the type of person that if I
need to talk, she'll be like "ok." No matter how boring it is or whatever, she'll
talk. So I know that I can depend on her and that I can trust her. . . . Everybody
else is like, well, I think I can trust them, you know, but then when it comes
down to me having a problem and stuff, everybody's running, you know, like,
"Well I ain't got nothing to do with it."

Robyn considers this friendship important because she believes that her
friend is the only person whom she can trust and upon whom she can
depend. She repeats this theme about the same best friend each year of
her interview. The girls in the study spoke just as frequently as the boys
about their peers betraying them or about their fears of betrayal by their

peers. However, the boys, unlike the girls, commonly stated that once their male peers had betrayed their trust (on one or more occasions), they refused not only to be close with those particular peers, but also to trust any of their peers—giving up, therefore, the possibility of having a close or best friend. The boys' sensitivity to betrayal from their same-sex peers seemed much more acute than that of the girls'.

## Desiring or Having Intimate Friendships

Victor, an African American student, says in his junior year interview:

*Do you have a close or best friend this year?*

I wouldn't say . . . I don't say I would. 'Cause . . . I feel that a friend is going to be there for you and they'll support you and stuff like that. Whether they're good and bad times . . . you can share with them you know you would share your feelings with them, your true feelings, . . . that's why I don't think I have any real close friends. I mean things can travel around in a school and things would go around, and the story would change from person to person. Yeah basically, I hate it, I hate it, 'cause you know I wouldn't mind talking to somebody my age that you know I can relate to 'em on a different basis.

Seven of the nine boys and all of the girls who did not have close, intimate friendships spoke about their desires for such friends.[7] Furthermore, only two of the six boys and none of the girls who had close or best friends during the study (six boys had close friends during the first year of the study) emphasized the activities they "did" with their close friends (such as playing basketball) rather than the thoughts or feelings they shared with their friends. Boys, who have been described as being primarily interested in "shared activity" or in status, leadership, and autonomy in their friendships (Buhrmester and Furman 1987; Caldwell and Peplau 1982; Deaux 1977; Epstein and Karweit 1983; Miller 1991), spoke repeatedly about wanting or, on occasion, having close or best friends with whom they could "really talk" and share their "true feelings" and problems. Although these boys came into our interview office *looking* cool, laid-back, and macho (pants riding low on their hips, Walkmans around their necks, sneakers untied), they did not *speak* in such ways when describing their friendships. Rather, they spoke with intensity about wanting or having same-sex friendships without whom you "feel lost," "deep depth" friends with whom you "share your secrets" and "tell everything." When discussing current or desired close or best friends, the girls *and* boys spoke a language of intimacy rather than a language of independence and autonomy.

Sonia, a Puerto Rican adolescent, says to her interviewer that her close friends are close to her because: "When I talk to them, they make me feel like I can really, you know, talk to them about anything." When Tito, who is also Puerto Rican, is asked if he would like to have a close friend (he claims that he does not have one), he says "I would like a friend that if I got anything to say to him or like any problems or anything I'll tell him and he'll tell me his problems you know." Marcus, who is from El Salvador, says that his friends are close to him because they "care" about him and they help him when he has problems at home—they "talk it out" with him. "We try to help [each other] get that anger out. . . . We don't keep anything from each other." While much of the existing research on friendships, including the present study, indicates that adolescent girls are more likely to *have* intimate, self-disclosing, and emotionally supportive friendships than are adolescent boys (see Berndt 1982; Caldwell and Peplau 1982; Camarena, Sarigiani, and Petersen 1990; Douvan and Adelson 1966; Furman and Buhrmester 1985; Reisman 1990; Savin-Williams and Berndt 1990; Sharabany, Gershoni, and Hofman 1981; Youniss 1980), this study suggests that both girls and boys have equally strong *desires* for such intimate and emotionally supportive relationships. The girls in this study appear, however, to have been more successful in finding and maintaining such friendships during their adolescence.

### Yearning for Earlier Friendships

The seven boys who expressed a desire for close, intimate friendships with other boys stated, furthermore, that they had enjoyed such friendships when they were younger (primarily in junior high school) and that they yearned to experience this type of friendship once again. When asked in his junior year whether he has a close or best friend, Alfredo, a Bolivian American adolescent, says:

Not really I think myself. The friend I had, I lost it. . . . That was the only person that I could trust and we talked about everything. When I was down, he used to help me feel better. The same I did to him you know so. I feel pretty lonely and sometimes depressed . . . because I don't have no one to go out with, no one to speak on the phone, no one to tell my secrets, no one for me to solve my problems.

*Why don't you think you have someone?*

Because I think that it will never be the same you know I think that when you have a real friend and you lose it, I don't think you find another one like him. That's the point of view that I have. . . . I tried to look for a person, you know, but it's not that easy.

Intimate and emotionally supportive male friendships—"chumships" according to Sullivan (1953)—are what Alfredo and six of his peers appear to have "lost." Malcolm, from whom we heard earlier in this chapter, told his interviewer that he "had a best friend when [he] was real young, around ten. . . . But right now, nobody really 'cause it seems that as I've grown, you know, everybody just talk behind your back." Albert says, in response to a question about whether he has a close or best friend, "No, I'm lonely here. . . . I was trying to find one . . . a good friend, you know, like my first one that I had back in New York [when he was in junior high school]." Although it is unclear just what those previous friendships were *really* like for these seven boys, they all remembered their early adolescent friendships as ones in which they could openly express themselves and that were mutually supportive and nurturing.

Whereas all of the girls who did not have close friendships expressed desires for such friendships, none of the girls expressed a yearning for an earlier type of friendship. Even the girls who had distanced themselves from their female peers by their third year interview did not indicate any such desire.

## Discussion

Four questions emerge as a result of the findings in this study: (1) Why do the boys who were interviewed have more difficulty than the girls in maintaining close or best friendships, especially given that many of these boys seem to desire such friendships? (2) Why do many of the boys yearn for friendships like those they experienced in early adolescence, while none of the girls have such yearnings? (3) Why is the theme of distrust in one's peers particularly prominent in the latter year interviews? and (4) Why are the majority of adolescents in this study reporting that they have difficulty trusting their peers?

In order to address the first and second questions, the culture in which these adolescents were raised, as well as their individual experiences, must be examined. Girls who grow up in a culture that does not discourage them from having close friendships with other girls may be more willing to sustain close and trusting relationships *even* when they have experienced betrayals and other violations in their friendships. Given that intimate behavior among girls is generally more rewarded and accepted in the United States than intimate behavior among boys, girls may have more motivation for continuing the relationship despite experiences of betrayal by their peers. In addition, girls, who have less power in the world than boys, may learn to be more tolerant of betrayal than boys. They may learn to forgive others quickly in the name of being a "good" or "nice" girl.[8] Girls, therefore, may learn to be more flexible—violations of trust in their friendships may not lead to the termination of all close friendships. While the girls' flexibility in friendships may ultimately lead to positive social behavior (e.g., close intimate friendships), the reasons behind this flexibility may not be as positive and in fact may undermine these girls' ability to discontinue those relationships in which they are not being cared for properly. Furthermore, girls may not yearn for the friendships they had in early adolescence because—given their flexibility—they know that even if presently they do not have close female friends, they will likely have such friends in the future (if they want them). As suggested by the adolescents in this study, the girls may not mourn a loss of intimacy with their same-sex peers because they do not perceive this loss—if they have experienced such a loss—to be final.

Adolescent boys who live in a largely homophobic culture that looks with ambivalence or suspicion on close, intimate male friendships may find it harder to maintain such friendships with other boys, *especially* when they have been betrayed by their male peers. Since the unspoken taboo against close male friendships only grows stronger as boys grow older, they may find it especially difficult to maintain close male relationships as they reach middle to late adolescence. During adolescence these boys may find themselves yearning not only for certain past relationships with boys, but also for a time when the taboo against same-sex intimacy was not as strong. Adolescent boys may decide that given both society's messages regarding intimate, close male friendships *and* their individual experiences of betrayal, it is neither worthwhile nor safe for them to pursue such friendships with other boys. Furthermore, adolescent boys in this society may be socialized to be less tolerant of betrayal or acts that undermine their self-esteem or self-worth than are girls; this may explain the seemingly acute sensitivity to betrayal evident among many of the boys.[9]

Cultural expectations and individual experiences, as well as physical and sexual maturation, may provide answers to the third question concerning the prominence of themes of distrust among the adolescents in their latter year interviews. Trusting one's same-sex peers may become increasingly difficult for both adolescent girls and adolescent boys as they become involved in romantic relationships and, consequently, spend less time with their friends, or "steal" each other's romantic partners. Some of the boys and girls in the study stated specifically that "stealing" occurrences—or their possibility—had led them not to trust their friends any longer. Moreover, adolescents may become more wary of same-sex peers as they reach middle to late adolescence simply because their experiences of betrayal are likely to be more numerous than when they were younger.

Adolescents' feelings of vulnerability and self-protection may also escalate as their bodies mature into fully grown adult bodies. These heightened feelings of self-protection and vulnerability may cause adolescents to become increasingly cautious about whom they trust among their peers, who are also physically and sexually maturing and, perhaps, becoming more wary and self-protected.

The fourth question, regarding the prevalence of distrust among this particular group of adolescents, can be addressed by examining both the familial and the cultural environments of these adolescents. Given that many researchers have noted that trust is one of the most important ingredients in adolescents' friendships and betrayal a commonly perceived threat to such friendships (see Brown and Gilligan 1992; Savin-Williams and Berndt 1990; Youniss and Smollar 1985), it was not altogether surprising that betrayal and distrust were pervasive concerns among the adolescents in this study. It *was* surprising, however, that the adolescents spoke so frequently about not trusting any or trusting very few of their peers. Twenty-one of the twenty-four adolescents stated that they had difficulty trusting their same-sex peers, and almost half of these adolescents stated, in at least one of their interviews, that they did not trust *any* of their peers. In an examination of the research literature on adolescent friendships, I could find no studies that suggested that distrusting one's peers was as pervasive a theme as in the present sample. James Youniss and Jaqueline Smollar (1985) found, in their quantitative assessment of friendships, that 30% of the primarily white middle-class adolescent boys in their studies did not have supportive and trusting relationships with their male peers. In the present study 75% of the boys reported, in at least one of their interviews, that they did not have such friendships, and 50% reported this in at least two of their interviews.

Reasons for the high level of distrust found in the present sample may indirectly or directly lie with the poverty, violence, and racism that shapes and pervades these adolescents' lives. When asked why it was that so many of his male peers do not trust each other, Malcolm responds:

> It's like certain areas affect the, you know, the whole. Like the environment . . . Like around [my neighborhood] mostly there's gangs and everybody talk about everybody. I don't know if there's still those in there that can like . . . hold their own and not think about talking about other people. . . . A baby's born innocent but it grows up in there and it does the same thing. . . .
>
> *So what do you think it is—the—what is it about the environment you live in now that makes—that causes this?*
>
> . . . The arrogance.

*The arrogance?*

Yeah. Most of the people you know it's like people wanna be number one and stuff. It's like like if somebody's downing me behind my back and somebody I know is with him, I might know both of them you know, but to make them both feel good, I guess they both gotta go along with it.

Malcolm locates the source of the problem in his community specifically with people wanting to "feel good" about themselves; his peers want to raise their standing among their peers, so they denigrate others. Wanting to be important, for boys such as Malcolm or for girls, appears to lead not only to betrayal but also to distrust. Although this pattern of betraying one's peers in order to feel important is likely to be evident in peer cultures across social class, race, and gender, it may be more frequent among adolescents like the ones in this study. These poor and working-class adolescents, who are constantly being given messages from the larger society regarding their lack of importance in the world, or at least who are rarely recognized as important, may find themselves having particularly strong desires to feel important. Such desires may lead some to attempt to feel important among those with whom they feel they can be important—their peers. Their desires to feel important may override, at times, their loyalty to their friends.

The school where this study was undertaken may further explain the pervasiveness of distrust among these adolescents. All of the participants in the study attended a particularly large, underfunded, and chaotic inner-city school that lacked any real means to create a community within the school. The rates of suspension and dropout within this school were among the highest in the city. Joyce Epstein and Nancy Karweit state: "Negative features in a school environment—ridicule, discrimination, low expectations, stereotypes, repressions, punishment, isolation—may increase the dissociative quality of the setting and affect the thought processes and social behaviors of the students" (1983, 60). Norris Haynes and Christine Emmons (1994) found, in their studies of the impact of school climate on students' psychosocial development, that students' peer relations are greatly affected by the climate in the school: A distrusting, negative environment was commonly associated with distrusting and negative peer relations. Although none of the students in the present study specifically discussed this issue, their social relations may have been deeply influenced by the school they attended and where they attempted to make close friends.

Finally, a third explanation for the prevalence of distrust found in this study may lie with the quality of the adolescents' relationships with their parents. Namely, those who do not have trusting, close relationships with their parents may not have such relationships with their peers (see Gold and Yanof 1985). However, among those students in the study who reported distrusting their peers, their stated feelings for their parents (or the persons with whom they resided) were as likely to be positive as they were to be negative. The only exception to this pattern were the girls who stated they did not trust *any* of their female peers. These four girls consistently described conflictual and tension-ridden relationships with their parents. Future research should explore further the association between trust of parents and of peers for urban adolescent girls and boys.

While considering the influence of parent-child relationships on friendships, it is important to note that some of the parents in this study specifically warned their children not to trust their peers (see Marie's interview). This type of message may reflect a belief system, considered to be common within many close-knit communities—especially within oppressed communities—that those who are not part of one's family or one's extended family should not be trusted (Salguero and McCusker, chap. 18 of this volume; Stack 1974). Such messages from parents and other family members may make it particularly difficult for adolescents from these communities to have close friends outside of their families.

These findings regarding trust, betrayal, and desire among urban adolescents raise critical questions. How can adolescents be supported to maintain trusting same-sex friendships? What are the developmental implications for adolescents' relationships (both friendships and romantic relationships) if boys are more likely to terminate their close relationships in response to betrayal, and girls are more likely to pursue intimacy despite betrayal? These types of seemingly gender-based responses may lead girls to stay in relationships that are not healthy, and may severely disrupt male friendships and male-female relationships. Furthermore, what are the implications for developmental theory if urban adolescent boys are indicating that they want intimate relationships as much as their female peers? Current developmental theory asserts that adolescent girls are more likely to value "being in relationship" than adolescent boys (see Miller 1991). The present study suggests that adolescent boys may *desire* relationships as much as their female peers; girls may simply be more encouraged, successful, and skillful in fulfilling such desires. None of the boys or girls in the sample discussed a desire to be independent or autonomous with their peers.

These findings indicate that there may be differences between urban, poor, and working-class adolescent boys and suburban, middle-class adolescent boys (the focus of most studies of adolescent friendships). These findings also suggest, however, that adolescent boys and girls from all different socioeconomic classes and ethnicities need to be listened to on their own terms. What would white middle-class adolescent boys or white, poor, and working-class adolescents say if they were interviewed in an open-ended format over time?; What would these boys and girls say if we entered into a relationship with them instead of administering questionnaires to them? Perhaps they, too, would speak about not having but desiring intimate male friendships.[10] Have we, as social science researchers, assumed that adolescent girls (and women) are more interested in intimate, self-disclosing, same-sex relationships because they are more likely than boys (and men) to have these types of relationships? The findings in this study underscore the need to reexamine adolescent development with diverse populations, using research methods that allow adolescents to express themselves in their own words.

NOTES

1. A notable exception to this pattern is the research that has been done by Ana Mari Cauce (see Cauce 1986, 1987).

2. Kurt Lewin (1951) and Uri Bronfenbrenner (1979) have written extensively about the importance of examining the research participant's "subjective experience" of his or her environment.

3. This project was a part of a larger cross-sectional project, funded by the National Institute of Drug Abuse (principal investigator, Perry London), examining the psychosocial correlates of risk-taking behavior. It was also a part of a longitudinal study examining the ways in which urban adolescents speak about their worlds, which was funded in part by the Henry Murray Research Center, Radcliffe College (see Way in press for a complete description of this latter project).

4. It is important to note the language in which these interviews were conducted, since some of the Hispanic adolescents spoke Spanish at home and with their friends (although they were all fluent English speakers). The stories told by these bilingual students may have been different had they been interviewed in Spanish.

5. Three of the boys, and none of the girls, discussed concerns about their peers stealing from them.

6. Many of the adolescents referred to being able to trust others "back then." Although this response seems to be referring to when they were younger, there is some indication that some of the adolescents may be referring to earlier generations of youth. Unfortunately, we never asked these adolescents what they meant by "back then."

7. I am defining "intimacy" as a feeling of emotional closeness stemming from the mutual sharing of thoughts and feelings (see Berndt 1982; Sullivan 1953).

8. This may be similar to the "perfect girl" phenomenon that Brown and Gilligan (1992) speak about in their studies of primarily white adolescent girls.

9. The impact of socialization pressures on adolescent girls' and boys' friendships has been noted by numerous researchers (see Clark and Reis 1988; Eder and Hallinan 1978; Leadbeater, Batgos, and Lin 1992; Rose 1985).

10. Reisman (1990) found in his quantitative study of male college undergraduates at a midwestern university that many males wished for "greater opportunities for personal disclosure" in their same-sex friendships.

## REFERENCES

Alan Guttmacher Institute. 1994. *Sex and America's teenagers*. New York: Alan Guttmacher Institute.

Apter, T. 1990. *Altered loves: Mothers and daughters during adolescence*. New York: St. Martin's Press.

Berndt, T. J. 1982. The features and effects of friendships in early adolescents. *Child Development* 53:1447–60.

Bronfenbrenner, U. 1979. *The ecology of human development*. Cambridge: Harvard University Press.

Brown, L. M., D. Argyris, J. Attanucci, B. Bardige, C. Gilligan, K. Johnston, B. Miller, R. Osborne, J. Ward, G. Wiggins, and D. Wilcox. 1988. *A guide to reading narratives of conflict and choice for self and moral voice*. Cambridge: Harvard Graduate School of Education, Project on Women's Psychology and Girls' Development.

Brown, L. M., and C. Gilligan. 1992. *Meeting at the crossroads: Women's psychology and girls' development*. Cambridge: Harvard University Press.

Buhrmester, D., and W. Furman. 1987. The development of companionship and intimacy. *Child Development* 58:1101–13.

Caldwell, M. A., and L. A. Peplau. 1982. Sex differences in same-sex friendships. *Sex roles* 8:721–33.

Camarena, P. M., P. A. Sarigiani, and A. C. Petersen. 1990. Gender-specific pathways to intimacy in early adolescence. *Journal of Youth and Adolescence* 19:19–32.

Campbell, A. 1984. *The girls in the gang*. Cambridge: Basil Blackwell.

Cauce, A. 1986. Social networks and social competence: Exploring the effects of early adolescent friendships. *American Journal of Community Psychology* 14 (6):607–28.

———, 1987. School and peer competence in early adolescence: A test of domain-specific self-perceived competence. *Developmental Psychology* 23(2):287–91.

Clark, M. L. 1989. Friendships and peer relations in black adolescents. In *Black adolescents*, edited by R. Jones. Berkeley, Calif.: Cobb and Henry.

Clark, M. S., and H. T. Reis. 1988. Interpersonal processes in close relationships. *Annual Review of Psychology* 39:609–72.

Deaux, K. 1977. Sex differences. In *Personality variables in social behavior*, edited by T. Blass. New York: Wiley.

Douvan, E., and J. Adelson. 1966. *The adolescent experience*. New York: Wiley.

DuBois, D. L., and B. J. Hirsch. 1990. School and neighborhood friendship patterns of Blacks and Whites in early adolescence. *Child Development* 61:524–36.

Eder, D., and M. T. Hallinan. 1978. Sex differences in children's friendships. *American Sociological Review* 43:237–50.

Epstein, J. L., and N. Karweit. 1983. *Friends in school: Patterns of selection and influence in secondary schools*. New York: Academic Press.

Fine, M. 1991. *Framing dropouts: Notes on the politics of an urban high school*. Albany: State University of New York Press.

Furman, W., and D. Buhrmester. 1985. Children's perceptions of the personal relationship in the social network. *Developmental Psychology* 21:1016–24.

Gallagher, C., and N. A. Busch-Rossnagel. 1991. Self-disclosure and social support in the relationships of black and white female adolescents. Poster presented at Society for Research on Child Development, March, Seattle.

Gilligan, C. 1982. *In a different voice: Psychological theory and women's development*. Cambridge: Harvard University Press.

Gold, M., and D. S. Yanof. 1985. Mothers, daughters, and girlfriends. *Journal of Personality and Social Psychology* 49 (3):654–59.

Hamm, J. V. 1994. Similarity in the face of diversity? African-American, Asian-American, European-American, and Hispanic-American Adolescents' best friendships in ethnically diverse high schools. Paper presented at the biennial meetings of the Society for Research on Adolescence, February, San Diego.

Hartup, W. 1993. Adolescents and their friends. In *Close friendships in adolescence,* edited by B. Laursen. San Francisco: Jossey Bass.

Haynes, N., and C. Emmons. 1994. Lecture given at the Developmental Psychology Luncheon Series, March 28, Yale University Department of Psychology.

Jessor, R. 1993. Successful adolescent development among youth in high-risk settings. *American Psychologist* 48 (2):117–26.

Jones, D. C., S. E. Costin, and R. J. Ricard. 1994. Ethnic and sex differences in best friendship characteristics among African-American, Mexican-American, and European-American adolescents. Poster presented at Society for Research on Adolescence, February 10, San Diego.

Ladner, J. 1971. *Tomorrow's tomorrow.* New York: Anchor Books.

Laursen, B., ed. 1993. *Close friendships in adolescence.* San Francisco: Jossey Bass.

Leadbeater, B. J., J. Batgos, and J. T. Lin. 1992. Gender differences in same- and cross-sex friendships: What counts as intimacy? Manuscript submitted for publication. Yale University, New Haven, Conn.

Lewin, K. 1951. *Field theory in social science.* New York: Harper.

Miller, B. 1988. Adolescent friendships: A pilot study. Qualifying paper, Harvard Graduate School of Education, Cambridge, Mass.

———. 1991. Adolescents' relationships with their friends. Ed.D. diss. Harvard Graduate School of Education.

Reis, H. T., M. Senchak, and B. Solomon. 1985. Sex differences in the intimacy of social interactions: Further examination of potential explanations. *Journal of Personality and Social Psychology* 48:1204–17.

Reisman, J. M. 1990. Intimacy in same-sex friendships. *Sex Roles* 23:65–82.

Rose, S. M. 1985. Same- and cross-sex friendships and the psychology of homosociality. *Sex Roles* 12:63–74.

Savin-Williams, R. C., and T. J. Berndt. 1990. Friendship and peer relations. In *At the threshold: The developing adolescent,* edited by S. Feldman and G. R. Elliot. Cambridge: Harvard University Press.

Selman, R. 1980. *The growth of interpersonal understanding: Developmental and clinical analyses.* New York: Academic Press.

Sharabany, R., R. Gershoni, and J. Hofman. 1981. Girlfriend, boyfriend: Age and sex differences in intimate friendship. *Developmental Psychology* 17 (6):800–808.

Shulman, S. 1993. Close friendships in early and mid adolescence: Typology and friendship reasoning. In *Close friendships in adolescence,* edited by B. Laursen. San Francisco: Jossey Bass.

Stack, C. 1974. *All our kin: Strategies for survival in a black community.* New York: Harper and Row.

Sullivan, H. S. 1953. *The interpersonal theory of psychiatry.* New York: W. W. Norton.

Sum, A. M., and W. N. Fogg. 1991. The adolescent poor and the transition to early adulthood. In *Adolescence and poverty: Challenge for the 1990s,* edited by P. B. Edelman and J. Ladner. Washington, D.C.: Center for National Policy Press.

Way, N. In press. *In their own words: Listening to urban adolescents speak about their worlds.* New York: New York University Press.

Youniss, J. 1980. *Parents and peers in social development: A Sullivan-Piaget perspective.* Chicago: University of Chicago Press.

Youniss, J., and J. Smollar. 1985. *Adolescent relations with mothers, fathers, and friends.* Chicago: University of Chicago Press.

# 11 Why Not Marry Your Baby's Father? Answers from African American and Hispanic Adolescent Mothers

Bonnie J. Ross Leadbeater,
Niobe Way, and Anthony Raden

Many have argued that the rise of adolescent parenting as a social problem stems less directly from concerns about the age of the mothers than from their marital status (Furstenberg, Brooks-Gunn, and Morgan 1987; Lawson and Rhodes 1993; Nathanson 1991). While the number of births to teenagers has actually declined since the 1950s, the number of out-of-wedlock births to teens has soared (Children's Defense Fund 1994). Along with declines in adolescent marriages, decreases in involvement among fathers of children born to teenage mothers have also been documented (Chase-Lansdale and Vinovskis 1987; Osofsky, Hann, and Peebles 1993). Decreased involvement becomes more pronounced as the children leave infancy (Furstenberg and Harris 1993; Leadbeater and Linares 1992; Unger and Wandersman 1988).

Public interest in the role of these fathers has focused mainly on their potential for providing child support in order to alleviate welfare dependency or poverty among single female heads of households. Fathers, however, may provide a range of formal or informal supports in addition to, or instead of, direct economic support. The support provided may include acknowledging paternity, maintaining contact or emotional bonds with their children, providing child care, or giving clothes, diapers, and so forth (Adams, Pittman, and O'Brien 1993). This study investigates the obstacles to and consequences of the biological fathers' support or involvement for adolescent mothers and their children.

The ethnicity or race of the mothers has been found to be related to differences in supports from male partners. Hispanic adolescent mothers are more likely to be married or living with a partner than are black or caucasian adolescent mothers (Wasserman et al. 1990). Black adolescent mothers are more likely to live with their families, remain single, or marry later than white adolescent mothers (Unger and Cooley 1992). Using 1986 National Longitudinal Survey of Youth data, Marsiglio (1987) reports that only 15% of black fathers of adolescent mothers' children lived with their firstborn children shortly after birth, compared to 48% of Hispanic and 58% of white fathers. For white fathers, residence with the child was positively related to older age, Catholic religion, and rural residence; however, none of these factors predicted father involvement among black and Hispanic men (Marsiglio 1987). Indeed, despite the social significance of their involvement, little research has focused on the fathers of black and Hispanic inner-city children.

Many involved fathers live with their own or the adolescent mother's family and typically depend on them for financial support (Marsiglio 1987). Yet, we know little of the stresses or supports that result from these living arrangements. Research has suggested that nonresidential fathers of the children of adult mothers may be more solicitous and affectionate toward their young children (McLoyd 1990). While some adolescent mothers and their children's fathers form stable and long-lasting marriages, these relationships are frequently transient (Chase-Lansdale and Vinovskis 1987; Furstenberg and Harris 1993). Some fathers enter new relationships, sometimes with additional children, and face the challenges of negotiating competing interests of more than one family. The extensive research literature on the effects of marital quality on child development suggests that marital conflict is an important predictor of children's problem behaviors (Hetherington and Clingempeel 1992; Miller et al. 1993). However, adolescent mothers are more frequently stereotyped as single mothers than as mothers with partners. The levels and nature of conflicts between adolescent mothers and their children's fathers and the impact of these conflicts on their children have not been investigated.

Longitudinal studies have demonstrated that support from the grandmothers relates positively to the adolescent mothers' educational achievement, financial status, living arrangements, day care assistance, and disciplinary practices (Cooley and Unger 1991; Crockenberg 1987; Spieker and Bensley 1994; Unger and Wandersman 1988). In contrast, support from a male partner is positively related to less tangible maternal outcomes, including residential stability, overall life satisfaction, psychological well-being, and social participation (Cooley and Unger 1991; Leadbeater and Linares 1992; Spieker and Bensley 1994; Unger and Cooley 1992; Unger and Wandersman 1988). On a less positive note, early marriages or living with a male partner are associated with lower levels of maternal education among both black and white mothers (Unger and Cooley 1992).

Research investigating the effects of father involvement for the children of adolescent mothers suggests both positive and negative outcomes. Cooley and Unger (1991) found that involvement of a male partner was associated with greater overall cognitive stimulation, which in turn was related to fewer problem behaviors and better academic achievement in the children of adolescent mothers at six to seven years of age. However, the researchers caution that these effects may be moderated by socioeconomic and racial differences and report that early marriages were weakly associated with higher levels of child problem behaviors for white mothers (Unger and Cooley 1992).

Following a group of adolescent children born to adolescent mothers in the late 1950s, Furstenberg and Harris (1993) report that youth who had long-term relations with a resident biological father or stepfather were more likely to have entered college or to have found stable employment after high school, were less likely to be teenage parents, or to have been in jail, and were less likely to report depressive symptoms. However, these close residential relationships were very rare. These findings did not hold for adolescents with close attachments to nonresidential fathers—which, in fact, predicted an increased likelihood of teenage childbearing, particularly for male children.

A great many gaps remain in our knowledge about the role of the biological fathers of the children of adolescent mothers. Some authors have argued that negative stereotypes and economic, educational, and residential circumstances hamper these fathers' involvement rather than their lack of concern for or commitment to their children (Adams, Pittman, and O'Brien 1993; Elster and Lamb 1986; Sander and Rosen 1987; Watson, Rowe, and Jones 1989). Most research has not considered the role of biological fathers separately from that of stepfathers or other male partners—despite the possibility that biological fathers may have reasons to be more invested in outcomes for their offspring (Kaplan et al. 1994). Measures of father involvement also generally tap their presence or absence, rather than qualitative differences in or closeness of their relationships to mother or child. In addition, we know little about the parenting skills, stresses, competencies, or problems of the fathers who are or who are not involved with their children (Lamb 1988). Most research has not considered the effects of father involvement beyond infancy (Furstenburg and Harris 1993). The father's reasons for *not* being involved with the child, the mother's reasons for *not* being involved with the father, and the quality of the relationships for those parents who remain involved all have important implications for both the durability of these relationships and their consequences for the children's development. Yet, these have not been systematically investigated. In this longitudinal study, quantitative and qualitative data were used to examine the obstacles to and consequences and quality of involvement of the biological fathers from the perspective of African American and Hispanic inner-city adolescent mothers. Individual interviews with the adolescent mothers were used to determine the presence or absence and quality of involvement of the biological fathers with their children when they were approximately 1, 12, and 28 to 36 months old. The effects of the fathers' involvement on their children's cognitive development at 12 months and behavioral problems at 28 to 36 months postpartum were assessed. In addition, interview data at 28 to 36 months were used to examine the quality of relationships for those parents who remain involved with each other (romantically or platonically). Self-reported depressive symptoms of the mothers were assessed in order to control for the effects of possible negative attribution biases in the mother's reports that may be associated with her depressed mood (see Leadbeater and Bishop 1994).

## The Study

### Participants

One hundred and twenty adolescent mothers and their children comprised the original sample. Mothers were thirteen to nineteen years old at delivery ($M = 17.1$, $SD = 1.2$) and were primarily African American (53.1%) or Puerto Rican (42.5%). All but two were primiparous, and most lived with their own mothers (71.7%) and came from families on welfare (64.6%). They had completed an average of 9.5 ($SD = 1.3$) years of school, and half remained in school or had graduated at delivery (Leadbeater in press). The majority of the children were from full-term deliveries and were of normal birth weight.

At an urban adolescent health care center in 1987–88, adolescent mothers were recruited consecutively at three to four weeks postpartum (time 1). The mothers in the original sample comprised 89% of those enrolled at the clinic during that time. Details of the sample, procedures, and measures are elaborated in previous publications (Leadbeater and Linares 1992; Linares et al. 1991). Mothers were interviewed again at 6 months (time 2), 12 months (time 3), 20–24 months (time 4), and 28–36 months (time 5) postpartum. Time 4 data were not used in these analyses.

Questionnaire data were collected from 113 mothers (94%) at times 2 and 3 and from 84 mothers (71%) at time 5. Data from an ethnographic interview (described below) conducted at time 5 were also available for 80 mothers (66%). Attrition was due to the mothers' out-of-state moves or researchers' inability to locate the mothers. Mothers not in the sample

at 28 to 36 months did not differ significantly from the remaining participants on any of the initial demographic or predictor variables except for
levels of depressive symptoms: mothers remaining in the study reported
more depressive symptoms ($M$ = 13.9, $SD$ = 7.8) than those lost to
follow up ($M$ = 10.7, $SD$ = 7.2) ($T[116]$ = 2.13, $p$ = .04). This
difference of three points is unlikely to be of practical or clinical significance.

## Procedure

At each time point, questionnaire data were collected in individual
interviews by researchers with at least a master's degree in social work,
counseling, or developmental psychology. At the time of the assessment
at 28 to 36 months an audiotaped, semistructured interview was also
conducted eliciting the mothers' descriptions of their lives since their
babies were born, their aspirations for themselves and their babies, their
plans to accomplish these goals, their views of themselves as women and
as mothers, and the stability and quality of their social support networks.
Interviews were transcribed and underwent content analyses as described
below. These data were unavailable for five of the mothers who completed questionnaires at time 5 (two mothers left before completing the
interview and three tapes were inaudible because of equipment
problems).

The children's biological fathers ranged in age from 15 to 33 at the
birth of the child and were on average 20.1 ($SD$ = 3.07) years old. They
had completed an average of 11.12 ($SD$ = 1.35) years of school, with a
range of 5 to 14 years. At one year postpartum, 21% of the fathers were
in school, 52.8% had graduated from high school, 60% were working
full or part time, and 12.2% lived with the adolescent mother and their
child. At 28 to 36 months postpartum, only six of the couples were
married. The data for fathers with no data at 28 to 36 months postpartum
did not significantly differ from those remaining in the sample on any of
the initial demographic, predictor, or outcome variables.

## Measures

*Maternal Depressive Symptoms.* The Beck Depression Inventory (Beck
1967) is a widely used, twenty-one-item questionnaire that assesses cognitive, behavioral, affective, and somatic symptoms of depression.
Weighted response categories are scored 0 to 3 for each item. Its psychometric properties have been established for minority adolescents (see
Leadbeater and Linares 1992).

*Father Involvement.* The involvement of the father was coded as "present" or "absent" at times 1, 3, and 5, with "present" indicating that the father either visited his child or contributed materially (i.e., diapers, clothes, money, etc.) to his child's care. As the fathers' relations with the mothers in many cases were unstable, this assessment was believed to be the best reflection of fathers' involvement with their children.

### Coding for the Ethnographic Data

The extent and quality of father involvement was coded qualitatively from the time 5 interview data ($N = 79$). The mother was asked to describe her child's relationship with his or her father. The extent and quality of the fathers' involvement with their children was coded on a 5-point scale, with 0 indicating no contact with child, 1 indicating rare or highly irregular contact and poor relationship with child (e.g., father does not pay attention to child or child and father constantly fight with each other when together), 2 indicating occasional contact and poor relationship, 3 indicating regular weekly or daily contact and an inconsistent relationship (e.g., sometimes the relationship is caring and loving and other times it is hostile, conflictual, or neglectful), and 4 indicating regular weekly or daily contact and a close relationship (e.g., father and child have a consistently enjoyable and caring relationship). There were no examples of fathers having irregular or occasional contact with their children and having close relationships with them or of fathers having regular weekly or daily contact with their children and having consistently poor relationships with them. Agreement for two coders for a third of the interviews was 95%.

The quality of the father's relationship with the adolescent mother was also coded from the time 5 interviews ($N = 79$). The mother was asked to describe her relationships with her child's father. The quality of their relationship was coded on a 5-point scale with 0 indicating no relationship, 1 indicating that the quality of the relationship is extremely poor (e.g., the relationship involves physical or emotional abuse or is particularly hostile), 2 indicating that the relationship is poor (e.g., the relationship is mostly hostile or negative, but father offers some emotional support to the adolescent mother), 3 indicating that the relationship is close (e.g., the relationship is emotionally supportive for the adolescent mother), and 4 indicating the relationship is very close (e.g., the relationship is highly emotionally supportive). Agreement between two coders for a third of the interviews was 89%.

The reasons for the fathers' lack of involvement were coded from the interview data. Problems mentioned in the relationships were coded as 0 = "no problems mentioned"; 1 = "immature, irresponsible, seeing other women"; 2 = "excessively macho, restrictive, or physically abusive;" 3 = "involved in selling or using drugs"; 4 = "in prison"; 5 = "dead." All categories mentioned were noted; however, the highest category number given was used in the analyses, reasoning that the problems overlapped (i.e., most prison terms and deaths were for drug-related reasons) and that higher category numbers reflected greater likelihood that fathers were unavailable. Agreement between two coders for all of the interviews was 84%.

### Child Outcomes

The Bayley Scales of Infant Development (Bayley 1969) were used to assess the child's mental development index (MDI) and physical development index (PDI) at twelve months of age. The scales were administered by a developmental psychologist with substantial previous experience in either Spanish or English, depending on the child's mother tongue.

Child behavior problems were measured with the Child Behavior Checklist (CBCL/2–3) at 28 to 36 months of age. This ninety-nine-item, mother-completed checklist yields scores for six syndromes: social withdrawal, depression, sleep problems, somatic problems, aggression, and destructive behavior; scores for two broader internalizing and externalizing dimensions; and a Total Behavior Problems score. Previous research has documented the reliability and validity of the CBCL/2–3 for lower- and middle-class samples (Achenbach 1992; Crawford and Lee 1991; Spiker et al. 1992) and with this sample in particular (Leadbeater and Bishop 1994).

## Results

### Father Involvement

For the eighty mothers with complete data at time 5, the involvement of the children's biological fathers with their children had declined over the three-year period of study from 77.5% at time 1 to 65.8% at time 3, and more substantially to 57.6% at time 5. Only four fathers described as initially not involved became involved by time 5.

Cross-tabulations and analyses of variance were used to compare involved ($N = 46$) and uninvolved fathers ($N = 34$) at time 5; these analyses yielded few significant differences. Both involved and uninvolved fathers had completed an average of grade eleven by the time their children were one year old, and they averaged twenty years of age ($SD$ = 3 years) when their children were born. At time 5 about half of each group had high school diplomas or equivalents (48.8% of involved and 55.2% of uninvolved), and 67.4% of involved fathers worked at least part time compared to 57.1% of uninvolved fathers. Mothers were equally likely to be receiving welfare at time 5 regardless of whether the father was involved (65.2%) or uninvolved (73.5%). Involvement was unrelated to the mothers' race or ethnicity in this sample. Fathers who remained involved were more likely to have contributed materially or financially to the children by one year of age (86.7%) than those who were not involved (50%) ($X^2$ = 12.6, $p$ < .001). All of the seven fathers who were living with the adolescent mothers at twelve months postpartum remained involved with their child by time 5. Fathers of female children (69.4%) were significantly more likely to be involved than fathers of males (47.7%) ($X^2$ = 11.8, $p$ < .001).

At 28 to 36 months postpartum only 18.8% of the mothers indicated that there was no contact between the children and their fathers. Another 23.8% said contact was rare or highly irregular and the quality of the relationship was poor; 12.5% indicated that their children had occasional contact and poor relationships with their fathers; 18.8% of the mothers indicated that their children saw their fathers regularly and had mediocre relationships; and 26.7% said their children saw their fathers on a weekly or daily basis and had close relationships. On the other hand, only 25.7% of the mothers described their own relationships with these fathers as close. An additional 41% were in a close relationship with a new romantic partner. The majority of the mothers (67.5%) were neither married nor planned to be.

The mothers' descriptions of problems encountered in their relationships with their children's fathers give some insight into why they did not remain involved with their children's fathers. Only 19.5% of the seventy-nine mothers reported no problems. The others said their children's fathers were immature, irresponsible, or seeing other women (32%); excessively macho, restrictive, or physically abusive (11.5%); selling or using drugs (14%); in jail (19.2%); or dead (3.8%).

## Outcomes for the Children

As shown in table 11.1, the children's cognitive and motor development at twelve months postpartum were not significantly related to the presence or absence of fathers' involvement prospectively (at time 1) or

TABLE II.I
*Mean Scores for Children with Involved and Noninvolved Fathers*

| | Involved N = 46 | Not involved N = 34 | t-statistics | p-value | N |
|---|---|---|---|---|---|
| Time 3[a] | | | | | |
| Mental development | 108 (SD = 12.2) | 108 (SD = 13.5) | ns | | 101 |
| Physical development | 106 (SD = 13.6) | 110 (SD = 13.1) | ns | | 101 |
| Time 5[a] | | | | | |
| CBCL (externalizing) | 26.8 (SD = 12.5) | 19.9 (SD = 9.9) | −2.63 | .01 | 79 |
| CBCL (internalizing) | 9.0 (SD = 5.5) | 7.0 (SD = 4.2) | −1.69 | .09 | 79 |

NOTES: [a]Cell numbers reflect occasional missing data.
CBCL = Child Behavior Checklist.

concurrently (at time 3). Levels of cognitive and motor development were also not significantly associated with the father's age ($r = -.11$ and .01) and educational attainment ($r = .01$ and 13).

Level of child problem behaviors at the 28-to-36 month period was related to the fathers' concurrent involvement (presence or absence) at time 5 (see table 11.1). Children of involved fathers had higher externalizing scores on the CBCL/2–3 than those with uninvolved fathers. A hierarchical regression equation was computed to assess the relative contributions of father involvement after accounting for the child's sex and the mother's race and ethnicity. (To facilitate interpretation of the findings, data for mothers identifying themselves as "other" for race/ethnicity ($N = 3$) were excluded from these analyses.) Maternal depressive symptoms were entered into the equation to control for possible negative reporting bias in the mothers' responses. This equation explained 23.6% of the variance in the children's externalizing behaviors ($F(4, 71) = 5.47$, $p < .001$). Results are displayed in table 11.2. Both being black and having higher levels of depressive symptoms contributed significantly to the explained variance, as expected. Greater father involvement also added significantly to the explained variance (5%). Follow-up analyses indicate that this model may be better at explaining data for the children of Hispanic ($N = 32$) than black ($N = 44$) adolescent mothers (see table

TABLE II.2
*Hierarchical Multiple Regression Analysis for Predictors of Children's Externalizing Behaviors*

| Step | Multiple R | R-square | R-square change | F change | Sig F change | Beta |
|---|---|---|---|---|---|---|
| 1. Ethnicity/race | .28 | .08 | .08 | 6.07 | .02 | .28 |
| 2. Child's sex | .29 | .09 | .01 | .94 | .33 | .11 |
| 3. Depressive symptoms | .43 | .18 | .09 | 8.19 | .005 | .31 |
| 4. Father's involvement | .48 | .23 | .05 | 5.07 | .02 | .24 |

For equation $F(4, 71) = 5.47$, $p < .001$

TABLE 11.3

*Hierarchical Multiple Regression Analysis for Predictors of Children's Externalizing Behaviors Separately for Black and Puerto Rican Families*

| Step | Multiple R | R-square | R-square change | F change | Sig F change | Beta |
|------|-----------|----------|-----------------|----------|--------------|------|
| Black families[a] | | | | | | |
| 1. Child's sex | .07 | .00 | .00 | ns | | − .08 |
| 2. Depressive symptoms | .17 | .03 | .03 | ns | | .16 |
| 3. Father's involvement | .25 | .06 | .03 | ns | | .17 |
| Puerto Rican families[b] | | | | | | |
| 1. Child's sex | .37 | .14 | .14 | 4.90 | .03 | .37 |
| 2. Depressive symptoms | .58 | .33 | .19 | 8.41 | .01 | .46 |
| 3. Father's involvement | .64 | .41 | .08 | 3.71 | .06 | .32 |

[a] For the equation $F_{(3,40)} = .86, p = .48$
[b] For the equation $F_{(3,28)} = 6.53, p = .002$

11.3); however, the small sample size for both groups suggests that caution should be used in this interpretation.

### Factors Influencing Children's Outcomes

To determine why the children with involved fathers were more likely than those with less involved fathers to exhibit externalizing behaviors, we returned to the adolescent mothers' interview data. Our qualitative data analysis focused exclusively on those interviews in which the mothers described their children's fathers as having regular, daily or weekly contact with their children (44.3% of the fathers). We examined specifically the mother's descriptions of her own and her child's relationships with the father. Content analyses of the data suggest three primary reasons for the association between father involvement and the children's externalizing behaviors: (1) there was considerable hostility and conflict in the relationship between the adolescent mother and the child's father (44.1%); (2) the adolescent mother and the child's father exhibited inconsistent parenting styles—the mother was typically the limit setter, whereas the father set few or no limits with the child (26.4%); and (3) the involved father's relationship with the child was compromised by the father's problematic behaviors (e.g., drug dealing) (12%). These three patterns frequently overlapped. For example, those parents who had considerable hostility and conflict in their relationship also commonly exhibited inconsistent parenting styles. Detecting one of these patterns in the father–adolescent mother relationship did not exclude the other patterns. Nineteen percent of the mothers indicated none of these patterns in their interviews. In the remainder of this chapter, we will elaborate on each of these three patterns.

According to mothers who described their own relationships with the fathers as being considerably hostile and conflictual (44.1%, $N = 15$), complex issues frequently arose with the father concerning visiting arrangements, financial support, and discipline. Of the involved fathers, 81% did not live with the mothers and their children. The tension and hostility between the mother and the father in many of these families was often severe and potentially extremely disruptive for the child. An example of this pattern is found in Eva's family. Eva, recently separated from her husband, lives with her sister-in-law. Her husband lives with their child and his own mother. Eva says:

Well, the reason that I separated from him was he liked to have a lot of girlfriends and I don't like that you know. I had talked to him and he would say he was sorry but then he would do it again. So I just got fed up and I don't think I'm worth that. So, I just left him.

Eva says that she and her husband are currently fighting over custody of their daughter. She believes that her husband loves his daughter, and she acknowledges that he spends time with her almost every day. However, she says he is not a responsible father because "all he thinks about is going out with his friends."

Such relational difficulties were typical among the adolescent mothers and the involved fathers. The adolescent mothers spoke of "hating" their child's father and of feeling "really hurt by" or very angry at him. However, many also believed that their children "should" have a close relationship with their fathers and that a father "should" be involved in his children's lives—a wish often fueled by the absence of a father in their own lives. Studies of divorced families have demonstrated that parental conflict before and after separation has a negative impact on the child's functioning (Hetherington and Clingempeel 1992; Miller et al. 1993). Numerous research projects have also documented associations between marital conflict, negative parenting behaviors, and problematic child behaviors (see Belsky and Vondra 1989; Miller et al. 1993). In addition, marital conflict has been shown to have a negative effect on the quality of the mother's and father's interactions with their children (Belsky and Vondra 1989). In the fragile, changing relationships of these adolescent mothers and fathers, the potential for conflict may be particularly high.

A second possible explanation for the association between father involvement and child problem behaviors relates to different disciplinary styles. Both mothers who were close with their children's fathers and those who were not described differences in indulgence and limit setting between themselves and the fathers of their children. These mothers complained that the fathers were "spoiling" their children by buying them anything they wanted or allowing them to do whatever they wanted. Some mothers specifically stated that when the children returned home from seeing their fathers, they were frequently uncooperative and unwilling to listen to them. This appeared particularly common for the fathers of female children (described by one mother as the father's "little princess"). For example, Sonia says her daughter's father sees his daughter frequently. She is frustrated, however, by his behavior with their daughter:

[My daughter's] father is nice. If I need something for her he gets it for her. If I need money he gives it to me. But he also, . . . like tries to buy [his daughter's] love. . . . Or tries to get it by giving her anything she wants. You know like when Mamma says no, Daddy says yes, like that. That makes me mad because sometimes she don't need it and sometimes you have to say no to the child. He never says no to her. I think that's why when she wants something she always asks him first 'cause she knows she'll get it. . . . That also sending her [the wrong] messages. . . . I don't like that.

The problems related to this splitting between indulgence and limit setting can also be exacerbated by other family members. For example, Tina lives with her grandmother and grandfather (her mother died when she was young), and she has a very close relationship with the child's father. The father visits daily. Tina describes her daughter as "spoiled rotten" by the child's father, grandmother, and grandfather:

If she asks me can she have something, if I say no, she'll go and ask her father can she have it and he'll give it to her. Else she'll do the same thing with my grandmother [or grandfather]. If I tell her no, she'll go and ask somebody else knowing that they gonna give it to her. . . . Whatever the little girl wants she can have.

The mothers typically had the roles of day-to-day disciplinarian and limit setter. The fathers, who commonly did not live with the children, often set few or no limits with them. The majority (62%) of the adolescent mothers also lived with older extended family members who could simultaneously increase the likelihood of variable limit setting and undermine the mothers' parental authority (see Apfel and Seitz, chap. 9 of this volume).

The parent-child role conflict between adolescent mothers and their own mothers and their mutual struggle for parental authority over the child has been written about extensively (Chase-Lansdale, Brooks-Gunn, and Zamsky 1994). Faced with such inconsistent limit setting, children often become unclear about the limits to their negative behaviors. Children whose fathers are not involved in their lives are less likely to receive conflicting messages about the rules and limits concerning unacceptable behaviors. Some previous research, reviewed by McLoyd (1990), suggests that low income fathers who do not reside with their families may be more indulgent with their infants than are resident fathers. Fathers who do not reside with their children can afford to be more affectionate and solicitous without the additional demands of the male provider role. Previous research has indicated that less control on the part of the fathers frequently leads to more externalizing behaviors among their children (Miller et al. 1993).

A third explanation for higher levels of externalizing behavior among children of involved fathers that was apparent in the interview data was related to problematic behaviors exhibited by the fathers. Only four (12%) of the mothers indicated such problems. These mothers variously described the involved father as "extremely jealous of the attention the child receives," or "continually arguing with his three year old child," or "addicted to drugs." In addition, Pam says her daughter feels very close to and sees her father frequently; however, she also mentions that her child's father is "really" depressed: "I guess [my child's father] had a really bad father. . . . His father was really cruel . . . wouldn't let them go outside when they were boys. He would abuse his children. So I guess [my child's father] still has that in his mind and I think he is still really depressed about it. He's a very depressed person." Although more research has addressed the consequences of maternal depression on child resilience and problem behaviors, paternal depression, in which inconsistent behavior and discipline toward the child are the results of the father's mood changes, is also known to contribute to child problem behaviors (McLoyd 1990).

Finally, it is important to emphasize that the degree or type of involvement of fathers of the children of adolescent mothers did not inevitably predict child problem behaviors. The amount of independent variance explained by father involvement in our data is in fact quite low. There are also examples in our interview data of adolescent parents who have clearly created a positive environment for their child. When Roshaunna describes the relationship between her child's father and her child, she speaks of the child's father with great admiration: "He takes time to read to her at night. He takes time to sit down and explain to her that when she does something wrong that it's wrong instead of screaming at her, or you know, or lashing at the kid. It, you know, makes me feel good." Nineteen percent of the mothers indicated that there were no problems in either their own relationships or their children's relationships with their fathers.

## Discussion

Previous findings for this sample indicate that father involvement is associated with fewer depressive symptoms in inner-city adolescent mothers at least in the first year postpartum (Leadbeater and Linares 1992). However, the effects of their involvement for their children may not be uniformly positive. Even after controlling for levels of depressive symptoms in the mothers, father involvement is associated with higher levels of externalizing problem behaviors in their children. In contrast to previous work showing that the presence of a male partner was associated with better cognitive stimulation for the children of black and Caucasian adolescent mothers (Cooley and Unger 1991), cognitive and physical development for the children in this sample were unrelated to involvement of their biological fathers.

Our qualitative findings suggest that the level of parental conflict, as well as inconsistent disciplinary practices, may explain the high levels of externalizing behaviors for those children whose fathers are involved in their lives. Educational programs focusing on enhancing parenting skills and stressing the importance of consistent discipline and limit setting may help. These parenting dynamics, however, are unlikely to be mere reflections of a lack of information about effective parenting skills. Rather, they are related to the more complex effects of poverty, stress, and psychological well-being on parenting (McLoyd 1990). Severe conflict in these frequently fragile relationships, negotiating visiting rather than live-in relationships, and dealing with the stress of poverty and unemployment may all contribute to inconsistent parenting styles and behaviors. As suggested in previous research (see Miller et al. 1993), interventions that help parents improve the quality of their relationship and their own adjustment may benefit not only their relationship but also their child's development.

Recent increases in the numbers of children who live in poverty (Strawn 1992), as well as simultaneous increases in births to fifteen- to nineteen-year-olds demand renewed attention to the fathers of the children of adolescent mothers. The effects of father involvement when there is little conflict and much affection in the parent's relationship needs to be studied. We also need to gain a better understanding of the effects of drug use, addiction, or drug trafficking by the fathers on the adolescent mothers and their families: disadvantages that stem from these activities (such as imprisonment and missed educational opportunities) decrease the possibilities for constructive involvement of the fathers. Such problems also compound the likelihood that these children will live in poverty by

limiting the probability of increasing the couple's financial security through marriage. For some young fathers, unemployment, relationships with new partners, restrictive or abusive behaviors, or drug-related crimes severely limit the likelihood that they will become long-term sources of support to their children.

Several of the adolescent mothers in the sample described the "ideal man" as a "provider" and "someone who accepts and is there for me and my child." The problems the mothers describe, together with high levels of unemployment among urban ethnic minority males, suggest that this ideal individual is not common in their social networks. Unemployment, underemployment, and declining earnings undermine these young men's ability to provide for their families (Adams, Pittman, and O'Brien 1993). Marriage, for adolescent mothers, is too often not a viable alternative. Many mothers also expressed their reluctance to become involved in new relationships, since, as one mother says: "I just came out of one relationship that ended bad, so I can't see myself in another one." The long-term effects of involvement in new relationships for both the mothers and their children are uncertain and indicate the need for follow-up research.

Most important, perhaps, is the need to question our standard conceptualization of unwed adolescent mothers as single parents. Our research demonstrates that this conceptualization inadequately represents the complexity of their family structures. Indeed, a majority of the biological fathers remained involved up to three years after the delivery. Moreover, many of the adolescent mothers believe the biological fathers *should* be involved with their children, and they try to foster the father's ties with the child. Our findings suggest a need to move beyond the limiting and potentially harmful stereotype of the absent, neglectful father. We need to reconceptualize our theories about adolescent mothers to take into account the problems experienced by adolescent mothers *and* fathers as they struggle to become economically and residentially independent at the same time as they are negotiating their transition to parenthood in the context of poverty, unemployment, and multigenerational families.

REFERENCES

The dedicated assistance of L. Oriana Linares and Pam M. Kato in data collection are acknowledged with appreciation. Our continuing thanks to all mothers who participated in the study. This research was supported in part by a grant from Smith-Richardson Foundation and a William T. Grant Faculty Scholars Award to Bonnie J. Ross Leadbeater.

Achenbach, T. M. 1992. *Manual for the Child Behavior Checklist/2–3 and 1992 profile.* Burlington, Vt.: University of Vermont Department of Psychiatry.

Adams, G., K. Pittman, and R. O'Brien. 1993. Adolescent and young adult fathers: Problems and solutions. In *The politics of pregnancy,* edited by A. Lawson and D. Rhodes, 216–37. New Haven: Yale University Press.

Bayley, N. 1969. *Manual for the Bayley Scales of Infant Development*. New York: Psychological Corp.

Beck, A. 1967. *Depression: Causes and treatment*. Philadelphia: University of Pennsylvania Press.

Belsky, J., and J. Vondra. 1989. Lessons from child abuse: The determinates of parenting. In *Child Maltreatment,* edited by D. Ciccetti and V. Carlson. New York: Cambridge University Press.

Brooks-Gunn, J., and F. F. Furstenberg. 1986. The children of adolescent mothers: Physical, academic, and psychological outcomes. *Developmental Review* 6:224–51.

Chase-Lansdale, P. L., J. Brooks-Gunn, and E. Zamsky. 1994. Young African-American multigenerational families in poverty: Quality of mothering and grandmothering. *Child Development* 65 (2):373–93.

Chase-Lansdale, P. L., and M. A. Vinovskis. 1987. Should we discourage teenage marriage? *Public Interest* 87:23–27.

Children's Defense Fund. 1994. Adolescent Pregnancy Prevention and Youth Development. In *The State of America's Children*. Washington, D.C.: Children's Defense Fund.

Cooley, M. L., and D. G. Unger. 1991. The role of family support in determining developmental outcomes in children of teen mothers. *Child Psychiatry and Human Development* 21:217–34.

Crawford, L., and S. W. Lee. 1991. Test-retest reliability of the Child Behavior Checklist ages 2–3. *Psychological Reports* 69:496–98.

Crockenberg, S. 1987. Predictors and correlates of anger toward and punitive control of toddlers by adolescent mothers. *Child Development* 58:964–75.

Elster, A. B., and M. E. Lamb, eds. 1986. *Adolescent Fatherhood*. Hillsdale, N.J.: Lawrence Erlbaum Associates.

Furstenberg, F. F., J. Brooks-Gunn, and S. P. Morgan. 1987. *Adolescent mothers in later life*. Cambridge: Cambridge University Press.

Furstenberg, F. F., and K. M. Harris. 1993. When fathers matter/Why fathers matter: The impact of paternal involvement on the offspring of adolescent mothers. In *The politics of pregnancy,* edited by A. Lawson and D. Rhodes, 189–209. New Haven: Yale University Press.

Garcia Coll, C. T. 1990. Developmental outcome of minority infants: A process-oriented look into our beginnings. *Child Development* 61:270–89.

Garcia Coll, C. T., J. Hoffman, and W. Oh. 1987. The social context of teenage childbearing: Effects on the infant's care-giving environment. *Journal of Youth and Adolescence* 16:345–60.

Hetherington, E. M., and W. G. Clingempeel. 1992. Coping with marital transition. *Monographs of the Society for Research in Child Development,* vol. 57, nos. 2–3, serial no. 227.

Kaplan, H. S., J. Lancaster, J. A. Bock, and S. E. Johnson. 1994. Manuscript. University of New Mexico, Albuquerque.

Kissman, K. 1990. Social support and gender role attitude among teenage mothers. *Adolescence* 99:709–16.

Lamb, M. E., ed. 1988. *The father's role: Applied perspectives*. New York: John Wiley.

Lawson, A., and D. Rhodes, eds. 1993. *The politics of pregnancy*. New Haven: Yale University Press.

Leadbeater, B. J. In press. School outcomes for minority group adolescent mothers at 28 to 36 months postpartum: A longitudinal follow-up. *Journal of Research on Adolescence*.

Leadbeater, B. J., and S. J. Bishop. 1994. Predictors of behavior problems in pre-school children of inner-city Afro-American and Puerto Rican adolescent mothers. *Child Development* 65:638–48.

Leadbeater, B. J., S. J. Blatt, and D. M. Quinlan. 1995. Gender-linked vulnerabilities to depressive symptoms, stress, and problem behaviors in adolescents. *Journal of Research on Adolescence* 5:1–29.

Leadbeater, B. J., and O. Linares. 1992. Depressive symptoms in black and Puerto Rican adolescent mothers in the first 3 years postpartum. *Development and Psychopathology* 4:451–68.

Linares, L. O., B. J. Leadbeater, P. M. Kato, and L. Jaffe. 1991. Predicting school outcomes for minority group adolescent mothers: Can subgroups be identified? *Journal of Research on Adolescence* 1:379–400.

Marsiglio, W. 1987. Adolescent fathers in the United States: Their initial living arrangements, marital experience, and educational outcomes. *Family Planning Perspectives* 19 (6):240–51.

McLoyd, V. C. 1990. The impact of economic hardship on black families and children: Psychological distress, parenting, and socioemotional development. *Child Development* 61:311–46.

Miller, N. B., P. A. Cowan, C. P. Cowan, E. M. Hetherington, and W. G. Clingempeel. 1993. Externalizing in preschoolers and early adolescents: A cross-study replication of a family model. *Developmental Psychology* 29:3–18.

Nathanson, C. A. 1991. *Dangerous passage. The social control of sexuality in women's adolescence.* Philadelphia: Temple University Press.

National Institute for Child Health and Human Development. 1990. *Adolescent pregnancy and childbearing: Rates, trends, and research findings.* Washington, D.C.: U.S. Government Printing Office.

Osofsky, J. D., D. M. Hann, and C. Peebles. 1993. Adolescent parenthood: Risks and opportunities for mothers and infants. In *Handbook of Infant Mental Health*, edited by C. H. Zeanah, Jr., 106–19. New York: Guilford Press.

Presser, H. B. 1989. Some economic complexities of childcare provided by grandmothers. *Journal of Marriage and the Family* 51:581–92.

Sander, J. H., and J. L. Rosen. 1987. Teenage fathers: Working with the neglected partner in adolescent childbearing. *Family Planning Perspectives* 19:107–10.

Spicker, S. J., and L. Bensley. 1994. Roles of living arrangements and grandmother social support in adolescent mothering and infant attachment. *Developmental Psychology* 30:102–11.

Spiker, D., H. C. Kraemer, N. A. Constantine, and D. Bryant. 1992. Reliability, validity of behavior problem checklists as measures of stable traits in low birth weight, premature, preschoolers. *Child Development* 63:1481–96.

Strawn, J. 1992. The states and the poor: Child poverty rises as the safety net shrinks. *Social Policy Report, Society for Research in Child Development* 6:1–19.

Unger, D. G., and M. Cooley. 1992. Partner and grandmother contact in black and white teen parent families. *Journal of Adolescent Health* 13:546–52.

Unger, D. G., and L. P. Wandersman. 1988. The relation of family and partner support to the adjustment of adolescent mothers. *Child Development* 59:1056–60.

Wasserman, G. A., V. A. Rauh, S. A. Brunelli, M. Garcia-Castro, and B. Necos. 1990. Psychosocial attributes and life experiences of disadvantaged minority mothers: Age and ethnic variations. *Child Development* 61:566–80.

Watson, B. J., C. L. Rowe, and D. J. Jones. 1989. Dispelling myths about teenage pregnancy and male responsibility: A research agenda. *Urban League Review* (Summer–Winter):119–27.

# IV

# Mentoring Relationships

As teachers, coaches, friends, and extended family members, nonparent adults or mentors have long played a central role in structuring adolescents' daily life experiences. Research concerning these relationships, however, is relatively new. A better understanding of how such individuals can affirm (or disconfirm) adolescent girls' talents and strengths would clearly assist in the reconceptualization of resources and interventions that could help to support the development of girls.

Rhodes and Davis's chapter (chapter 12) presents research findings that affirm the positive influence of natural and volunteer mentors for pregnant and parenting urban adolescent girls. Findings from their longitudinal studies of African American girls suggest that natural mentors enhance girls' ability to appreciate the positive aspects of their social support networks, cope with problems in their family relationships, and pursue activities related to their career goals. The research with volunteer mentors also points to their success in enhancing outcomes for some adolescent mothers, but it raises questions about the ability of volunteers to sustain enduring and influential relationships that emulate the positive effects of natural mentors.

In chapter 13, Sullivan contrasts the traditional role of mentor as one who teaches or acts as a role model or father figure for the inexperienced apprentice with the role of the muse as one who listens, understands, respects, and validates the knowledge, experiences, and feelings of a young person. From her qualitative interviews with eighth grade urban girls, Sullivan argues that the latter types of relationships with nonparenting adults may be especially beneficial in supporting the resources that adolescent girls have within themselves to speak about their own ideas and to assertively participate in creating their own futures.

# 12

# Supportive Ties between Nonparent Adults and Urban Adolescent Girls

## Jean E. Rhodes and Anita B. Davis

Adolescents who have adjusted well in spite of profound, ongoing stress often attribute their success to the influence of a natural mentor, such as a special aunt, neighbor, or teacher. Anecdotal reports of mentors' protective qualities are corroborated by a growing body of literature that has underscored the positive influence of nonparent adults in the lives of adolescents. Despite the promise of mentoring, as well as the recent growth in volunteer programs, many questions remain concerning the nature and effects of mentor relationships. This chapter presents findings from an ongoing investigation of the influence of mentors on pregnant and parenting minority adolescent girls. Preliminary results from a mentoring intervention are also presented. Implications of these findings for future research and preventive intervention are discussed.

## Background

Although adolescents' relationships with their parents have been the subject of extensive research, few studies have examined the role of nonparent adults. Nonetheless, such adults appear to be quite prominent in the lives of adolescents (Bryant 1985; Coates 1987; Galbo 1986; Hirsch et al. 1994; Gottlieb and Sylvestre 1994). Garbarino and his colleagues (1978), for example, found that adults other than parents comprised 22.3% of all persons listed by adolescents as significant others. Similarly, Blyth, Hill, and Thiel (1982) found that nonparent adults comprised 25.8% of adolescents boys' social networks and 27.2% of adolescent girls' social networks.

Relationships with adults appear to be especially important for adolescent girls (Konopka 1986; Strommen 1977). Gilligan contends that "relationships between girls and adult women may be particularly critical during the transition into adolescence," because girls at this juncture are eager to "seek out and listen attentively to advice from women" ("Girls at 11" 1990, 6). In this capacity the adults may play a critical role in mediating adolescent girls' paradoxical needs for both independence and guidance. With adults other than their parents, adolescents can gain some autonomy while simultaneously obtaining needed emotional support and advice (Allen, Aber, and Leadbeater 1990). Chodorow also notes the influential role of adults in the lives of adolescent girls. From childhood, girls are more likely than boys to participate in an intergenerational world with their mothers, including their grandmothers, aunts, and other female kin. Older women "become mediators between mother and daughter, by providing a daughter with alternative models for personal identification and objects of attachment" (1992, 62).

These intergenerational relationships have long been recognized as an important resource in many urban African American communities (Martin and Martin 1978; Wilson 1986). Collins (1987), for example, has described the protective influence of African American women, referring to them as "othermothers." These women provide guidance to younger members of the community, often acting as surrogate parents. Woman-centered networks typically extend beyond the boundaries of biologically related extended families to include "community othermothers" and "fictive" kin (i.e., nonkin who have been absorbed into an existing family structure) (Collins 1987; Stack 1974).

Similarly, many Latino families are embedded in extended kinship systems that include not only blood relatives but other important adults as well (de Anda 1984; Escobar and Randolph 1982; Ramirez 1989). For example, godparents often function as substitute parents for children and adolescents *(padrinos/matrinas)* and as "co-parents" to young mothers *(compadres/commadres)* (Mindel 1980; Sena-Rivera 1979; Becerra and de Anda 1984). These relationships are often formalized through the ritual of infant baptism, which obligates godparents to provide the children and their families with economic assistance, encouragement, and guidance (Garcia-Preto 1982). "Child-keeping," or the informal fostering of children, is common in both African American and Latino families (Dore and Dumois 1990).

Despite their prominence, little is known about the role that these intergenerational ties play in the lives of urban adolescent girls. In the following sections we present results from a series of studies on supportive relationships between urban African American and Latina adolescent girls and nonparent adults. Most of our work has been conducted with pregnant and parenting minority adolescents—young women who are particularly receptive to adult support and guidance (Hayes 1987). We also describe an intervention program that is currently under way, in which pregnant minority adolescents are being paired with volunteer adult mentors.

## Conceptual Framework

Our work on mentoring has been driven by the concept of resilience. Investigators of resilience attempt to understand youth who have adjusted well despite profound, ongoing stress associated with poverty and hazardous life circumstances. Within this context nonparent adults and other extrafamilial sources of support have been consistently identified as contributing to resilience (Cowen and Work 1988; Garmezy and Neuchterlein 1972; Luthar and Zigler 1991; Rutter 1979, 1987). Werner and Smith (1982), for example, conducted a longitudinal investigation of children who were exposed to poverty, biological risks, and family instability. Children who developed into competent and autonomous young adults showed an ability to locate an adult in addition to their parents for support. Werner noted that "without exception, all the children who thrived had at least one person who provided them with consistent emotional support—a grandmother, an older sister, a teacher, or neighbor" (cited in Goleman 1987).

These findings raise a number of important questions concerning the influence and characteristics of nonparent adult relationships. For example, it is unclear whether such relationships actually contribute to better functioning or whether they are simply correlated with this outcome (i.e., resilient youth may have the social skills to better seek out support). Similarly, it is not known whether nonparent relationships supplement healthy parental bonds or compensate for their absence. It is also important to consider the extent to which these relationships can be arranged through volunteer mentoring programs. Our research is attempting to address these and related issues.

## Current Studies

In a preliminary investigation, the influence of nonparent adults, or natural mentors, on the adjustment of 129 African American adolescent mothers was examined (Rhodes, Ebert, and Fischer 1992). The literature on mentoring (e.g., Bronfenbrenner 1986 [cited in Hamilton 1990]; Levinson et al. 1979) served as a basis for our definition of a natural mentor. The mothers were asked, "Other than your parents or whoever raised you, is there an older person in your life (a mentor or positive role model) who you go to for support and guidance?" Four characteristics of the relationship were then listed as criteria for persons to be nominated as mentors. These included (1) that you can count on this person to be there for you, (2) that he or she believes in you and cares deeply about you, (3) that he or she inspires you to do your best, and (4) that knowing him or her has really influenced what you do and the choices that you make. Participants who nominated natural mentors were then asked how long and in what capacity they had known them, what the qualities and importance of the relationships had been, and what had been their frequency of interaction.

Several additional measures were employed, including the depression subscale of a self-report symptom inventory (the SCL-90-R) (Derogatis 1983) and a checklist of major stressors occurring in the past year (Life Events Survey) (Sarason, Johnson, and Siegel 1979). In addition participants' levels of economic strain (Pearlin et al. 1981) and social network characteristics (Rhodes et al. 1994) were assessed. Participants were asked to nominate individuals from whom various types of support (i.e., tangible, emotional, social, cognitive, instrumental, or child care) were elicited in the past month, to rate their satisfaction with this support and to cite any problems that they experienced in their relationships (i.e., conflict, disappointment, criticism, or intrusiveness). The amount of support was calculated as the total number of persons who were nominated as providing support. (Further details about the measures and procedures are reported in Rhodes, Ebert, and Fischer 1992).

Forty-five percent of the participants in this study nominated natural mentors, ranging from their boyfriends' female relatives to their grandmothers, aunts and uncles, older friends, sisters, teachers, church staff, counselors, and neighbors. Most (85%) of the mentors were women, over half (53%) lived in the same neighborhood as the adolescent, and 95% were seen at least once per week. Adolescents with and without mentors were exposed to comparable levels of life stress and economic strain and, when mentor support was removed from the analyses, there were no group differences in the amount of social support that was available to the participants. Nonetheless, adolescents with mentors were less depressed than adolescents without mentors ($t = 2.00, p < .05$).

In the next set of analyses, we sought to further understand the processes by which mentors may be associated with lower levels of depression. Hierarchical multiple regression analyses revealed that for participants with mentors both the amount of social support (mentor support excluded) and satisfaction with this support were negatively related to depression. Problems with network members did not predict depression in this group. For participants without mentors, however, neither the amount of social support nor satisfaction with this support was related to depression. Instead, those who reported greater problems in relationships reported higher levels of depression (see table 12.1).

Similar findings emerged in a study of mentoring relationships among adolescent Latina (predominantly Puerto Rican and Mexican) mothers (Rhodes, Contreras, and Mangelsdorf 1994). Thirty-five percent of the participants in the study nominated natural mentors, most of whom (89%) were women. Most of the participants (94.7%) interacted with their mentors at least once per week, nearly half (46.4%) had known their mentors for at least sixteen years, and most (84.2%) expected to maintain the relationships for the rest of their lives. Despite similar levels of stress exposure and overall support (mentor support excluded), adolescents with mentors reported lower levels of depression ($t = 2.00$, $p < .05$) and anxiety ($t = 2.15$, $p < .05$) and greater satisfaction with support resources ($t = -2.00$, $p < .05$). A hierarchical multiple regression analysis, performed only with mentored adolescents, revealed that mentor support was not significantly associated with symptomology levels. As in the previous study, hierarchial multiple regression analyses were then run separately for participants with and without mentors. For the group with mentors, none of the predictor variables (i.e., amount of support, satisfaction with support, problems in relationships) were related to anxiety or depression. For the group without mentors, however, relationship problems significantly predicted anxiety and depression (see table 12.2).

In both studies mentor relationships appeared to provide adolescent girls with a context for understanding relationship problems. This pattern is consistent with Collins's observations concerning othermothers, who "often play a central role in defusing the emotional intensity between bloodmothers and their daughters" (1987, 8).

TABLE 12.1

*Hierarchical Multiple Regression Analysis for African American Mothers with and without Mentors*

| | Degree of symptomatology | | | |
| | Mentor | | No mentor | |
| Predictor variables | Beta | $R^2$ chg | Beta | $R^2$ chg |
| --- | --- | --- | --- | --- |
| Step 1: Amount of support | −.28 | .08[a] | −.16 | .001 |
| Step 2: Satisfaction with support | −.41 | .16[b] | −.13 | .017 |
| Step 3: Relationship problems | .12 | .013 | .43 | .17[a] |
| Step 4: Support × problems | .34 | .001 | 1.0 | .035 |
| | Overall $R$-square = .26[b] | | Overall $R$-square = .24[b] | |
| | $F = 4.66$[b] | | $F = 5.21$[b] | |

SOURCE: Rhodes, Ebert, and Fischer 1992.
[a] $p < .05$
[b] $p < .01$

TABLE 12.2

*Hierarchical Multiple Regression Analysis for Latina Mothers with and without Mentors*

| | Degree of symptomatology | | | |
| | Mentor | | No mentor | |
| Predictor variables | Beta | $R^2$ chg | Beta | $R^2$ chg |
|---|---|---|---|---|
| Step 1: Amount of support | −.16 | .03 | −.029 | .00 |
| Step 2: Satisfaction with support | .002 | .00 | −.088 | .01 |
| Step 3: Relationship problems | .11 | .01 | .351 | .12[a] |
| | Overall $R$-square = .04 | | Overall $R$-square = .13 | |
| | $F$ = .208 | | $F$ = 1.54 | |

SOURCE: Rhodes, Contreras, and Mangelsdorf 1994.

[a] = $p < .05$

Mentors may enhance the young women's capacity to elicit and appreciate the positive aspects of their social support networks and more effectively cope with relationship problems.

The latter study also provided some insights into factors that may have led certain youths to be responsive to or even seek out the support and guidance of natural mentors. Although the young women with and without mentors were equally satisfied with their current maternal relationships, those with mentors reported feeling more accepted by their mothers when they were younger ($t = -2.20$, $p < .05$). This suggests that their early primary relationships may have predisposed them to develop later mentor relationships.

Participants, whether or not they had mentors, perceived equal levels of support and problems in their maternal relationships. Mentors, then, may not be compensating for these unsatisfactory maternal relationships but may instead be supplementing the participants' support resources. Similarly, in both studies participants with and without mentors perceived equal levels of overall support and problems, suggesting that the differences in depression and anxiety were not a function of increased support resources among participants with mentors. Thus, having a mentor does not appear to be simply a proxy for greater social competence.

Taken together, the results of these studies provide some insights into the circumstances surrounding the formation of mentor relationships and the underlying processes by which they influence psychological adjustment. We have also attempted to examine the extent to which natural mentors are associated with vocational outcomes (Klaw and Rhodes in press). This line of research is particularly relevant because, as young minority women approach early adulthood, they often experience a widening gap between their career aspirations and their actual expectations. Mentors can sometimes serve as credible role models and alter young women's beliefs about available opportunities (Bowman 1991; Hamilton and Hamilton 1990; Mickelson 1990; Schmidt and Wolfe 1980). We found that African American adolescents who identified natural mentors were more likely to be engaged in activities related to their career goals. Moreover, mentor support was associated with the girls' belief in education as a link to opportunities and with their heightened optimism about the future (Klaw and Rhodes in press).

## Implications

Although these findings are promising for those adolescents with natural mentors, a larger proportion of adolescents in each study did not identify natural mentors. To address the needs of these young women, it might be worthwhile to pair them with volunteer mentors. Rather than attempting to substitute for problematic support figures, volunteer mentors might teach young mothers strategies for minimizing the escalation of relationship problems or offsetting their deleterious effects. In doing so, volunteer mentors might offer adolescents some of the protection that natural mentors seem to afford.

Hundreds of mentoring programs, modeled after the Big Brothers/Big Sisters prototype, have emerged in the last few years. Many of these programs have been designed to meet the needs of pregnant and parenting adolescents. Although such programs tend to engender considerable enthusiasm, we know little about their effectiveness (Freedman 1993). Most evaluations have relied on participants' retrospective accounts (Carden 1990). Where participants have been compared to nonparticipants, it has been difficult to determine whether group differences were the result of self-selection (reflecting underlying motivational differences) or actual intervention effects.

It is also unclear whether assigned mentoring relationships can be as protective as natural mentor relationships. Whereas natural mentor relationships typically emerge from within the youth's social support system, assigned mentor relationships tend to be grafted onto the extant network. These and other differences are likely to influence the nature and course of the relationship.

To address these issues, we are currently conducting a longitudinal study at an alternative school for pregnant and parenting students, located in a low-income Chicago community. Every student in the school is being randomly assigned to an experimental (assigned mentor) or control (no mentor) condition. The assigned mentors are encouraged to meet with adolescents at least once per week. Both outcome data (adolescents' health, academic, and psychological functioning) and process data (mentor and adolescent relationship diaries) are being collected.

## Preliminary Results and Reflections

Although the study is still in its early stages, preliminary observations provide an opportunity for us to reflect on this intervention approach. First, we have seen some extraordinary examples of successful assigned mentor relationships. For example, Latrice, sixteen, describes what is clearly an important relationship with her assigned mentor of eleven months:

Patricia takes an interest in what I like and what I think—not because she has to but because she cares about me and my daughter. If she feels that I'm disturbed about something, we usually go for a walk and talk about what's on my mind. I really love our conversations because she listens to whatever I have to say and she doesn't think any less of me and she doesn't tell me how I should handle things. When Patricia introduced me to her family and friends she introduced me as her daughter—as one of her kids. It meant so much. Meeting Patricia is one of the best things that ever happened to me.

This example suggests that even after a relatively short time, assigned mentors may become as influential to adolescents as natural mentors. It also raises important questions about our definition of successful relationships and the measurement of outcomes. We often conceive of mentoring relationships in terms of their influence on young people's academic and career success. In one of the most influential works on mentoring, *The Seasons of a Man's Life* (Levinson et al. 1979), *mentor* is defined in terms of the person's role in facilitating men's career goals. From the perspective of these writers mentor relationships progress through predictable stages of intimacy, ultimately leading to a developmentally appropriate "crisis" and termination.

This conceptualization contrasts with many of the mentor relationships that we have observed, which tend to endure indefinitely and are not always oriented toward particular goals. In addition, the relationships often proceed quite slowly, marked by issues of trust and intimacy. This can been seen in fifteen-year-old Sonia's discussion of her natural mentor of five years:

I look up to her so much that there are times I would like to talk to her about something personal, but have too much respect for her thoughts to do so. What will she think of me? How would she feel about me asking her such things? Does she think that we're that close that I can talk to her about anything? These are questions that I constantly ask myself.

This insecurity is reminiscent of the themes that emerged in Brown and Gilligan's interviews (1992) with adolescent girls. Despite the girls' desire for connection and responsiveness, they often censored themselves—fearing that their openness might somehow jeopardize the relationship. Clearly, our understanding of mentoring and the assessment of outcomes need to encompass the complexity of adolescent girls' ways of being in relationship.

Our evaluations should also consider the benefits that adults may derive in their role as mentors. This course of inquiry is driven by Riessman's helper-therapy concept (1965), that is, that people help themselves through the process of being helpful to others. Many mentors have found that by helping an adolescent find solutions to her struggles with family, academic, and professional issues, they reinforce in themselves the positive messages they are trying to give and actually make progress on their own goals. The increased self-awareness (Brown and Gilligan 1992) and sense of empowerment (Roberts and Rappaport 1989) that derive from helping adolescents may well be a driving force in the positive changes that are often observed in mentors' lives. Although most discussions of mentoring acknowledge the benefits to the mentor, such benefits are typically viewed as an unexpected by-product. More recently researchers have begun to recognize mutual benefit as integral to the relationship (Healy and Welchert 1990; Sullivan, chap. 13 of this volume).

## Alternatives to Mentoring Programs

Despite some clear successes, our preliminary data also suggest that volunteer relationships may not be as influential or enduring as those that form naturally. For example, a sizable proportion (20%) of the volunteer relationships terminated after only a few months. High termination rates are common in mentoring programs and appear to be partially influenced by the expectations and characteristics of the volunteers. Whereas some mentors allow their partners to take an active role in determining the direction and activities of the relationship, others enter the project with a more rigid, prescriptive agenda (Styles and Morrow 1992).

Similarly, some young women complain that their mentors seem out of touch with their experiences and problems. This problem sometimes stems from the social distance that exists between middle-class volunteers and urban adolescent girls. Flaxman, Ascher, and Harrington have noted that in settings where middle-class adults are attempting to work with urban adolescents, the mentors' world can easily seem "irrelevant or even nonsensical" to the youngsters, "and their goals for mentees naive" (1988, 3). Adults who live or work in urban communities, and who are familiar with the circumstances confronting youth, are likely to be better able to give advice that is consistent with the cultural norms, options, and constraints of a given setting.

One implication of these observations is that, compared to assigning volunteer mentors, a more effective intervention approach may ultimately lie in teaching adolescents techniques for recruiting support from helpful adults within their own social networks. Potential natural mentors already exist in many extended families, schools, churches, and neighborhoods, but many girls are hesitant to approach them. With training and encouragement, adolescents might be taught techniques for identifying, meeting, and establishing relationships with existing sources of support (Balcazar and Fawcett 1992). Adolescents can then use their acquired skills to find different adults to assist them in dealing with various concerns over time.

Unfortunately, even when young women are predisposed toward finding mentors, settings are often structured in ways that discourage intergenerational contact, particularly for young women of color (Gottlieb and Sylvestre 1994; Hamilton 1991; Lipsitz 1977). Many professionals who work with urban adolescents are burdened with excessive classroom sizes or caseloads, leaving them with little time to develop meaningful individual relationships. Specific strategies, such as reducing the ratios between professionals and adolescents, might go a long way toward increasing the accessibility of natural mentors.

## Conclusions

Enthusiasm for any of these approaches to working with urban adolescent girls (assigned mentoring, recruitment training, and increasing natural mentor availability) must be tempered with realism about their potential limitations. As noted earlier, we found that individuals who did not already have natural mentors reported having experienced less accepting early relationships with their primary caregivers. This suggests that the adolescents who are perhaps most in need of mentors may, by virtue of their early relationships, be the least likely to trust the overtures of caring adults.

It is also important to consider that, although roughly 45% of the young women in our studies identified natural mentors, a far smaller proportion could be classified as truly "resilient." For example, at least 20% of the participants with mentors in our study have had subsequent unplanned pregnancies or have dropped out of school. This should come as no surprise. It is unrealistic to expect that one relationship can counter all of the stressors and negative influences confronting many urban adolescents. Until the basic resources in urban communities are improved—the schools, neighborhoods, health care settings, employment opportunities, and so forth—the influence of adult supports or any other supplementary resources on the life trajectories of most youths will remain limited.

On the other hand, we should not minimize mentors' potentially positive influences. Indeed, our findings and observations provide us with considerable hope about the capacity of mentors to transform some young women's lives. These observations challenge us to further understand the complexities of nonparent adult relationships and the conditions under which they have protective effects.

REFERENCES

Allen, J. P., J. L. Aber, and B. J. Leadbeater. 1990. Adolescent problem behaviors: The influence of attachment and autonomy. *Psychiatric Clinics of North America* 13:455–67.

Balcazar, F. E., and S. B. Fawcett. 1992. *Recruiting mentors and potential helpers*. Lawrence: University of Kansas Press.

Becerra, R., and D. de Anda. 1984. Pregnancy and motherhood among Mexican American adolescents. *Health and Social Work* 9:106–23.

Blyth, D. A., J. P. Hill, and K. S. Thiel. 1982. Early adolescents' significant others: Grade and gender differences in perceived relationships with familial and nonfamilial adults and young people. *Journal of Youth and Adolescence* 11:425–50.

Bowman, P. J. 1991. Joblessness. In *Life in Black America,* edited by J. S. Jackson, 156–78. Newbury Park, Calif.: Sage Publications.

Brown, L. M., and C. Gilligan. 1992. *Meeting at the crossroads: Women's psychology and girls' development*. Cambridge: Harvard University Press.

Bryant, B. K. 1985. *The neighborhood walk: Sources of support in middle childhood*. Monographs of the Society for Research in Child Development, vol. 50 (3).

Carden, A. D. 1990. Mentoring and adult career development: The evolution of a theory. *Counseling Psychologist* 18:275–99.

Chodorow, N. 1992. *Feminism and psychoanalysis*. San Francisco, Calif.: Jossey-Bass.

Coates, D. L. 1987. Gender differences in the structure and support characteristics of black adolescents' networks. *Sex Roles* 17:667–86.

Collins, P. H. 1987. The meaning of motherhood in black culture and black mother/daughter relationships. *Sage* 4:3–10.

Cowen, E. L., and W. Work. 1988. Resilient children, psychological wellness, and primary prevention. *American Journal of Community Psychology* 16:591–607.

Davis, A. A., and J. E. Rhodes. 1994. African American teenage mothers and their mothers: An analysis of supportive and problematic interactions. *Journal of Community Psychology* 2:12–20.

de Anda, D. 1984. Informal support networks of Hispanic mothers: A comparison across age groups. *Journal of Social Service Research* 7:89–105.

Derogatis, L. R. 1983. *SCL-90: Administration, scoring, and procedures manual-I for the R version*. Baltimore, Md.: Author.

Dore, M. M., and A. O. Dumois. 1990. Cultural differences in the meaning of adolescent pregnancy. *Journal of Contemporary Human Services* 2:93–102.

Escobar, J. I., and E. T. Randolph. 1982. The Hispanic and social networks. In *Mental health and Hispanic Americans, clinical perspectives,* edited by R. M. Becerra, M. Karno, and J. I. Escobar. New York: Grune and Stratton.

Flaxman, E., C. Ascher, and C. Harrington. 1988. *Youth mentoring programs and practices*. New York: Institute for Urban and Minority Education, Teachers College, Columbia University.

Freedman, M. 1993. *The kindness of strangers: Adult mentors, urban youth, and the new volunteerism*. San Francisco: Jossey-Bass.

Galbo, J. J. 1986. Adolescents' perceptions of significant adults: Implications for the family, the school, and youth serving agencies. *Children and Youth Services Review* 8:37–51.

Garbarino, J., N. Burston, S. Raber, R. Russell, and A. Crouter. 1978. The social maps of children approaching adolescence. *Journal of Youth and Adolescence* 7:417–28.

Garcia-Preto, N. 1982. Puerto Rican families. In *Ethnicity and family therapy*, edited by M. McGoldrick, J. K. Pearce, and J. Giordano. New York: Guilford Press.

Garmezy, N., and K. Neuchterlein. 1972. Invulnerable children: The fact and fiction of competence and disadvantage. *American Journal of Orthopsychiatry* 42:328–29.

Girls at 11: An interview with Carol Gilligan. 1990. *Harvard Education Letter*, July–August, 6.

Goleman, D. 1987. Thriving despite hardship: Key childhood traits identified. *New York Times*, October, C1, 11.

Gottlieb, B. H., and J. C. Sylvestre. 1994. Social support in the relationships between older adolescents and adults. In *Social networks and social support in childhood and adolescence*, edited by F. Nestmann and K. Hurrelman. Berlin: de Gruyter.

Hamilton, C. F. 1990. *Apprenticeship for adulthood*. Cambridge: Harvard University Press.

Hamilton, S. F. 1991. *Unrelated adults in adolescents' lives: Perspectives from four countries*. Ithaca, N.Y.: Cornell University Western Societies Program.

Hamilton, S. F., and M. A. Hamilton. 1990. *Linking up: Final report on a mentoring program for youth*. New York: Cornell University, College of Human Ecology.

Hayes, C. D., ed. 1987. *Risking the future: Adolescent sexuality, pregnancy, and childbearing*. Washington, D.C.: National Academy Press.

Healy, C. C., and A. J. Welchert. 1990. Mentoring relations: A definition to advance research and practice. *Educational Researcher* 12:17–21.

Hirsch, B. J., R. Boerger, A. E. Levy, and M. Mickus. 1994. The social networks of adolescents and their mothers: Influences on Blacks and Whites in single- and two-parent families. In *Social networks and social support in childhood and adolescence*, edited by F. Nestmann and K. Hurrelman. Berlin: de Gruyter.

Klaw, E., and J. E. Rhodes. In press. Natural mentors and the career activities of urban youth. *Psychology of Women Quarterly*.

Konopka, G. 1986. *Young girls: A portrait of adolescence*. Englewood Cliffs, N.J.: Prentice-Hall.

Levinson, D. J., C. N. Darrow, E. B. Klein, M. H. Levinson, and B. McKee. 1979. *The seasons of a man's life*. New York: Alfred A. Knopf.

Lipsitz, J. 1977. *Growing up forgotten: A review of research and programs concerning early adolescence*. Lexington, Mass.: Lexington Books.

Luthar, S. S., and E. Zigler. 1991. Vulnerability and competence: A review of research on resilience in childhood. *American Journal of Orthopsychiatry* 61 (1):6–22.

Martin, E. P., and J. M. Martin. 1978. *The black extended family*. Chicago: University of Chicago Press.

Mickelson, R. A. 1990. The attitude-achievement paradox among black adolescents. *Sociology of Education* 63:44–61.

Mindel, C. H. 1980. Extended familism among urban Mexican Americans, Anglos, and Blacks. *Hispanic Journal of Behavioral Sciences* 2:21–34.

Pearlin, L., E. G. Menaghan, M. A. Lieberman, and T. J. Mullan. 1981. The stress process. *Journal of Health and Social Behaviors* 22:337–56.

Ramirez, O. 1989. Mexican American children and adolescents. In *Children of color: Psychological interventions with minority youth*, edited by J. T. Gibbs and L.N. Huang. San Francisco, Calif.: Jossey-Bass.

Rhodes, J. E., J. M. Contreras, and S. C. Mangelsdorf. 1994. Natural mentor relationships among Latina adolescent mothers: Psychological adjustment, moderating processes, and the role of early parental acceptance. *American Journal of Community Psychology* 22:211–28.

Rhodes, J., L. Ebert, and K. Fischer. 1992. Natural mentors: An overlooked resource in the social networks of adolescent mothers. *American Journal of Community Psychology* 20:445–61.

Rhodes, J. E., A. B. Meyers, A. A. Davis, and L. Ebert. 1994. *The Social Support Network Questionnaire: A method for assessing social support and social strain.* Manuscript.

Riessman, F. 1965. The 'helper' therapy principle. *Social Work* 10:27–32.

Roberts, L. J., and J. Rappaport. 1989. *Empowerment in the mutual help context: An empirical analysis of the value of helping others.* Paper presented at the Second Biennial Conference on Community Research and Action, East Lansing, Michigan.

Rutter, M. 1979. Protective factors in children's responses to stress and disadvantage. In *Primary prevention of psychopathology.* Vol. 3, *Social competence in children,* edited by M. W. Kent and J. E. Rolf, 49–74. Hanover, N.H.: University Press of New England.

———. 1987. Psychosocial resilience and protective mechanisms. *American Journal of Orthopsychiatry* 57:57–72.

Sarason, I. G., J. H. Johnson, and J. M. Siegel. 1979. Assessing the impact of life changes: Development of the life experiences survey. In *Stress and anxiety,* edited by I. G. Sarason, and C. D. Spielberger. New York: Wiley.

Schmidt, J. A., and J. S. Wolfe. 1980. The mentor partnership: Discovery of professionalism. *National Association of Student and Personnel Administration* 17:45–51.

Sena-Rivera, J. 1979. Extended kinship in the United States: Computing models and the case of the la familia Chicana. *Journal of Marriage and the Family* 41:121–29.

Stack, C. B. 1974. *All our kin.* New York: Harper and Row.

Strommen, E. A. 1977. Friendship. In *Women: A psychological perspective,* edited by E. Donelson and J. Gullahorn, 154–67. New York: Wiley.

Styles, M. B., and K. V. Morrow. 1992. *Understanding how youth and elders form relationships: A study of four linking lifetime programs.* Philadelphia, Pa.: Public/Private Ventures.

Werner, E. E., and S. Smith. 1982. *Vulnerable but invincible: A study of resilient children.* New York: McGraw-Hill.

Wilson, M. N. 1986. The black extended family: An analytical consideration. *Developmental Psychology* 22:246–58.

# 13 From Mentor to Muse: Recasting the Role of Women in Relationship with Urban Adolescent Girls

Amy M. Sullivan

Although mentoring programs are frequently promoted as strategies to "reduce problem behavior and foster healthy development among adolescents" (Hamilton 1991, 7–8), there is reason to question whether the traditional role of mentor is appropriate or sufficient for women in relationship with adolescent girls. The role of mentor, as described in literature on "at risk" teens, is devoted to teaching, socializing, and acting as a role model for the adolescent. My research with urban adolescent girls considered to be at risk for dropout or school-age motherhood, however, suggests that important and health-sustaining relationships with women are overwhelmingly characterized by women's ability to listen, understand, and validate the knowledge, experience, and feelings of the adolescent. Efforts at teaching without acknowledging and respecting girls' perspectives may discount rather than enhance their experience and knowledge; attempts at socialization can be similarly destructive if they enforce social conventions that are harmful to girls and women.

The model upon which mentoring is based, originating in early Greek literature and myth, illustrates some of the limits that the prevailing mentoring model presents for girls. Advisor to Odysseus, Mentor was charged with the care and education of Odysseus' son, Telemachus, during his father's long absence. Descriptions of mentoring retain the essential characteristics of the relationship between Mentor and Telemachus: the mentor's role is one of teacher and father substitute, with the mentor relationship most commonly formed between a man and a boy. My research with girls points to another metaphor that shares its linguistic roots with *mentor*—that of *muse*. Muses were women in mythology who acted as sources of inspiration; their role was to recognize and to help spark or draw out the genius or artistry of their charges. The metaphor of *muse* shifts the focus to the inner resources and potentials of girls—strengths that might well be missed in relationships that seek primarily to teach girls what they do not know. Thus instead of a *helping model* of mentoring, which often assumes deficiencies in the adolescent, research with urban girls supports a *relational model* that recognizes the diversity of needs and resources among girls of varied backgrounds, assumes that both adolescent and adult possess vulnerabilities and strengths, and values the contributions of both partners in the relationship.

Using the guiding metaphors of *mentor* and *muse,* this chapter outlines two models of relationships between adolescents and nonparental adults. Described first is the current framing of the mentor role and relationship—what it is, why and how it is considered helpful, and where it may fall short in meeting the developmental needs of girls. Following this is a preliminary formulation of relationships between women and girls that has arisen from my research with urban girls, centering on why and how the role of muse may benefit girls as well as the women with whom they are in relationship. Data for this discussion are drawn from the Understanding Adolescence Study—a study of the relational development of urban adolescent girls considered to be at risk. This project was carried out by members of the Harvard Project on Women's Psychology and Girls' Development (Gilligan et al. 1992; Taylor, Gilligan, and Sullivan 1996). Although this chapter specifically addresses relationships between women and this particular group of girls, the types of relationships that these girls describe may be equally beneficial in other adolescent-adult relationships, including those with urban (as well as nonurban) girls who are not considered to be at risk, those between girls or boys and men, and those between boys and women. Future research may determine whether or not the role of muse applies as well to these other varieties of adolescent-adult relationships.

This chapter does not seek to dismiss the value of the mentoring role; rather, it offers possibilities for expanding or recasting existing formulations of the mentor relationship; it also suggests alternatives for creating meaningful and mutually beneficial relationships with urban adolescent girls. Such recastings of roles for women in relationship with girls not only point to new directions for research on relationships between all adults and adolescents; they also offer practical models of relationship that may be of immediate value to women who work with girls in formal and informal educational settings and to any women who share part of their lives with adolescent girls.

## The Mentor

Mentoring has received considerable attention in discussions of how adults can serve in the social, psychological, and educational development of adolescents (Darling 1991; Galbo 1983; Hamilton and Darling 1989; Hurrelmann 1991). Mentors are believed to be of particular value to adolescents who are at high risk for dropping out, school-age parenthood, delinquency, or emotional distress. This belief is supported by research on resilience in adolescence, which documents an association between positive relationships with adults and avoidance of these negative outcomes (Rutter 1980; Werner 1987). Summarizing this research, Stephen Hamilton describes how investigations of adolescents "who overcame the problems they faced and successfully negotiated the transition to adulthood have found that a key factor in their 'resilience' is the presence of a nonparental adult who gives guidance and encouragement, doing what a parent would be expected to do under better conditions or complementing parental influence" (1991, 1).

Mentoring can be described as primarily an *instrumental relationship*. Mentors are characterized as teachers and guides (Daloz 1983; Levinson et al. 1979); they provide information and advice to their students or protégés, guiding them in decision making, teaching them particular skills, and identifying areas in which they might improve their behavior or competency (Hamilton and Darling 1989). Stephen Hamilton and Linda Darling describe the prototypical mentor relationship as "a special bond between an inexperienced or naive student and someone more skilled than himself or herself who is willing to act as a guide in a new or unfamiliar situation" (1989, 121). Thus, the relationship tends to be primarily unidirectional, reflecting a helping model in which the focus is on the behaviors of the mentor that are directed toward the student. It is also likely to be a transitional relationship, aimed at bringing the student or protégé to a level of development at which the mentor role is no longer needed. The mentor role is therefore one that is future oriented, focusing on what or who the protégé can become or is becoming.

There is some evidence that relationships that fit the description of mentoring are relatively uncommon among young women. Hamilton and Darling (1989) found that female college students were less likely than were male students to have an unrelated adult mentor (defined as an adult who acted as a "teacher," "challenger," and "role model"). Slightly more than one-third of these college women (those perhaps most likely to have mentors) had mentors; among those students who named a significant adult, 43% of female students identified this adult as a mentor, whereas 72% of male students said the same. Hamilton observes that "distinctions flowing from gender and class call attention to the likelihood that mentors are . . . harder to find for young women, working class youth, and members of minority groups who seek to find a place among the dominant white males." Hamilton therefore recommends efforts to make mentors more available to these adolescents, for whom mentors are also "more critical because such pioneers need more help to take advantage of opportunities that are easier for the dominant group to acquire" (1991, 8).

From the perspectives of cognitive, educational, and career development, urban girls may indeed benefit from greater access to the kinds of instrumental support provided by the mentor relationship. Other research concurs that greater access to opportunity and to more information and guidance on educational plans and career development may be a need shared by all girls (American Association of University Women [AAUW] 1992; De León, chap. 21 of this volume; Sadker and Sadker 1994; Sullivan, with Snee and Weinger 1994). However, the social and emotional health and development of girls (and perhaps boys as well) may not be equally well served by a primarily instrumental mentor relationship. It may be that girls are less likely to report having mentor relationships not only because of the social inequities of gender, race, and class that may make mentors less accessible to them, but also because this type of relationship with adults is one that girls themselves are less likely to seek out.

More research is needed on the role of nonparental adults in all adolescents' lives, including the specific role of women in the lives of urban girls. While some progress is evident in the years since Dale Blyth, John Hill, and Karen Smith Thiel stated that "relations with adults other than parents have, for the most part, been ignored in empirical studies" (1982, 426), there is still much to be learned about what constitutes positive and health-sustaining relationships between adolescents and adults. Research has identified relationships with adults as key factors in adolescents' resilience, but it has yet to specify the kinds and qualities of relationships that are most beneficial. Social network studies have explored a range of adolescents' relationships with others, including adults; however, they have not investigated the psychological dimensions of these relationships (Salzinger, Hammer, and Antrobus 1988). Few studies offer a developmental perspective on these relationships, and little is known about the relationships of adolescents who are not white and of the middle class. (Some notable exceptions include Garbarino et al. 1978; Rhodes and Davis, chap. 12 of this volume; Rhodes, Ebert, and Fischer 1992.) At present, discussions of why relationships with mentors might be important for adolescents rarely reflect a recognition of the needs and wants that might be specific to urban girls in adolescence. As Galbo concluded in a comprehensive review of research on relationships between adolescents and adults, "much has been assumed about who really are the significant adults in adolescents' lives" (1984, 958).

## The Muse

My analysis of interviews from the Understanding Adolescence Study begins to address some of the gaps in knowledge about the significant women in girls' lives. The purpose of this qualitative, longitudinal study was to contribute to an understanding of the relational development of a racially and ethnically diverse group of urban adolescent girls who were at risk for high school dropout or adolescent motherhood, or both. Although not asked explicitly about connections with women other than their mothers, 85% ($N = 22$) of girls in this sample cited at least one such relationship. Aunts, adult sisters, sisters-in-law, older friends, and neighbors were among the women who figured prominently in these girls' lives.

## The Study

Eighth grade girls from three elementary schools in racially and ethnically diverse working-class and low-income sections of a large urban area were asked to participate in this study. Students who were included were designated "at risk" for school dropout or teen pregnancy by their teachers and also met our criteria of "risk" (see Taylor, chap. 7 of this volume, for description of these criteria). Although the label of risk is problematic because it is commonly used to imply deficit or deviance, I use it here for the purpose of identifying the particular girls in this study because not all urban adolescent girls are at equal risk for the outcomes of school dropout or pregnancy. The shorthand label "at risk" is kept in quotation marks, however, to reflect the caution with which the term should be interpreted.

The twenty-six girls in the final sample—eight African American girls, four Latina girls (whose families were from Central America), eight Portuguese girls, and six white girls (of varied ethnicities)—were interviewed annually over the course of three years, from 1988 to 1990.[1] When possible, girls and interviewers were matched by race (no Latina or Portuguese women were available to conduct interviews). The interview guide used in this study was developed by members of the Harvard Project to elicit narratives of relationships in and out of school, decision-making strategies in conflicts and dilemmas, and future plans. Students were administered the pencil-and-paper Washington University Sentence Completion task (Loevinger and Wessler 1970) in the eighth and tenth grades to provide supplementary data to the interviews. Two methods were used to carry out the interview analysis: (1) content coded, conceptually clustered matrices (Miles and Huberman 1984), and (2) a narrative listening guide (Brown et al. 1988). Analyses of these interviews were conducted with attention not only to evidence of psychological distress and health but also to evidence of risk and resilience. Reliability of coding and validity of interpretations were assessed through ongoing discussions with the research team and in periodic review with colleagues whose personal and professional experience afforded them insight into a variety of social and cultural contexts.

The first method entailed creating matrices to code and organize major aspects of the girls' descriptions of their relationships with women and to chart the progress of themes in these descriptions over time. Categories included relational roles (for example, aunt or neighbor), types of shared experiences (such as being the oldest sibling or running away from home), duration of relationships, uniqueness of relationship, types of interactions (such as listening or talking), and content of communication (school problems, dating, or future plans).

In contrast and complement to the first method's focus on breaking down and organizing narratives into summary descriptions of themes in relationships across girls, the second method—the narrative listening guide—retains the coherence and integrity of individual narratives by moving through four different levels of analysis of the same text (see Taylor, chap. 7 of this volume, for description). For this analysis each of the four readings were undertaken with portions of text describing girls' relationships with women. The third and fourth readings, for psychological health and distress, traced evidence of when relationships with women either seemed to support girls' psychological health and development or to increase girls' distress and level of psychological risk (guidelines for psychological distress and health were drawn from Rogers, Brown, and Tappan 1993). Examples of psychological health include feeling free to voice a range of thoughts and feelings (especially those not shared in other relationships) and being able to resist debilitating racial, ethnic, class, or gender stereotypes. Increases in these capacities over time in the context of these relationships would be noted as evidence of psychological development. Only a few girls spoke explicitly about relationships with women that caused them distress; most evidence of distress was found in women's failure to connect with girls or in their diminished presence in girls' narratives over time.

Many narratives about important relationships with women other than mothers occurred in response to the question that followed inquiries about relationships with mothers, namely, *Can you tell me about someone else who is important to you?* Narratives about relationships with women also arose in response to questions about girls' experiences of feeling good or bad about themselves and in response to questions about who helped them think about their futures. Based on previous research—my own and that of my colleagues at the Harvard Project—I have organized the discussion of findings around three possible implications of this relationship: health, healing, and transformation.

### Health

Maria, a Portuguese American girl in the tenth grade, completes a sentence that begins with the phrase "a girl has a right to———" by writing "talk and express her feelings." Eighth grade Donna, who is Italian American, expresses a similar sentiment when she asserts a girl's right to "speak for herself and tell what she means." Yet the girls' sentence completions also describe a dilemma: alongside a recognition of their right to voice their feelings is the knowledge that speaking up can lead to trouble. Maria completes the sentence that begins "what gets me into trouble is———" with the words "my big mouth." More than half of the girls who did the sentence completion task complete this sentence stem describing the same idea; in fact, they also use the same words, "my mouth" or "my big mouth," to define the source of their trouble.

Research with girls conducted by Carol Gilligan and her colleagues has highlighted the key role that *voice* and *relationship* play in psychological health and resilience (for example, Gilligan [1982] 1993; Brown and Gilligan 1992; Gilligan, Ward, and Taylor 1988; Rogers 1993). Connections with others and with one's own feelings and knowledge are forged and fostered by expressing feelings and speaking for one's self. At adolescence, however, girls' relationships with themselves and others may be placed at risk, and as Maria and Donna describe, girls may find that voicing their thoughts and feelings lands them in trouble.

Lyn Mikel Brown, Carol Gilligan, and Annie Rogers have described how prior to adolescence, many young girls demonstrate a strong sense of self, an ability to know and voice their feelings and to trust in the authority of their own experience (Brown and Gilligan 1992; Gilligan [1982] 1993, 1990; Rogers 1993). Relationships with others are often characterized by a full range of experiences and expressions, including love, anger, closeness, jealousy, joy and sadness, trust and betrayal. At adolescence, however, girls' voices may be silenced or suppressed, and authentic relationships put at risk, by increased cultural pressure to conform to dominant images of femininity or by culturally mandated ideals of separation. Ideals of femininity and the "perfect girl" encourage girls to suppress feelings such as anger and to control or deny physical needs such as hunger or sexual desire. Conventional ideals that equate development with increasing levels of separation from others can also discourage girls from bringing the full range of their thoughts and feelings into relationship with others. These new demands may create an impasse for many girls, who face "psychological dilemmas in which they [feel] that if they said what they were feeling and thinking no one would want to be with them, and if they didn't say what they were thinking and feeling they would be all alone, no one would know what was happening to them" (Gilligan [1982] 1993, xx).

Resisting these losses by speaking or acting out against relationships that feel false, or against conventions that would require self-sacrifice, silence, or disavowal of one's own experience, may have costly social or personal consequences. Thus, girls' resistance to disconnection from self and others constitutes both a strength and a risk. Gilligan and her colleagues suggest that women can hinder girls' healthy development by supporting and enforcing cultural conventions that are harmful to girls. Alternatively, women can foster healthy development by validating girls' feelings and experiences even when they are at odds with convention and by assisting girls' efforts to recognize and resist idealized social norms (Gilligan 1990).

Writer Brenda Ueland tells a parallel story of psychological resilience and risk in her vivid account of the vibrancy and spontaneity of young girls—and of how this creative energy can be stifled:

You know how all children have this creative power. You have all seen things like this: the little girls in our family used to give play after play. They wrote the plays themselves (they were very good plays too, interesting, exciting and funny). They acted in them . . . made the costumes themselves, beautiful, effective . . . contriving them in the most ingenious way out of attic junk and their mothers' best dresses. They constructed the stage and theater. . . . They drummed up the audience, throwing out a drag-net for all the hired girls, dogs, babies, mothers, neighbors within a radius of a mile or so. . . .

They were working for nothing but fun, for that glorious inner excitement. . . . It was hard, hard work but there was no pleasure or excitement like it. . . . But this joyful, imaginative, impassioned energy dies out of us very young. Why? Because we do not see that it is great and important. . . . Because we don't respect it in ourselves and keep it alive by using it. And because we don't keep it alive in others by *listening* to them. ([1938] 1987, 5–6)

Ueland invokes the image of the muse when she adds, "The only way to love a person is . . . by listening to them and seeing and believing in the god, in the poet, in them. For by doing this, you keep the god and the poet alive and make it flourish." Ueland writes about keeping the creative impulse alive both in writing and in life; as the girls in this study describe, women who listen to and believe in them—who do not focus on what they lack but value who they are—help girls resist disconnection from this "joyful, imaginative, impassioned energy" ([1938] 1987, 6, 5). Other research suggests that girls can have a similar, and equally powerful, effect on women (Brown and Gilligan 1992; Dorney 1991).

Listening to the diverse group of "at risk" girls involved in the current study suggests that relational risk and resilience may play out differently for girls of differing culture, background, and experience. Variations in cultural conventions, patterns of socialization, school standing, and relational resources seem to contribute to different psychological strengths and vulnerabilities among these girls. Understanding the risks faced by these girls and the resources and strategies they use to manage these risks requires an understanding of the cultural contexts in which they live, as well as knowledge of the multiple and often contradictory conventions that they learn.

Both the black girls and the white girls in this study, for example, tended to maintain their ability to speak their minds and express disagreement or anger. This is not surprising, as African American girls are likely to be socialized to resist the internal and external manifestations of racism (Ward, chap. 5 of this volume), to adopt conventions of womanhood that include being strong and self-sufficient, and to expect to work outside the home (Reid and Comas-Diaz 1990). Although research is sparse on the development of white low-income and working-class urban girls, Jewelle Taylor Gibbs (1985) has suggested that they may have more in common with black girls of the same class than they do with white girls in middle-income groups. Among many of the more outspoken girls, however, maintaining strong voices throughout this period of adolescence carried with it distinct risks. For many, by the time they reached tenth grade, "being strong" or "self-confident" (their words) also meant covering over a need for relationships and curtailing the willingness or ability to voice their fears or concerns. For girls in the frightening position of being close to dropping out of school, the need to "stand alone" or keep their feelings to themselves seemed only to bring them closer to the edge of leaving school, and it certainly put them in danger of increased isolation and psychological distress.

Among the Latina and Portuguese girls traditional conventions of femininity and being a "good woman," rooted in cultural values emphasizing goodness and virtue (Falicov 1982; Moitoza 1982), revolved around maintaining loyalty to families and adhering to restrictions in speaking about or engaging in sexual activity. Although these conventions may have protected them from becoming teen mothers or dropping out of school—only one Latina girl eventually dropped out to have a baby—they also may place the girls at risk for the covering over or loss of voice and desire documented in earlier work among girls in more privileged educational or social settings (Brown and Gilligan 1992).

The girls in this study speak clearly about both their needs in relationships and how adult women can join with them in healthy and potentially health-sustaining relationships. Their narratives also hint at what distinguishes women who are able to be present with them, to listen and "really talk" without giving "a lecture." For example, Lilian, a Latina girl, frames many of her relational needs with other women in terms of what she is unable to discuss with her mother. She does not talk to her mother about boys "because she's strict about that"—a restriction cited repeatedly, often with unconcealed frustration, by a number of the Latina and Portuguese girls. Lilian's neighbor Joan, however, gives her an opportunity in eighth grade to discuss what is forbidden to her at home: "Yah, I talk to her. It's more easy to talk to her [than to my mother . . . because] my mother's strict and Joan really likes to hear what we think, kids our age and our time, because she said she used to be that way when she was young, just like me. It's good to talk to her." Connection with a woman who listens to her, who is interested in her, and whose experience resonates with her own is a source of pleasure and support for Lilian. Like many of the women described by these girls, Joan matches Ueland's profile of "the only good teachers for you": they are "those friends who love you, who think you are interesting, or very important, or wonderfully funny; whose attitude is: 'Tell me more. Tell me all you can. I want to understand more about everything you feel and know and all the changes inside and out of you. Let more come out' " ([1938] 1987, 8).

Connection with Joan is particularly important for Lilian in light of the many difficulties she describes at home with her mother and brothers and the lack of opportunity she has elsewhere to share her thoughts and feelings. Joan also helps Lilian to think about her future and how she might respond to her family by asking questions and sharing her own experience and learnings:

She always asks me, what do I want to be when I grow up. And how am I going to live my life, am I going to make mistakes like with my family—like her family, they don't like what she did. She ran away from home when she was 16, if I was going to do that. She ran away from home and she asked me if I was going to do the same thing and I said no, I'd just work it out. . . . She says, "Don't make the same mistakes I did." . . . She just came to realize that running away, she wasn't as close to her father as she used to be. . . . She was sad because she always wanted to get along with her father, and her father never wanted to come down and visit her.

For Lilian, as for many of the girls in this study, the transition from eighth grade to high school brought with it heightened concerns about the trustworthiness of peers, as rumors and gossip became a daily threat at school. Emerging issues of and interest in sexuality also became a point of tension and contention in many girls' relationships with their mothers and with peers. In this context, knowing an adult with whom they could speak openly and in whom they could trust implicitly became a valuable and much needed resource.

In tenth grade Lilian speaks of how she feels good about a close relationship with her older cousin, a woman in her early twenties. Again, the trust and identification that Lilian feels with her cousin create a relationship in which she can speak freely; they "really can talk." Lilian draws a distinction between giving advice and delivering lectures:

We're able to talk about anything. I can tell her anything I want. You know, with mothers . . . some daughters are close to their mothers, others are not. . . . My cousin seems to understand more . . . she's been through it. . . . She understands more and she can give me more advice while my mother's just more like, "Oh, you shouldn't do that." . . . Yet you try to tell her, "But Mom that's what I'm asking you, for advice," and then they don't understand. With [my cousin] I can tell her anything and she'll understand. She gives me advice, I give her advice, you know. So this, we really can talk. [With my mother] it's not advice, it's more like, um, a lecture with my mother, you know.

Ana, who is Latina like Lilian, also prefaces the discussion of an important relationship with an adult woman by describing the subjects that cannot be understood by, or broached with, her mother: boys and sex are again off-limits for discussion. Ana says that the differences between her and her mother are not only those of generation and culture. A limited understanding of English also precludes her mother's understanding of the "pressures" and "temptations" Ana faces:

My mother doesn't know about school things, she's, she doesn't hardly even know English, okay. It's different from her country. . . . It's different now, you know, she doesn't know what pressures we're having in school, what temptations, a lot of problems, you know. So let's say um, we can't really talk . . . about it, you know. Because [she doesn't] understand it. Like my mother doesn't know English. It's hard to tell her. And if I tell her in Spanish, it won't come out so good, you know, how it really is in English.

Ana says that her aunt has been in this country for a longer period of time than her mother; thus the differences of experience, culture, and language seem to be attenuated:

She's so different. She'll listen to you. She knows how it is because um, see, she knows more, even though she's from a foreign country too, she knows more English, she understands more of the words what I'm trying to say. She married an Italian guy, so . . . she knows things, right. . . . She came [here] when she was around 17 or something and . . . she's like more used to here, she knows what things go on in school.

Ana's cousins seem to find similar sanctuary in the company of their aunt:

All my girl cousins . . . that are 14, 15, they all go to her. . . . A lot of my cousins just find it so easy. . . . Because sometimes their mothers don't understand it and they get a different wrong idea . . . of what you're trying to say. You know, they think you are saying one thing, they'll say, "Oh, she must be telling me this, this and this." They understand it wrong. . . . All my cousins go to her and they say . . . their mothers would probably get mad. . . . And so . . . she won't tell your mother. . . . She won't say, "No, don't do this," she's just, "You make the decision whether its right or wrong."

Like Lilian's neighbor, Ana's aunt does not instruct or tell her nieces what to do; rather, by simply listening as they describe their experience, she helps them stay connected to their own knowledge in deciding what is right or wrong. Ana's description also suggests that a woman to whom girls can turn is easily recognized by girls. With Lilian, Ana builds a portrait of such a woman: she is someone who "likes to hear what we think," who may be "just like me," who "understands" and has "been through it," who "listens" and "knows what things go on." Ana also notes, however, that relationships like this with an adult are a rarity when she says of her aunt, "she's so different."

Christina is a Portuguese girl who has also experienced sanctions at home about what she can and cannot say. Christina conveys a need to express herself but seems by tenth grade to have learned to keep her feelings to herself: "I usually keep my feelings bottled up. You know, I don't usually say anything, but when something bad happens, like I get into a fight, it all comes out, knocks against me. If I don't talk about it, it all stays inside, all my feelings stay inside and I don't really say anything about them." Adding that she needs to "get [her feelings] out" so that "one day I just won't blow up you know," Christina also indicates that this need has not been well met. She describes liking the interview, for example, because "you could talk to somebody, somebody listens to you for once." Christina experienced the loss of her father in ninth grade, and by the tenth grade she seems increasingly cut off from her friends and family and seems to be struggling with some level of depression. Speaking and listening, as Gilligan has observed, are "a form of psychic breathing" ([1982] 1993, xvi), and tenth grade Christina seems to be in particular need of this life-sustaining process.

Mary is an Italian American girl who dropped out of school in ninth grade and later returned. Her narrative tells a story of a failed opportunity for connection with a woman and suggests that the continued presence of someone who could listen to her might have helped forestall some of the losses she experienced. In eighth grade Mary described herself as surrounded by people to whom she could turn: "If I have a school problem, then I'd go to my father. If I have a boyfriend problem, then I go to my mother. . . . [And] I always have my best friends to go to." Over the three years of this study, however, these connections lose their prominence in her narratives. Mary increasingly takes on conventions of autonomy that are flagged in her narrative with the phrase "you should." In tenth grade, for example, she says she no longer discusses her problems with others: "I just like to deal with [things] myself. . . . I don't want to feel like I have to depend on other people. . . . You should be able to deal with it yourself." These conventions of autonomy and independence propel Mary increasingly out of relationship with others, and by tenth grade she says, "I really don't tell anybody about anything."

The reasons for Mary's adoption of these conventions become evident when she speaks of how she has been "hurt in relationships . . . so many times" and how speaking her mind has led to "trouble and fights." Mary's solution is to resist revealing her feelings to others, and in the tenth grade she says, "I just can't be honest or open anymore. I'm afraid that if I just open up to everybody, I'll end up getting hurt again." While she is wise to avoid "opening up to everybody"—for indeed such indiscriminate openness would leave her vulnerable to considerable hurt—her strategy of not opening up to *anybody* proves equally costly. If, as Robert Stevenson and Jeanne Ellsworth suggest, the "culture of individualism," so prominent in white middle-class ideology, is an even "more powerful influence" in the white working class (1993, 270), such cultural forces may potentiate the effects of Mary's personal experience and increase her risk of psychological isolation.

In the past Mary's ability to connect with and voice her feelings had enabled her to express herself creatively through writing. After returning to school, however, Mary says that she "lost [the] ability to do some things": "I used to be a great writer, write great stories. But now, I read my stories and . . . I don't really know what happened. . . . They don't feel the same. When I used to read my stories, no matter what . . . I was a messup, but I wrote some damn good stories, let me tell you." Mary says she used to "automatically . . . have a story in my head," but in her recent attempts to protect herself things have changed:

Now I think of nothing, and it takes me a long time to write down a story. . . . I don't feel as comfortable as I did last year, writing about my stories . . . because if [people reading them] didn't like 'em, I think I'd die. You know what I mean. If I wrote down all my feelings on a piece of paper and somebody said "I don't like this," I really think I would die.

Mary told these things to her writing teacher, but "she didn't comment. She didn't say what she thought." Venturing for a moment out from "dealing with things" herself, Mary shared with her teacher the magnitude of her fears about having her feelings, her story, rejected—"I really think I would die"—only to have these feelings themselves met with silence. By Mary's teacher's apparent reluctance to share her thoughts, and by her seeming failure to respond to Mary's concerns, she may have missed a critical opportunity to assist Mary in reconnecting with others, with her feelings, and with her creative abilities to write "some damn good stories."

Despite her stated caution, Mary's readiness to connect with someone she could trust was evident in her interview. Like Christina, who liked having "somebody listen to you for once," Mary said that she liked the interview because she was able "to sit down and like talk to somebody and have them understand, without them turning around and laugh and say, 'Oh, that was stupid,' or stuff like that." Describing the positive impact of such interactions, Mary added that the interview itself might help her in the future "to be more open and honest." Her comments not only reveal the need to be listened to, but they also highlight the risks in speaking, where there is ever present the prospect of being hurt by someone who might "laugh and say . . . that was stupid."

Mary dropped out again in eleventh grade. Although the continued presence of someone with whom Mary felt safe to voice her feelings may not have prevented this outcome, it may have provided her opportunities to stay connected to her writing and may have diminished some of the emotional distress and isolation she was experiencing. That she was capable of taking advantage of opportunities for such a relationship was evident in her interviews; as Mary commented at the end of her tenth grade interview, "It's good to tell how you feel." That such opportunities had become rare for Mary, however, was equally, and distressingly, apparent.

Ruby is an African American girl who became pregnant and dropped out of school, despite her reported intentions in tenth grade to do otherwise. Like Mary, Ruby begins to move away from confiding relationships in ninth grade and begins to speak of the ability to "stand alone" as a sign of strength. Also like Mary, Ruby's increasing psychological distance from others is accompanied by an increasing level of psychological distress. When asked about a time she felt good outside of school—a question she responded to with ease in the eighth grade—Ruby in tenth grade is unable to recall any examples: "I don't know, I can't remember any, but I know there must have been times when I felt really good."

In eighth grade, when Ruby speaks of the burdens and privileges of being the oldest in a large family, she says she can go to her aunt for advice on a problem: "She's the oldest, too, so she sort of understands me better. She says if I need to come over there on weekends to talk about things, that I can come over and tell her." As it is for Lilian and Ana, a relationship with a woman who can understand and share her experience is important for Ruby. In the ninth grade, however, Ruby's aunt receives only brief mention, and by the tenth, women drop out altogether from the stories that Ruby tells about her life. Ruby's interviews over the three years sound progressively more guarded; she speaks more frequently of keeping to herself and about how it has become increasingly difficult to find people she can trust. By tenth grade Ruby says, "I really don't talk to nobody."

Although concerned about failing her classes in school, Ruby has kept this information from her teachers: "I'm worried about it. They don't know that, though." Like Mary, Ruby says she does not share her feelings with others, but she nevertheless is willing to speak in the interview about her concerns, and this in turn seems to help Ruby clarify her feelings. Ruby says that the interview "lets you know a lot about yourself and how you feel about things. I mean I leave out the door and I'm like, 'Wow, I didn't think I thought that,' you know. . . . I didn't know I really felt that way." Speaking about her life "let me know how I felt" and, she adds, "I think that's good." Ruby's need for relationships—both for her emotional well-being and to cope with her difficulties at school—is clear, and her loss of connection places her at greater psychological and academic risk.

What seems to be shared by the women with whom these girls felt free to speak—including the interviewers—is that they are relatively unencumbered by conventions that would dictate or constrain their roles in these relationships. Ana's aunt, for example, has no children of her own; this may enable her to be free to listen to her adolescent nieces without feeling compelled to tell them what they should do or needing to report these conversations to their mothers. Without children—especially daughters—Ana's aunt may not feel the pull to enforce rules of the dominant culture or the family culture with her nieces. Lilian's neighbor and cousin and Mary's and Ruby's interviewers may be in similarly advantageous positions. They are free to listen to these girls without the need to change them, and they can allow them to share their experiences and express their feelings in a climate of trust. These women, because they are "not their mothers, teachers, or therapists" may have "the advantage of standing outside of what are sometimes painfully complex and difficult relationships for girls at this time in their lives" (Rogers 1989).

Patricia Hill Collins remarks on this connection for women in the role of "othermothers" with girls in black communities:

Othermothers often help to defuse the emotional intensity of relationships between bloodmothers and their daughters. In recounting how she dealt with the intensity of her relationship with her mother, [one writer] describes the women teachers, neighbors, friends, and othermothers she turned to—women who, she observes, "did not have the onus of providing for me, and so had the luxury of talking to me." (1990, 128)

For the girls in this study—especially those who are experiencing tension or restrictions in their relationships with their mothers, who become cautious with friends in a school climate of rumors, gossip, and distrust, and who find themselves caught up in trying to adopt the role of "good daughter" or "strong woman"—relationships with women they can trust in and talk with may play a vital role in sustaining and supporting their psychological health and resilience.

### Healing

The 1992 AAUW report on education and girls stated that "incest, rape, and other physical violence severely compromise the lives of girls and women all across the country. These realities are rarely, if ever, discussed in schools" (1992, 3). Psychiatrist Judith Herman describes research documenting the extent of "these realities":

The results of these investigations confirmed the reality of women's experiences that Freud had dismissed as fantasies a century before. Sexual assaults against women and children were shown to be pervasive and endemic in our culture. The most sophisticated epidemiological survey was conducted in the early 1980s by Diana Russell, a sociologist and human rights activist. Over 900 women, chosen by random sampling techniques, were interviewed in depth about their experiences of domestic violence and sexual exploitation. The results were horrifying. One woman in four had been raped. One woman in three had been sexually abused in childhood. (1992, 30)

For many girls in adolescence, healing from trauma is a crucial aspect of their development. There is evidence, in fact, that girls who are identified as "at risk" may be even more likely than other girls to have been sexually abused. One investigation involving girls who had become pregnant as teenagers found that two-thirds of the girls had experienced at least one unwanted sexual experience: molestation, attempted rape, or rape (Boyer and Fine 1992). A girl who has experienced sexual abuse is likely to have a complicated relationship with her family and thus might be in particular need of a safe and supportive relationship with an adult woman. Herman describes research that identifies relationships as central to recovery: "Many of the women who had escaped without permanent harm remembered particular people who had helped them to integrate and overcome their sexual trauma. Most frequently cited were supportive friends and family members, who assured these women that they were not at fault" (Tsai, reported in Herman 1981, 33). A woman who can listen to and understand a girl's experience may offer a safe and healing presence not easily found elsewhere.

Although the current study with girls "at risk" was not designed to assess whether or not girls had an abuse history, several spoke about experiences of some kind of abuse. Sandy, for example, is a white girl who described ongoing problems with her stepfather. The specifics of abuse were not articulated in her interview, but Sandy was unambiguous about her desire "to leave the house because he's bothering me a lot"; she was reluctant, however, to leave her mother alone in a dangerous situation. For Sandy, important relationships are with women who can offer her some protection from her stepfather. In ninth grade, for example, she finds support and sanctuary with her neighbor: "My downstairs neighbor, she is like a mother to me, too. And when I have problems she helps me out and she doesn't really like my [step]father that much, so she's always on my side." Sandy's neighbor shares her experience: "She went through a lot of things like that, related to that. Her boyfriend . . . used to do this stuff to her." Although Sandy does not provide details of what "this stuff" is, she provides a sense of the severity of the problem by describing how she routinely goes to her neighbor's apartment to call for help from the police.

In tenth grade Sandy seems no longer to have anyone to whom she can turn. She speaks longingly of how her grandmother had once been a source of protection:

My grandmother [was important to me], but she passed away a year ago. I guess she was close to me, too. . . . She was just so nice and everything. I always wish that she's still alive and I could talk to her and I know she wouldn't let my stepfather treat me the way he does. I know she wouldn't. It's just that she had ways. I think she had like powers or something to just take people over and just boss them around. . . . Yah, she could. My stepfather wouldn't ever try to get wise with her and talk back to her because he knows better, I know.

Sandy's wish in tenth grade is for a relationship with a woman who, like her grandmother, has "powers" to do something on her behalf, with whom she could talk and in whom she could trust. Her interviewer joined this lineage, for a short time at least, by listening to Sandy and helping her contact a counselor shortly after their interview. Since that last interview, Sandy has moved out of her parents' home and away from her stepfather. Sandy ultimately became pregnant and dropped out of school.

Evidence has also begun to accumulate suggesting that many symptoms of extreme psychological distress that become more prominent in adolescence—depression, eating disorders, suicide, self-mutilating behaviors—can in fact often be traced to experiences of sexual abuse in childhood or adolescence (Herman 1992). At this crucial time for adolescent girls, adult women may indeed be in a unique position to mitigate or prevent these negative outcomes. The intention is not for women to be therapists, but rather to foster relationships that are therapeutic: to create a safe place to speak, to listen and share their own experience, to use their power when necessary to stop continuing abuse, and to make it possible for girls to speak the unspeakable and thus regain a sense of their own power.

Alongside evidence of the prevalence of abuse among girls and the essential place of relationships in recovery from this trauma, the absence of discussions about sexual abuse in the current literature on mentoring for adolescents "at risk" is notable. The literature focuses on preventing pregnancy but not sexual abuse; certainly if sexual abuse coexists with higher risks of pregnancy, it should be raised as an issue to consider both in research and in program development. Relationships with women may have considerable potential for healing among girls deemed "at risk"; the healing potential for these kinds of relationships, however, is sharply diminished if the silence that has historically surrounded sexual abuse persists.

### Transformation

The transformative potential of connections between women and adolescent girls "at risk" has many faces. As this chapter has suggested thus far, these include transforming the present and future quality of girls' lives by supporting their healthy development and, when necessary, acting as partners in their healing. These relationships also have the potential to foster change in the social sphere. Collins describes how the othermother tradition in some black communities has already transformed mentoring relationships between black teachers and their students to a "fundamentally radical" enterprise: "This community othermother tradition . . . explains the 'mothering the mind' relationships that can develop between Black women teachers and their Black students. Unlike the traditional mentoring so widely reported in educational literature, this relationship goes far beyond that of providing students with either technical skills or a network of academic and professional contacts." Collins cites feminist cultural critic bell hooks's description of this transformative aspect of mentoring: "'I understand from the teachers . . . that the work of any teacher committed to the full self-realization of students [is] necessarily and fundamentally radical, that ideas [are] not neutral, that to teach in a way that liberates, that expands consciousness, that awakens, is to challenge domination at its very core' " (1990, 131). The potential for developing a critical consciousness that can inspire challenges to oppressive social structures and conventions that silence girls and women does not, however, appear in mentoring models aimed at correcting deficits, preventing high risk behaviors, or maintaining the status quo.

In her analysis of programs and policies that affect adolescents, Millicent Poole points out that "what has largely been missing from the discourse and action has been a concern to empower young people; to make them more socially critical or more able to participate in social transformation or social analysis and questioning." In the same way, instead of focusing on empowerment and on developing a healthy critical perspective, some of the more traditional notions of mentoring emphasize socializing, teaching, and modeling functions that, however well-intentioned, function to preserve the status quo—despite the ill effects that some existing social structures may have on the adolescent. As Poole stresses, "agency and self-empowerment [are] of vital significance for individual and societal futures" (1989, 80).

Yet for girls "at risk" the costs of speaking up may be high, including expulsion from the school system, as Michelle Fine (1991) has documented. This is particularly true when speaking up constitutes a challenge to prevailing norms. These girls need to know the risks that they face and to know how to formulate strategies that can minimize these risks without losing connection with their own voices, thoughts, and feelings. At the same time, adult women need to use their power in the system as adults to reduce the material and psychological risks that these girls confront.

Connections between girls and women contain the potential to let girls *and* women know that they matter and that they can make a difference. Unfortunately, while there are many positive stories of relationships with women in this study, there are also repeated stories of girls' receiving messages that they do not matter, messages that cut across lines of race and ethnicity. Valerie, an African American girl, conveys this when she describes what she especially liked about the interview: "Being listened to. You just feel like there is someone out there that's really paying attention to me." Christina voices a similar thought when she says the interview was important because "a lot of people don't ask. . . . I think a lot of people should ask more questions . . . What do we think about something." Donna, in the presence of an aunt who doubts she will go to college, feels "like I'm nothing. Like she doesn't have any confidence in me." Tiffany, a black adolescent mother, says she felt good helping a friend because "someone listened to me for once. . . . No one ever listens to me." Bettina, who is Latina, describes why she does not talk to anyone about her future: "I just think about my future by myself . . . , it's my ideas, I don't want anybody to take them away from me. . . . If you tell somebody your ideas, they might be like, 'Oh, that's stupid,' put you down and then you'd be like, 'Oh, I don't want to do that anymore.' " And Ana, describing the singular experience of feeling good during a job interview "because I was like, 'Oh boy, they're listening to me.' . . . The lady talked to me as if I was a regular person." Rather than dismissing such comments as variations on a typical adolescent lament, when taken seriously they point to a real and pressing need for these girls.

For women to be in authentic, healthy relationship with girls requires courage to question the ways in which women's attempts at being "role models" may have separated them from girls and perpetuated traditions in the culture that are unhealthy for girls:

[Women] may discover that they have succumbed to the temptation to model perfection *by trying to be perfect role-models for girls* and thus have taken themselves out of relationship with girls—in part to hide their imperfection, but also perhaps to keep girls from feeling their sadness and their anger. . . . And it may be that women, in the name of being good women, have been modeling for girls repudiation—teaching girls the necessity of a loss or renunciation. (Gilligan 1990, 531, emphasis added)

Women who are mentors can still socialize, teach, challenge, and be role models for girls, but they must also be able to think critically about these roles with an awareness of both what is helpful to girls and what is harmful. For any women in relationship with adolescent girls "at risk"—mentor or not—clearly what is central is the act and art of listening, of meeting girls where they are.

Across the lines of race and ethnicity in this study, the character of meaningful relationships remains a constant: they are distinguished by girls' ability to speak freely; by women's ability to listen to, understand, and validate girls' feelings and experience; and by women's willingness to share their own experience as well. The focus of this relationship is on confirming or drawing out girls' experience, feelings, and knowledge. In contrast with the more instrumental nature of mentoring, the role of muse that emerges from girls' narratives forms what can be called an *evocative relationship*. Unlike mentoring, which may be more unidirectional, transitional, and ultimately facilitative of separation, these are relationships that are decidedly more mutual, marked both by constancy and connection.

bell hooks, quoting the Vietnamese Buddhist monk Thich Nhat Hahn, provides a description of communities of resistance that can arise from relationships such as these:

Resistance means opposition to being invaded, occupied, assaulted and destroyed by the system. The purpose of resistance, here, is to seek the healing of yourself in order to be able to see clearly. . . . I think that communities of resistance should be places where people can return to themselves more easily, where the conditions are such that they can heal themselves and recover their wholeness. (1990, 43)

Relationships between girls and women can help girls develop a healthy critical perspective, to be able to develop, with women, strategies of resistance that maintain health and manage the inevitable losses, both psychological and material, in a social system stratified by race, class, and gender. By creating relationships that are not simply instrumental but evocative as well, and by creating connections that encourage girls and women to bring themselves more fully into relationship, relationships between women and girls "at risk" might indeed become "places where people can return to themselves more easily, where . . . they can heal themselves and recover their wholeness."

NOTE

1. In this group, three African American girls, one Latina girl, and two white girls dropped out of high school. All of these six except one of the white girls became adolescent mothers.

REFERENCES

I gratefully acknowledge the substantive contributions and editorial assistance of George Horner. Thanks also to Kathryn Geismar, Katie Weinger, and Mary Peckham for their helpful feedback.

American Association of University Women. 1992. *The AAUW report: How schools shortchange girls.* Washington, D.C.: American Association of University Women Educational Foundation and National Education Association.

Blyth, D. A., J. P. Hill, and K. Thiel. 1982. Early adolescents' significant others: Grade and gender differences in perceived relationships with familial and nonfamilial adults and young people. *Journal of Youth and Adolescence* 11 (6):425–50.

Boyer, D., and D. Fine. 1992. Sexual abuse as a factor in adolescent pregnancy and child maltreatment. *Family Planning Perspectives* 24 (4):4–11.

Brown, L., D. Argyris, J. Attanucci, B. Bardige, C. Gilligan, K. Johnston, B. Miller, D. Osborne, M. Tappan, J. Ward, G. Wiggins, and D. Wilcox. 1988. *A guide to reading narratives of conflict and choice for self and moral voice.* Cambridge: Harvard Graduate School of Education, Project on Women's Psychology and Girls' Development.

Brown, L., and C. Gilligan. 1992. *Meeting at the crossroads.* Cambridge: Harvard University Press.

Clark-Lempers, D. S., J. D. Lempers, and C. Ho. 1991. Early, middle, and late adolescents' perceptions of their relationships with significant others. *Journal of Adolescent Research* 6 (3):296–315. Newbury Park, Calif.: Sage.

Collins, P. H. 1990. *Black feminist thought: Knowledge, consciousness, and the politics of empowerment.* Boston: Unwin Hyman.

Daloz, L. A. 1983. Mentors: Teachers who make a difference. *Change* 15 (6):24–27.

Darling, N. 1991. Challenging and supportive relationships and the academic achievement of adolescents. In *Unrelated adults in adolescents' lives,* edited by S. Hamilton, 12–30. Occasional Paper no. 29. Ithaca, N.Y.: Cornell University Western Societies Program.

Dorney, J. 1991. "Courage to act in a small way": Clues toward community and change among women and girls. Ph.D. diss., Harvard University.

Falicov, C. 1982. Mexican families. In *Ethnicity and family therapy,* edited by M. McGoldrick, J. Pearce, and J. Giordano, 134–63. New York: Guilford Press.

Fine, M. 1991. *Framing dropouts: Notes on the politics of an urban high school.* New York: State University of New York Press.

Galbo, J. 1983. Adolescents' perceptions of significant adults. *Adolescence* 18 (70):417–27.

———. 1984. Adolescents' perceptions of significant adults: A review of the literature. *Adolescence* 19 (76):951–70.

Garbarino, J., N. Burston, S. Raber, R. Russell, and A. Crouter. 1978. The social maps of children approaching adolescence: Studies of the ecology of growth development. *Journal of Youth and Adolescence* 7 (4):417–28.

Gibbs, J. T. 1985. City girls: Psychosocial adjustment of urban black adolescent females. *SAGE* 2 (2):28–36.

Gilligan, C. [1982] 1993. *In a different voice: Psychological theory and women's development.* Reprint, Cambridge: Harvard University Press.

———. 1990. Joining the resistance: Psychology, politics, girls and women. *Michigan Quarterly Review* 29 (4):501–36.

Gilligan, C., J. Taylor, D. Tolman, A. Sullivan, J. Dorney, and P. Pleasants. 1992. *Understanding adolescence: A study of urban teens considered to be at-risk.* Cambridge: Harvard Graduate School of Education, Project on Women's Psychology and Girls' Development.

Gilligan, C., J. Ward, and J. Taylor, eds. 1988. *Mapping the moral domain: A contribution of women's thinking to psychological theory and education*. Cambridge: Harvard University Press.

Hamilton, S. F., ed. 1991. *Unrelated adults in adolescents' lives: Perspectives from four countries*. Occasional Paper no. 29. Ithaca, N.Y.: Cornell University Western Societies Program.

Hamilton, S. F., and L. Darling. 1989. Mentors in adolescents' lives. In *The social world of adolescents*, edited by K. Hurrelmann and U. Engel. New York: Walter de Gruyter.

Herman, J. 1981. *Father-daughter incest*. Cambridge: Harvard University Press.

———. 1992. *Trauma and recovery*. New York: Basic Books.

hooks, b. 1990. *Yearning: Race, gender, and cultural politics*. Boston: South End Press.

Hurrelmann, K. 1991. Parents, peers, teachers, and other significant partners in adolescence. In *Unrelated adults in adolescents' lives: Perspectives from four countries*, edited by S. F. Hamilton, 31–39. Occasional Paper no. 29. Ithaca, N.Y.: Cornell University Western Societies Program.

Levinson, D., with C. Darrow, E. Klein, M. Levinson, and B. McKee. 1979. *The seasons of a man's life*. New York: Alfred A. Knopf.

Loevinger, J., and R. Wessler. 1970. *Measuring ego development*. San Francisco: Jossey-Bass.

Miles, M., and A. Huberman. 1984. *Qualitative data analysis: A sourcebook of new methods*. Beverly Hills, Calif.: Sage.

Moitoza, E. 1982. Portuguese families. In *Ethnicity and family therapy*, edited by M. McGoldrick, J. Pearce, and J. Giordano, 412–37. New York: Guilford Press.

Poole, M. E. 1989. Adolescent transitions: A life-course perspective. In *The social world of adolescence*, edited by K. Hurrelmann and U. Engel, 65–85. New York: Walter de Gruyter.

Reid, P., and L. Comas-Diaz. 1990. Gender and ethnicity: Perspectives on dual status. *Sex Roles* 22 (7/8):397–408.

Rhodes, J., L. Ebert, and K. Fischer. 1992. Natural mentors: An overlooked resource in the social networks of adolescent mothers. *American Journal of Community Psychology* 20:445–61.

Rogers, A. 1989. Translating girls' voices. Paper presented at the Big Brothers/Big Sisters of America National Conference, Norfolk, Va.

———. 1993. Voice, play, and the practice of ordinary courage in girls' and women's lives. *Harvard Educational Review* 63 (3):265–96.

Rogers, A., L. Brown, and M. Tappan. 1993. Interpreting loss and ego development in girls: Regression or resistance? In *The narrative study of lives*, edited by R. E. Josselson and A. Lieblich. Newbury Park, Calif.: Sage.

Rutter, M. 1980. *Changing youth in a changing society: Patterns of adolescent development and disorder*. Cambridge: Harvard University Press.

Sadker, M., and D. Sadker. 1994. *Failing at fairness: How America's schools cheat girls*. New York: Charles Scribner's Sons.

Salzinger, S., M. Hammer, and J. Antrobus. 1988. From crib to college: An overview of studies of the social networks of children, adolescents, and college students. In *Social networks of children, adolescents, and college students*, edited by S. Salzinger, J. Antrobus, and M. Hammer, 1–16. Hillsdale, N.J.: Lawrence Erlbaum Associates.

Stevenson, R., and J. Ellsworth. 1993. Dropouts and the silencing of critical voices. In *Beyond silenced voices: Class, race, and gender in United States schools*, edited by L. Weis and M. Fine, 259–71. Albany: State University of New York Press.

Sullivan, A. M. 1993. Connections of promise: Women in the lives of adolescent girls considered to be at risk. Doctoral qualifying paper, Harvard University Graduate School of Education.

Sullivan, A. M., with E. Snee, and K. Weinger. 1994. How equal is opportunity in Indiana? A report on girls. In *High hopes, long odds*, edited by G. Orfield and F. Paul. Indianapolis: Lilly Endowment.

Taylor, J., C. Gilligan, and A. Sullivan. 1996. *Between voice and silence: Women and girls, race and relationships*. Cambridge: Harvard University Press.

Ueland, B. [1938] 1987. *If you want to write*. Reprint, Saint Paul: Graywolf Press.

Werner, E. 1987. Vulnerability and resiliency in children at risk for delinquency: A longitudinal study from birth to adulthood. In *Prevention of delinquent behavior*, edited by J. Burchard and S. Burchard, vol. 10, 16–43. Newbury Park, Calif.: Sage.

# Sexuality

The premarital sexual activity of young women (and young men) has come to be of greater social concern than it was in earlier generations because today's young people are not only reaching sexual maturity and initiating intercourse earlier, they are also marrying later than they did previously. Almost all adolescents (96%) initiate sexual intercourse before they are married, and 56% of women and 73% of men have had intercourse before their eighteenth birthday. Although the prevalent view of ethnic minority poor urban girls is that they are more likely to be sexually active than their white, rural or higher-income counterparts, in reality the percentages of fifteen- to nineteen-year-old girls having sex are similar in these groups (Alan Guttmacher Institute 1994, 20, 26).

Despite the prevalence of teenage sexual activity, there remains considerable controversy about the desirability of sex education in the United States. Moreover, studying the sex education curriculum of a number of New York City schools, Michelle Fine (1988) concluded that a hidden curriculum teaches girls that the consequence of sexual maturation is becoming vulnerable to male predators who cannot control their raging hormones and to unwanted pregnancies and sexually transmitted diseases. Managing sexuality is seen as the moral choice of good and bad girls. The "problem" of girls' sexuality is not an issue of girls' taking responsibility in wanting or not wanting sex, but that they must decide whether to resist or receive boys' desires—"just say no" or "let" him go all the way. Fine (1988) also notes the absence of discussion in sex education classes about girls' desire and about girls as agents of their sexual behavior. She notes with some irony that, lacking a view of themselves as desiring agent, girls also fail to see themselves as having responsibility for initiating or negotiating sexual situations.

Youth magazines, television, and movies also teach girls that a woman's sexuality is not about having agency. Rather, it is a matter of appearance. The message that preadolescent girls (and indeed adult women) hear from the media is at once inviting, confusing, and shaming. At puberty girls must accommodate to their growing, rounding, sexual bodies while aspiring to become as thin and sexy as the super models. They must also remain as chaste and wholesome as a preadolescent or risk a "bad" reputation. The possibility of girls controlling their bodies and their sexuality is undermined by confusing messages about the negative consequences both of their actions (appearing to be sluts) and their inaction (not protecting themselves). Yet, girls are unambiguously held responsible for these consequences.

Beliefs that equate sexual promiscuity with poor urban girls of color also stem from historical and current racist images of black women, from conditions of poverty that make the negative consequences of adolescent sexuality in these communities more visible, and from research that has focused on racial rather than socioeconomic differences in investigations of adolescent sexuality. In the voices of urban girls in this section, we hear concerns about victimization and the dangers of not silencing their desire (chapter 14) as well as about the risks of not acting on it (chapter 16). Characteristics of girls who successfully avoid pregnancy, despite sexual activity, are also discussed (chapter 15).

In chapter 14, Tolman counters the stereotype of the sexually promiscuous poor urban girl with the words of a racially and ethnically diverse sample of urban and suburban girls. When asked to speak about their experiences of sexual desire, these girls describe silencing, highly self-regulating, or denying their sexual feelings in the name of protecting themselves against diseases, sexual abuse, and bad reputations. Tolman asks whether the costs of closing off sexual feelings are not too high for adolescent girls.

Research abounds on the changing rates of sexual activity among adolescent girls, as well as on their birth control use and on their risks for contracting sexually transmitted diseases. Murry, in chapter 15, reviews this extensive literature and suggests that biological (e.g., race, early maturation), social control (e.g., parental supervision), and social structural (e.g., access to reproductive health care) factors explain differences in sexual activity in adolescent girls. She uses data from the 1988 National Survey of Family Growth Cycle VI, which included 1,246 urban black and Hispanic sexually active nonmothers, ages fifteen to twenty-one, to investigate factors that influence their ability to avoid pregnancy during adolescence. The strongest predictors in multivariate analyses included lower family income, current sexual activity, early menarche, and their mothers' levels of education.

Vera, Reese, Paikoff, and Jarrett conducted focus groups with African American preadolescents, parents, and community leaders to elaborate the details of the social context in which preadolescents from an inner-city Chicago housing development begin to make choices about sexual activity. Their research, presented in chapter 16, raises questions about how exposure to chronic poverty and violence affects decision making around high risk sexual behaviors. The authors argue that prevention efforts cannot succeed if they fail to consider the broader picture of these preadolescent's lives and fail to integrate their early knowledge about sexual activity and concerns about personal safety with their decisions about engagement in early sexual activity.

## REFERENCES

Alan Guttmacher Institute. 1994. *Sex and America's teenagers.* New York: Author.

Fine, M. 1988. Sexuality, schooling, and adolescent females: The missing discourse of desire. *Harvard Educational Review* 58 (1):29–53.

# 14 Adolescent Girls' Sexuality: Debunking the Myth of The Urban Girl

Deborah L. Tolman

## Sex and The Urban Girl

When the nation's ills are bemoaned by politicians, the media, and many social scientists, the twin crises of "teenage promiscuity and pregnancy" inevitably make the short list. This cry of moral decay is, in fact, a code. Cracking this code, "teenage" really means girls (not boys, who are never considered promiscuous and cannot get pregnant), but not all girls—this problem affects "certain" girls. The brows of the browbeaters are furrowed on behalf of The Urban Girl. Like drawing a police sketch from fractured recollections of features, it is not hard to flesh out a single face, a single body, for The Urban Girl. This stereotype is not a real person but a unidimensional stick figure who lives in the public imagination rather than on the streets of urban America. On the body of The Urban Girl, social context becomes confused and confounded with race: she is a girl of color, and so she must be poor (Painter 1992). She is the daughter of a single mother. She is incapable of delaying gratification, fails in school, does not secure employment, and most of all she is sexually promiscuous, lacking in morality or family values, and out of control. She is at risk and at fault. She embodies the problem of teenage pregnancy.

Social theorists have suggested that teenage pregnancy pushes the panic button not only because of concern with economic burdens or negative outcomes for individual teenage mothers and society, but because it makes teenage sexuality real (Petchesky 1990). We live in a society in which displays of sexuality are not well tolerated and in which displays of female sexuality are especially anxiety-provoking (Vance 1984). Because adolescent girls' sexuality is rarely contained within monogamous marriages, it is particularly distressing. For girls, "sexual" is split from "good" and "normal." The Urban Girl is bad and not normal: she *is* female adolescent sexuality. So imagined and constructed, she bears the brunt of society's collective anxiety in altered, punitive forms. She is the dumping ground for the strongest and most suppressed fears and desires regarding sexuality. Researchers have been complicit in the cultural myth that she is, indeed, the root of most social problems. This equation of The Urban Girl with forbidden sexuality has come at the expense of urban girls themselves, both in the narrow venue society expects and offers them and in fueling ignorance of their complex lives. This parochial association of sexuality with The Urban Girl is also a disservice to all other girls, whose sexuality is not identified as important or even existent.

Why is The Urban Girl a girl of color? The Urban Girl has deep roots in the American psyche's constructions of women and of sexuality. In the dominant culture of this country, black women have been historically connected with sexuality, while white women have been thought to embody asexual virtue, racially encoding a segregation of women labeled "good" and "bad." These categories are reinforced by the association of blackness with poverty, the other realm of "bad" sexual women in this ideology (Painter 1992). Hyperbolic images of black women's sexuality include the castrating matriarch, the overly sexual young Jezebel and her not-too-distant adolescent cousin, the welfare queen or cheat. All are characterized as sexually out of control, instigators and temptresses, bad girls and women who are therefore never considered to be sexually vulnerable (Caraway 1991; Painter 1992; Daniel in press).

The persistent focus on The Urban Girl as the embodiment of (teenage) sexuality is more nuanced than a simple equation of sexuality with blackness, poverty, or Otherness (Daniel in press). It reproduces deep historical and interlocking ideas not only about black women but also about white women (Hall 1983; Caraway 1991; Collins 1991). The "goodness" of white women rests on the constructed "immorality" of black women (Caraway 1991). In a misogynist culture that offers dubious rewards to virtuous women and unequivocally punishes even the presumably errant, a (white) woman knows her "goodness" by knowing she is not that Other. A seductive and impoverished privilege thus accrues to white women on the bodies of black women as well as at the expense of their own psyches and vitality. This complex interplay of oppressions depends on keeping women divided into good vs. bad, normal vs. out-of-control categories, coded by race and class. The legacy of the desexualized white woman, who is above all else not black, underpins The Urban Girl.

Researchers are not immune to these constructions of women, as is amply evident in research on adolescent sexuality. In a society myopically focused on individual characteristics, the quest to identify "bad" girls and predict their egregious behavior (premarital sexual intercourse) dominates the study of adolescent sexuality. Since the social and educational dislocation of many urban girls makes the consequences of sexuality more costly for them than for adolescents who have functioning safety nets (Petchesky 1990), their sexuality and their pregnancy are more visible and more easily vilified. Unlike most research on adolescent development, where urban girls are ignored or eclipsed by the perpetual use of white, economically and educationally advantaged samples, The Urban Girl has historically been, and continues to be, the subject of choice for research on adolescent sexuality (Scott-Jones and White 1990).

Recent demographic trends raise questions, however, about why a focus on The Urban Girl persists in studies of adolescent sexuality. The reality is that the majority of adolescent girls, be they urban or suburban, white, black, or Hispanic (or other racial or ethnic groups rarely mentioned), become sexually active in adolescence (Alan Guttmacher Institute 1994; Gullotta, Adams, and Montemayor 1993). The differential observed in the 1970s, when a higher percentage of black than white girls were sexually active, was negligible in the 1980s. Most of the increase in female sexual activity in the 1980s was among white teenagers and those in higher income families, narrowing the previous racial or ethnic and income differences (Forrest and Singh 1990; Zabin and Hayward 1993). When race and class are not confounded, black adolescents are not more sexually active than whites (Scott-Jones and White 1990). In research on adolescent sexuality published between 1987 and 1993, race is consistently examined as a correlate of sexual activity with no theoretical justification (e.g., Foshee and Bauman 1992; Muram et al. 1991). Even more prevalent is the exclusive use of samples of urban black and, more recently, Hispanic girls (e.g., Ensminger 1990; Holmbeck, Waters, and Brookman 1990; Handler 1990; Keith et al. 1991).

The difference between understanding adolescent sexuality and preventing adolescent pregnancy has not been well articulated, precisely because the underlying agenda has not been to understand adolescent sexuality but to prevent adolescent pregnancy (Petchesky 1990). Research on adolescent girls' sexuality arouses such anxiety and controversy that woeful neglect of this topic has been tolerated (Tolman 1994). While much is known about adolescents' rates of sexual intercourse and pregnancy, and about their contraceptive practices, adolescent sexuality is defined as initiation of sexual intercourse rather than in terms of the meanings various aspects of sexuality have for adolescents (Brooks-Gunn and Furstenberg 1989; Zaslow and Takanishi 1993). Sexual behavior is persistently equated with deviance rather than with development (e.g., Flannery, Rowe, and Gulley 1993). Since it is The Urban Girl who is considered deviant and sexual, it is her sexual activity that comes under scrutiny. Rates of black adolescent pregnancy are higher than rates of pregnancy among white adolescents (Zabin and Hayward 1993), but the fact that these rates have diminished more rapidly among Blacks than among Whites in the last decade (Alan Guttmacher Institute 1994) or that there are larger numbers of white than black adolescent births (Child Trends 1994) is rarely mentioned.

The few studies suggesting any positive psychological or social outcomes of girls' sexual activity or adolescent pregnancy quickly disappear from the discourse on adolescent sexuality. The exclusive focus on preventing pregnancy shores up The Urban Girl, enabling ongoing ignorance of and resistance to the sexuality of adolescent girls. Theoretically relevant differences among urban girls, such as religiosity, quality of sexual and relational experiences, contexts of sexual encounters, and the meanings of those encounters for different girls are virtually unexplored. This body of research is also oddly silent about the potential negative outcomes for all girls of failing to understand, acknowledge, or integrate sexuality into a positive sense of themselves and their relationships (e.g., hooks 1993; Lorde 1984).

Michelle Fine offers a partial corrective in initiating a discourse about adolescent sexuality that is not overwhelmed by adolescent pregnancy; in her study urban girls have a voice that conveys the complexity of their lives. She observes that urban girls talk about desire and danger as interwoven aspects of their sexuality (Fine 1988). In this chapter I flesh out how a group of urban girls understand their own sexual feelings and how they deal with the conflicts and consequences of their own sexuality. An unintended outcome of this research is compelling evidence for debunking The Urban Girl myth. First, urban girls who are learning to negotiate their sexuality are not all black or of color. Secondly, suburban girls experience and negotiate their sexuality as well. Finally, the association of urban girls with pregnancy and promiscuity obscures a far more complex psychological process of how girls deal with their own and their partners' sexuality.

## The Study

My goal was to develop an understanding of girls' experiences of their own sexual desire as described by a purposefully heterogeneous sample of twenty-eight girls from urban and suburban public school settings.[1] Theoretically and psychologically compelling similarities and differences in how they express their desire emerged among these two groups of girls, challenging The Urban Girl as sole proprietor of female adolescent sexuality. They represent a range of class, cultural, educational, racial or ethnic, and religious backgrounds, as well as a variety of family situations, histories of sexual abuse or violence, histories of closeness and safety, physical appearances, and sexual experiences. In the urban sample, seven girls are black (four African Americans and three Caribbeans), three are Hispanic, and five are white. They are from poor or working-class backgrounds. Fourteen of the suburban girls are white and one is Hispanic. This confounding of race and class is typical of urban and suburban communities.

I conducted in-depth semistructured interviews with each of them, utilizing an approach to psychological inquiry that is explicitly relational; the interviewer attends to the participant's experience as the guide for inquiry (Brown and Gilligan 1992). These girls said that no adult woman had ever talked directly or in such depth to them before about their sexual desire and pleasure; more than half had never spoken with anyone about it. For the urban girls, research unrelated to pregnancy was a novelty; for the suburban girls, acknowledgement of their sexuality in any form was new. I analyzed the narrative told by each girl about a time when she experienced sexual desire using a variation of a qualitative approach, the Listening Guide, an interpretive analysis that focuses on a girl's voice and the layered meanings that inhere in any story of lived experience (Brown et al. 1991). Each narrative is read several times, each time privileging and underlining a particular voice or point of view. The result is a visual mapping of the multiple aspects of a girl's experience that retains the context of the narrative rather than breaking it apart to evaluate the frequency of themes. This map is used to create an interpretation of the girl's experience, as understood by the researcher. Using these interpretations, I then developed conceptually clustered matrices (Miles and Huberman 1984), a qualitative analytic technique for organizing and displaying data according to designated concepts, to identify patterns within and between the urban and suburban groups.

## Not for The Urban Girl Only: An Erotic Voice

For all these girls, sexual desire is a feature of and a way of being in relationships. While feelings of sexual desire most often arise in the context of relationships, they distinguish sexual desire from wanting relationships. Rather, for the majority of these girls, regardless of urban or suburban location, sexual desire is a specific, powerful "feeling" of wanting. Their descriptions resonate with what African American poet and essayist Audre Lorde has described as the power of the erotic, "the *yes* within ourselves, our deepest cravings . . . how fully and acutely we can feel in the doing" (Lorde 1984, 54). Lorde writes that in this society women have been systematically kept from this power in ourselves, because, she surmises, the power of the erotic makes women dangerous: women so empowered will challenge an oppressive status quo. She encourages women to reclaim and reconnect with this affirmative force that resides inside them, so that they will be able to glean pleasure in all arenas of their lives.

The majority of this group of white, black, and Hispanic girls, from both urban and suburban settings, could describe their own feelings of sexual desire. Inez knows she is feeling desire when "my body says yes." Lily calls feeling desire "amazing." Rochelle feels it "so, so bad . . . I wanna have sex so bad, you know . . . you just have this feeling, you just have to get rid of it." In speaking about her sexual desire, Liz explains: "I just wanted to have sex with him really badly and I just, and we just took off our bathing suits really fast (laugh) and it was almost like really rushed and really quick." For Barbara, it is "very strong . . . an overwhelming longing" and "a wicked urge"; Paulina's heart "would really beat fast"; she is "extremely aware of every, every touch and everything." Alexandra speaks of being "incredibly attracted" to her friend. Jane calls the power of her desire "demanding" and says "the feelings are so strong inside you that they're just like ready to burst." Cassandra evidences the strength and the urgency of her feeling in narrating what she does not want to do, "stop": "he just like stopped all of a sudden and I was like what are you doing? cause I didn't want to stop at all"; she says that for her, desire is "powerful." Lily contrasts not being "in the mood to do anything . . . because I just have all my clothes on . . . because it's just too inconvenient" with the power of her desire when she feels it, "once in a while": "even though it's inconvenient for me, sometimes I just have this feeling, well I just don't care, if I have to put my pantyhose on or not," the power of her desire overriding her usual concern about looking proper.

## Listening to Urban Girls Voice Desire

When the urban girls describe their responses to their own sexual desire, themes of self-control, caution, and conflict predominate. They make explicit connections between their sexual desire and danger, acknowledging conflicts between their desire and their physical vulnerability to AIDS and to pregnancy, as well as their social vulnerability to getting a "bad reputation." In a social context in which danger and violence are palpable, visible, and unavoidable, most of these girls make conscious choices to sacrifice pleasure to protect themselves from danger. This self-protective strategy may cost them a connection to themselves and to their own bodies and may provide little real safety. The only glimpse I caught of The Urban Girl in this sample of urban girls was of her lurking discreetly in the girls' psyches, in their attempts to avoid her, not to become her.

Ellen is a soft-spoken seventeen-year-old black woman from Trinidad, whose intelligent eyes look bashfully back at me, safe behind her glasses. She describes herself as very religious, a Baptist who attends church regularly. Ellen tells me that she made a promise to God, at age eleven, not to have relationships, "particularly that kind of relationship" until she had graduated from high school. When I ask her directly if sexual desire is something she has experienced, she responds, "Ummmm, no." When I ask her again—"A feeling of wanting?"— she replies "Yes." I am not sure how to hear these responses: is she guessing for the "right" answer, the one she thinks I want to hear? Is she speaking, yet not telling me about whether sexual desire is something she experiences? Is she unsure? I notice how polite she is; I sense that, just as she wants to be a successful student, she wants to be a good participant. I ask her to speak about her experience, hoping that specifics will shed some light.

At first, when I ask Ellen if she could tell me about a time when she experienced sexual desire, she begins to tell me a sparse story about a time when she started "thinking about him . . . having sex, kissing him." When I ask her if she can tell me more, she answers "I can't, I just forgot about it, I really didn't." I sense that Ellen's story, a short story that ends abruptly because she "just forgot about it," relays in its structure what sexual desire may be like for her. Even thinking about kissing initiates a process in her mind that could lead to sexual desire in her body. The logic of her promise to God is revealed when Ellen interrupts her sparse desire narrative with another story, about how her friend wanted to have sex, got pregnant, and had an abortion. Ellen explains that she "didn't want that happening to me, just because of a boy." I am thus not surprised to hear that regarding sexual desire, Ellen's body is absent: "I don't feel very much in my body, it's like very few is physical." She may prevent her thoughts about sex from moving into her body by "forgetting it," an astute psychological move to try to dissociate from what for Ellen appear to be dangerous feelings.

Yet the way Ellen speaks of what does not happen in her body makes me think that she may have some "physical" feelings at times, feelings that are not very strong, perhaps, or not very frequent. This interpretation of Ellen's words is supported when she describes how her resolve is threatened; when one particular boy is persistent in his wish to be with her, feelings occur in her body that make her want to break her promise. This experience causes Ellen distress:

I didn't like it. You know, well, I didn't want it to happen . . . sex, or kissing, or whatever, my feelings, cause, you know, it wasn't the right time, you know . . . liking the person so much . . . I'm afraid that, you know, liking the person so much, or maybe that something will happen . . . my desires, or, that, I might act upon it, you know.

I come away from speaking with Ellen with the distinct sense that she would prefer not to feel desire, because such feelings make it hard for her to keep her promise. Ellen helps me understand her reticence by explaining how her family context fleshes out the danger of her desire:

See, I'm afraid of sex, cause I mean I've seen what happens to my friends, to my family. . . . I don't want that happening to me, the situation [my sisters] are both in, having a baby at a young age, and not prepared for it. And my older sister has a boyfriend that don't care if she is having a baby or if she's not, because all he cares about is the sex, you know, and the desire, his desire, he doesn't care about her.

Ellen's psychological and social moves to protect herself from herself and from being hurt by others appear to reflect the "internal self-censoring mechanisms which come into play to thwart Black women's desire, pervert their pleasures and suppress their sexuality" (Caraway 1991, 97). For Ellen, sexuality offers only danger and the threat of deviance; the power of the erotic is carried out of her life on the back of The Urban Girl.

Inez, who is sixteen years old and Puerto Rican, knows she is feeling desire when "my body gets into the pleasure mood." Inez speaks of her sexual desire in terms of her body—she knows she is feeling desire "when my body says yes." She lays out the relationship she experiences between her mind and her body saying: "My body does not control my mind. My mind controls my body, and if my body gets into the pleasure mood, my mind is gonna tell him no. And it can happen, because I said so, because I control you, and my mind is lookin' towards my body." When Inez speaks of her experiences of sexual desire, she speaks of knowing and feeling pleasure and of knowing, fearing, and avoiding danger. While she knows that having her breasts touched "feels so wonderful," Inez also thinks and speaks about the physical dangers that make her vulnerable, saying: "Let's say you don't have no kind of contraceptives like a condom, and he has AIDS and you don't know that, you can get AIDS just by having sex with him, because your body said yes, your mind said no, but your body said yes." Inez speaks about how listening and responding to the "yes" of her body can lead to pregnancy and AIDS. She explains that her "mind is lookin towards my body" and acts as a shield to protect her body from vulnerabilities about which she is very aware. Knowing what she knows about pleasure, she nevertheless explains how the "no" in her mind must unequivocally drown out her body's "yes" to protect her from disease and death.

Throughout this interview Inez voices her knowledge of her own sexual desire and her choice to keep herself out of danger by silencing her body. Knowing the power of her own desire both from her experience and from watching other girls, she tries to avoid getting into situations in which she might begin to have sexual feelings:

Desire? Yes, because [a girl] is probably in one of those, like let's say she's just drunk and she doesn't know what she's doin', and she's dancing with this guy, you know how they dance reggae, ever seen somebody dance reggae? How they rubbin' on each other? Well that gets a guy real, I'll say, hard. And it gets a girl very horny. And they could just be dancin' together for like five minutes, and all the sudden, [snaps fingers] they just, they, something just snaps in 'em and they say "oh, let's go to the bedroom." And, it'll just happen, just because they were dancing. That's why I don't dance reggae with guys.

Although she describes dancing as something she enjoys and is good at, to keep her body safe, Inez keeps her body still, trying to avoid situations in which she will feel desire, minimizing the moments when she will have to cope with this mind–body conflict, in which she might be mistaken for The Urban Girl.

Sixteen-year-old Barbara, who is white and has blue eyes framed by long blond hair that falls across the back of her track jacket, tells a story about a time with her boyfriend "before [they] had sex, cause I wasn't sure how he looked at sex":

There was this time, he was giving me a backrub, and all I could think about is what I wanted him to do besides have backrubs [laugh] and he has to rub my body, forget the back, just do the whole body. . . . It was a very strong desire just to have him rub all over, and that was the one time I can think of I've really had it bad [laugh]. . . . I'm laying there thinking this, and I didn't want to tell him that, cause I didn't know him that well at the time, and its like, noooo, no, we'll just wait [laugh].

She explains how she comes to her decision not to speak or act in concordance with what she is feeling and wanting:

I didn't know him well enough. I subtly like to initiate, I don't like to come outright and say, oh let's go do this, I just like doing things very subtly, cause I'm not a very, when it comes to sex, the first few times with the person, I'm not very forthright about anything, until after I've gotten to know them, and I trust them a little bit more, and I know that they're not going to look at me funny when I say I want to do something like this.

Barbara narrates a retreat to what Carol Gilligan has called the "underground," a metaphor for how some girls consciously keep their true thoughts and feelings protected, out of relationships where saying what they really think and feel can be dangerous (Gilligan 1989). Barbara knows her own feelings and chooses to keep them out of this relationship as a way of protecting herself from having her boyfriend judge her. Barbara's sense that she needs to keep herself from being known as a young woman who "want[s] to do something," who knows and wants to act in response to her own desire, comes from her own experience:

That was like with oral sex, I never thought I would meet a guy that didn't like oral sex, and I met a guy. Cause I hadn't had oral sex with this boyfriend, but the boyfriend before that I was wanting to attempt that, and, he would have no part in that. And so I was kind of, you feel really embarrassed after you've asked to do something, and it's like, and then they're, 'oh no, no, no, get away.' And so I came to this boyfriend I'm thinking, I was very [laugh] subtle about doing this 'cause I wanted to make sure I wasn't going to make a fool of myself. It depends on the guy, if I'll be forthright or not.

To avoid being taken for a "fool," Barbara must temper her curiosity and desire; she has figured out that she can avoid embarrassment by being "subtle." This process not only consumes her energy but supports the discipline her mind exerts over her body, a discipline that puts her at risk for dissociating from key information about this relationship.

Rather than silence the "yes" in her body, Barbara continues to feel her desire for what she wanted besides backrubs, keeping it alive in the underground world of her real thoughts and feelings, but chooses consciously not to pursue it: "It's kinda depressing in its own way afterwards, cause you're like sitting there, well I, you know, I should have said something, or, you know, actually left and gone home, you're laying there, well I should have said something [with small laugh] cause later on it's like, well, I didn't fulfill it (moan) [laugh]." Perhaps precisely because Barbara does not silence her body, she holds onto other knowledge about herself; not listening to her body is "kinda depressing," being fully aware of the pleasure she has sacrificed, bemoaning the frustration she now feels, in the wake of her choice not to respond to her sexual feeling and curiosity. In telling this desire narrative, Barbara describes the doubt and regret surrounding her choice to respond to her desire by silencing her body and herself. These costly efforts to regulate her sexual desire silently and keep The Urban Girl at bay prove an ill-fated strategy: Barbara reveals that she is four months pregnant at the time of this interview.

Rather than give credence to the sexually out-of-control Urban Girl, these urban girls portray a vigilant caution regarding their own sexual desire, investing energy in efforts to insure their safety. These girls disconnect from or dampen any curiosity associated with their sexual desire. Curiosity, the pleasure of feeling and learning about themselves and others in relationship, staying in connection with the power of the erotic, seems a luxury for these girls, one they cannot reconcile with dangers they perceive. The one exception is seventeen-year-old Paulina, a recent immigrant from Eastern Europe, who describes a response to her sexual desire in which caution and curiosity comingle:

[That feeling] makes me like really aware of what somebody's doing. . . . You're like aware of every move he makes, you just know it. . . . I don't mind touching the other person, I mean, I don't feel like any part of the other person is dirty in any way. And like, I like guys chests especially, especially if it's broad, and I like touching the chest, especially if it smells nice, I like it. And I like playing just like especially if it's like little hairs, I just like playing with it, I don't mind.

Paulina knows what she likes: experiencing, through "touch," "smell," and "play," the pleasure of a man's body. But there is a distinct note of caution in how Paulina speaks about her enjoyment; she seems to curb her pleasure and enjoyment, telling me repeatedly that when she feels desire, she doesn't mind. This unsolicited caveat suggests that she knows or feels that perhaps she should mind. When I ask her about it, she explains that she knows girls are aware of how others view and judge them if they explore and express sexual desire:

Because there's a lot of girls that I know who just wouldn't do it, they're kind of like, they wouldn't have oral sex with somebody because the person might think something of them. And I don't really care what the person will think, because the person will know me well enough, so I just do it.

*Because?*

Because I would want to.

Paulina voices a resistance to other people's opinions, not "really car [ing]" if "something" is thought or said about her if she is exploring her desire, doing what she wants to do. Yet her insistence on explaining to me that she "doesn't feel like any part of the other person is dirty in any way" belies her sense that she is under pressure to modulate her desire and her response to it to fit the picture of what girls who want to avoid becoming The Urban Girl should do. In order to stay with the pleasure of her senses, Paulina maintains an active program of "not caring" about the potentially painful social stigma of being talked about—or shunned—

which constantly threatens her ability to stay connected with the power of the erotic. If she is to stay connected with the erotic, she must engage in an active resistance against the social pressure she feels to silence herself.

## Listening to Suburban Girls Voice Desire

In contrast, when the suburban girls told me about their responses to sexual desire, they spoke more frequently of pursuing sexual curiosity. While for the urban girls the need to protect and control themselves consistently won out over their curiosity, in the suburban girls this conflict was expressed and often resolved differently. Rather than problems of physical dangers or spoiled reputations, the suburban girls voiced an internal conflict between what they felt in their bodies and the cultural messages about appropriate female sexual behavior that had been instilled in them. Instead of silencing their bodies in response to this conflict, these suburban girls describe their struggle to stay in connection with themselves and their bodies. Themes of romance and being a "good" girl resounded more centrally in their stories. By asking girls to speak about their sexual feelings and their responses to these feelings, rather than about their sexual activity, I begin to reconstitute what "counts" as sexuality, supplanting whether or not a girl has had sexual intercourse with knowing oneself as sexual.

Seventeen-year-old Sophie,[2] who is white, speaks easily about a time she experienced sexual desire. She describes what sounds like an episode from a romance novel, in which she embodies The Urban Girl's alter ego, the "good and normal" girl who is not supposed to feel desire:

My friend [Eugenia] was on the phone, and he was like chasing me around, like we were totally joking. He was like chasing me with some like bat or something like that? And I like went to get away, and he like pinned me down. It sounds like cruel and like ferocious, but he was like holding me down, and I was like, Eugenia! But I was literally like, I was like, Eugenia! But she knew that I liked him, [laughing] so she was just staying on the phone. And he was just right above me and had both my arms down, and it was like, I knew that I was acting like I just wanted to get away, but really I just would've wanted to just totally kiss him or something? And it is those great brown eyes, he just looked right at me, and he's just so—it's that sexual desire thing, you just feel a certain way, and it was just like, it's almost like a waiting feeling?

In compliance with her role in this drama, Sophie is not only passive, but she pretends she is not feeling desire and keeps her real feelings disguised as cries of distress.[3] Yet Sophie is in fact quite knowledgeable about her own sexual desire. She explains why she waits rather than acts in this situation: "Maybe that's because I'm a female and usually, guys make the first move. That isn't always the way, but a lot of times it's that way. . . . It just tends to happen that way? Like they tend to, maybe they tend to just get to it faster or, I don't know." Sophie connects her feeling of "waiting" and her conscious decision to "act" as if she wants to escape when in fact she wants to "totally kiss him or something" to being female. For Sophie the prerogative of sexual action is male—"usually, guys make the first move." Sophie says she "does not know" why this is so.

While not spoken about directly by Sophie, the vulnerability embedded in this role is also apparent as Sophie describes this boy's "cruel" and "ferocious" behavior. In fact, a melding of fear and excitement is evident in Sophie's story and makes sense in a culture that eroticizes danger and women's vulnerability. Because she is safe in this particular situation, Sophie can enjoy this play. What is cause for concern, however, is Sophie's seeming lack of conscious awareness or concern about the violence in her story and the vulnerability to danger, as well as disconnection, to which she exposes herself by covering up her true feelings. In telling this story in this way, Sophie seems both to know and not know (or may not wish to know) the potential for danger that is braided into pleasure for her, "that sexual desire thing," in this situation.

The suburban girls did not speak overtly about danger when they voiced their sexual desire, a striking contrast to how the urban girls spoke. Getting a bad reputation did not seem to be as much a concern among the suburban girls, and few spoke about fears of getting pregnant or contracting AIDS. A few of these girls, like Sophie, indirectly acknowledged an association between their sexual desire and the potential for physical violence or violation by men. The suburban girls seemed to know unconsciously, yet not have conscious awareness, about a real danger that they could encounter, and in fact that many of them had encountered. In this study, ten of these thirty girls told me that they had experienced sexual abuse or violence in childhood or in adolescence. Both the urban and the suburban girls reported such incidents. Statistics indicate that sexual violence is prevalent and real in the lives of all female adolescents (e.g., Kelly 1991). Whereas the urban girls are keenly aware of and may try to protect themselves from physical danger by dissociating from their desire, the suburban girls failed to acknowledge the dangers that can be associated with exploring their embodied sexual curiosity, suggesting a lack of awareness that could leave them vulnerable to these dangers. This differential highlights the conundrum of sexuality for all girls and women in this society: to be sexually empowered, that is, to feel entitled to act on one's own sexual desire responsibly, is at the same time to be in danger in a society that resists women's empowerment.

## Conclusion

The voices of flesh-and-blood urban and suburban girls speaking the realities of sexuality for them in adolescence offer a challenge to the stereotype of The Urban Girl, which has pervaded this society's collective psyche and research on adolescent sexuality. The Urban Girl obscures the real lives of girls who are struggling to develop a sense of themselves as good and normal, while juggling their changing bodies and relationships. The Urban Girl can be thought of as living in the psyches of these urban girls, creating for them the burden of insuring that they do not become her as they negotiate their own complex stories of self and desire. By beginning to understand how all girls learn to know and respond to their own sexual feelings in adolescence, we develop the evidence needed to deconstruct The Urban Girl as the contaminated container of female adolescent sexuality. This is not to say that sexual activity is never associated with negative social and economic consequences for girls, or that urban girls are not at more risk for these consequences, given the absence of social and economic safety nets available to them. It is the social context, rather than the embodiment of The Urban Girl, that offers up meanings of adolescent sexuality and controls the material resources of education and contraception. It is the social context that must change to insure the safe integration of sexuality into a whole sense of an empowered self, enabling girls to have agency in their own lives.

The psychological and possibly physical dangers that are associated with girls' difficulty in incorporating their sexuality into their identity and their relationships have not been acknowledged or discussed by researchers. We have not asked what the costs of denying sexuality might be for their development. To do so, we need, at least conceptually, to unhitch sexuality from pregnancy and deviance. We also need to reconceptualize what sexuality is. Such a new framework includes reclaiming "sexual activity" from the realm of having intercourse; it involves encouraging girls—and boys—to know their sexuality as feelings as well as actions, feelings to which they are entitled, feelings that are in fact not necessarily the same as actions. One attempt at safety for girls is to deny their sexual desires, to be the models of control of their own and boys' sexual feelings. But this approach keeps in place a system of oppression that requires girls to sacrifice a part of themselves in the name of saving themselves (Gilligan 1989). The experiences of the girls in this study suggest that this gap in research and in education must be addressed.

It behooves us to listen to scholars who have named the necessity for and power of the erotic in women's lives. As bell hooks observes, "we lose sight of the way in which the ability to experience and know pleasure is an essential ingredient of wellness" (1993, 116). We must formulate different research questions about all girls' sexuality. When girls engage in sexual encounters, are they experiencing pleasure? Do they know what they want or desire sexually? In what contexts can they act on their own feelings? Are there differences in psychological vitality between girls with positive sexual self-concepts and those without? By challenging the myth of The Urban Girl with the real lives of urban and suburban girls, we open avenues for embodied knowledge of self and resistance to oppression not only for urban girls, but for all women.

NOTES

1. The next three sections of this chapter are adapted in part from Tolman (1994).

2. The downside of offering one example is the tendency to reify the group as being all alike. There was a great deal of difference in how the suburban girls spoke about their sexual desire within the group, and a great deal of similarity across the two groups. Sophie's interview does typify some tendencies that arose among these girls.

3. In this situation Sophie narrates that her objections in fact are a kind of encouragement—that in this case her "no" does in fact mean "yes." The notion that girls say "no" when they really mean "yes" has been described as a false stereotype about female sexuality that has been used to hurt girls and women. This construction has been strongly rejected and resisted by a multitude of feminist scholars and activists, and this critique is important in the struggle to end sexual violence. What Sophie's story illustrates, however, is that despite feminist claims to the contrary, often "no" can mean "yes" for young women. Without meaning to reinforce a stereotype, it is essential not to dismiss a reality of girls' lives that lines up with a stereotype that makes girls and women vulnerable. Rather, by listening to Sophie's not atypical story in which her cries of "no" belie her own desire, I emphasize that, because the only allowable scripted response for girls attempting to see themselves and be seen as "good" or "normal" remains "no," sometimes "no" does mean "yes." The point to be emphasized here is that until girls really can say "yes," "no" will always be suspect and will also be used by girls when they mean "yes." This narrative exemplifies that oppressive stereotypes about female sexuality can often become the storyline on which girls and women rely to construct their experiences, relationships, and bodies when there is no recourse to alternative, empowering stories by which they can resist potentially dangerous interactions.

REFERENCES

Alan Guttmacher Institute. 1994. *Sex and the American teenager*. New York: AGI.
Brooks-Gunn, J., and F. Furstenberg. 1989. Adolescent sexual behavior. *American Psychologist* 44 (2):249–57.

Brown, L., E. Debold, M. Tappan, and C. Gilligan. 1991. Reading narratives of conflict for self and moral voice: A relational method. In *Handbook of moral behavior and development: Theory, research, and application,* edited by W. Kurtines and J. Gewirtz. Hillsdale, N.J.: Lawrence Erlbaum.

Brown, L., and C. Gilligan. 1992. *Meeting at the crossroads: Women's psychology and girls' development.* Cambridge: Harvard University Press.

Caraway, N. 1991. *Segregated sisterhood.* Knoxville: University of Tennessee Press.

Child Trends. 1994. *Facts at a glance (January).* Washington, D.C.: Child Trends.

Christian-Smith, L. 1990. *Becoming a woman through romance.* New York: Routledge.

Collins, P. H. 1991. *Black feminist thought: Knowledge, consciousness, and the politics of empowerment.* New York: Routledge.

Daniel, J. In press. The discourse on Thomas v. Hill: A resource for perspectives on the black woman and sexual trauma. *Feminist Family Therapy and International Forum* 7 (1–2).

Ensminger, M. 1990. Sexual activity and problem behaviors among black urban adolescents. *Child Development* 61:2032–46.

Fine, M. 1988. Sexuality, schooling and adolescent females: The missing discourse of desire. *Harvard Educational Review* 58 (1):29–53.

Flannery, D., D. Rowe, and B. Gulley. 1993. Impact of pubertal status, timing, and age on adolescent sexual experience and delinquency. *Journal of Adolescent Research* 8 (1):21–40.

Forrest, J., and S. Singh. 1990. The sexual and reproductive behavior of American women, 1982–1988. *Family Planning Perspectives* 22:206–14.

Foshee, V., and K. Bauman. 1992. Gender stereotyping and adolescent sexual behavior: A test of temporal order. *Journal of Applied Social Psychology* 22 (20):1561–79.

Gilligan, C. 1989. Teaching Shakespeare's sister. In *Making connections: The relational world of adolescent girls at Emma Willard School,* edited by C. Gilligan, N. Lyons, and T. Hamner. Cambridge: Harvard University Press.

Gullotta, T., G. Adams, and R. Montemayor, eds. 1993. *Adolescent sexuality.* Newbury Park, Calif.: Sage.

Hall, J. 1983. The mind that burns in each body. In *The power of desire,* edited by A. Snitow, C. Stansell, and S. Thompson. New York: Monthly Review Press.

Handler, A. 1990. The correlates of the initiation of sexual intercourse among young urban Black females. *Journal of Youth and Adolescence* 19 (2):159–70.

Holmbeck, G., K. Waters, and R. Brookman. 1990. Psychosocial correlates of sexually transmitted diseases and sexual activity in black adolescent females. *Journal of Adolescent Research* 5 (4):431–48.

hooks, b. 1993. *Sisters of the yam.* Boston: South End Press.

Keith, J. B., C. McCreary, K. Collins, and C. P. Smith. 1991. Sexual activity and contraceptive use among low-income urban black adolecent females. *Adolescence* 26 (104):769–85.

Kelly, L. 1991. *Surviving sexual violence.* Minneapolis: University of Minnesota Press.

Lorde, A. 1984. *Sister Outsider.* Freedom, Calif.: Crossing Press.

Miles, M., and A. Huberman. 1984. *Qualitative data analysis: A sourcebook of new methods.* Beverly Hills, Calif.: Sage.

Muram, D., T. Rosenthal, E. Tolley, and M. Peeler et al. 1991. Race and personality traits affect high school senior girls' sexual reports. *Journal of Sex Education and Therapy* 17 (4):231–43.

Painter, N. 1992. Hill, Thomas, and the use of racial stereotypes. In *Racing justice, engendering power,* edited by T. Morrison. New York: Pantheon.

Petchesky, R. 1990. *Abortion and women's choice.* Boston: Northeastern University Press.

Scott-Jones, D., and A. White. 1990. Correlates of sexual activity in early adolescence. *Journal of Early Adolescence* 10 (2):221–38.

Tolman, D. 1994. Daring to desire: Culture and the bodies of adolescent girls. In *Sexual cultures: Adolescents, communities, and the construction of identity,* edited by J. Irvine. Philadelphia, Pa.: Temple University Press.

Vance, C. 1984. More danger, more pleasure. In *Pleasure and danger: Exploring female sexuality,* edited by C. Vance. Boston: Routledge and Kegan Paul.

Zabin, L., and S. Hayward. 1993. *Adolescent sexual behavior and childbearing.* Newbury Park, Calif.: Sage.

Zaslow, M., and R. Takanishi. 1993. Priorities for research on adolescent development. *American Psychologist* 48 (2):185–92.

# 15

# Inner-City Girls of Color: Unmarried, Sexually Active Nonmothers

Velma McBride Murry

Birth control is probably the most important thing for young people to know about sex, because to enjoy sex and make it a part of caring, it is absolutely essential to be sure you won't produce a baby unless you want one.

—A. Comfort and J. Comfort

Over the past fifteen years a plethora of studies have been published about adolescent sexuality. Attention has been devoted to (a) identifying trends regarding changing rates of sexual activity among unmarried adolescents, (b) understanding why adolescents are becoming sexually active at younger ages, (c) identifying factors associated with ineffective contraceptive use, and (d) developing a profile of those at greatest risk for early pregnancy, childbearing, and motherhood. In addition, much concern has been expressed about the extent to which adolescents of color are disproportionately represented in rates of sexual activity, pregnancy, and childbearing. Researchers have suggested that black girls become sexually active younger than whites (Newcomer and Udry 1985; Zelnik, Kantner, and Ford 1981), with an average age of onset of sexual activity at about 14.4 years (Zabin et al. 1986; Zelnik and Shah 1983). In addition, compared to white adolescents, black girls are more likely to experience pregnancy during adolescence (Henshaw and Van Vort 1989; National Center for Health Statistics 1989), are 2.5 times as likely to carry the pregnancy to term, and are 5.5 times as likely to be single mothers (Bumpass and McLanahan 1987; U.S. Bureau of the Census 1987). The majority of these studies, however, use research designs that are unbalanced with regard to family structure and socioeconomic status.

Research studies of sexual activity among Hispanic youths were almost nonexistent until the mid-1980s. Recent reports indicate that approximately half of never-married Hispanics of ages fifteen to nineteen have experienced sexual intercourse. Further, Hispanics tend to be older than Blacks, yet younger than Whites, at sexual onset. Although the fertility rates among Hispanic and black adolescents are quite similar, over half of Hispanics are married at the time of first birth (Aneshensel, Fielder, and Becerra 1989; Brindis 1992; Darabi, Dryfoos, and Schwartz 1986).

Recognizing that Hispanics are not a homogeneous ethnic group, some researchers have conducted within-group investigations. A national study (Durant, Pendergrast, and Seymore 1990) of Hispanic adolescents living in the United States revealed that the greatest proportion of Cubans had experienced sexual intercourse (69%); they were followed by adolescents of Central or South American (56%), Puerto Rican (40%), and Mexican American (39%) origins. Average age at sexual onset, across Hispanic groups, was 15.3 years. In terms of adolescent fertility rates, Puerto Ricans had the highest rate of births (62.4 per 1,000), followed by Mexican Americans (42 per 1,000), and Cubans (7 per 1,000).

The widely publicized adolescent pregnancy "epidemic" of the 1980s resulted in a major research emphasis to determine why children are having children. The urgent need to understand this trend seems to have placed other aspects of adolescent sexuality on the back burner. Yet, statistics clearly illustrate that not *all* sexually active adolescents get pregnant and have children. Virtually nothing is known about those who avoid pregnancy and early motherhood. This is especially true of adolescents of color. In fact, Jones and Philliber have pointed out that when minority adolescent females "who are sexually active, but not pregnant, are studied, they are often not carefully questioned for the insights they may offer into the avoidance of adolescent childbearing" (1983, 236).

In this chapter I report on an investigation of a group of girls who are at high risk for early childbearing because of their place of residence and their sexual histories, but who have nevertheless avoided this life transition. A study of this nature seems important because, whereas many urban adolescents are caught up in the drug culture, gang activity, early sexual activity, and adolescent parenthood (Hogan and Kitagawa 1985; Rhodes and Jason 1990), the majority choose not to become mothers at this developmental stage.

The chapter is divided into three sections. In the first section I briefly discuss theories of adolescent sexual behavior. A conceptual framework for the present study is presented in the second section. Supportive empirical findings regarding selected components of that framework are also included in this section. Next, using data obtained from a national probability sample, the conceptual model is empirically tested. I conclude the chapter by briefly summarizing the major findings of the study and offering suggestions concerning how our society can be instrumental in preparing adolescents to make responsible sexual decisions. As readers explore the areas discussed in this chapter, they should be reminded that the majority of research on adolescent sexuality is based on nonrepresentative data obtained from low-income Blacks and middle-income Whites, with few investigations of Hispanics, other adolescents of color, or middle-income Blacks. It is also important to mention that research on the psychosexual development of gay, lesbian, and bisexual adolescents is virtually invisible. Lack of attention to these youths has been attributed to the "assumed heterosexuality" of our society (Savin-Williams and Rodriguez 1993).

## Theoretical Explanations

Studies on adolescent sexuality are generally atheoretical and provide descriptive and correlational information only. Given the large body of past research, it is somewhat surprising that limited attention has been given to developing explanatory principles or theories of adolescent sexuality (B. C. Miller and Fox 1987). In an extensive review, Murry (1991) used an inductive approach to identify the theoretical assumptions inherent in the empirical research on black adolescent female sexuality. Three paradigms were identified. The first paradigm explains sexual behavior as inner drives, motivated by biological maturation (i.e., onset of puberty). According to this perspective, there is a greater likelihood of early sexual onset among girls who reach menarche at an early age. The next two paradigms view sexual behavior as socially shaped and learned behavior. Proponents of the second paradigm suggest that young people learn to conform to societal expectations regarding sexual behavior patterns. Established rules and norms are enforced by supervision from parents and significant others (e.g., peers, religious leaders, and teachers). The third paradigm focuses on changes in social structure that impact adolescent sexual behavior. Premarital sexual experiences are, according to this view, associated with (1) increased autonomy for adolescents to engage in activities with limited adult supervision, (2) pervasive sexuality in mass media, (3) more divorces and single-parent families, (4) greater acceptance of sex outside of marriage, (5) legalization of abortion, (6) technological advances in contraception, and (7) a widening gap between physical maturation and age at first marriage, referred to as the "sexual maturity gap" (Davis 1989; Franklin 1988). A more detailed discussion

| General Context Areas | Biological | Social control | Social structure |
|---|---|---|---|
| Specific Variables | Sexual maturation | a) Parental control<br>b) Religion | a) Social autonomy<br>b) Family planning services |
| Examples of Variables | Age at menarche | a) Disciplinary strategies<br>b) Church attendance<br>c) Religious affiliation | a) Employment status<br>b) Access to reproductive health care services |

Other dimensions
  Family structure
  Family income
  Sexual knowledge
  Contraception use pattern
  Family sexuality socialization

*Figure 15.1.* A Conceptual Model for Studying Adolescent Sexuality

and integration of these paradigms provides the conceptual framework for this study.

## A Conceptual Framework

This framework includes three broad areas (biological, social control, and social structure) for which specific variables are identified (see figure 15.1). These variables are intended to be illustrative of the broad categories rather than exhaustive.

### Biological Factors

One common perspective of adolescent sexual activity is that age at sexual onset is a result of instinctual, biologically driven sexual impulses that are initiated during puberty. Thus, declining age at first coitus and increased incidence of pregnancy and childbearing among adolescents can be attributed to the occurrence of early sexual maturation among today's females. This finding, however, seems more germane to white adolescents than to black adolescents (Magnusson, Stattin, and Allen 1986). Similar studies of black youth are inconclusive. Although Blacks reach sexual maturity slightly earlier than Whites do, research suggests that biological maturation has little or no influence on timing of sexual intercourse (Moore, Simms, and Betsey 1986; Westney et al. 1984). In contrast, based on an examination of black adolescents included in a nationally representative sample, research has shown that early sexual maturation was significantly related to sexual onset among black females (Leigh, Weddle, and Loewen 1988; Murry 1992). Similar findings have been reported for white adolescent girls (Moore, Simms, and Betsey 1986). The significance of pubertal development for sexual activity among Hispanics has been mostly ignored.

275

### Social Control

Social control theory maintains that premarital sexual activity occurs when family, schools, and religious groups have inadequate control over adolescents. It is through these mechanisms that adolescents learn to conform to societal expectations regarding appropriate and inappropriate behavior. The extent to which social constraint or control impacts the sexual behavior of adolescents is unclear. Results from several studies have indicated that when black parents define limits, supervise their daughters' dating habits, and have open talks about sexual issues, their daughters are more likely to delay sexual onset, pregnancy, and childbearing (Abrahamse, Morrison, and Waite 1988; Murry 1994b; Scott-Jones and Turner 1988). However, Wilson (1982) and others (Hogan and Kitagawa 1985; Zelnik, Kantner, and Ford 1981) have pointed out that protecting urban adolescents from the negative influences of their environment may be difficult for parents. The task becomes even more difficult for adolescents living in poverty, for whom the traditional pathways to adulthood status (i.e., employment, independent living arrangements, and marriage) are not readily available.

Using one aspect of parental control, B. C. Miller and associates (1986) found a curvilinear relationship between degree of parental strictness and adolescent sexual activity. That is, parents who are very lenient in imposing rules and restrictions and those who exert a high degree of control tend to have daughters who engage in sexual activity at an earlier age. The lowest level of sexual activity was found among daughters of parents who exercised moderate control.

Religious institutions are central within the black and Hispanic communities and have been viewed as influential in defining morality and values in family members. It has been suggested that religious teachings influence adolescent sexual behavior by providing meaning to and defining norms for sexual conduct, thus constraining sexual behavior through fear of institutional sanctions (DeLamater 1981). Empirically, the relationship between church attendance and sexual behavior patterns among adolescents of color has not been well substantiated. Available studies provide some evidence suggesting that black and Hispanic adolescents who attend church frequently are less likely to engage in premarital sexual activities (Durant, Pendergrast, and Seymore 1990; Murry 1994a; Zelnik, Kantner, and Ford 1981). Moreover, according to Hayes (1987), those who frequently participate in religious services may have stronger social supports to enforce more conservative behavior norms. However, some researchers have pointed out that highly religious adolescents may actually be more vulnerable to pregnancy and parenting than their nonreligious counterparts. Religious adolescents tend to be more ambivalent about their sexuality and may, therefore, be less inclined to select effective contraceptive methods that require advance planning or a doctor's appointment (Abrahamse, Morrison, and Waite 1988; Studer and Thornton 1987; Zelnik, Kantner, and Ford 1981).

## Social Structure

According to Davis (1989) adolescent sexual behavior is socially shaped, and it is therefore an outcome of changes in modern society. For example, social changes including the increased divorce rate, the greater incidence of single-parent households, the separation of work and home, urbanization and mobility, the increased access to cars, as well as technological advances have greatly increased the likelihood that adolescents' activities take place outside direct parental or other adult supervision (Beeghley and Sellers 1986). This decreased supervision also allows adolescents to plan their social lives, including opportunities to have sex, with greater autonomy.

*Labor Force Participation.* Increased adolescent participation in the labor force is also associated with greater independence among adolescents and may influence adolescents' sexual behavior. Researchers have suggested that adolescents who work more than fifteen hours per week are more distant from their parents, tend to have less ambition for college, and are more likely to engage in high risk behaviors (Mortimer and Finch 1986; Steinberg et al. 1982). Yet, for urban youths, the benefits of employment may outweigh the costs. According to Alter (1987), having a job after school appears to decrease urban adolescents' vulnerability to the pressures of their neighborhoods. Moreover, Moore and Werthheimer (1984) have pointed out that a major predictor of fertility rates among minority youths is their perception that future opportunities decline as a result of early childbearing. According to these researchers, the lowest fertility rates occur among adolescents who have the best alternatives to motherhood (e.g., education, employment, and economic independence). Results from a recent investigation also provide support for this finding. Specifically, employed black adolescent females were more likely to delay sexual onset than were those who were unemployed or had never worked (Murry 1994a). One explanation offered for this finding is that employed adolescents may have more limits placed on their independence and greater regulation of their free time, resulting in fewer opportunities to engage in sexual activities.

*Family Characteristics.* Several aspects of the family have been identified as important antecedents of adolescent sexual behavior, including parents' characteristics, family income, and family structure (B. C. Miller and Jorgensen 1988; Murry 1994b). One characteristic often associated with an adolescent girl's sexual behavior is her mother's age at first birth. Adolescents whose mothers had their first child during adolescence seem to have a greater risk of early motherhood (Hogan and Kitagawa 1985; Newcomer and Udry 1985).

Further, having middle to high incomes and educated parents appears to place adolescents at less risk of early sexual onset, pregnancy, and motherhood (Forste and Heaton 1988; Hogan and Kitagawa 1985). One explanation for this finding is that these families tend to place a higher value on achievement, therefore encouraging their adolescents to delay sexual activities in order to accomplish future goals (B. C. Miller and Sneesby 1988). A second reason is that these adolescents may also see a more direct connection between achievement and employment than adolescents who do not have educated or employed parents.

In addition, most studies have found single-mother households to be a significant factor in adolescent sexual behavior patterns (Evans 1987; Grief 1985; Zelnik, Kantner, and Ford 1981). Compared to those in two-parent households, daughters of single mothers appear to be at greater risk of early sexual onset, pregnancy, and childbearing for several reasons. First, their mother's dating practice may enhance the acceptability of sex outside of marriage (Moore, Peterson, and Furstenberg 1986; Newcomer and Udry 1985). Second, daughters of female-headed families may be given the message that husbands are not essential to raise a family. Father-absent families may also give sons distorted views about raising a family. For instance, sons may receive the message that one does not have to be committed to marriage or child rearing in order to father children (Gibbs 1992). There are, however, no empirical data to substantiate these explanations.

Thornton (1980) and others (Ladner 1971; McLanahan and Booth 1991) have suggested, though, that norms are not directly transmitted from parental status. The decreased parental supervision, availability, and guidance often associated with single-mother households may explain variations in the sexual behavior of their daughters as compared to those in two-parent households (Hogan and Kitagawa 1985).

*Demographic Characteristics.* Several social and demographic characteristics are related to contraceptive use among adolescents. These include race, socioeconomic status, family stability, and religiosity. Researchers frequently report that adolescents of color are less effective contraceptive users than their white counterparts (Darabi, Dryfoos, and Schwartz 1986). This difference, however, seems to disappear when such factors as socioeconomic status and family stability are taken into account (Hofferth 1987; Zelnik and Kantner 1977). Greater evidence of contraceptive use occurs among black and white girls with higher socioeconomic status, greater family stability, and higher levels of religiosity (Zelnik, Kantner, and Ford 1981). In fact, results from a within-group comparison of black adolescents in Chicago revealed that as socioeconomic status increased, the likelihood of the girls having used contraception at first coitus also increased (Hogan and Kitagawa 1985). Further, studies have also shown that when blacks girls do use contraception, they are more likely to select a prescribed method at first sexual intercourse. In contrast, their counterparts from other racial backgrounds tend to select less reliable over-the-counter methods (Zelnik, Kantner, and Ford 1981).

*Sexual Knowledge.* Going beyond models of factors influencing sexual behavior, a great deal of research has focused on the role of knowledge about contraception and reproduction in the sexual activity of adolescent girls. It has been well documented that most adolescents have limited and often incorrect information about contraception and reproduction (Freeman et al. 1982; Zelnik and Kantner 1977). Inadequate sexual knowledge puts adolescents at risk of pregnancy and sexually transmitted diseases because, more often than not, they believe that they *know* what they are doing. On the contrary, results from a national study revealed that only 43% of white, 17% of black, and 24% of Hispanic adolescent girls knew the least fertile period in a woman's cycle (Palmer and Murry 1994). Similar findings were reported by Zelnik and associates over a decade ago (Zelnick, Kantner, and Ford 1981).

Studies evaluating the influence of sexual knowledge on adolescent sexual behavior have been less consistent. Some researchers report that adolescents who are adequately informed about sexual matters are more likely to delay sexual onset. Further, those with accurate contraception and reproductive knowledge are more likely to be effective contraceptive users and tend to be less vulnerable to unintended pregnancies (Murry 1992; Scott-Jones and Turner 1988). Another view is that providing factual knowledge increases curiosity, thereby encouraging sexual experimentation (Rossa 1983). Finally, there are those who suggest that sexual knowledge neither fosters nor inhibits sexual experimentation among adolescents (Newcomer and Udry 1985).

### Avoiding Motherhood: Testing the Conceptual Model

Are there differences between black and Hispanic urban adolescent females who are sexually active but have avoided pregnancy and motherhood? To what extent do biological factors, social control, and social structure factors influence their ability to avoid motherhood during adolescence?

The data set utilized to test these questions is the 1988 National Survey of Family Growth Cycle VI (NSFG). These data were collected by the National Center for Health Statistics, with a nationally representative sample of presumed heterosexual females of childbearing age (fifteen to forty-four) living in the United States. Completed questionnaires were obtained from 8,450 women. The NSFG includes an array of highly structured questions about the contraception and pregnancy histories, the reproductive knowledge and sex education, the sexual activity patterns, and a wide range of social, economic, and family characteristics of women living in the United States. The NSFG data define urban as an area that has at least 50,000 inhabitants located inside a county that has 100,000 residents, based on the census definition of areas.

### Sample Selection

A total of 1,246 urban females, 884 blacks and 362 Hispanics, were selected for this study. They were ages fifteen to twenty-one, unmarried, and did not have children. This age range was selected because the extant data set does not include women younger than age fifteen. Second, within the American society twenty-one is the most consistently recognized age at which individuals have adult privileges and responsibilities. Third, the need for advanced education in order to obtain employment delays the time at which individuals *usually* marry or become parents, both symbols of adulthood status in America.

*Race or Ethnicity Differences in the Sample.* A number of demographic factors differentiated the Blacks and the Hispanics in this sample.

*Age.* Black adolescents were, on average, slightly older than their Hispanic counterparts (age 18.5 years [$SD = .06$] and 18.3 years [$SD = .10$], respectively) at the time of the questionnaire administration ($F(1,1,245) = 5.06$, $p = .03$). This slight age difference, however, may not be meaningful in relation to the prediction of the girls' sexual activity.

*Family Structure.* Most of the Hispanic adolescents (67.2%) lived with both biological parents, 22% lived in mother-only families, and 11% lived in stepfather families. Among Blacks, 43% lived with their biological mothers and fathers, 47% lived in mother-only families, and 9% lived in stepfather families ($X2 = 72.78$, $df = 2$, $p < .001$). Although many of these urban girls lived with both their mothers and their fathers, the NSFG did not include information about the fathers' characteristics in their data collection.

*Economic Status.* At the time of the interviews, 53% of the Blacks and 27% of the Hispanics reported that their family incomes were 0–99% below the poverty line (low income). Those in the middle-income status group (100–199% above the poverty line) included 26% of the Blacks and 32% of the Hispanics, with 21% of the Blacks and 41% of the Hispanics reporting incomes greater than 200% above the poverty line (upper incomes) ($X2 = 83.55$, $df = 2$, $p < .001$). According to national data, in 1988 200% of the poverty line was equivalent to a total income of $23,222 for a family of four (U.S. Bureau of the Census 1989).

*Mother's Education and Employment Status.* Urban black girls reported that their mothers had completed 11.6 years of schooling, and 20% had attended college. Their Hispanic counterparts reported 11.3 years of education for their mothers, and 23% of their mothers had attended college. These differences were not statistically significant. Black adolescents were more likely to report that their mothers were employed than were Hispanics. Furthermore, 64% of the black girls indicated that their mothers were employed full-time, compared to only 17% of the Hispanics ($X2 = 34.79$, $df = 2$, $p < .001$).

*Religion.* Most of the Hispanic girls (69%) were Catholic, and the majority of the black girls (65%) were Baptist. The remainder reported that they practiced no religion (7.3% of the Blacks and 4.5% of the Hispanics) or did not specify a particular Protestant denomination (15.8% of the Blacks and 15% of the Hispanics). Most of the urban black girls (61.1%), but less than half of the Hispanic girls (48.6%) indicated that they attended church once per week ($X2 = 48.13$, $df = 3$, $p < .001$).

## Sexual Activity and Knowledge

*Age at Menarche.* There was a slight difference, not statistically significant, between Blacks (12.5 years) and Hispanics (12.3 years) with regard to age at menarche.

*Onset of Sexual Activity.* Black girls became sexually active at slightly younger ages than did Hispanics. Mean age at first sexual intercourse for the black girl was 15.5 years, ranging from 9 to 20. Hispanic girls became sexually active, on average, at age 15.8 years, ranging from 11 to 20 ($F(1,1245) = 21.77$, $p < .001$). In addition, when asked about their current sexual activity status, 81% of the Blacks and 65% of the Hispanics indicated that they had had sex within the last three months before the interview ($X2 = 39.17$, $df = 1$, $p < .001$).

*Contraceptive Use Pattern.* Most of the girls were ineffective contraceptive users. Slightly over 45% of both black and Hispanic girls indicated that they did not use contraception at first sexual intercourse, and 60% of each group indicated that they used no method at last intercourse. When methods were selected, Blacks (45%) tended to use medically prescribed methods, whereas Hispanics (41%) were more likely to select over-the-counter methods ($p < .001$). A greater proportion of black girls (45%) than Hispanic girls (29%) had become pregnant.

*Sexual Knowledge.* Regardless of race or ethnicity, these urban girls were generally not knowledgeable about reproduction and contraception. Only 20% of the Hispanics and 18% of the Blacks knew the correct answer to the question "When during a woman's monthly cycle is she most likely to get pregnant?" Approximately 49% of the Hispanic girls and 45% of the black girls were able to select correctly the least effective and the most effective contraception.

*Source of Sexual Information.* Mothers were the leading source of sexual information for these girls. Overall, black girls seemed to engage in more conversations about contraception and issues regarding sexually transmitted diseases with their mother than did the Hispanic girls. Regardless of race or ethnicity, contraception was the most common sexual topic that the girls had discussed with their mothers; 73.3% of the Blacks and 50% of the Hispanics had discussed it ($X2 = 11.27$, $df = 1$, $p < .001$). Fifty-four percent of the black girls and about 40% of the Hispanic girls indicated that they had talked with their mothers about sexually transmitted diseases ($X2 = 28.24$, $df = 1$, $p < .001$). Both groups reported having received limited information from their mothers about how pregnancy occurs.

*Access to Reproductive Health Care.* Most of the girls (50% of the Blacks and 71% of the Hispanics) reported that they did not utilize family planning services. Among those who did, more Blacks (26%) sought the services of private doctors, and more Hispanics (16.2%) attended clinics ($[[(X2 = 28.24$, $df = 1$, $p < .001])$.

*Contraceptive Use and Pregnancy Status.* Although all these girls had avoided motherhood, some of them had had previous pregnancies, and many were engaging in unprotected sex. A more in-depth examination of within-group differences was conducted. The sample was stratified into eight groups based on their degree of sexual risk, which was calculated by cross-tabulating the girls' *contraceptive use pattern* (never used, used at first coitus but not at last coitus, used at last coitus but not at first coitus, or used at both first and last coitus) and their *pregnancy status* (never pregnant or pregnant once). Results are presented for black and Hispanic girls in table 15.1. Not surprisingly, this cross-tabulation indi-

TABLE 15.1
*Groups Configuration according to Contraception Use and Pregnancy Risk Status*

| | Pregnancy status[a] | | | |
| | Never | | Once | |
| Contraceptive use pattern | Black | Hispanic | Black | Hispanic |
|---|---|---|---|---|
| Never used | 14.0 | 19.6 | 16.6 | 13.9 |
| Not used at first coitus | 0.0 | 0.0 | 16.1 | 7.8 |
| Used at last coitus | 10.3 | 16.7 | 0.0 | 0.0 |
| Both, first and last coitus | 32.0 | 32.1 | 11.0 | 9.9 |
| Totals | 56.3 | 68.4 | 43.7 | 31.6 |

[a]Percentages reflect proportion based on 884 Blacks and 362 Hispanics.
NOTE: All of those who did not use contraception at first coitus were in the once pregnant group. All of those who used contraception at last coitus were in the never pregnant group.

cates that the greatest proportion of the Blacks and the Hispanics who reported never having been pregnant also reported using contraception at both first and last coitus (32%).

A discriminant function analysis (multivariate regression procedure) was used to identify variables that distinguish the six groups identified by cross-tabulations (contraceptive use pattern and pregnancy status). Results of these analyses are shown in table 15.2.

The discriminant function analysis produces canonical coefficients for each predicting variable. The canonical coefficients are the correlations between the discriminant function and each variable. The interpretation of the coefficients is similar to that used in multiple regression and can be

TABLE 15.2
*Factors Associated with Contraceptive Use and Pregnancy Status*

| Variables[a] | Standardized canonical coefficients | Wilks Lambda |
|---|---|---|
| Biological | | |
| Menarche | −0.476 | 0.508 |
| Race or ethnicity | 0.051 | 0.462 |
| Social control | | |
| Parental disciplinary strategies | 0.143 | 0.496 |
| Religious affiliation | −0.053 | 0.468 |
| Church attendance | 0.116 | 0.473 |
| Social structure | | |
| Employment opportunities | | |
| adolescents | 0.233 | 0.582 |
| mothers | 0.138 | 0.487 |
| Reproductive health care | −0.321 | 0.735 |
| Other Dimensions | | |
| Family characteristics | | |
| family structure | 0.284 | 0.480 |
| family income | 0.494 | 0.794 |
| mother's education | 0.458 | 0.611 |
| Sexual information | | |
| STDs | 0.283 | 0.529 |
| Sexual knowledge about | | |
| pregnancy | 0.325 | 0.555 |
| contraception | 0.270 | 0.646 |
| Current sexual activity status | 0.485 | 0.885 |

[a]Variables included reached significance at $p < .001$ level.

examined to assess the importance of an individual variable in predicting group membership. To interpret the magnitudes of the coefficients as indicators of relative importance, variables with the largest standardized coefficients contribute more to the overall discriminant function. The actual signs of the coefficients are arbitrary. Thus, to ascertain the relative importance of each variable in predicting group membership, the magnitude of each standardized canonical coefficient should be considered.

The standardized discriminant function coefficients for adolescents included in the present study are included in table 15.2. An examination of standardized canonical coefficients revealed that the variable providing the greatest contribution in classifying girls into groups by contraceptive use and pregnancy status is family income ($R^2_c = .494$), followed by current sexuality status, menarche, and mother's education. Other variables providing moderate contributions include adolescents' knowledge about how pregnancy occurs ($R^2_c = .325$), access to reproductive health care, family structure, level of knowledge about contraception, and having received information from parents about sexually transmitted disease. As shown in table 15.2, race and ethnicity, as well as religious affiliation, provided the least amount of contribution to group membership based on contraceptive use and pregnancy status.

## Chapter Summary

It has been well documented that urban girls of color are at risk for early motherhood. Given that they do not *all* become mothers, studying those who are sexually active but avoid motherhood can offer insights into how to encourage others to delay childbearing during adolescence. Biological, social control, and social structure theories served to construct a conceptual framework for this investigation of factors associated with contraceptive use patterns and pregnancy status of a nationally representative sample of urban Hispanic and black girls.

Several noteworthy findings emerged. First, there are within- and between-group differences among urban girls of color—urban adolescents of color are not monolithic. Between-race comparisons of Hispanics and Blacks indicate that sexually active urban Black girls are more likely to be poor and live in mother-only households. Blacks attended church more frequently, became sexually active at younger ages, and were more likely to have been pregnant than the Hispanic girls. These between-group differences have been reported in previous studies (Aneshensel, Fielder, and Becerra 1989; Brindis 1992; Darabi, Dryfoos, and Schwartz 1986).

When steps are taken to unravel the relative importance of race or ethnicity in understanding high risk sexual activity among urban girls, race or ethnicity appears to play a very small role. The most significant predictor of contraception use pattern and pregnancy status was family income. Regardless of race, urban girls who were least at risk for pregnancy had family incomes of middle to high levels. Other researchers have reported similar findings for groups of lower- and middle-class black adolescents (Hogan and Kitagawa 1985; Zelnik, Kantner, and Ford 1981). Living in urban areas is not synonymous with living in poverty. However, results from the present study suggest that family income does play a determinant role in urban girls' vulnerability to pregnancy.

Findings presented here also substantiate other studies reporting that adolescent girls are still *not* receiving accurate information about reproduction and pregnancy (Freeman et al. 1982; Zelnik and Kantner 1977). Less than 25% of the urban girls could correctly identify when during her menstrual cycle a woman is the most or least fertile.

It is no surprise that adolescents are misinformed, when one considers what often occurs in sex education classes. Results from an ethnographic study of inner-city youths revealed that in these classes students watch films on hygiene, work individually, and construct outlines from their hygiene books; they have little opportunity to discuss human reproduction or to interact with other students or the teachers (Williams and Kornblum 1985). "Under these circumstances not much learning is taking place. When they do get accurate information about reproduction and contraception, it is usually from health-care professionals" (Williams and Kornblum 1985, 86).

An even more disturbing finding is that most of these urban girls were not getting reproductive health care. Though sexually active, over 50% of the black girls and 71% of the Hispanics indicated that they had not had pap smears, pelvic examinations, or breast examinations within the past year. According to other research (Chilman 1980; E. F. Jones et al. 1985), the limited use of reproductive health care services by adolescents may be attributed to costs associated with such facilities, especially if they consult a private doctor. Family planning services may be stigmatized as services for "poor" people. Adolescent girls who attend family planning or prenatal clinics may also be concerned that the purpose of their visit is all too obvious, and they may not trust that their privacy will be protected; they may believe that their parents or other family members will find out (E. F. Jones et al. 1985).

Although successful in avoiding motherhood, most of these urban girls were not taking precautions to protect themselves from sexually transmitted diseases. This behavior can have deadly consequences. The spread of HIV cases among adolescents is a growing concern. Parents, educators, the media, and medical practitioners can no longer ignore feelings and relationships in counseling, teaching, and advising adolescents about sexuality. Rather than taking the position that adolescents should "just say no," initiatives are needed to educate adolescents about effectively protecting themselves from STDs. Encouraging youth to "wait until you are married to have sex " is not working. The latest survey figures indicate that a majority of adolescents have already engaged in sexual intercourse by the time they complete high school (Centers for Disease Control 1992; Forrest and Singh 1990). If we as a society are serious about combatting sexual risk-taking among our youths, we must begin to acknowledge that most of them do not view sexual activity before marriage as wrong. Because of this we must give adolescents permission to protect themselves. "Programs serving adolescents do best when they integrate medical care into a network of education and counseling" (Zabin and Hayward 1993, 105).

The answer to the question of which sexually active urban girls of color are most likely to delay pregnancy is complex. A number of biological, social control, and social structure factors help to predict level of risk. Yet, two clear patterns emerge from this research. First, it is the sexually active urban girls of color with the greatest economic and family resources who are at the least risk for pregnancy. It has been well documented that girls growing up in middle-income homes are more likely than others to have high educational and occupational aspirations. These aspirations also increase their level of awareness and their conscientious effort to eliminate barriers that may prevent them from accomplishing their future goals (see McLoyd and Jozefowicz, chap. 20 of this volume). In fact, Hogan and Kitagawa (1985) found that urban Chicago adolescents of color (black), ages thirteen to nineteen, with high career aspirations were less at risk for pregnancy than those with low career aspirations. A similar pattern was found for black adolescent females who anticipated a higher socioeconomic status compared to those who anticipated they would do less well (P. Y. Miller and Simon 1974).

In the present study, most of the urban girls who had successfully avoided pregnancy were raised in families where issues of pregnancy and contraception were discussed. Providing sex education to their daughters may result from parents' concern about the increased vulnerability of urban youth with respect to childbearing. At the same time, receiving sex education in the home not only prepared these girls to make more responsible decisions about their sexual activity, but it also may have transmitted messages, indirectly or directly, about their parents approval of their daughters using contraceptives to protect themselves from unplanned pregnancies.

The second pattern that emerged is that urban girls who appeared to be at least risk of pregnancy were slightly older at the time of sexual maturation and were older at the time of sexual onset. In general, adolescents of color, particularly Blacks, reach puberty earlier than their white counterparts. However, as noted earlier, the relationship between biological maturity and age at first sexual intercourse has primarily been substantiated among white adolescents only. No differences in age of menarche were found in this study, and Blacks were only slightly earlier in their age of onset of sexual activity than Hispanics.

Being older at the time of sexual onset may also decrease girls' vulnerability to pregnancy because they may be able to more fully comprehend the risks they are taking (Rodman, Lewis, and Griffith 1984). Further, age at sexual onset plays an integral role in adolescents' decisions regarding contraceptive use. Older sexually active teens are more likely to be effective contraceptive users and are more likely to use low risk methods (e.g., birth control pills) (J. Jones and Philliber 1983; Murry 1994a). In this study never-pregnant urban girls were more likely to be consistent users of contraception.

The important conclusion from this study is that a substantial number of sexually active urban girls of color have successfully avoided pregnancy. Their motivation to postpone motherhood is similar to what is frequently reported of their nonurban counterparts. These factors are primarily related to access to opportunities to obtain adulthood status through more traditional pathways, as well as avenues to prevent unplanned pregnancies.

## REFERENCES

Abrahamse, A. F., P. A. Morrison, and C. J. Waite. 1988. Teenagers' willingness to consider single parenthood: Who is at greater risk? *Family Planning Perspectives* 20:13–18.

Alter, C. F. 1987. Preventing family dependency. *Society* 24:12–16.

Aneshensel, C. S., E. V. Fielder, and R. M. Becerra. 1989. Fertility and fertility-related behavior among Mexican-American and non-Hispanic White females. *Journal of Health and Social Behavior* 30:56–76.

Beeghley, L., and C. Sellers. 1986. Adolescents and sex: A structural theory of premarital sex in the United States. *Deviant Behavior* 7:313–36.

Brindis, C. 1992. Adolescent pregnancy prevention for Hispanic youth: The role of schools, families, and communities. *Journal of School Health* 62:345–51.

Bumpass, L. L., and S. McLanahan. 1987. Social background, not race, conditions for black premarital childbearing. *Family Planning Perspectives* 19: 219–20.

Centers for Disease Control. 1992. Sexual behavior among high school students. *Morbidity and Mortality Weekly Report* 40:882–85.

Chilman, C. S. 1980. Social and psychological research concerning adolescent childbearing, 1970–1980. *Journal of Marriage and the Family* 42:793–805.

Comfort, A., and J. Comfort. 1979. *The facts of love*. New York: Crown.

Darabi, K. F., J. Dryfoos, and D. Schwartz. 1986. Hispanic adolescent fertility. *Hispanic Journal of Behavioral Sciences* 8:157–71.

Davis, R. 1989. Teenage pregnancy: A theoretical analysis of a social problem. *Adolescence* 93:19–28.

DeLamater, J. 1981. The social control of sexuality. *Annual Review of Sociology* 7: 263–90.

Durant, R. H., R. Pendergrast, and C. Seymore. 1990. Sexual behavior among Hispanic female adolescents in the United States. *Pediatrics* 85:1051–58.

Evans, R. C. 1987. Adolescent sexual activity, pregnancy, and childbearing: Attitudes of significant others as risk factors. *Child and Youth Services* 9:75–93.

Forrest, J. D., and S. Singh. 1990. The sexual and reproductive behavior of American women: 1982–1988. *Family Planning Perspectives* 22:206–14.

Forste, R. T., and T. B. Heaton. 1988. Initiation of sexual activity among female adolescents. *Youth and Society* 19: 250–68.

Franklin, D. L. 1988. Race, class, and adolescent pregnancy: An ecological analysis. *American Journal of Orthopsychiatric* 58:339–54.

Freeman, E. W., K. Rickels, E. B. Mudd, and G. R. Huggins. 1982. Never-pregnant adolescents and family planning programs: Contraception continuation and pregnancy risk. *American Journal of Public Health* 72:815–22.

Gibbs, J. T. 1992. The social context of teenage pregnancy and parenting in the Black community: Implications for public policy. In *Early parenthood and coming of age in the 1990's,* edited by M. K. Rosenheim and M. F. Testa. New Brunswick, N.J.: Rutgers University Press.

Grief, G. 1985. Children and housework in the single father family. *Family Relations* 34:353–57.

Hayes, C., ed. 1987. *Risking the future: Adolescent sexuality, pregnancy, and childbearing.* Vol. 1. Washington, D.C.: National Academy Press.

Henshaw, S. K., and J. Van Vort. 1989. Teenage abortion, birth, and pregnancy statistics: An update. *Family Planning Perspectives* 21:84–88.

Hofferth, S. L. 1987. Factors affecting initiation of sexual intercourse. In *Risking the future: Adolescent sexuality, pregnancy and childbearing,* edited by S. L. Hofferth and C. D. Hayes. Vol. 2, 7–35. Washington, D.C.: National Academy Press.

Hogan, D. P., and E. M. Kitagawa. 1985. The impact of social status, family structure, and neighborhood on the fertility of black adolescents. *American Journal of Sociology* 19:825–55.

Jones, E. F., J. D. Forrest, N. Goldman, S. K. Henshaw, R. Lincoln, J. I. Rosoff, C. F. Westoff, and D. Wulf. 1985. Teenage pregnancy in developed countries: Determinants and policy implications. *Family Planning Perspectives* 17:53–65.

Jones, J., and S. Philliber. 1983. Sexually active but not pregnant: A comparison of teens who risk and teens who plan. *Journal of Youth and Adolescence* 12:235–51.

Ladner, J. A. 1971. *Tomorrow's tomorrow: The black woman*. Garden City, N.Y.: Doubleday.

Leigh, G. K., K. Weddle, and I. R. Loewen. 1988. Analysis of timing of transition to sexual intercourse for black adolescent females. *Journal of Adolescent Research* 3:333–45.

Magnusson, D., H. Stattin, and V. L. Allen. 1986. Differential maturation among girls and its relation to social adjustment in a longitudinal perspective. In *Life-span development,* edited by D. L. Featherman and R. M. Lerner. Vol. 7. New York: Academic Press.

McLanahan, S., and K. Booth. 1991. Mother-only families: Problems, prospects, and politics. In *Contemporary families: Looking forward, looking back,* edited by A. Booth. Minneapolis: National Council on Family Relations.

Miller, B. C., and G. L. Fox. 1987. Theories of adolescent heterosexual behavior. *Journal of Adolescent Research* 2:269–82.

Miller, B. C., and S. R. Jorgensen. 1988. Adolescent fertility-related behavior and its family linkages. In *Social stress and family development*, edited by D. Klein and J. Aldous. New York: Guilford Press.

Miller, B. C., J. K. McCoy, T. D. Olson, and C. M. Wallace. 1986. Parental discipline and control attempts in relation to adolescent sexual attitudes and behavior. *Journal of Marriage and the Family* 48:503–12.

Miller, B. C., and K. R. Sneesby. 1988. Educational correlates of adolescents' sexual attitudes and behavior. *Journal of Youth and Adolescence* 17:521–30.

Miller, P. Y., and W. Simon. 1974. Adolescent sexual behavior: Context and change. *Social Problems* 22:58–76.

Moore, K. A., J. L. Peterson, and F. F. Furstenberg. 1986. Parental attitudes and the occurrence of early sexual activity. *Journal of Marriage and the Family* 48:777–82.

Moore, K. A., M. C. Simms, and C. L. Betsey. 1986. *Choice and circumstance*. New Brunswick, N.J.: Transaction Books.

Moore, K. A., and R. F. Werthheimer. 1984. Teenage childbearing and welfare: Prevention and ameliorative strategies. *Family Planning Perspectives* 16:285–91.

Mortimer, J., and M. Finch. 1986. The effects of part-time work on adolescent self-concept and achievement. In *Becoming a worker*, edited by P. Borman and J. Reisman. Norwood, N.J.: Ablex.

Murry, V. M. 1991. Socio-historical study of black females' sexuality: Transition to first coitus. In *Black family: Essays and studies*, edited by R. Staples, 78–87, 4th ed. Belmont, Calif.: Wadsworth.

———. 1992. Sexual career paths of black adolescent females: A study of socioeconomic status and other life experiences. *Journal of Adolescent Research* 7:4–27.

———. 1994a. Black adolescent females: A comparison of early versus late coital initiators. *Family Relations* 43:342–48.

———. 1994b. Socio-historical study of African American adolescent females' sexuality: Timing of first coitus 1950 through 1980. In *The black family: Essays and studies*, edited by R. Staples, 52–65. Belmont, Calif.: Wadsworth.

National Center for Health Statistics. 1989. *Trends in teenage childbearing: United States 1970–81*. Series 21, no. 41. Hyattsville, Md.: U.S. Department of Health and Human Services.

Newcomer, S. F., and J. R. Udry. 1985. Parent-child communication and adolescent sexual behavior. *Family Planning Perspectives* 17:169–74.

Palmer, J. T., and V. M. Murry. 1994. Sexual knowledge and sexual behavior: Tri-ethnic comparison of black, Hispanic, and white adolescents. Manuscript.

Rhodes, J. E., and L. A. Jason. 1990. A social-stress model of substance abuse. *Journal of Consulting and Clinical Psychology* 58:395–401.

Rodman, H., S. H. Lewis, and S. B. Griffith. 1984. *The sexual rights of adolescents: Competence, vulnerability, and parental control*. New York: Columbia University Press.

Rossa, M. W. 1983. A comparative study of pregnant teenagers, parenting attitudes, and knowledge about sexual and child development. *Journal of Youth and Adolescence* 12:213–23.

Savin-Williams, R., and R. G. Rodriguez. 1993. A developmental, clinical perspective on lesbian, gay male, and bisexual youths. In *Adolescent sexuality*, edited by T. P. Gutllotta, G. R. Adams, and R. Montemayor. Newbury Park, Calif.: Sage.

Scott-Jones, D., and S. L. Turner. 1988. Sex education, contraceptives and reproductive knowledge, and contraceptive use among Black adolescent females. *Journal of Adolescent Research* 3: 171–87.

Steinberg, L., E. Greenburger, L. Garduque, and S. McAuliffe. 1982. Adolescents in the labor force: Some costs and benefits to schooling and learning. *Education and Policy Analysis* 4:363–72.

Studer, M., and A. Thornton. 1987. Adolescent religiosity and contraceptive usage. *Journal of Marriage and the Family* 49:117–28.

Thornton, A. 1980. The difference between first generation fertility and economic status of second generation fertility. *Population and Environment* 3:51–72.

U. S. Bureau of the Census. 1987. *Statistical abstract of the United States: 1986.* 107th ed., no. 84. Washington, D.C.: U.S. Government Printing Office.

———. 1989. Current population reports. Series P-60, no. 166. Washington, D.C.: U.S. Government Printing Office.

Westney, O. E., R. R. Jenkins, J. D. Butts, and I. Williams. 1984. Sexual development and behavior in black adolescents. *Adolescence* 9:557–68.

Wilkinson, D. 1993. Family ethnicity in America. In *Family ethnicity: Strength in diversity,* edited by H. P. McAdoo, 15–59. Newbury Park, Calif.: Sage.

Williams, T., and W. Kornblum. 1985. *Growing up poor.* Lexington, Mass.: Lexington Books.

Wilson, W. J. 1982. Inner-city dislocations. *Society* 21:80–86.

Zabin, L. S., and S. C. Hayward. 1993. *Adolescent sexual behavior and childbearing.* Newbury Park, Calif.: Sage.

Zabin, L. S., E. A. Smith, M. B. Hirsch, and J. B. Hardy. 1986. Ages of physical maturation and first intercourse in Black teenage males and females. *Demography* 23: 595–605.

Zelnik, M., and J. F. Kantner. 1977. Sexual and contraceptive experiences of young unmarried women in the United States, 1971 and 1976. *Family Planning Perspectives* 9:55–71.

Zelnik, M., J. F. Kantner, and K. Ford. 1981. *Sex and pregnancy in adolescence.* Beverly Hills, Calif.: Sage.

Zelnik, M., and F. K. Shah. 1983. First intercourse among young Americans. *Family Planning Perspectives* 2:64–70.

# 16 Contextual Factors of Sexual Risk-Taking in Urban African American Preadolescent Children

Elizabeth M. Vera, Le'Roy E. Reese,
Roberta L. Paikoff, and Robin L. Jarrett

Urban children living in poverty are faced with the challenge of growing up in increasingly dangerous environments. Threats of violence, substance abuse, teenage pregnancy, and sexually transmitted diseases are but a few of the factors that place poor children at risk for adverse mental and physical health consequences (Kazdin 1993). However, children and adolescents who reside in poor urban communities, many of whom are also members of ethnic and racial minority groups, are among those most understudied and underserved by mental health researchers (Jessor 1993; Kazdin 1993; Spencer and Dornbusch 1990).

Sexual risk-taking behavior is of particular concern in these communities because of the alarming incidence of problems such as teenage pregnancy and AIDS and other sexually transmitted diseases. Although both children of color and Caucasian children are at risk for these problems, significant ethnic or racial differences are noteworthy: U.S. youths overall are having heterosexual intercourse at earlier and earlier ages (the median age for urban youth is 12–13 years of age, according to Levy et al. 1993), but higher prevalence rates are found for African American adolescents than for Caucasians (Brooks-Gunn and Paikoff 1993). African American youth are also more likely to move directly from kissing to intercourse than their Caucasian counterparts (Udry 1988). Pubertal maturation on average occurs earlier in African American children (Brooks-Gunn and Reiter 1990). African American boys report more frequent sexual activity than do Caucasian boys, Caucasian girls, or African American girls (Sonenstein, Pleck, and Klu 1989).

Urban African American adolescents are at increased risk for HIV infection (Centers for Disease Control 1992), partly because of the earlier onset of sexual intercourse and experience with more sexual partners.

Fifty percent of all teens infected with the virus and 75% of all babies born to infected mothers are African American (Dryfoos 1990). In Chicago, where the research for this chapter was conducted, the percentage of African Americans with AIDS shifted dramatically from 30% in the mid-1980s to 50% in the early 1990s. In addition, infection via intravenous drug use has increased, while infection via male sex with men has decreased (AIDS Chicago 1992).

Teenagers also represent 19% of all women having children in Chicago, and 89% of the teenage mothers are unwed (Moore 1991). Urban children are also more likely to live in environments plagued by violence and crime. In 1991 one public housing development in Chicago experienced 89 murders, 319 sexual assaults, 3,690 aggressive assaults, and 3,536 robberies (Chicago Police Department, personal communication, 1991).

Although these numbers indicate dramatically the high prevalence of problems within poor urban minority communities, they also indicate that significant numbers of young women and young men grow up in these communities *without* becoming pregnant or fathering a child. Approximately half of all urban youth delay initial intercourse past the early adolescent years. From a primary prevention perspective, knowledge about the normative development of adolescents living with urban poverty is critical. Descriptive data are needed, as well as an understanding of factors that distinguish those who experience negative events or engage in high-risk behaviors from those who do not. Very little work has been conducted that focuses on normative behavior in urban youths; rather, most work has focused on the problems of teenagers, such as pregnancy and STDs (Brooks-Gunn and Paikoff 1993; Spencer and Dornbusch 1990). The work described here is an initial attempt to understand adolescent sexuality from the perspectives of young adolescents and adults living in an impoverished urban African American community.

## Project Goals

The current project was conducted in collaboration with members of an inner-city Chicago community. Together we aimed to design a developmentally appropriate, culturally and socially relevant curriculum for preventing health-compromising risk behaviors (such as alcohol and drug abuse, unsafe sexual behavior, and violence) in urban African American preadolescents and young adolescents living in poverty. A major component of the project was to assess the needs of the children residing in the target community and to develop an understanding of the community's perceptions of risk to their children. A qualitative approach was selected, using focus groups to explore the meanings of specific concepts to the group members (Polkinghorne 1994). Focus groups of four to twelve participants are most useful when orienting to a relatively new field of study or generating hypotheses based on participants' insights (Morgan 1988). Information gathered through the needs assessment was used to design a prevention curriculum that integrated information from the community with successful components of previously developed prevention programs.

## Focus Group Participants

A sample of sixty fourth- and fifth-grade boys and girls (ranging in age from eight to twelve years) and seventeen interested parents and adult community leaders were invited to participate in the project. The parents of the children and the community leaders were contacted through the school's community liaison. The decision to include significant members of the children's support system was based on evidence that multicomponent programs that involve multiple sources of information and support are greatly needed (Kazdin 1993). The selected elementary school students came from classrooms designed to provide specialized educational assistance (i.e., having a smaller teacher-to-student ratio) because of low reading levels. They were identified by the school personnel as being at risk for future behavioral problems. All of the children were African American and resided in a large public housing development in Chicago, where the average family income was below the poverty level. These children lived with chronic threats of random violence and gang warfare in their everyday lives. In comparison with other poor urban neighborhoods in the city, these families were residing in a particularly beleaguered environment.

## Methods

Seven focus groups were held to assess the perceived needs and concerns of the participants on the topic of risky behaviors. These groups were conducted in a semistructured manner, with the goal of developing a safe and comfortable environment. The groups were divided by grade level and gender of the children and included two groups of girls (one each for fourth- and fifth-grade girls) and three groups of boys (one for fourth graders and two for fifth graders). The number of participants in the groups ranged from eight to twelve. Each session lasted approximately one hour and a half. The children's groups were each run by a same-gender, Ph.D.-level psychologist who had training in clinical child psychology and group work. The group leaders worked weekly for several months as teaching assistants in the children's classrooms in order to establish a degree of familiarity with them before the focus groups were convened.

Two parents' focus groups were facilitated by a female Ph.D. sociologist who had considerable experience in conducting focus groups. The number of participants in the parent groups ranged from four to ten, and they met for one and a half hours each. The majority of the parent participants were mothers.

A series of open-ended questions structured the content of all focus groups. Children and parents were asked about their plans for the future, their perceptions of potential obstacles to their plans, their perceptions of risks concerning sexual activity, and drug or alcohol involvement. These issues guided the research from the investigators' point of view, but the conversation also included topics that emerged in the discussions.

Following focus group participation, a random sample of children were interviewed individually by the primary investigator to discuss their direct experience with sexual experimentation (see Paikoff 1995), including the frequency of sexual experiences. An individual interview was opted to preserve confidentiality because of the sensitive nature of these questions.

## Data Analytic Plan

The focus group discussions were videotaped to facilitate data analysis. The content of the conversations was transcribed from the videotape by research assistants, and the transcripts were coded thematically according to topic area. Some of the themes were anticipated prior to data analysis by the researchers (e.g., issues of HIV infection and teenage pregnancy), whereas other categories arose out of the material introduced by the participants (e.g., gang violence and rape). A theme, or topic, was defined as a discrete unit of discussion among the participants. In most cases the theme or topic was discussed by several participants in each of the groups, so that a cluster of dialogue was generated. Key issues and themes were derived from these data and are presented in what follows.

## Themes in the Data

### Age of Onset for Initial Sexual Experimentation

Both the children and the parents agreed that children were likely to begin sexual experimentation by ten to twelve years of age. Individual interview data collected on a subsample of the children indicated that many of the girls had witnessed "sexual activity" (defined as intercourse),[1] but none had engaged in sexual intercourse themselves. For the boys, individual interview data suggested that approximately one out of four had already initiated sexual activity (Paikoff 1995). This gender difference suggests that it is necessary to implement prevention programs earlier with boys if the aim is to intervene with nonvirgins.

### Parental Perceptions of Factors Influencing Early Experimentation

*Exposure to Sexual Activity.* Parents articulated several factors that increased the likelihood of early sexual experimentation in their children. The first factor was that of modeling or social learning. They reported that it was common to see individuals engaging in sexual activity in public places. Given that the children frequently witnessed this behavior, many parents felt that discouraging sexual activity was difficult. One mother expressed this sentiment by saying, "We all know that we can go downstairs on the first floor of any of these buildings and see somebody's hand up somebody's daughter's skirt."

*Misinformation.* A second factor influencing early sexual experimentation cited by the parents was a lack of proper information regarding sexual activity. Some of the parents expressed concern that misinformation on the streets is passed around among children about pregnancy prevention, prevention of sexually transmitted diseases, and similar topics. There was a fear that children would be exposed to this misinformation before parents or educators provided correct information. A related concern was the possibility that children would come into contact with other individuals who would purposely misinform them in order to have sex with them. One mother described her concern by saying:

When your daughter is hanging with them (a group) the first thing they going to tell her is "Well, you don't have to go and ask your mother," they'll give her a condom and try and tell her "Well you do it this way and won't have a problem, you won't get pregnant." But her girlfriend don't know any more about sex than she knows. That's why you have to tell her to come and talk to you (the parent) about anything.

*Low Self-Esteem.* The mothers believed that a third factor influencing early sexual activity was low self-esteem. Many mothers believed that girls who got pregnant thought that a baby would provide them with attention and love lacking in their own lives. One mother summarized her views by saying: "Some of the teenagers having babies, especially some of the younger ones, feel that if you get a baby, you can get love, but that is not necessarily true, you've got to give love to get love, if you don't know how to give love, you'll never get love."

*Gang Protection.* Parents pointed out another problem: the use of sex to obtain protection from gang members. Girls in particular were having unsafe sex with gang members in order to "buy" safety from violence in the community. Although perhaps not being an official member of a gang, a young girl might feel a sense of greater safety by having a gang affiliation in a community where violence is commonplace. One of the parents reflected her understanding of this problem by saying, "I was going to say that with all the gang activity going on, a lot of girls are looking for protection, so that they don't get hurt, so the boys want their rewards and will say, 'Hey, I ain't kept them off you for nothin'."

*Coercion.* The parents' groups also discussed the potential for children to be persuaded into sexual intercourse to prove their love or affection for their boyfriends or girlfriends. This scenario seemed particularly salient for girls, in the perceptions of the parents. One mother summarized the situation: "What's risky is listening to boys say 'Oh baby I love you' when tomorrow he'll want to move on to somebody else, and she'll get her heart broke listening to him, and worse maybe."

### Aspects of Sexual Risk-Taking for Child Focus Group Participants

In response to the question, "What might be risky about being sexually active (having sex)?" the children's responses were categorized as follows:

*Teenage Pregnancy.* A concern that was identified by the girls, but not the boys, was teenage pregnancy. Not only was this perceived by girls as a major risk of being sexually active, but it also was seen as a barrier to vocational achievement. Many of the girls either had relationships with other girls (family or friends) who had dropped out of school to have children, or knew of teenage girls who could not get jobs because they had no one to watch their children. There was a high degree of awareness and familiarity with the negative aspects of unplanned teenage pregnancy, and the desire to avoid such a situation was also expressed by the girls' group members. The fact that the boys did not perceive this as a risk suggests that there may be an assumption that teenage pregnancy is a problem only for females or that it may more greatly affect the lives of young women. Since boys do not become pregnant, it may not be an issue they think about at this age.

*AIDS and Other Sexually Transmitted Diseases.* Contracting the AIDS virus was a concern identified by all group participants, reflecting the awareness that AIDS does not discriminate between genders. The children also expressed the sentiment that one is most likely to contract AIDS by being deceived by one's sexual partner (i.e., an HIV-positive individual does not disclose his or her status to the intended partner). Children stated that they were fearful of encountering sexual partners who knew they had the virus but chose not to disclose that information.

The children understood the likelihood of dying from AIDS, but they lacked a sense of control in preventing themselves from contracting the virus. This may reflect an absence of information about safe sex or the inability to feel a sense of mastery over their lives, or it may reflect a cultural difference in locus of control (Gurin, Gurin, and Morrison 1978), resulting from historical and ongoing experiences of oppression, discrimination, and community violence. One of the fifth grade girls reported: "My godsister got the virus from a boy she didn't know and he told her [he was HIV-positive] when they got through. She thought it was funny because she thought he was kidding. A week later she went to the hospital and they told her, and she's pregnant now."

*Sexual Assault and Rape.* Sexual victimization also emerged as a theme during the discussion. The children perceived a relationship between being sexually active and being more susceptible to sexual assault and abuse. A fourth-grade member of the girls' group, discussing why "fast" girls were at greater risk for sexual assault, stated: "It's important not to wear tight pants, when you walk down the street all fancy, 'cause he won't mess around, he'll rape you, then shove you in the garbage can." Another fourth-grader supported her statement, saying: "I think it's dangerous for this little girl to be shaking her butt and poppin' it in front of grown men, cause when they snatch you, it's cause they see what kind of a body you got in there."

These illustrative comments may reflect the socialization or greater cultural influences that blame women who are victims of sexual assaults and absolve men of responsibility for abusive actions toward them (Koss, Gidycz, and Wisniewski 1987).

The boys also saw themselves as being vulnerable to rape. Several of the fourth-grade boys recalled stories they had heard about young boys being chased and sexually assaulted by men who lived in their buildings. Both girls' and boys' groups expressed feelings of vulnerability and fear of victimization in their immediate surroundings. However, the girls also identified a subgroup of girls who were at higher risk for attacks, whereas the boys did not. This mindset may be protective, although unrealistic, in its function. It is easier to deflect a perception of risk away from oneself by identifying ways in which a "type" of person may have "deserved" the attack or brought it on herself. This "Just World" hypothesis (Lerner and Miller 1978) allows children to believe that bad things cannot happen to them, since bad events are not perceived as random. Unfortunately, we know this to be far from the reality of the situation.

*Sex for Drugs Bartering.* Sex was also perceived by the children as having economic value. These girls recounted stories of women they knew who used sex as a way of receiving drugs. Sex could be used as a commodity that could be offered or received as a form of payment for drugs. The existence of this type of arrangement is well documented by data coming from the culture of crack houses and illicit drug users (Inciardi, Lockwood, and Pottieger 1993). That children participating in this project saw sex and drugs as being so closely related suggests a high level of awareness or witnessing of such activities. One fifth-grade girl described a situation she knew of: "This lady, one time she told this boy she would suck his thing for a rock (a piece of crack cocaine), and he gave her two dollars, 'cause she said she was hungry too."

*Gang Initiation or Activity.* Sexual activity was cited as a component or a "rite of passage" associated with gang membership. Gangs were reported to be a major force in the community and were seen as largely responsible for the violence in the community. The girls and boys discussed the random violence associated with gang initiation. Sexual behavior was also identified as a part of gang initiation for girls. Having sex with a gang member was reported to be a requirement for girls' initiation into gangs. This requirement not only applied to girls wishing to become members or associates of the gang, but it also applied to girls who wished to receive protection from physical harm from a specific gang. Sex was again conceptualized as a commodity, in this case one that could be exchanged for an increased sense of safety in an increasingly violent environment.

*Domestic Violence and Sex.* During our discussion of the risks of having sex, some of the girls raised the issue of the risk of *not* having sex. Several of the group members identified that there were many situations in which refusing to have sex could result in physical harm. According to the stories related by the children, it was their perception that this could be the case in marital and nonmarital or dating relationships. Many of the girls described instances of domestic violence that they had either witnessed or heard about. Girls who did not comply with requests for sex from a marital or romantic partner were again blamed or seen as responsible for the abuse they experienced. Risk-taking decisions can clearly have multiple or ambiguous consequences, regardless of the choice.

*Misinformation.* Children also cited lack of information as a factor influencing early sexual activity. In fact, it was their only response to the question of what factors might explain early sexual activity. They were not able to elaborate on issues of misinformation, but they did believe that providing them with correct information would help them to make healthy choices. They stated that having access to information in health classes would give them more knowledge upon which to base future decisions.

## Why Have Prevention Efforts Failed?

Historically, prevention researchers in the area of health-compromising risk behavior have focused attention on developing cognitive, individually based strategies to promote health and decrease risk-taking. Specifically, interventions have been designed to help adolescents choose more effectively in situations that put their health at risk. Such strategies include providing educational information (e.g., sex education), practicing assertiveness skills through role playing (e.g., practicing saying "no"), and values identification exercises (see Howard and McCabe 1992; Kavanagh et al. 1990). Despite the frequency with which intervention strategies have been introduced, the effectiveness of the current programs has been inconsistent at best. Even very high-quality programs evidence considerable variability in their degree of impact and success (Kazdin 1993). There are many reasons that past prevention efforts have had so little effect on inner-city children.

First, previous approaches to prevention have failed to take a developmental approach to curriculum design, despite evidence of its promise (Brooks-Gunn and Paikoff 1993). In other words, programs are designed to provide children with a broad scope of information or skills without considering normative developmental issues that have implications for the quantity and manner in which such material should be presented. There has also been a lack of consideration of cultural and other group differences (e.g., generational, gender, ethnic and racial, and socioeconomic). Recent evidence suggests that children are entering puberty earlier today than in past generations (Brooks-Gunn and Reiter 1990; Zigler and Finn-Stevenson 1987) and that urban children and adolescents are sexually active at relatively younger ages (Levy et al. 1993). Indeed, many urban children's initiation into sexual activity occurs before they have access to most sexual risk-taking prevention programs.

Pregnancy prevention programs work very differently with adolescents who have and have not yet initiated sexual intercourse: Such programs are more effective with virgins than with nonvirgins (Miller et al.

1992). Thus, an earlier starting point is required if researchers are to truly target nonactive children for prevention programs.

Prevention curricula have often focused on singular risk behaviors in efforts to isolate the individual variables salient to them. It is common to see "HIV prevention" or "alcohol and drug abuse prevention" (see Botvin et al. 1990). These efforts may overlook contextual factors that interconnect multiple, coexisting risk situations (e.g., how drug abuse influences sexual risk-taking). When risks are closely related, singular approaches are likely to lead to few, if any, changes in risk behaviors (Kazdin 1993).

Several recent prevention programs (Allen, Philliber, and Hoggson 1990; Kavanagh et al. 1990) that have attempted to address co-occurring risks and the interaction of such risks have documented some success. These programs acknowledge that risk behaviors are interrelated, and although they may not necessarily co-occur, such behaviors tend to come in "packages" (Kazdin 1993; Jessor 1993).

In spite of efforts to understand the complexity of co-occurring risk-taking behaviors, however, many programs continue to ignore the effects of violent environments on individual behaviors. In fact, there has been little systematic research on the psychological consequences for children of being raised in chronically violent neighborhoods or on how exposure to chronic violence affects decision making around risky behavior in children (Martinez and Richters 1993). This is a critical challenge for prevention of high-risk behaviors in urban children.

A final problem inherent in many prevention efforts has been the failure to address critical social context (e.g., economic, cultural, ethnic, and racial) influences that affect urban youth (Kazdin 1993). For example, the availability of financial and institutional resources has a significant impact on individuals' perceptions of their ability to control their destinies (Gurin, Gurin, and Morrison 1978). An important challenge for prevention efforts is to identify culturally appropriate, relevant, and acceptable methods of intervention (Kazdin 1993).

## Implications of Our Data for Augmenting Prevention Efforts

The results of our research have many implications for prevention planners and practitioners alike. Although the sampling methods of focus groups limit the generalizability of our findings (Morgan 1988), we have identified some issues relevant to urban children living in poverty that warrant further consideration.

The level of sophistication of knowledge illustrated by these children was striking. Most of these eight- to twelve-year-old children had witnessed, experienced, or had knowledge of sexual activity and violence.

For urban children many of the factors we think of as compromising to health seem to be interrelated. With regard to sexual risk-taking, neither children nor parents perceived the issue as involving only pregnancy or teenage parenting. Violence, AIDS, sexual abuse, and drug abuse overlapped with or were perceived as being closely related to sexual activity.

References to the threat of violence were abundant throughout the focus group discussions. This finding raises the question of health priorities. When physical safety is in constant jeopardy, unsafe sex may become a secondary, and by default, less important consideration. Such an interpretation has been supported historically by hierarchy of needs theorists such as Maslow (1954). Previous research has shown that children who are exposed to violent incidents are significantly more likely than those not exposed to suffer from a wide range of social and emotional problems that may impair decision making. Evidence of the negative effects of exposure to chronic community violence (e.g., distress symptoms) has been found in children as young as six (Martinez and Richters 1993).

The challenge to prevention researchers is to integrate overall safety and protection with risk-specific prevention. For example, it seems naive to teach urban children to abstain if we do not also help them to maneuver the consequences of "saying no." In addition, the impact of peer pressure takes on a new meaning when one's safety is in constant flux. Not only do children look to each other to assess what it takes to "fit in," but they also may look to each other to figure out how to stay alive. Faced with multiple, coexisting risks, urban children must learn to choose between the lesser of two (or more) evils. "Avoidance" of health risks or "abstinence" may not be a truly tenable choice in the absence of more viable, or functional, alternatives that meet basic safety or survival needs.

Teaching children to say no to one risk situation may expose them to greater risks in another situation. When a girl is faced with engaging in sex without knowledge of her partner's sexual history, in exchange for feeling safer because of the "protection" that activity will buy, she may choose current gains over future risks. It behooves professionals dedicated to improving the lives of urban children to recognize the need for alternative health strategies (e.g., how to use a condom). In other words, it is critical that we tell children what *to* do, not just what *not* to do. We also need to measure the wisdom of our advice against the level of potential danger involved in the child's daily context.

## Implications for Future Research

Complex questions and issues need to be addressed by prevention researchers working with urban youth living in poverty. Sexual risk-taking behaviors cannot be seen as isolated behaviors. Prevention strategies are needed that take into account a full spectrum of risks and help our children to learn self-protective strategies that can help to keep them safer from multiple, coexisting risks. We must make a commitment to understanding how urban children can maneuver their way through multiple risks and keep themselves alive, so that staying healthy is relevant. This may involve devising interventions that are not only school based, but also include family and community intervention, since many problems have community roots (Snowden 1987).

It is also important that professionals target prevention efforts toward preadolescents and younger children (Hammond and Yung 1993; Kazdin 1993). In doing so we must confront the challenge of preparing relatively young children for multifaceted, complex issues, keeping in mind the limits of their cognitive processing of information.

This requires that we rethink our approach to risk prevention and that we go beyond prescribing generic solutions. For example, if we teach abstinence, we must be prepared to answer the questions, "Then what?" or "What happens if when I say no I face another decision?" We are not necessarily required to present "an answer" as much as a process of decision-making that encompasses multiple risks and multiple consequences of varying decisions. This multifaceted approach to health promotion and sexual risk prevention may seem complex, but anything less is unlikely to reflect the needs of urban children and adolescents.

It is essential to allow inner-city communities to educate us about the realities of their lives. We cannot assume that the current body of knowledge we have about sexual risk-taking, or any other area of human functioning, represents the reality for every child (Kiesler 1966). Cultural and developmental factors must be assessed and integrated into prevention efforts and curricula. Many urban communities are overwhelmed with violence and inadequate access to resources, and these factors permeate physical and mental health considerations at every level. We must rise to the challenges of designing developmentally sensitive and culturally appropriate curricula in order to improve the health and safety of children and families.

NOTE

1. Sexual activity was defined explicitly for children in the interview; however, it was undefined in the focus group setting. Although this may undoubtedly restrict our ability to focus on heterosexual intercourse, it allowed the children to focus on issues important to them, probably including but not restricted to intercourse.

REFERENCES

AIDS Chicago. 1992. AIDS surveillance program report. Office of AIDS Prevention, City of Chicago. June.

Alexander, J., and B. V. Parsons. 1982. *Functional family therapy*. Monterey, Calif.: Brooks/Cole.

Allen, J. P., S. Philliber, and N. Hoggson. 1990. School-based prevention of teen-age pregnancy and school dropout: Process evaluation of the national replication of the Teen Outreach Program. *American Journal of Community Psychology* 18:505–24.

Botvin, G. J., E. Baker, A. D. Filazzola, and E. M. Botvin. 1990. A cognitive-behavioral approach to substance abuse prevention: One year follow-up. *Addictive Behaviors* 15:47–63.

Brooks-Gunn, J., and R. L. Paikoff. 1993. "Sex is a gamble, kissing is a game": Adolescent sexuality and health promotion. In *Promotion of health behavior in adolescence*, edited by S. P. Millstein, A. Petersen, and E. Nightengale. New York: Oxford University Press.

Brooks-Gunn, J., and E. O. Reiter. 1990. The role of pubertal processes in the early adolescent transition. In *At the threshold: The developing adolescent*, edited by S. Feldman and G. R. Elliot. Cambridge: Harvard University Press.

Centers for Disease Control. 1992. Selected behaviors that increase risk for HIV infection among high school students—United States 1990. *Morbidity and Mortality Weekly Reports* 41 (14):231–40.

Dryfoos, J. G. 1990. *Adolescents at risk: Prevalence and prevention*. New York: Oxford University Press.

Guerra, N., and A. Panizzon. 1992. *Viewpoints: Solving problems and making effective decisions*. Santa Barbara, Calif.: Center for Law-Related Education.

Gurin, P., G. Gurin, and B. M. Morrison. 1978. Personal and ideological aspects of internal and external control. *Social Psychology Quarterly* 41 (4):275–96.

Hammond, W. R., and B. Yung. 1993. Psychology's role in the public health response to assaultive violence among young African American men. *American Psychologist* 48 (2):142–54.

Howard, M., and J. McCabe. 1992. An information and skills approach for younger teens: Postponing sexual involvement program. In *Preventing Adolescent Pregnancy*, edited by B. C. Miller, J. J. Card, R. L. Paikoff, and J. L. Peterson. Newbury Park, Calif.: Sage Publications.

Inciardi, J. A., D. Lockwood, and A. E. Pottieger. 1993. *Women and crack-cocaine*. New York: Macmillan.

Jarrett, R. L. 1993. Focus group interviewing with low-income minority populations: A research experience. In *Successful focus groups: Advancing the state of the art*, edited by D. Morgan. Newbury Park, Calif.: Sage Publications.

Jessor, R. 1993. Successful adolescent development among youth in high-risk settings. *American Psychologist* 48 (2):117–26.

Jessor, R., and S. L. Jessor. 1977. *Problem behavior and psychological development: A longitudinal study of youth*. San Diego: Academic Press.

Kavanagh, M., A. S. Jackson, J. Gaffney, M. Caplan, and R. P. Weissberg. 1990. *The New Haven social development program: Sixth-grade human growth development, AIDS prevention, and teen pregnancy prevention module*. New Haven: Yale University.

Kazdin, A. E. 1993. Adolescent mental health: Prevention and treatment programs. *American Psychologist* 48 (2):127–41.

Kiesler, D. J. 1966. Some myths of psychotherapy research and the search for a paradigm. *Psychological Bulletin* 65:110–36.

Koss, M.P., C. A. Gidycz, and N. Wisniewski. 1987. The scope of rape: Incidents and prevalence of sexual aggression and victimization in a national sample of higher education students. *Journal of Clinical and Consulting Psychology* 55 (2):162–70.

Lerner, M. J., and D. T. Miller. 1978. Just world research and the attribution process: Looking back and ahead. *Psychological Bulletin* 85:1030–51.

Levy, S. R., C. Lampman, A. Handler, B. R. Flay, and K. Weeks. 1993. Young adolescent attitudes toward sex and substance use: Implications for AIDS prevention. *AIDS Education and Prevention* 5 (4):340–51.

Martinez, P., and J. E. Richters. 1993. The NIMH Community Violence Project Part 2, Children's distress symptoms associated with violence exposure. *Psychiatry: Interpersonal and Biological Processes* 56 (1):22–35.

Maslow, A. 1954. *Motivation and personality*. New York: Harper and Row.

Miller, B. C., J. J. Card, R. L. Paikoff, and J. L. Peterson, eds. 1992. *Preventing adolescent pregnancy: Model programs and evaluations*. Newbury Park, Calif.: Sage Publications.

Moore, C. 1991. *A state by state look at teenage childbearing in the U.S.* Report prepared for the Charles Stuart Mott Foundation. Flint, Michigan.

Morgan, D. L. 1988. *Focus groups as qualitative research*. Newbury Park, Calif.: Sage Publications.

———. 1993. *Successful focus groups: Advancing the state of the art*. Newbury Park, Calif.: Sage Publications.

Paikoff, R. L. 1995. Early heterosexual debut: Situations of sexual possibility during the transition to adolescence. *American Journal of Orthopsychiatry* 65 (3):389–401.

Polkinghorne, D. 1994. Qualitative Research. Workshop conducted at the Division 17 Great Lakes Conference, April, Notre Dame, Indiana.

Richters, J. E., and P. Martinez. 1993. The NIMH Community Violence Project: I. Children as victims of and witness to violence. Special issue children and violence. *Psychiatry: Interpersonal and Biological Processes* 56 (1):7–21.

Snowden, L. R. 1987. The peculiar successes of community psychology: Service deliveries to ethnic minorities and the poor. *American Journal of Community Psychology* 15 (5):575–86.

Sonenstein, F. L., J. H. Pleck, and L. C. Klu. 1989. Sexual activity, condom use, and AIDS awareness among adolescent males. *Family Planning Perspectives* 21:152–58.

Spencer, M. B., and S. M. Dornbusch. 1990. Challenges in studying minority youth. In *At the threshold: The developing adolescent,* edited by S. S. Feldman and G. R. Elliott. Cambridge: Harvard University Press.

Udry, J. R. 1988. Biological predispositions and social control in adolescent sexual behavior. *American Sociological Review* 53:709–22.

Wilson, W. J. 1987. *The truly disadvantaged*. Chicago: University of Chicago Press.

Zigler, E. F., and M. Finn-Stevenson. 1987. *Children: Development and social issues*. Lexington, Mass.: D. C. Health.

# VI

# Health Risks

The 1990 American Medical Association report *Healthy Youth 2000* outlines national health promotion and disease prevention objectives for adolescents. These objectives typically focus on "young people" or males (except when considering issues of sexuality or pregnancy). Although substantial gender differences exist in adolescent health risks, research and policy specific to girls' health problems (not related to their sexuality) lags behind studies of boys' problems. Boys are more likely to exhibit externalizing symptoms (aggressive or delinquent behaviors), whereas girls are more likely to exhibit internalizing symptoms (somatic disorders, depression, and anxiety) (Leadbeater, Blatt, and Quinlan 1995). Males in the United States are three times more likely to die from violent causes (accidental death, suicides involving guns or hanging, and homicide) than females. On the other hand, 90% to 95% of anorexics and bulemics are female; girls appear more likely to attempt suicide, and after puberty, girls are twice as likely as boys to show depressive symptoms (Leadbeater, Blatt, and Quinlan 1995).

Major adolescent health risks primarily reflect sets of social problems that stretch well beyond the risk-taking behaviors of individual adolescents. Accidents, suicides, and homicides rank highest as causes of death in teenagers (U.S. Congress Office of Technology Assessment 1991). Many of the health risks that compromise normal adolescent development today have complex psychosocial and environmental causes rather than or in addition to biological causes (Jessor 1993). The following chapters illustrate the importance of taking account of social and family contexts in understanding drug use and depression in adolescent girls.

Gibbs, in chapter 17, reports on an investigation of the correlates of cigarette, alcohol, and drug use in an economically and racially diverse sample of young urban adolescents. Despite stereotypes of the greater vulnerability of urban black girls to substance abuse, her findings suggest that white and middle-class adolescent girls (perhaps those who can more afford the substances) are using alcohol and drugs more often than their black peers. Her findings also indicate that engagement in more serious levels of substance abuse is associated with a problem behavior profile that included higher levels of family conflict, school problems, negative perceptions of heath problems (more somatic complaints), delinquent activities, more liberal sexual attitudes, and less positive attachments to friends.

In chapter 18, Salguero and McCusker explore the processes by which cultural differences affect symptom expression in a group of Puerto Rican girls who were seen in an urban, community-based outpatient clinic in the Northeast. The authors caution against ascribing girls' mental health problems to characteristics of traditional Puerto Rican culture (e.g., excessive strictness with girls). Rather, they argue that it is disruptions in the efficient working of cultural traditions that underlie many immigrant parent-child conflicts: unemployment undermines the traditional role of the father as provider, immigration isolates families from extended family networks, and intergenerational acculturation lags make it necessary for immigrant families to cope with the contradictions between cultural and mainstream values. Salguero and McCusker also argue that symptom expression in Latina adolescents may be a sign of healthy resistance to a dysfunctional situation.

Allen, Denner, Yoshikawa, Seidman, and Aber, in chapter 19, also assess the effects of acculturation on the expression of depressive symptoms in a community-based sample. Their sample includes 137 Latina girls, predominantly from Puerto Rican and Dominican backgrounds. Using extent of English use as a proxy for acculturation, Allen and her coauthors confirm the association between lower levels of acculturation and higher levels of depressive symptoms. They also explore moderators of this association and find that low levels of English use are associated with more depressive symptoms when levels of daily stresses are high and when the family has fewer economic resources. The interactions of these risk variables with acculturation gives credence to the hypothesis that the compounding of stresses related to poverty with low levels of acculturation, rather than cultural attributes alone, contribute to symptom expression in Latina adolescents.

REFERENCES

Jessor, R. 1993. Successful adolescent development among youth in high-risk settings. *American Psychologist* 48 (2):117–26.
Leadbeater, B. J., S. J. Blatt, and D. M. Quinlan. 1995. Gender-linked vulnerabilities to

depressive symptoms, stress, and problem behaviors in adolescents. *Journal of Research on Adolescence* 5(1):1–29.

U.S. Congress Office of Technology Assessment. 1991. *Adolescent health,* Vol. 1, *Summary and policy option, OTA-H-468.* April. Washington, D.C.: U.S. Government Printing Office.

# 17 Health-Compromising Behaviors in Urban Early Adolescent Females: Ethnic and Socioeconomic Variations

Jewelle Taylor Gibbs

## Introduction and Literature Review

The use of cigarettes, alcohol, and other illicit drugs among early adolescents is of concern to health professionals not only because of its immediate behavioral consequences, but also because of its potential for health-damaging effects (Dryfoos 1990; Newcomb and Bentler 1988). Those effects can range from negative short-term consequences for physical and mental health, including higher risks for self-destructive behaviors and accidental death, to long-term consequences such as cancer, emphysema, and coronary and circulatory diseases (Coates, Peterson, and Perry 1982).

The major purpose of this chapter is to report the findings of a study of health-compromising behaviors of urban early adolescent females, with a specific focus on their use of illicit substances and an analysis of the psychosocial and demographic factors associated with that use. Self-reports of health status, feelings of depression, levels of somatic complaints, and sexual attitudes and behaviors are described in relation to participants' substance use.

Studies of drug use in late adolescence and young adulthood have consistently shown that initial experimentation with drugs, particularly cigarettes, alcohol, and marijuana, begins in junior high school and even earlier (Kandel and Logan 1984; Newcomb and Bentler 1988; Oetting and Beauvais 1990). Although these studies have traditionally focused on older adolescents, in recent years an increasing number of researchers have investigated patterns of drug use among teens and preteens in junior high and middle schools (Coombs, Fawzy, and Gerber 1986; Thomas et al. 1990; Zastowny et al. 1993). Drug use among eighth graders has increased, according to a recent report from the University of Michigan Institute for Social Research (Johnston, O'Malley, and Bachman 1994).

*Incidence of Substance Use*

It is difficult to estimate the incidence of substance use in this twelve-to-fifteen-year-old age group for several methodological and practical reasons, including difficulties accessing school samples, the need for parental consent for minors, the possibility of social desirability responses, and concerns over the limits of confidentiality of the data. Estimates of substance use have been made by disaggregating statistics from large-scale surveys of twelve-to-seventeen-year-olds and from a series of cross-sectional studies with smaller samples (Dryfoos 1990; Mott and Haurin 1988; Oetting and Beauvais 1990; Skager 1986).

*Cigarette Smoking.* Incidence rates reported in recent community studies of junior high school samples ranged from 5.7% to 67% for females in the twelve-to-fifteen age group who had ever smoked cigarettes. Rates for "regular users" ranged from 5% to 30%, but many studies do not differentiate levels of use. In analyzing rates from a number of studies with early adolescent samples, ages twelve to fifteen, Dryfoos (1990) estimated that 20% in this age group are cigarette smokers.

*Alcohol Use.* In large-scale studies of alcohol use among students in junior high school or ninth grade, self-reported rates have ranged from 43% to 53% ever using hard liquor and 6% to 79% ever using beer or wine (Barnes and Welte 1986; Harford 1986; Kandel and Logan 1984; Rachal et al. 1980). Smaller samples drawn from the Midwest, the South, the West, and rural New England have reported rates ranging from 12% to 66% ever using hard liquor and 23% to 96% ever using beer or wine (Bloom and Greenwald 1984; Gleaton and Smith 1981). According to Dryfoos (1990), about 46% of early adolescents, ages twelve to fifteen, across a range of studies, have reported ever drinking alcoholic beverages. Regular users of hard liquor, however, accounted for a minor fraction of this group.

*Marijuana Use.* Experimenting with marijuana also begins in junior high school, where one study found up to 50% of the students reporting pressure to try it by seventh grade (Skager 1986). In other surveys of early adolescents (ages twelve to fifteen) since 1982, reported incidence rates for marijuana use have ranged from 0.0% to 51% (Carlisi 1984; Newcomb et al. 1987; Segal 1989). "Regular" users range from 7% to 15% in these studies. Marijuana use in this age group has fluctuated over the past two decades (1970–90), reaching its peak in the mid-1980s and leveling off since then, with an average estimate of 15% of the twelve-to-fifteen age group having ever used it (Dryfoos 1990).

*Other Drugs.* Use of the hard drugs, such as cocaine, heroin, and PCP, usually is not widespread before high school (Kandel and Logan 1984; Oetting and Beauvais 1990). However, the incidence and patterns of use of these substances vary greatly across communities. Reliable data on these drugs are even more difficult to obtain because of the different labels they have, the perception that they are more dangerous, and the fear of possible sanctions if confidentiality is abridged. In the New York City survey only 2% of the seventh graders reported using "other drugs" as contrasted with 10% of the tenth graders (New York State Division of Substance Abuse Services 1984). Estimates from other studies of early adolescents range from 2% to 15% for use of "other drugs" or "hard drugs" or a combination, but Dryfoos (1990) concludes from studies published through 1985 that only about 1% of the twelve-to-fifteen age group had ever used hard drugs.

### Risk Factors for Adolescent Substance Use

Risk factors that precede and/or predict the use of cigarettes, alcohol, and other illicit drugs in adolescence have been identified and enumerated in a number of studies (National Institute of Drug Abuse [NIDA] 1986; Howard, Boyd, and Zucker 1994; Segal 1989; Vega et al. 1993; Way et al. 1994; Windle 1990).

These risk factors and predictors include family factors, such as dysfunctional family patterns of behavior and communication, parental modeling of substance use, family conflict, lack of parental support or affection, and child physical or sexual abuse; social and environmental factors, including neighborhoods with high rates of substance use and availability of drugs, substance-using peer networks, and school settings with easy access to drugs; behavioral risk factors, such as early delinquent or acting-out behaviors, low school achievement, truancy, rebelliousness against authority figures, low involvement in religious and extracurricular activities, and frequent involvement in high-risk behaviors; and psychological risk factors, including feelings of depression, somatic complaints and symptoms, symptoms of anxiety or stress, low educational and occupational aspirations, low perceived risk of negative consequences of substance use, and acculturation stress particularly for immigrant and Native American adolescents.

Although these factors have been identified in numerous studies of adolescent substance abuse, it is important to note that, when multiethnic samples have been used, differences have been found in the number and pattern of risk factors or predictors of substance use among adolescents from different ethnic and socioeconomic groups. In fact race and ethnicity, socioeconomic status, parental marital status, and household composition yield conflicting evidence as antecedents or predictors of adolescent substance use and show differential effects across different combinations of variables (see Barrera, Li, and Chassin 1993; Barnes, Farrell, and Banerjee 1994; Newcomb et al. 1987; Wallace and Bachman 1991; Way et al. 1994).

### Correlates of Illicit Substance Use

Demographic factors associated with adolescent substance use include age (use increases with age), sex (males have higher rates than females, except for cigarette smoking), and geographic region (higher rates in the Northeast and the Northwest, lower rates in the Midwest and the South) (Newcomb and Bentler 1988; Zastowny et al. 1993). The findings on the relationship of ethnicity and socioeconomic status to adolescent substance use are somewhat unclear.

Studies have generally found that Asian, black, and Hispanic females consistently report lower rates of both alcohol and drug use as compared with white and American Indian girls (Barnes, Farrell, and Banerjee 1994; Wallace and Bachman 1991). Studies also show socioeconomic differences in rates and patterns of illicit substance use (Farrow and Schwartz 1992; Newcomb et al. 1987; Velez and Ungemack 1989; Way et al. 1994). Within-group comparisons indicate that low-income black female adolescents generally report higher rates of illicit substance use than middle- and upper-income black females do, but the reverse is true among Whites (Gibbs 1982; Oyemade and Washington 1990). Since most youth drug use surveys are conducted with in-school samples, these results probably do not accurately reflect the incidence of substance use of school dropouts and institutionalized adolescents, whose rates may be even higher.

Behavioral correlates of illicit substance use in early adolescence have been identified as low school achievement, delinquent activities, running away, conflict with parents, and general rebelliousness and nonconforming behaviors (Beschner and Friedman 1986; Newcomb et al. 1987; NIDA 1986). The profile developed by Jessor and Jessor (1977) of the "deviant-prone" adolescent who engages in multiple problem behaviors, including substance abuse, has been supported by many subsequent studies.

Psychological correlates of illicit substance use in this age group include low self-esteem, external locus of control, inability to delay gratification, depression, anxiety, low educational and career aspirations, and deviant social attitudes (Beschner and Friedman 1986; Newcomb et al. 1987; NIDA 1986). The relationship between substance use and depression has been shown to differ across different socioeconomic groups (Farrow and Schwartz 1992; Way et al. 1994).

Illicit substance use is also associated with a host of physical problems among adolescents, including premature sexual activity, psychosomatic complaints, excessive dieting, mouth cancer and dental problems, and accidents and self-destructive behaviors (Mott and Haurin 1988; Newcomb and Bentler 1988). In fact, 75% of all fatal car and motorcycle accidents among adolescents are drug related. Some studies have found that adolescents who use drugs report more health-related problems or have a more negative perception of their current health status (Brunswick, Merzel, and Messeri 1985; Millstein et al. 1992). Conversely, in a study of eleventh graders in Ohio, it was found that females with a higher perception of drugs as harmful to health had a lower incidence of drug use (Pascale, Trucksis, and Sylvester 1985).

Although many studies have found gender differences in the incidence rates of substance use in adolescents, few take the next step, asking how the correlates of substance use might differ between girls and boys. This study focuses specifically on the correlates of substance use for adolescent girls. It cannot be assumed that prevention or intervention efforts will lead to healthy behaviors among girls if the efforts are not appropriately targeted to meet their particular needs.

The following discussion has three goals: (1) to describe the use of illicit drugs among a multiethnic sample of urban early adolescent females, (2) to discuss the relationship between substance use and selected psychosocial and demographic factors, and (3) to suggest implications for prevention and early intervention in order to foster positive health behaviors in this age group.

## Study Design

### Sample

The sample was composed of 387 female adolescents recruited from four public junior high schools in a San Francisco Bay Area community. The participants were in grades seven through nine, and the sample included a multiracial student population in schools located in three geographically and socioeconomically diverse areas. The participants all volunteered, with parental consent. The data were collected during the academic year of 1982–83. While drug use among high school students (except LSD) has declined over the last decade, recent reports using national statistics from the University of Michigan Institute for Social Research (Johnston, O'Malley, and Bachman 1994) suggest that alcohol and drug use has increased in young adolescents. Hence, the drug use estimate here may be conservative. Correlates of drug use specific to early adolescent girls continue to be underexplored.

*Demographic Characteristics of the Sample.* The girls ranged in age from 12–16, with a mean age of 14.0. The group included 38 Asians (9.8%), 204 Blacks (52.7%), 23 Hispanics (5.9%), 116 Whites (30.0%), and 6 American Indians and multiracial girls (1.6%). The largest proportion (39%) were in the eighth grade, with 35% in ninth grade and 26% in seventh grade; 47.5% were from intact families and 43.5% from divorced or separated families; 5% lived with widowed parents, and 4% with never-married families. They had an average of 2.4 siblings.

Using the Center's Occupational Scale to determine socioeconomic status, we rated them as 55% upper middle and middle class, 23% working class, and 22% low income. They reported their religious affiliations as 57% Protestant, 20% Jewish, 18% Catholic, and 5% "other/unaffiliated."

*Measures*

The following measures were used in this study:

1. *A brief demographic questionnaire:* questions on age, race or ethnicity, religion, grade level, parental marital status, parental occupation and education, number of siblings, and number of household moves.

2. *Beck Depression Inventory (BDI):* a twenty-one-item self-administered inventory that measures cognitive, behavioral, affective, and somatic aspects of depression. Scores can be converted to a depression rating in one of four levels ranging from nonminimal to severe depression (Beck and Beamesderfer 1974).

3. *Mooney Problem Check-List (Junior High School Form):* a 210-item self-administered inventory that measures the number of problems or concerns in seven areas of adolescent psychosocial functioning. This instrument has been widely used with adolescent samples, and its psychometric properties are described in the author's manual (Mooney and Gordon 1950).

4. *Offer Self-Image Questionnaire for Adolescents (Female Form):* a 130-item self-administered questionnaire that yields scores in eleven areas of adolescent personality and psychological functioning, as well as a total score of overall psychosocial adjustment (Offer, Ostrov, and Howard 1981).

5. *Adolescent Biographical Questionnaire:* a self-administered question-

naire, designed by the author to obtain personal, family, social and behavioral data in eight major areas of adolescent psychosocial functioning.

Participants were asked to rate their overall level of satisfaction with themselves on a five-point scale from "very satisfied with myself" to "very dissatisfied with myself." This rating was used as a proxy measure of current self-esteem. Participants were also asked to state the highest level of education they expected to complete and the highest occupational level they expected to achieve in the future, as indicators of their educational and occupational aspirations.

6. *Incidence and Frequency of Substance Abuse:* an inventory of illicit substances with a five-point frequency scale ("never" to "frequent") on the Adolescent Biographical Questionnaire. Participants were asked about their use of cigarettes, marijuana, alcohol, and a list of other drugs included in standard questionnaires on adolescent substance use.

## Administration of the Study

The study was conducted in each junior high school during the regular school day. The self-administered instruments took approximately two hours to complete. In order to minimize ethnic and age effects, the study was administered by the author, an African American, and two female graduate students, one white and one Hispanic. Participants were given standardized instructions and were assisted in completing all instruments if they encountered any difficulties with vocabulary or comprehension of questions on any of the measures.

## Findings

### Use of Illicit Substances

In this multiethnic sample of urban early adolescent females, 33.8% reported ever smoking cigarettes, 23.3% drinking alcoholic beverages, 23.3% using marijuana, and 11.6% using one or more other drugs (see table 17.1). Among those girls in the current study who reported using illicit substances, the proportion who used any substance regularly (one or more times per week) ranged from 7% for cigarettes, 5%–7% for beer and wine, 4% for marijuana, and 2% for "other drugs," which included cocaine, amphetamines, hashish, valium, codeine, dexedrine, and benzedrine. Fewer than 2% reported ever using sedatives, heroin, LSD, PCP, or quaaludes. These statistics are somewhat higher than those recently

TABLE 17.1
*Use of Illicit Substances by Race/Ethnicity*

| | Black (N = 204) | | White (N = 116) | | Total Sample (N = 387) | |
|---|---|---|---|---|---|---|
| | users | % of group | users | % of group | users | % of total |
| Cigarettes | 67 | 33.0 | 45 | 38.7 | 131 | 33.8 |
| Alcohol[a, b] | 28 | 13.7 | 51 | 43.9 | 90 | 23.3 |
| Marijuana | 52 | 25.4 | 29 | 25.0 | 90 | 23.3 |
| Other drugs[c] | 15 | 7.3 | 22 | 18.9 | 45 | 11.6 |

NOTES: Blacks and Whites constituted 82.6% of the total sample of 387 participants. Total rates in text include the entire sample, except where otherwise noted.
[a]Alcoholic beverages include beer, wine, mixed drinks, and hard liquor.
[b]Whites had a significantly higher rate of alcohol use than Blacks ($x^2$ = 18.81, 3 *d.f.*, $p < .001$).
[c]Whites had a significantly higher rate of "other drug" use than Blacks ($x^2$ = 7.89, 3 *d.f.*, $p < .05$).

reported by the Institute for Social Research at the University of Michigan (Johnston, O'Malley, and Bachman 1994) of all eighth grade students in the last month (15.5% reported smoking cigarettes, 26.1% drinking alcoholic beverages, 3.7% using marijuana, and 7% using other drugs). These differences demonstrate the methodological difficulties of assessing incidence of adolescent drug use.

White girls were significantly more likely than black girls to use alcohol (44% vs. 14%). A similar pattern held true across all alcoholic beverages. Patterns of marijuana were nearly identical in the two groups, but white girls were significantly more likely than black girls to report using "other drugs." Compared to black girls, white girls were somewhat more likely to smoke cigarettes and to smoke on a regular basis, but the differences were not significant (see table 17.1).

Socioeconomic status was also related to use of these illicit substances, with middle- and higher-income girls significantly more likely to use alcoholic beverages and "other drugs" than lower-income girls (see table 17.2). Patterns of cigarette smoking and marijuana use did not vary significantly between these two groups, but the higher-income girls had slightly higher rates of usage for both cigarettes and marijuana than the lower-income girls, a pattern found in both black and white groups.

*Behavioral Correlates of Illicit Substance Use*

Several problem behaviors were associated with substance use in these girls. Black and white users of all illicit substances were significantly more likely to skip classes, to break school rules, and to have been suspended or expelled than nonusers. They were significantly more likely than nonusers to engage occasionally in shoplifting small items. They were also somewhat more likely than nonusers to be sexually active and to report a greater number of sexual partners ($p < .10$) (see table 17.2).

TABLE 17.2
*Correlates of Illicit Substance Use*

| Variable | Cigarettes | Alcohol | Marijuana | Other Drugs |
|---|---|---|---|---|
| 1. Age | — | $r = .283^c$ | — | $r = .234^c$ |
| 2. Race/ethnicity | $.116^b$ | $r = .283^c$ | $r = .086^a$ | $r = .189^c$ |
| 3. SES | — | $r = .200^a$ | — | $r = .127^b$ |
| 4. Relationship with mother | $r = -.149^c$ | $r = -.116^b$ | $r = -.115^b$ | $r = -.175^c$ |
| 5. Relationship with father | $r = -.222^c$ | — | $r = -.133^b$ | $r = -.135^b$ |
| 6. Living with natural parents | — | — | $r = -.144^b$ | — |
| 7. Skips classes | $r = .349^c$ | $r = .287^c$ | $r = .363^c$ | $r = .421^c$ |
| 8. Breaks rules | $r = .276^c$ | $r = .289^c$ | $r = .269^c$ | $r = .279^c$ |
| 9. Suspensions/expulsions | $r = .185^c$ | $r = .088^a$ | $r = .198^c$ | — |
| 10. Shoplifting small items | $r = .279^c$ | $r = .288^c$ | $r = .366^c$ | $r = .333^c$ |
| 11. Frequency of social activities | — | — | $r = .148^b$ | — |
| 12. Moving from friends | $r = .130^b$ | — | $r = .148^b$ | — |
| 13. Perception of adolescent health | $r = -.161^b$ | $r = -.135^b$ | $r = -.223^c$ | $r = -.200^c$ |

NOTES: Variables 1–13 from the Demographic Data and Adolescent Biographical Questionnaire were analyzed in a correlation matrix, as represented by Pearson $r$ values.

Key for levels of significance:
$^a p = <.05$
$^b p = <.01$
$^c p = <.001$

## Psychological and Psychosocial Correlates

Psychological correlates of illicit substance use are shown in table 17.3. Overall scores on the Beck Depression Inventory were not significantly related to the use of cigarettes, drugs, or alcohol. However, those girls who reported smoking cigarettes frequently and using "other drugs" frequently were somewhat more likely than nonusers to complain on the Adolescent Biographical Questionnaire of "feeling depressed."

Frequency of cigarette smoking was also related to the total number of problems reported on the Mooney Problem Checklist, with heavy smokers reporting significantly more family, social, school, and behavioral problems than nonsmokers. A two-way analysis of variance showed that girls who smoked more frequently were also significantly more likely than nonsmokers to have more liberal attitudes on the Sexual Attitudes Scale of the Offer Self-Image Questionnaire (OSIQ), to experience more communication problems with their parents on the Family Relations Scale of the OSIQ, and to have lower aspirations in educational and career planning on the Vocational-Educational Goals Scale of the OSIQ (see table 17.3).

Girls who used marijuana more frequently were significantly more

TABLE 17.3

*Psychological and Psychosocial Relationships to Substance Use*

| Variable | Cigarettes | Alcohol | Marijuana | Other Drugs |
|---|---|---|---|---|
| 1. Total problems (M.P.C.L.) | $F = 7.30^c$ | — | — | — |
| 2. Sexual attitudes scale (OSIQ) | $F = 13.95^c$ | $F = 13.51^c$ | $F = 19.27^c$ | $F = 11.66^c$ |
| 3. Family relations scale (OSIQ) | $F = 12.08^c$ | — | $F = 7.75^c$ | $F = 4.53^a$ |
| 4. Vocational-educational goals (OSIQ) | $F = 5.61^b$ | — | $F = 4.22^a$ | — |
| 5. Impulse control scale (OSIQ) | — | — | $F = 2.89^a$ | — |

NOTES: Variables 1–5 from the Mooney Problem Check List and the Offer Self-Image Questionnaire were analyzed by a two-way analysis of variance, as represented by *F*-ratio values.

Key for levels of significance:

$^a p = <.05$
$^b p = <.01$
$^c p = <.001$

likely to show greater problems in the areas of family relationships and vocational goals on the OSIQ; they were also more likely to exhibit lower frustration tolerance and inability to delay gratification on the Impulse Control Scale of the OSIQ.

Black and white users of all illicit substances were significantly more likely than nonusers to report problems in getting along with their families, particularly conflicts with their mothers. Whites were somewhat more likely than Blacks to describe their fathers as unhelpful with their problems and disinterested in their activities, while their mothers were described as strict and as giving them infrequent positive feedback, but these differences were not significant ($p < .10$). Users of alcohol also more frequently described their parents as strict and were significantly more likely than nonusers to report problems in getting along with their mothers. Users of marijuana and "other drugs" also were significantly more likely than nonusers to report conflicts with their mothers and to complain that their mothers rarely praised them. There were no significant ethnic differences in these findings.

Marijuana use was the only one of the four categories of illicit substance use that was significantly related to family structure, that is, marijuana users were less likely to live with both natural parents than users of the other substances. Marijuana and cigarette smokers were also significantly more likely to have moved away from friends than other users and nonusers of illicit substances.

Both black and white drinkers were significantly more likely to have fewer friends and less frequent social activities than the nondrinkers; by contrast, the marijuana users were significantly more likely than nonusers to report more frequent social activities and to have a wider circle of friends.

*Perceptions of Health*

Girls who smoked cigarettes and drank alcoholic beverages were significantly more likely than nonsmokers or nondrinkers to perceive their physical health as "fair" or "poor" rather than "good." In accordance with their more negative perception of their current health status, users of all four categories of illicit substances were somewhat more likely than nonusers to complain of frequent menstrual cramps and a variety of somatic symptoms, including headaches, stomachaches, sleep problems, and fatigue, but these differences were not significant ($p < .10$).

Finally, girls who were frequent users of multiple drugs were significantly more likely to have negative perceptions of their current health status than those who used fewer drugs or no drugs. Although black girls were significantly more likely than white girls to be sexually active, ethnicity did not interact significantly with sexual activity as a correlate of substance abuse.

## Discussion

In this sample of urban early adolescent females, the majority do not smoke cigarettes or use any drugs. However, with the exception of lower reported rates of using alcoholic beverages, the incidence of illicit substance use in this sample of urban junior high school females is still somewhat higher than the average usage rates for the twelve-to-fifteen age range reported in other surveys of early adolescent substance use. The facts that one-third have ever smoked cigarettes, about one-fourth have ever used alcohol (primarily beer and wine) or marijuana, and even fewer have used other drugs, support the model of initiation to substance use proposed by Kandel and Logan (1984).

The high rate of cigarette smoking in this sample (33.8%) mirrors the trend among adolescent females in the rest of the nation. Whereas smoking cigarettes has declined in nearly every age and sex subgroup in the population, it has increased among teenage girls. A higher proportion of this sample reports cigarette smoking as compared to drinking alcoholic beverages and using marijuana. This pattern also may reflect a national trend in the leveling off of marijuana use and the increasing attraction of alcohol consumption among teenagers.

The relationship between drug use and participants' negative perception of their health and reports of multiple somatic symptoms is consistent with results of other studies cited previously. While the direction of the relationship is unclear, that is, whether drug use precedes or follows somatic symptoms and negative perceptions of health, this information could be a useful clue in the assessment of those adolescent females who are judged to be at high risk for progressing from initial experimentation to heavier substance use.

The psychological and psychosocial correlates of substance use in this sample suggest that there are different patterns associated with each drug. Cigarette smoking alone was significantly more likely than use of alcohol or marijuana to be associated with a greater number of reported problems. Given that cigarette smoking usually precedes experimentation with other drugs, its initiation in early adolescence may be associated with rebelliousness and may be a predictor of girls who are more problem-prone.

Use of marijuana alone was significantly associated with living in a nonintact family, greater frequency of social activities, and lower scores on the Impulse Control Scale of the OSIQ; this suggests that family breakdown, excessive socializing with peers, and impulsivity might predispose an early adolescent to experiment with marijuana. Marijuana use for this group may be a way of facilitating social acceptance and forming alternative peer networks to create a sense of social support (Barnes, Farrell, and Banerjee 1994).

The combination of cigarette smoking and use of marijuana was significantly related to lower scores on the Family Relations and the Vocational-Educational Goals Scales of the OSIQ, as well as to moving away from friends. Thus, issues of family conflict, lower aspirations, and loss of meaningful attachments may be precursors of substance use in early adolescence.

Use of cigarettes, alcohol, marijuana, and other drugs was significantly associated with the highest number of psychological and behavioral factors, including truancy, breaking school rules, suspensions and expulsions, shoplifting, problems in getting along with mothers, more liberal sexual attitudes, and more negative perceptions of their current health status. Conflictual relations with fathers were significantly associated with use of all illicit substances except alcohol. Multiple drug use in early adolescent girls may be a maladaptive attempt to reduce anxiety and cope with chronic stress or feelings of inadequacy caused by family, personal, school, or social problems.

Despite differences in their incidence rates and patterns of substance use, characteristics associated with regular or frequent drug use were similar for both black and white girls. For example, black and white girls who were sexually active were significantly more likely to smoke cigarettes and to use alcohol than their non–sexually active peers. However, there were some trends ($p < .10$) in interaction effects that are suggestive of differences in demographic and behavioral antecedents to drug use in black and white girls. For example, black girls in integrated schools were *less* likely than white girls in the same schools to use alcohol and "other drugs." Black girls who were involved in extracurricular activities were *less* likely than similarly involved white girls to use alcohol and marijuana. Yet, black girls who had moved away from friends were *more* likely to use marijuana and cigarettes than were Whites in similar situations. White girls who were sexually active, involved in minor delinquency, and who had highly conflictual relations with their mothers were somewhat more likely to use alcohol and other drugs than Blacks who reported similar situations ($p < .10$).

Despite the public perception of drugs as primarily a problem of minority and low-income girls, the results of this study show that overall rates of drug use for in-school girls are higher for white and middle-income girls than for black and lower-income girls. These findings of ethnic and socioeconomic differences in substance use are also in agreement with those studies that have reported differential patterns of use in different ethnic groups (Wallace and Bachman 1991). In this sample, white and higher-income girls reported more frequent use of a wider variety of all substances, except marijuana, than black and lower-income girls. Such findings suggest that income is a factor in determining usage patterns, particularly in the purchase of the more expensive drugs and alcoholic beverages. Further, membership in an affluent peer group may provide girls with more funds to pool for greater access to the more expensive drugs (Farrow and Schwartz 1992).

White girls were more than twice as likely to use "other drugs" as black girls. Although these multiple drug users constituted only about one of nine girls in this sample, they tended to be the most troubled. They were significantly more likely to be older, to report conflictual relations with both parents, to have a history of truancy, and to report incidents of shoplifting minor items.

Although the conventional stereotype portrays urban adolescent girls as more vulnerable than nonurban girls to substance use, the findings of this study suggest that there are a number of moderating factors that must be evaluated in predicting adolescent substance use. In addition to ethnicity and socioeconomic status, these factors include family structure, family conflict, school problems, negative perceptions of health status, delinquent activities, sexual activity, and moving away from friends (Peterson et al. 1994).

Risk factors for substance use in this sample are consistent with the "problem profile" of adolescent substance users in previous studies, results that suggest that urban residence per se is not a major risk factor for adolescent females, but rather the behavioral, psychosocial, and family characteristics of the females themselves. In fact, several studies of adolescent substance use have found that rural adolescents actually may have equal or higher rates of use, perhaps exacerbated by social isolation and the lack of recreational activities, family and youth services, and drug prevention and treatment programs in these areas (Gleaton and Smith 1981; Segal 1989; Skager 1986).

Conversely, some factors appear to be protective and to militate against the use of illicit substances in early adolescence. These factors include non-drug-using peer group networks, less frequent involvement in social activities, more conservative sexual attitudes, and higher career aspirations.

To summarize: The majority of urban early adolescent females in this sample were not involved in substance abuse, but white and higher-income girls were significantly more likely to have used both alcohol and other drugs than blacks and lower-income girls. Furthermore, Blacks and Latinas may currently be at higher risk than white girls to initiate cigarette smoking. The recent intensified efforts of major tobacco companies to target this population by advertising heavily in minority communities and sponsoring recreational activities in these areas may contribute to this trend. Compared to white girls, black and Latina girls tend to have poorer nutritional habits, less knowledge about preventive health care, and less access to health care; thus, the industry campaigns to increase cigarette sales among minority adolescents have very serious implications for the long-term health of these girls (Falkner 1993; Lieu, Newacheck, and McManus 1993).

## Implications for Prevention and Early Intervention Programs

Since 1980, reviews of programs to educate teenagers about cigarette smoking and the use of alcohol, marijuana, and hard drugs—those programs that have the aim of preventing or substantially reducing their use—have concluded that the efforts have generally failed, primarily for three reasons: their target groups were not well defined, their goals were not clearly articulated, and their strategies were not appropriate to the developmental needs and attitudes of adolescents (Barnes 1984; Goldstein and DiNitto 1982; Evans and Raines 1982). However, intervention research, particularly focusing on prevention, is expanding (Howard, Boyd, and Zucker 1994).

The findings of this study support the recommendations of several of these investigators concerning important features that should be incorporated into an effective substance abuse prevention or early intervention program, such as the following:

1. Drug-use prevention programs should begin in elementary school, since initial experimentation with cigarettes and drugs begins in fifth or sixth grade, well before entry to junior high school.

2. Programs should be aimed at single-drug use in early grades (six through eight) because there are different factors associated with each drug, but in later grades (nine through twelve) the programs should be aimed at poly-drug users, since that is the more typical pattern and would be more cost effective. In this sample white girls were more likely to be poly-drug users than black girls, so it is essential to identify those girls who are most at risk for poly-drug use in early adolescence.

3. Programs should be targeted to specific subgroups of drug users with different usage patterns, for example, females, Blacks, Hispanics, and rural groups. Prevention and early-intervention programs for young black females might increase their success rates by focusing on improving their school environments, increasing their involvement in extracurricular activities, and strengthening their family resources (cf. Wallace and Bachman 1991).

4. Programs should pay attention to the social context of drug use, involving parents, teachers, school counselors, community leaders, adult role models, and peers in educational and counseling activities. Parent involvement is particularly important for young black females in order to decrease the influence of drug-using peers and to improve parent–daughter communication patterns.

5. Programs should also focus on cultural attitudes about drugs and the function they serve for early adolescents, particularly in low-income minority schools and communities, with the goal of providing alternative recreational and social activities to promote positive health behaviors among these youths.

## Implications for Research

Findings from this study indicate the need for more complex research designs to investigate the ethnic and socioeconomic differences in rates, patterns, and correlates of early adolescent female illicit substance use. While incidence rates and patterns of usage provide an overall picture of substance use in this population group, it is particularly important to determine differential antecedents and correlates of substance use in order to target prevention and intervention programs more effectively.

Since the majority of black and white adolescent females grow up in different sociocultural environments, attend different kinds of schools, and have access to different types of community recreational facilities and social service programs, it is reasonable to hypothesize that the demographic, psychosocial, and behavioral antecedents and correlates of substance use in these two ethnic groups also might be different.

Although significant ethnic differences in antecedents or correlates of substance use were not found in this study, there are trends in the data that indicate that black girls might be more vulnerable to certain patterns of illicit substance use because of socioenvironmental factors (schools, activities, residential mobility), while white girls might be more vulnerable to other patterns of substance use because of psychosocial factors (sexual activity, maternal conflict, minor delinquency). Dembo and his colleagues (1990) have found such ethnic differences in antecedents of delinquency and drug use among a group of high-risk youth in a regional detention center in Florida.

With more representative samples and finely tuned research instruments, future studies should be able to tease out the relationships of ethnicity, demographic, psychosocial, and behavioral factors to patterns of illicit substance abuse in early adolescent females. A commitment to research on girls' health that not only includes them as participants but also investigates the correlates of their health problems would be a positive first step.

REFERENCES

Barnes, G. 1984. Evaluation of alcohol education—A reassessment using socialization theory. *Journal of Drug Education* 14:133–50.

Barnes, G. M., M. P. Farrell, and S. Banerjee. 1994. Family influences on alcohol abuse and other problem behaviors among black and white adolescents in a general population sample. *Journal of Research on Adolescence* 4 (2):183–201.

Barnes, G. M., and J. W. Welte. 1986. Patterns and predictors of alcohol use among 7–12th grade students in New York state. *Journal of Studies in Alcohol* 47:53–61.

Barrera, M., S. A. Li, and L. Chassin. 1993. Ethnic group differences in vulnerability to parental alcoholism and life stress: A study of Hispanic and non-Hispanic Caucasian adolescents. *American Journal of Community Psychology* 21:15–35.

Beck, A., and A. Beamesderfer. 1974. Assessment of depression: The Depression Inventory. *Psychological Measurements in Psychopharmacology* 7:151–69.

Beschner, G., and A. Friedman, eds. 1986. *Teen drug use*. Lexington, Mass.: Lexington Books.

Bloom, M., and M. Greenwald. 1984. Alcohol and cigarette use among early adolescents. *Journal of Drug Education* 14:195–205.

Brunswick, A. F., C. Merzel, and P. Messeri. 1985. Drug use initiation among urban black youth: A seven-year follow-up of developmental and secular influences. *Youth and Society* 17:189–216.

Carlisi, J. 1984. *Drug abuse among white ethnic adolescents*. Washington, D.C.: National Center for Urban Ethnic Affairs.

Coates, T., A. Petersen, and C. Perry, eds. 1982. *Promoting adolescent health*. New York: Academic Press.

Coombs, R. H., F. Fawzy, and G. Gerber. 1986. Patterns of cigarette, alcohol, and other drug use among children and adolescents: A longitudinal study. *International Journal of the Addictions* 21:897–913.

Dembo, R., L. Williams, E. Berry, A. Getreu, M. Washburn, E. Wish, and J. Schmeidler. 1990. Examination of the relationships among drug use, emotional problems, and crime among youths entering a juvenile detention center. *International Journal of the Addictions* 25:1301–40.

Dryfoos, J. G. 1990. *Adolescents at risk: Prevalence and prevention*. New York: Oxford University Press.

Evans, R., and B. Raines. 1982. Control and prevention of smoking in adolescents: A psychosocial perspective. In *Promoting adolescent health*, edited by T. Coates, A. Petersen, and C. Perry. New York: Academic Press.

Falkner, F. 1993. Obesity and cardiovascular disease risk factors in prepubescent and pubescent black and white females. *Critical Reviews in Food Science and Nutrition* 33:397–402.

Farrow, J. A., and R. H. Schwartz. 1992. Adolescent drug and alcohol usage: A comparison of urban and suburban pediatric practices. *Journal of the National Medical Association* 84:409–13.

Gersick, K., K. Grady, E. Sexton, and S. M. Lyons. 1981. Personality and sociodemographic factors in adolescent drug use. In *Drug abuse in the American adolescent*, edited by D. J. Lettieri and J. P. Ludford, 39–56. National Institute of Drug Abuse, U.S. Department of Health and Human Services. N.I.D.A. Research Monograph no. 38. Rockville, Md.: U.S. Government Printing Office.

Gibbs, J. T. 1982. Psychosocial factors related to substance abuse among delinquent females: Implications for prevention and treatment. *American Journal of Orthopsychiatry* 52:261–71.

Gleaton, T., and S. Smith. 1981. Drug use by urban and rural adolescents. *Journal of Drug Education* 11:1–8.

Goldstein, H., and D. DiNitto. 1982. Some methodological problems, solutions, and findings from evaluating risk reduction projects. *Journal of Drug Education* 12:241–53.

Harford, T. C. 1986. Drinking patterns among black and non-black adolescents: Results of a national survey. *Annals of the New York Academy of Sciences* 472:130–41.

Howard, J., G. M. Boyd, and R. A. Zucker. 1994. Overview of issues. *Journal of Research on Adolescence* 4 (2):175–81.

Jessor, R., and S. Jessor. 1977. *Problem behavior and psychological development: A longitudinal study of youth*. San Diego: Academic Press.

Johnston, L., J. Bachman, and P. O'Malley. 1986. *Monitoring the future, 1985*. Ann Arbor: Institute for Social Research, University of Michigan.

Johnston, L., P. O'Malley, and J. Bachman. 1994. *National survey results on drug use from the monitoring the future study, 1975–1993*. Ann Arbor: Institute for Social Research, University of Michigan.

Kandel, D. B. 1982. Epidemiological and psychosocial perspectives on adolescent drug use. *Journal of American Academy of Child Psychiatry* 21:328–47.

Kandel, D. B., and J. Logan. 1984. Patterns of drug use from adolescence to young adulthood: 1. Periods of risk for initiation, continued use, and discontinuation. *American Journal of Public Health* 74:660–67.

Lieu, T. A., P. W. Newacheck, and M. A. McManus. 1993. Race, ethnicity, and access to ambulatory care among U.S. adolescents. *American Journal of Public Health* 83:960–65.

Millstein, S., C. Irwin, N. Adler, L. Cohn, S. Kegeles, and M. Dolcini. 1992. Health-risk behaviors and health concerns among young adolescents. *Pediatrics* 89:422–28.

Mooney, L., and L. Gordon. 1950. *Manual for the Mooney problem check-lists*. New York: Psychological Corporation.

Mott, F. L., and R. J. Haurin. 1988. Linkages between sexual activity and alcohol and drug use among American adolescents. *Family Planning Perspectives* 20:128–36.

National Institute of Drug Abuse. 1986. *Etiology of drug abuse: Implications for prevention.* D.H.H.S. Pub. no. (ADM) 86-1335. Washington, D.C.: U.S. Government Printing Office.

————. 1988. *National household survey on drug abuse: Main findings, 1985.* D.H.H.S. Pub. no. (ADM) 88-1586. Rockville, Md.: U.S. Government Printing Office.

Newcomb, M., and P. Bentler. 1988. *Consequences of adolescent drug use: Impact on the lives of young adults.* Newbury Park, Calif.: Sage Publications.

Newcomb, M., E. Maddahian, E. Skager, and P. Bentler. 1987. Substance abuse and psychosocial risk factors among teenagers: Associations with sex, age, ethnicity, and type of school. *American Journal of Drug and Alcohol Abuse* 13:413–33.

New York State Division of Substance Abuse Services. 1984. *Substance abuse among New York State Public and Private School students in grades 7 through 12, 1983.* Albany, N.Y.: Division of Substance Abuse Services.

Oetting, E. R., and F. Beauvais. 1990. Adolescent drug use: Findings of national and local surveys. *Journal of Consulting and Clinical Psychology* 58:385–94.

Offer, D., E. Ostrov, and K. Howard. 1981. *The Offer self-image questionnaire for adolescents: A manual.* Rev. ed. Chicago: Michael Reese Hospital.

Oyemade, U., and V. Washington. 1990. The role of family factors in the primary prevention of substance abuse among high-risk black youth. In *Ethnic issues in adolescent mental health,* edited by A. R. Stiffman and L. E. Davis, 267–84. Newbury Park, Calif.: Sage Publications.

Pascale, P. J., F. E. Trucksis, and J. Sylvester. 1985. Regional trends and sex differences in drug use and attitudes of high school students in Northeast Ohio 1977–1983. *Journal of Drug Education* 15:241–51.

Peterson, P. J., J. D. Hawkins, R. D. Abbott, and R. F. Catalano. 1994. Disentangling the effects of parental drinking, family management, and parental alcohol norms on current drinking by black and white adolescents. *Journal of Research on Adolescence* 4 (2):203–27.

Rachal, J. V., L. L. Guess, R. L. Hubbard, S. A. Maisto, E. R. Cavanaugh, R. Waddell, R., and C. D. Benrud. 1980. *Adolescent drinking behavior.* Vol. 1, *The extent and nature of adolescent alcohol and drug use.* Research Triangle Park, N.C.: Research Triangle Institute.

Riggs, S., and T. Cheng. 1988. Adolescents' willingness to use a school-based clinic in view of health concerns. *Journal of Adolescent Health Care* 9:208–13.

Segal, B. 1989. Drug-taking behavior among school-aged youth: The Alaska experience and comparisons with lower 48 states. *Drugs and Society* 4:1–174.

Skager, R. 1986. *A statewide survey of drug and alcohol use among California students in grades 7, 9, and 11.* Sacramento, Calif.: Office of the Attorney General.

Thomas, S. M., A. O. Fick, J. Henderson, and K. Doherty. 1990. Tobacco, alcohol, and marijuana use among black adolescents: A comparison across gender, grade, and school environment. *Journal of the Louisiana State Medical Society* 142:37–42.

Torabi, M. R., W. J. Bailey, and M. Majd-Jabbari. 1993. Cigarette smoking as a predictor of alcohol and other drug use by children and adolescents: Evidence of the "gateway drug effect." *Journal of School Health* 63:302–6.

Vega, W., R. Zimmerman, G. Warheit, E. Apospori, and A. Gil. 1993. Risk factors for early adolescent drug use in four ethnic and racial groups. *American Journal of Public Health* 83:185–89.

Velez, C. N., and J. A. Ungemack. 1989. Drug use among Puerto Rican youth: An exploration of generational status differences. *Social Science and Medicine* 29:779–89.

Wallace, J. G., and J. M. Bachman. 1991. Explaining racial/ethnic differences in adolescent drug use: The impact of background and lifestyle. *Social Problems* 38:333–57.

Way, N., H. Y. Stauber, M. J. Nakkula, and P. London. 1994. Depression and substance use in two divergent high school cultures: A quantitative and qualitative analysis. *Journal of Youth and Adolescence* 23:331–57.

Windle, M. 1990. A longitudinal study of antisocial behaviors in early adolescence as predictors of late adolescent substance use: Gender and ethnic group differences. *Journal of Abnormal Psychology* 99:86–91.

Zastowny, T., E. Adams, G. Black, K. Lawton, and A. Wilder. 1993. Sociodemographic and attitudinal correlates of alcohol and other drug use among children and adolescents: Analysis of a large scale attitude tracking study. *Journal of Psychoactive Drugs* 25:223–37.

# 18

# Symptom Expression in Inner-City Latinas: Psychopathology or Help Seeking?

## Carlos Salguero and Wendy R. McCusker

Anita, a twelve-year-old Latina, was described as very disrespectful by her mother, who brought her to the clinic. Anita would not listen to her. She would not help with family chores, and the family had to scream at her to make her obey. The mother's husband wanted Anita to assume a lot of responsibilities because her mother was very sick. In addition, Anita had no friends outside of her home. In the initial interview Anita disclosed that she had recently learned that her father was really a stepfather, and she was very upset about this. It was the stepfather who was screaming at her and her younger siblings, and she was rebelling against him and protecting her siblings. The family had moved to the U.S. mainland from Puerto Rico seven months before coming to the clinic. The mother had AIDS and the stepfather was HIV positive. Her two step-siblings, aged one and two and a half years old, were also HIV positive. Anita told the therapist that she felt very sad about her mother's and her siblings' illness. She had constant nightmares in which her mother was dying and would return to take Anita with her. She felt tired and nervous or anxious during the day and could not stand listening to her stepfather screaming at her. The therapist met with the stepfather, who admitted his own confusion and sadness while he watched his wife die. The therapist believed that Anita wanted to express her angry feelings through oppositional behavior rather than directly confronting the mother, as she knew this was not acceptable. The therapist recommended individual and family therapy, but the family did not return in spite of several attempts to reach them.

In this chapter we report the findings from our study of the clinical symptoms of a sample of Latina adolescent girls. Few researchers or clinicians have discussed the symptomatology of Latino children. A notable exception is I. A. Canino and colleagues (1986), who reviewed the symptoms and diagnoses in Latino and black children aged five to sixteen years from an outpatient mental health clinic in New York City. The Latino children reported experiencing more psychosocial stressors in their lives than their black peers. Of the twenty-two clinical variables examined by I. A. Canino and colleagues, morbid depression and unhappiness, fears and phobias, anxiety and panic, school refusal, and disturbed relationships with other children were significantly higher in the Latino than in the black children. The authors inferred that these differences could, in part, be explained by cultural factors.

Latinas come from a collectivist background (Hofstede 1980), in which family unity and allegiance is the norm (Triandis 1988, 1990, 1994). Consequently, living in an indivualistic culture such as that in the mainland United States commonly creates acute tensions between opposing value systems (Berry 1990; Ulaszek and Triandis 1994). Lowered mental health status (especially confusion, anxiety, and depression), feelings of marginality and alienation, heightened psychosomatic symptoms, and identity confusion may be experienced by acculturating individuals (Berry 1974). First generation parents typically have a more difficult time than their children in adjusting to the foreign culture (Berry 1989); this situation may lead to miscommunication and additional tension between generations. For example, the parents may wish for respect involving control over their children's dating activities, whereas the children may feel that these values impose on their autonomy and individual privacy.

Along with cultural and generational clashes, Latina adolescents also have to deal with the common struggles associated with adolescence. Adolescence can be a tumultuous period, with hormonal, psychological, and external factors playing significant roles in shaping the adolescent's inner psyche as well as her or his ability to cope with future life events. Family support and nurturing are known contributors to positive outcomes for adolescents. On the other hand, urban poverty and weakened familial support have been found to be associated with higher symptomatology (G. J. Canino et al. 1987; McLoyd 1990; McLoyd and Jozefowicz, chap. 20 of this volume).

We argue that to fully understand the Latina adolescents in our sample, one must place their symptoms not only within the context of Latino culture, but also within the context of urban poverty. The internal conflict and psychosocial stressors experienced by young Latinas living in inner-city poverty often challenge their coping abilities. They have to deal with multiple, often adverse circumstances, yet they have to continue to function in their roles as students, children, and, at times, surrogate parents to their siblings. In light of these contextual factors, we believe that the symptoms expressed by the Latina girls in our sample display a unique type of resilience that questions the implied pathology of their symptoms. Their resilience is demonstrated by their ability to seek help and by their belief that something can be done to alleviate their suffering.

## The Study

The sample was comprised of forty-one adolescent Latina girls ages fourteen to eighteen, seen for an initial screening evaluation at a child and family guidance clinic from 1993 to 1994. The clinic, located in a low income neighborhood of New Haven, Connecticut, provides comprehensive physical and mental health services to a mostly indigent ethnic minority population. In order to assess the girls' symptomatology, we examined their initial screening charts, which contained demographic data and standardized information on symptomatology, family makeup, basic school background, and past and current occurrence of physical, sexual, and drug abuse.

Fourteen girls (34%) out of the 41 were twelve to fourteen years old; 13 (32%) were fifteen years old, and 14 (34%) were sixteen to eighteen years old. Many of the girls were Puerto Rican and had experienced multiple moves between Puerto Rico and the mainland United States. Four of the adolescents had been living in the United States for less than six months. Ten of the 41 youths (24%) spoke Spanish only, 21 (51%) spoke both Spanish and English, and 10 (24%) spoke English only. All of the girls were attending school, and six girls were in a special education program. The mothers of 28 of the youths (68.3%) were living in the same household as their daughters, and the fathers of 12 of the youths (29%) were present in the household. Legal guardians tended to be mothers (51%). In other cases the guardians were both parents (24%), aunts (14.6%), fathers (2.4%), or grandmothers (2.4%). A main reason for an adolescent not to be living with her mother was the mother's involvement with drugs and the subsequent neglect of the adolescent, resulting in the removal of the child from her mother's home. The majority of the adolescents were brought to the clinic by their mothers (49%) or by other family members (17%). Conflict at home played a significant role in the decision of the mothers or relatives to bring the adolescent girls to the clinic.

TABLE 18.1
*Percentages of Latina Adolescents Exhibiting Different Types of Clinical Symptoms*

| Symptoms | Total sample (N = 41) | Language ability | | |
|---|---|---|---|---|
| | | Spanish (N = 10) | Spanish and English (N = 21) | English (N = 10) |
| Depression | 49 | 70 | 52 | 20 |
| Anxiety | 44 | 50 | 38 | 50 |
| Eating disturbances | 15 | 30 | 9 | 10 |
| Suicide ideation/attempt | 49 | 70 | 48 | 30 |
| Sleep disturbances[a] | 20 | 40 | 19 | 0 |
| Aggression | 24 | 30 | 33 | 0 |
| Oppositional behaviors | 44 | 70 | 38 | 30 |
| Physical abuse | 15 | 0 | 19 | 20 |
| Sexual abuse | 29 | 0 | 38 | 40 |
| Neglect | 17 | 10 | 19 | 20 |
| Encopresis | 2 | 10 | 0 | 0 |
| Enuresis | 2 | 0 | 5 | 0 |

[a]missing data for 3 of the girls.

## Results

Table 18.1 shows the percentages of the Latina adolescents who experienced different types of clinical symptoms. Symptoms that were reported by 40% or more of the sample included depression, anxiety, suicidal ideation or attempts, and oppositional behaviors (e.g., refusal to obey parental or teacher rules). Almost one-fourth of the girls also exhibited aggressive behaviors (i.e., physically hitting or assaulting parents, teachers or peers). One-third of the girls reported a history of sexual abuse, 15% reported a history of physical abuse, and 17% reported neglect. Somatic problems such as eating disturbances, encopresis, and enuresis were less frequent.

As seen in table 18.1, differences in symptom expression among the girls appeared to be related to level of acculturation, using language spoken as an indicator of level of acculturation (see also Allen et al., chap. 19 of this volume). The girls who spoke only Spanish or who spoke both Spanish and English were more likely than their peers who spoke English only to exhibit depression, suicidal ideation or attempts, and oppositional and aggressive behaviors. The English-speaking girls were as likely as the Spanish-speaking girls to exhibit anxiety, but they were more likely to report sexual abuse. The less acculturated girls (Spanish-speaking only) were more likely to experience multiple symptoms than were the more acculturated girls (English-speaking only) (see table 18.2). Depression co-occurred with oppositional behaviors or aggression, or both, for eight (20%) of the girls in the sample, of whom four spoke Spanish and the other four were bilingual.

As seen in table 18.3, serious family problems were reported in many

TABLE 18.2
*Frequencies of Girls Reporting 1, 2, 3, or 4 or More Symptoms*

| | | Language ability | | |
|---|---|---|---|---|
| Number of symptoms | Total sample (N = 41) | Spanish (N = 10) | Spanish and English (N = 21) | English (N = 10) |
| 1 | 8 (20%) | 1 (10%) | 4 (19%) | 3 (30%) |
| 2 | 10 (24%) | 1 (10%) | 5 (24%) | 4 (40%) |
| 3 | 11 (27%) | 5 (50%) | 4 (19%) | 2 (20%) |
| 4 or more | 12 (29%) | 3 (30%) | 8 (38%) | 1 (10%) |

of the interviews, including drug abuse by a family member (44%), domestic violence (20%), family illness or death due to AIDS (17%), and homicide attempted or completed by a family member (12%). Fewer families (10%) who spoke only Spanish reported family problems than those who were bilingual or spoke English only, perhaps reflecting a cultural norm deterring the discussion of family business with strangers.

## Discussion

The Latinas of this sample lived with parents who, for the most part, were first-generation immigrants to the mainland United States. These parents upheld the traditions and values of their culture. Spanish, for example, was spoken in the majority of the youths' homes. In Puerto Rico, an intact nuclear family has a father who commonly plays the role of breadwinner and decision maker, albeit detached from daily family transactions. The mother's primary role is to carry out the daily child-rearing tasks and other duties, such as counseling her children, looking out for their well-being, and serving as a role model. Respect for authority is a very important cultural value. Children are often discouraged from looking their fathers or mothers in the eye or challenging their parents' authority when reprimanded. In Puerto Rico, the extended fam-

TABLE 18.3
*Percentages of Latina Adolescents with Reported Family Context Variables*

| | | Language ability | | |
|---|---|---|---|---|
| Variables | Total sample (N = 41) | Spanish (N = 10) | Spanish and English (N = 21) | English (N = 10) |
| Drug abuse by family member | 44 | 20 | 48 | 60 |
| Domestic violence | 20 | 20 | 19 | 20 |
| AIDS in family | 17 | 10 | 14 | 30 |
| Homicide attempted/completed by family member | 12 | 10 | 19 | 0 |
| Family problems reported | 88 | 10 | 86 | 80 |
| School problems reported | 56 | 60 | 57 | 50 |
| Peer problems reported | 32 | 20 | 38 | 30 |

ily participates in the family support network, acting as buffers for stress-producing changes.

From a developmental perspective, the difficulties of adolescence may be magnified for Latinos living in the United States when traditional family structures break down, leaving family members no longer able to rely on relatives to deal with conflicts. Although occurring less frequently in the mainland United States than in Puerto Rico, Latino aunts, uncles, and grandparents may attempt to act as advocates or as primary care givers when an adolescent needs assistance.

Contact with an Anglo society in which there is an emphasis on individuality and a strong pull to relate to a peer group increases the likelihood of a conflict between Latina adolescents and their parents. Latina girls frequently live in two communities: one at home with family and its demands for obedience and respect, and the other in the Anglo world, which encourages separation and individuation. Furthermore, many Puerto Rican mothers view with a great deal of trepidation the burgeoning sexuality of their young adolescent daughters (Salguero 1985). In contrast to dating practices of adolescents in the United States, dating in Latino families follows established rituals according to which the boyfriend must visit the Latina's parents to communicate his good intentions. The demands by the Latinas to be allowed to date like their Anglo peers may be misinterpreted by the parents or other relatives as a lack of respect, as the following vignette illustrates.

Naomi was a thirteen-year-old brought to the clinic by her grandmother. She had been suspended from school for hitting a teacher, and she had apparently been similarly aggressive toward her peers. At home she physically fought with family members. Past history revealed a chaotic family life in Puerto Rico with her mother. In addition, Naomi had been involved with a married man. . . . On examination, Naomi expressed suicidal ideation. . . . One year later Naomi revealed that her mother did not want her to date an older Mexican adolescent because he was too old and came from a different country. A compromise was reached, under which she could see the boyfriend only at her home so that her family would know what kind of person he was.

Aggression and oppositional behavior were common symptoms exhibited by our sample. The high rate of aggressive and oppositional behavior—especially among those who were less acculturated—may reflect a desperate attempt by the Latina girls to communicate their distress to their families. If this is true, oppositional behavior and aggression have a healthier, more adaptive quality than the pathological connotation that their psychiatric diagnoses suggest.

Naomi's aggression, illustrated above, and Anita's disrespectful or oppositional behavior, seen in the opening vignette of this chapter, are perhaps adaptive reactions to very adverse circumstances. The Latina adolescents in our sample often witnessed family violence and drug use or experienced the loss of loved ones through homicide, AIDS, or abandonment. Family stress was so severe that it elicited symptomatic signals from the adolescents. Oppositionality and aggression may signify a cry for help or rebellion against a very troubled family situation.

Depression and sadness were also common symptoms exhibited by the adolescents. In trying to understand these symptoms, we must remember that a Latina adolescent's quest is not for total individuation but for interdependence with her family—to become an adult like her mother and to maintain the value system that the adolescent knew as a child. As a young girl, a Latina often feels it is important to live according to the idealized image of her mother. On the other hand, a mother also wishes for her daughter to grow up and marry someone who can take care of her and respect her, just as she had wished for herself.

Deviations from these traditional sets of expectations, as brought forth by stresses of poverty, family problems, and acculturation, frequently result in conflict for the adolescent. Unable to resolve this conflict in a satisfactory manner, the adolescent may find herself experiencing a variety of feelings—feelings of abandonment, anger, and hopelessness, as the following vignette illustrates.

Ada, a fifteen-year-old ninth grader from an intact family, was brought to the clinic after stealing from her mother, running away, and performing increasingly poorly in school. She claimed that her parents were too strict and that she wanted more freedom. Ada felt frustrated and angry. As therapy progressed, she became aware that she had always been very close to her mother and that her mother's decision to go back to college had changed the family routines. Ada's parents did not want her to be influenced by her friends. Her mother was afraid that Ada would get pregnant or raped as the mother later revealed had happened to herself. During the session Ada said she just could not communicate with her mother. She did not communicate with her father because he was an alcoholic. Ada expressed that she wished people could hear all that was going on inside her. She became depressed and expressed hopelessness and a desire to kill herself.

Depression, anxiety, and the presence of somatic symptoms are more acceptable symptoms in Latin culture than oppositional behavior, as they do not involve open confrontations or disrespectful acts with one's parents. The cultural acceptablity of symptoms such as depression may explain the high rate of such symptoms among the girls in this sample, particularly among the less acculturated adolescent Latinas. These symptoms may mobilize the mother or other family members to seek help from others. This often results in moving the mother-daughter relationship to a more egalitarian level, in which a mother may also reveal some of her own past disappointments.

The Latina adolescents in our sample exhibited their symptoms in a context of significant family conflict. They wanted to be understood and nurtured, and they commonly felt abandoned by their parents. A circumstance that may further exacerbate conflicts within the Latino family is created by the public assistance that many in our sample received. All but two of the mothers of the Latina adolescents in our sample were on AFDC (Aid to Families with Dependent Children), which is awarded to the heads of households. This shifts the financial support, traditionally provided by the father, to the mother and may alienate the father who is poorly prepared to hold a job and support the family. According to Abad, Ramos, and Boyce (1974), Latino men are highly sensitive to any situation that threatens their machismo image. One of the characteristics of machismo is that the man is the head of the house and the protector of the family. Any change in this cultural value may trigger "acting out." Many of the fathers in this sample appeared to act out by drinking, doing drugs, and in some cases, abusing their children or stepchildren. It appeared that the familial, cultural, and social mechanisms that typically played a role in preserving the family homeostasis had failed and that the adolescents had developed symptoms that, in some respects, were efforts on their part to express their pain.

As serious as the symptoms expressed by this group of adolescent girls may be, these symptoms also have a resilient quality. Coping and resilience should not only be viewed as the ability to do well under adverse circumstances, but also as the ability to avoid more catastrophic outcomes. In their willingness to seek help, these Latinas revealed an extraordinary degree of resilience. One facet of competence has to do with the child's capacity to make "meaningful sense" out of the chaotic, traumatic events that confront him or her (Anthony 1987). The Latinas in this sample, in the midst of their suffering, were trying to make meaningful sense of their own situations. As Inclán and Herron (1989) believe, parents may be trying to reassert their authority as a means to deal with their children's often problematic behavior. The purpose of therapy with Latina adolescents, therefore, should be to intervene in a way that helps adolescents understand the cultural origins of their parents' expectations and the reasons for their possible conflicts with mainstream Anglo values.

Conflicts concerning sexuality, identity, autonomy, and dependency, among other things, are expressed by Latinas within the contexts of family dynamics, acculturation, psychosocial conditions, and the stressors of poverty and an inner-city milieu. All of these factors help shape the symptoms presented by this sample of urban adolescents. Nevertheless, resilience is evident within this group of girls. Their resilience is suggested by their ability to ask for help for their struggles. Further longitudinal studies of larger samples of Latinas from diverse socioeconomic backgrounds are needed to further explore the themes we have suggested in this chapter.

## REFERENCES

Abad, V., J. Ramos, and E. Boyce. 1974. A model for delivery of mental health services to Spanish-speaking minorities. *American Journal of Orthopsychiatry* 44 (4):584–95.

American Psychiatric Association. 1984. *Diagnostic and statistical manual of mental disorders.* 3d ed., revised. Washington, D.C.: American Psychiatric Association.

Anthony, E. J. 1987. Risk, vulnerability, and resilience: An overview. In *The invulnerable child,* edited by E. J. Anthony and B. J. Cohler. New York: Guilford Press.

Berry, J. W. 1974. Ecology, cultural and psychological differentiation. *International Journal of Psychology* 9:173–93.

———. 1989. Psychology of acculturation. In *Nebraska symposium on motivation, 1989,* edited by J. Berman, 201–34. Lincoln: University of Nebraska Press.

———. 1990. Psychology of acculturation: Understanding individuals moving between cultures. In *Applied cross-cultural psychology,* edited by R. W. Brislin, 232–53. Newbury Park, Calif.: Sage Publications.

Canino, G. J., M. Rubio-Stipec, P. Shrout, M. Bravo, R. Stolber, and H. R. Bird. 1987. Sex differences and depression in Puerto Rico. *Psychology of Women Quarterly* 11:443–59.

Canino, I. A., M. Gould, S. Prupis, and D. Shaffer. 1986. A comparison of symptoms and diagnoses in Hispanic and black children in an outpatient mental health clinic. *Journal of the American Academy of Child Psychiatry* 25 (2):254–59.

Hofstede, G. 1980. *Culture's consequences.* Beverly Hills, Calif.: Sage Publications.

Inclán, J. E., and D. G. Herron. 1989. Puerto Rican adolescents. In *Children of color: Psychological interventions with minority youth,* edited by J. T. Gibbs and L. N. Huang, 251–77. San Francisco: Jossey-Bass.

McLoyd, V. C. 1990. The impact of economic hardship on black families and children: Psychological distress, parenting, and socioemotional development. *Child Development* 61:311–46.

Salguero, C. 1985. The role of ethnic factors in adolescent pregnancy and motherhood. In *Adolescent Parenthood,* edited by N. Sugar. New York: New York Spectrum.

Triandis, H. C. 1988. Collectivism vs. individualism: A reconceptualization of a basic concept of cross-cultural psychology. In *Cross-cultural studies of personality, attitudes, and cognition,* edited by G. K. Verma and C. Bagley, 60–95. London: Macmillan.

———. 1990. Cross-cultural studies of individualism and collectivism. In *Nebraska symposium on motivation, 1989,* edited by J. Berman, 41–133. Lincoln: University of Nebraska Press.

———. 1994. *Culture and social behavior.* New York: McGraw-Hill.

Ulaszek, W. R., and H. C. Triandis. 1994. *Cultural differences in the perception of stress.* Paper presented at the meeting of the Midwestern Psychological Association, May, Chicago.

# 19 Acculturation and Depression among Latina Urban Girls

LaRue Allen, Jill Denner, Hirokazu
Yoshikawa, Edward Seidman,
and J. Lawrence Aber

Depression and other affective disorders are the most commonly diagnosed mental health problems leading to hospitalization among American adolescents. In 1986 these disorders made up approximately 31% of admissions among those adolescents who were ten to fourteen years old and 34% among those who were fourteen to seventeen. Treatment of depression accounted for a significant portion of the roughly $3.5 billion spent in 1986 on treating adolescent mental health problems (a figure that does not include indirect costs, such as losses of productivity). Although specific estimates of the social and economic costs of depression are not available, it is clear that they are considerable (U.S. Congress 1991).

Women predominate among adults with depressed mood or diagnosed depression; the female-male ratio across studies averages 2:1 (McGrath, Keita, Strickland, and Russo 1990). Prior to adolescence, depression affects boys more frequently than girls (Kashani and Schmid 1992). In adolescence, though, the trajectory toward the almost epidemic rates of adult female depression begins to accelerate, peaking for girls at higher rates than for boys (Nolen-Hoeksema and Girgus 1994). Little is known about the continuity of this symptom or syndrome across the adolescent years. Even less is known about how rates of depression may differ across adolescent racial or ethnic groups.

The shift in the gender balance has been attributed to factors such as changes associated with puberty or sex role socialization (Petersen et al. 1993). However, the current lack of clarity regarding how these factors are related to depression suggests that more studies that focus on the specific precursors or correlates of depression among adolescent girls are needed.

Poverty is an established risk factor for depression among women. A recent study using a national probability sample found that the relative risk of depression in the lowest socioeconomic status (SES) group was 1.79 times that in the highest SES group (Holzer et al. 1986). A variety of poverty-related conditions with particularly strong impact for women—gender gaps in income and employment opportunities, increases in single-parent families, lack of adequate child support, child care and family support policies—can bring about the increases in stress and decreases in social support that are associated with the onset of depressive symptoms (Belle 1982) as well as other mental health problems (Holzer et al. 1986). Despite the clear risk that poverty represents for female depression, there is virtually no information available on correlates of depression among poor adolescent girls, let alone for racial or ethnic minority girls, who are more than twice as likely to live in poverty as their white counterparts (Children's Defense Fund 1993).

This chapter presents an investigation of correlates of depressive symptoms among a sample of poor urban Latina girls in early adolescence. Two broad inquiries guide our research. First, we examine the relationship between level of acculturation to mainstream culture (or, said another way, attachment to one's culture of origin) and depression. Our second research question concerns the degree to which traditionally found correlates of depressive symptoms are related to the prevalence of depressive symptoms in this understudied group.

Before presenting our model, we discuss the relationship between cultural factors and depressive symptoms. Following that we present a brief review of theories regarding the relationship between acculturation and mental health. We then review literature relevant to our second question, regarding the degree to which correlates of depressive symptoms that are found in primarily white groups also exist among our understudied groups. The findings of these reviews are then combined in our model of person-centered and contextual correlates of depressive symptoms in Latina adolescent females.

## Racial or Ethnic Background and Depression

Among members of racial or ethnic minority groups, depressive symptoms may be related to (1) the socioeconomic factors that interact with ethnic group membership to affect the kinds of stress experienced, as well as (2) the coping resources available for dealing with stress. Culturally relevant stressors include racism and the experience of conflicting value orientations between minority family traditions and those of the larger society. Exposure to racist attitudes and symbols can contribute to a child's alienation from society, both directly and indirectly, through the limitations it can place on a parent's resources and opportunities (Spurlock 1973).

A feeling of cultural marginality can result from these differences in social values between one's group and the mainstream; that feeling, in turn, may lead to anxiety that is expressed in either withdrawal or acting-out behaviors. Intergenerational conflict, for example, is a developmentally specific source of conflict in which more integrated ethnic-group adolescents may experience an increase in conflict with their traditional families. For both girls and boys, adolescent relationships outside the family may lead to a questioning of parental authority, particularly for children whose parents hold traditional values (Meswick 1992).

Young females may feel the impact of family-level conflict more than young males (see Waters, chap. 4 of this volume). In the socialization of girls there are more differences between Latino cultures on the one hand, and middle-class white culture on the other, than there are between the two cultures in socialization of young males. For example, Latina girls are often expected to be self-sacrificing, to remain at home and care for younger siblings. These roles can conflict with expectations at school. Inconsistency between the traditional cultural role for women in the family and the societal role can create distress for female adolescents (Vazquez-Nuttall and Romero-Garcia 1989). Girls who experience disparate expectations, and who are not allowed to express their discontent, are prime candidates for the kind of internalizing that leads to depression.

## Acculturation as a Cultural Explanation for Depression

The measurement of acculturation among minority groups in the United States has focused largely on language minority groups such as people of Latin American or Asian origin, and the Latinos have definitely been the predominant focus of these studies (Sodowsky, Lai, and Plake 1991). The form of the relationship between acculturation and adaptation is not at all clear from existing research. Rogler, Cortes, and Malgady (1991) have reviewed the current evidence for and against three hypotheses, positing either a negative, a positive, or a curvilinear relationship between acculturation and mental health problems among Latinos.

In the negative relationship hypothesis, those who are new to the culture (less acculturated) are at increased risk for depression because of recent losses in social support, economic and social stresses associated with their new environment, and subsequent declines in self-esteem (Rogler, Cortes, and Malgady 1991). In the positive relationship, increases in acculturation lead to higher risk for depression through exposure to negative mainstream attitudes toward minorities, alienation from supportive immigrant communities, and subsequent internalized low self-regard. In the third pattern, risk for depression is greatest at extremes of low and high acculturation. A balance between retention of traditional values and ties and knowledge of the host culture is thought to protect against psychological distress and depression.

Rogler and his colleagues note a lack of consistent support for any of the three hypotheses. Of three studies that included measures of depression in particular, two found a positive relationship between acculturation and depression among Latinos (Burnam et al. 1987; Griffith 1983), and one found a negative relationship (Warheit et al. 1985). None of these studies included adolescents.

In this study we explore how acculturation to the United States relates to depression among young adolescent females. Our measure of acculturation is extent of English use, which we consider a measure of contact with mainstream culture. This does not imply, however, that it is inversely related to identification with Latino heritage.

## Depressive Symptoms: Definitions and Precursors

Our second question focuses on risk and protective factors found in the literature on depressive symptoms in mainstream populations, and the degree to which these play a role in the modulation of depressive symptoms in poor urban Latinas.

### Definitions

The most prevalent method of diagnosing adolescent depression is outlined in the *Diagnostic and Statistical Manual of Mental Disorders (DSM-IV)* (American Psychiatric Association 1994). The diagnosis relies more heavily on clinical consensus on categorical judgments than on empirical data (Achenbach and McConaughy 1992). Symptoms include depressed mood for most of the day, loss of interest in activities, weight loss or gain, insomnia or oversleeping, agitation or lethargy, loss of energy, feelings of worthlessness or guilt, lack of concentration, and recurrent thoughts of death or suicide. Five of these nine symptoms are necessary for a diagnosis of a major depressive episode. In contrast to the categorical classification approach of the *DSM-IV*, measures of depressed mood and depressive syndromes attempt to quantify the severity of symptoms (for example, on a scale of one to seven). Measures of depressive mood are usually restricted to self-report of sad feelings, whereas those of depressive syndromes include other symptoms that have been found to cooccur with sadness, such as anxiety, self-consciousness, and feeling unliked (Petersen et al. 1993). These taxonomic or dimensional approaches thus enable one to investigate the "degree to which each child manifests each syndrome" (Achenbach and McConaughy 1992). Women in poverty (and, by extension, adolescent girls in poverty) may be at particular risk for the chronic, moderate levels of depression (Belle 1982) best captured by dimensional measures of depressive syndromes.

Investigation of risk and protective factors can reveal causal mechanisms crucial to understanding and preventing mental health problems such as adolescent depression. What does the available literature tell us about risk and protective factors for depressive symptoms among adolescents?

### Risk and Protective Factors for Depressive Syndromes

*Life Stress.* The effect of life stress on depression has been considered by assessing both major life events and day-to-day hassles. Comparisons of the influence of these two kinds of stress on psychological symptoms have generally found that the effect of stressful life events on psychological symptoms occurred through the effect of increased daily hassles (Wagner, Compas, and Howell 1988). Both cross-sectional and longitudinal data from a study of low-income adolescents have shown a positive relationship between daily hassles and depressive symptoms (Dubois et al. 1992). In the present study we use daily hassles as our measure of stress.

*Social Support.* Perceived social support has been shown not only to protect against the development of depressive symptoms, but to have a direct effect on well-being. However, it appears that the kind and the quality of support make a crucial difference in this relationship. For example, the number of nonrelatives in the network has been positively related to psychological well-being in both low income African American children and adolescents (McLoyd and Wilson 1990) and Mexican American adults (Vega and Kolody 1985). There is some indication that satisfaction with support (McLoyd and Wilson 1990) and the presence of instrumental support (i.e., helping to solve specific problems) in addition to expressive support (i.e., affection) are negatively related to psychological distress (Valle and Bensussen 1985).

*Self-Esteem.* Low general self-worth has been consistently related to both childhood and adolescent depression (Kashani and Schmid 1992). Some researchers have even called for inclusion of poor self-attitudes in diagnostic definitions of child and adolescent depression (Harter 1990). In their white middle-class sample, Allgood-Merten, Lewinsohn, and Hops (1990) found that, after controlling for initial levels of depression, negative body image and low self-esteem were still significant predictors of depression one month later. There is little research, however, on the relationship between self-esteem and depression among poor urban adolescents.

## Our Model

On the basis of our review of the literature, we examined a set of variables related to depressive symptoms in adolescent females, and we determined the relative contribution of each variable to the prediction of depression. We hypothesize that there are both additive (direct and indirect) and synergistic (interactive) effects between acculturation and other predictors on self-reports of depressive symptoms. We use hierarchical multiple regression analyses to allow us to control the order in which variables and the interaction of one variable with another were examined.

The first block of variables includes demographic background factors. Although our sample of Latina females is from poor neighborhoods, level of poverty was entered into the equation first to control for any variation. Age is also a control variable entered in the first block. The final variable assesses the direct effects of acculturation on reports of depression. Block two consisted of daily hassles and social support. The first is expected to increase depression, the second to decrease depressive symptoms. The interaction of hassles and social support is entered next, to examine the possibility that social support buffers or attenuates the negative effects of hassles. Block four looks at the direct effects of self-esteem, which is expected to be low when reports of depression are high. Block five addresses our primary question concerning the moderating effects of acculturation on the relationship between the traditional predictors and depression for this poor urban sample. The interactions of acculturation with poverty, hassles, social support, and self-esteem are entered. These interactions will tell us to what degree we must qualify our interpretation of any main effects of poverty, hassles, social support, and self-esteem if we learn that their interaction with acculturation leads to varied patterns of outcome.

## Method

The data for this study were drawn from the Adolescent Pathways Project, a longitudinal study tracking youth in Baltimore, Washington, D.C., and New York City (for a more complete description of the sample, see Seidman et al. 1994). In these cities schools were selected with mainly black, Latino, or white student populations, and with a minimum of 63% of the students eligible for reduced or free lunch (adolescents in the study lived for the most part in low income neighborhoods). All adolescents in the grade before junior high school (fifth grade in some schools, sixth grade in others) were recruited from these twenty-four schools. The sample for this study includes 137 Latina girls. Of the 99 Latinas who specified their country of origin, 33% indicated Puerto Rico, 39% the Dominican Republic, 6% Central America, 4% South America, 2% Mexico, 2% Cuba, and 13% some combination of these. In terms of marital status, 45.4% had mothers with partners, and 54.6% had mothers without.

Information was collected in group settings at school. Members of multiracial or multiethnic research teams read instructions, each question, and all possible responses aloud to the group; other team members circulated to answer students' questions and to spot-check answers on measures for which directions were more complicated.

We used the following measures in this study:

Acculturation, operationalized as extent of English use, was measured for Latinas through a five-item questionnaire on language used at home, with friends, and during childhood (adapted from Marín et al. 1986). Response choices ranged from 1 (another language only) to 3 (both English and another language equally) to 5 (English only). The alpha coefficient (a) for this measure, an index of internal consistency, was .83. Although language use is clearly not all there is to acculturation, the authors of this shorter measure recommend its use as a proxy for acculturation and report that it correlates .78 with a fifteen-item measure tapping additional dimensions of acculturation (e.g., food and music preferences).

Poverty was operationalized with a measure of household economic resources, composed of questions on whether the adolescent's family was female-headed, whether the family owned a car, and the number of people in the family with part- or full-time jobs. The last two variables were reverse coded; then the mean of all three standardized variables was computed. These variables were used as indicators of constraints on the household's economic resources to provide for the adolescent.

A twenty-three-item measure of daily hassles was created, tapping hassles in the family, school, and peer settings (items included whether the adolescent experienced "trouble with parents over how you spend your time after school and on weekends," "school being too hard," and "trouble with friends over beliefs, opinions, and choices"). The scale ranged from 2 (not at all a hassle) to 5 (a very big hassle) (1 was scored as "didn't happen") (a = .81).

The mean of a twenty-one-item measure of social support (adapted from Cauce, Felner, and Primavera 1982) explored how helpful the adolescent's family, teachers, and peers were with personal problems and needs for "money and other things," as well as whether the girl has fun with these people (a = .68). For the first two questions, response choices were 1, "not at all," 2, "sort of," and 3, "very." For the question about whether she has fun with these people, response choices were 1, "never," 2, "sometimes," and 3, "often."

Six questions on self-esteem (adapted from Harter 1987) measured how happy the adolescent was with herself (a = .72). Girls were asked to "pick the item that best describes you" from two opposite choices (e.g., "Some teenagers are very happy being the way they are" vs. "Some teenagers wish they were different"), and then indicate whether their selection was "sort of true" or "really true" of them. Items were scored on a four-point scale.

Finally, the outcome measure was the fourteen-item depression sub-scale from the Youth Self Report by Achenbach and Edelbrock (1987) (a = .83). The response choices were "not true," "somewhat or sometimes true," and "very true or often true." The measure taps the constellation of symptoms making up the depressive syndrome and includes items describing feelings of loneliness, self-consciousness, being unliked, and suicide.

## Results

In both regression equations, the direct effects of household economic resources, age, and extent of English use on depressive symptoms were considered first, followed by the effects of hassles and social support. Third, the interaction of hassles and social support was entered, next the effects of self-esteem, and finally the effects of interactions between acculturation and household economic resources, hassles, social support, and self-esteem.[1] Means and standard deviations for all measures are summarized in table 19.1, and summaries of the results of the regression analyses are presented in table 19.2.

The overall equation predicting depressive symptoms accounted for 33% of the variance in depressive symptoms. Again, the overall $F$ was significant ($F$ (11, 125) = 7.09, $p$ < .001). There were direct effects for age, in which younger girls reported more depressive symptoms and a trend for extent of English use ($p$ < .08) in which adherence to their

TABLE 19.1
*Descriptive Statistics for All Variables*

| | Latinas (N = 137) | | | |
| --- | --- | --- | --- | --- |
| | Mean | SD | Min | Max |
| Depressive symptoms | .65 | .38 | .00 | 1.85 |
| Age | 11.45 | .99 | 10.00 | 14.00 |
| Language use (higher = more English use) | 3.31 | .75 | 1.00 | 5.00 |
| Household economic resources (higher = less resources) | .21 | .68 | −.98 | 1.73 |
| Daily hassles | 3.16 | .59 | 2.00 | 4.60 |
| Social support | 2.10 | .27 | 1.33 | 2.81 |
| Self-esteem | 2.85 | .74 | 1.00 | 4.00 |

culture of origin tended to be associated with higher depressive symptom scores (see table 19.2). Daily hassles and self esteem were both related to depressive symptoms. But these direct effects were qualified by significant interactions with acculturation.

There was evidence of a moderating effect of Latinas' extent of English use on the traditional predictors of depressive symptoms. Based on the work of McClelland and Judd (1993), which suggests that it is more difficult to detect moderator effects in field studies than in experiments because of the nature of the distributions of the interaction variables,

TABLE 19.2
*Summary of Hierarchical Multiple Regression Analyses: Depressive Symptoms Regressed onto Demographic Variables, Daily Hassles, Social Support, and Self-Esteem*
(N = 137)

| Steps | $\Delta R^2$ | Final b (SE b) | Final Beta |
| --- | --- | --- | --- |
| 1. Demographic variables | .08[b] | | |
| Houschold cconomic resources (higher = fewer resources) | | −.02 (.04) | −.03 |
| Age | | −.09 (.03) | −.24[c] |
| Language use (higher = more English use) | | −.07 (.04) | −.14[a] |
| 2. Hassles and social support | .14[d] | | |
| Daily hassles | | .17 (.05) | .27[d] |
| Social support | | −.03 (.11) | −.02 |
| 3. Hassles × social support interaction | .01 | −.21 (.18) | −.08 |
| 4. Self-esteem | .12[d] | −.20 (.04) | −.37[d] |
| 5. Interactions of language usc with predictors | .04[a] | | |
| Language use × household economic resources | | −.10 (.06) | −.13[a] |
| Language use × hassles | | −.15 (.07) | −.16[b] |
| Language use × social support | | .03 (.14) | .02 |
| Language use × self-esteem | | −.14 (.07) | −.16[b] |

[a] $p < .10$
[b] $p < .05$
[c] $p < .01$
[d] $p < .001$

significance level for interactions was set at $p < .10$. There was a significant interaction between extent of English language use and hassles in the prediction of depressive symptoms for Latinas. At low levels of hassles, there appeared to be no differences in depressive symptom scores for those with different levels of English use. But at high levels of hassles, Latinas low in English use reported higher depressive symptom scores than those high in English use. Those highest in English use appeared to show no differences in depressive symptoms across the range of hassles reported.

There was also a significant interaction between self-esteem and extent of English use among Latinas. At low levels of English use, there was no significant relation between self-esteem and depressive symptoms. But for girls who indicated higher levels of English use, high self-esteem was associated with lower levels of depressive symptoms, and low self-esteem with higher levels of depressive symptoms.

In the final interaction, at high levels of English use, high levels of poverty were associated with lower levels of depressive symptoms. For those at low levels of English use, on the other hand, high levels of poverty were associated with higher levels of depressive symptoms.

Thus, for all three of the interactions, the moderating effects of acculturation are always in the positive direction. High levels of acculturation may serve a protective function against the effects of low esteem on depressive symptoms. On the other hand, low levels of acculturation may increase the risk effect of daily hassles and may increase the risk effect of poverty. Confirmation of the causal direction of these findings would require longitudinal data.

## Discussion

We investigated how useful traditional predictors of depression were in understanding levels of depressive symptoms among poor Latina females. We were also interested in how acculturation, operationalized here as extent of English use, modified the relations between traditional correlates and depression. Our findings are consistent with previous studies of the relation between life stress and psychological symptoms in low income adolescents. For our sample of Latinas, being faced with a greater number of daily stressors is related to more depressive symptoms. In addition, our data suggest that the negative relationship between self-esteem and depressive symptoms found in mainstream samples may also hold for poor inner-city girls. Future studies should investigate whether this relationship is due in part to the role that ethnic identity plays in the acculturation conflict sometimes experienced by Latinos (Szapocznik and Kurtines 1993).

Consistent with findings on other low income adolescents (Taylor, Casten, and Flickinger 1993), this study failed to demonstrate a significant relationship between social support and depressive symptoms. Our explanation for this is threefold. First, there may be an optimal amount of contact and support, which, when exceeded, may increase stress. This curvilinear relationship, suggesting that low and high amounts of support are associated with depressive symptoms, while moderate amounts of support reduce symptoms, would not be detected by our multiple regression technique. Also, the range of support found among studies in the mainstream literature (often based on white middle-class samples) may be very different from the levels of support reported by adolescents in our sample, as shown by our small standard deviation; this suggests a restricted range of support. Second, adolescents may ascribe different meanings to support from family compared with support from friends, a distinction that is not made by our measure (Way, chap. 10 of this volume). Lastly, first generation Latina adolescents trying to fit in with their peers may experience conflict as a result of high support from immigrant parents who hold values that differ from the values of their peers (Meswick 1992; Waters, chap. 4 of this volume). Thus, they may ascribe different meaning to support from parents than do youths whose parents are more acculturated.

Our findings also suggest that among Latinas there are culturally influenced coping styles in the presence of external stressors or hassles and internal resources or self-esteem. Further, there does not appear to be a simple, or direct, relationship between extent of English use and psychological symptoms. The findings suggest that although hassles are a common factor in adolescent depression (Dubois et al. 1992), including for these poor Latina females, their negative impact is even greater for Latinas who use the English language less often. The interaction showed little difference in depression across increasing hassles for girls who had high levels of acculturation, but an increase in depression as hassles increased for girls without this protective factor. This suggests that the use of English may serve as a protection against the negative effects of exposure to hassles, perhaps by increasing one's ability to benefit from external resources. Low use of English in the United States may decrease the ability to seek support outside the family. This is suggested in a study by Sabogal and colleagues (1987), who find that more acculturated Mexican, Cuban and Central American adults (those with greater English use) perceived fewer obligations to support or seek the approval of family members than less acculturated adults. On the other hand, those less acculturated may feel that they have fewer options for dealing with the hassles. In addition, report of depression appears to be more common in younger Latinas, who may possess fewer help-seeking skills.

Poverty-related risks associated with recent immigration may explain the interaction of daily hassles and language use. Those using less English than Spanish may come from Latino families that have more recently immigrated to the United States. These families may be under higher levels of poverty-related stress, and the daughters in turn may be more vulnerable to daily hassles (Vega, Hough, and Miranda 1985). A recent study by Aber and colleagues (submitted for publication) found, among Latinos in this particular sample, that the effects of poverty-related risks, such as negative life events and being in a single-parent underemployed household, on psychological symptoms were partially mediated by daily hassles.

The interactions are synergistic (suggesting a "piling up" of multiple risks' effects, such that in the presence of one, the relationship of the other to the outcome is strengthened). They may reflect the cumulative effect of poverty-related risks (daily hassles and household economic resources) and factors associated with recent immigration (less English use) on depressive symptoms. It is well known that the effects of multiple psychosocial risks on developmental problems are additive and possibly multiplicative (Yoshikawa 1994); however, there has been little exploration of whether such cumulative risk processes operate among minority populations, or whether they explain the development of depressive symptoms in particular. Our findings may represent part of such a risk process, explaining depressive symptoms among poor Latina girls. If so, promising avenues for prevention of Latinas' depressive symptoms include reducing poverty-related hassles among recently immigrated families.

It appears that language acculturation may also be a protective factor in the relationship between self-esteem and depression. We found that for more acculturated youths, high self-esteem greatly reduces the incidence of depression, whereas less acculturated youth benefit little from this internal resource. High self-esteem in the presence of greater acculturation may minimize the problems that can result from conflict between less acculturated families and more acculturated adolescents (Szapocznik and Kurtines 1993). Soto and Shaver (1982) found an indirect relationship between generation or age at arrival and neurotic or stress-related symptoms in first and second generation Puerto Rican women. Their findings suggest that acculturation affects symptoms through its association with education, traditional sex roles, and assertiveness. Our findings suggest that there is an effect of acculturation and that it varies by hassles and self-esteem. Low acculturation is associated with close family relationships, which have positive effects for children (Taylor, Hurley, and Riley 1986) but may have different effects on adolescents (see Waters, chap. 4 of this volume).

These findings suggest that some degree of acculturation, at least in terms of English language usage, may buffer the negative effects of hassles and low self-esteem on Latina adjustment. Greater use of English does not necessarily indicate rejection of culture that leads to family conflict. It may, rather, be an indication of empowering economic and social transformations within and outside the community (Szapocznik and Kurtines 1993). In particular, language acculturation may say less about one's identification with the Latino culture and more about one's knowledge of mainstream culture.

In summary, our findings suggest that acculturation is a protective factor in the development of depressive symptoms in Latinas. Because the analyses we used are designed to look for simple relationships between variables, we are unable to conclude whether there is an optimal balance of acculturation and maintenance of cultural values that is associated with lowered depression.

Our findings add to the literature on minority mental health and the effects of minority culture background on symptom formation. Although we look at depressive symptoms rather than clinical depression, our findings may also have implications for the prevention of adolescent depression. The use of English may be a skill that protects one in interactions with the mainstream culture. As we indicated earlier, we were not able to directly test the effects of attitude toward one's own culture combined with integration into mainstream culture (measured by use of English), because we did not measure the former. However, future research should test our suggestion that, for Latinas, use of English may facilitate adaptation to the mainstream.

Clearly, the strength of these findings for suggesting preventive pathways would be increased by the addition of measures of acculturation that assess behaviors beyond language use. We also need longitudinal information if we are to understand the process by which the protective aspects of language use are activated. It would also be enlightening to collect data within Latinas to assess the impact of subgroup cultural variations further. For Latinas, the most effective prevention efforts, based on our findings, would facilitate some level of acculturation to the mainstream, as well as reduce external stressors and poverty among recent immigrants.

NOTE

1. A variable of life events related to family loss was included in initial analyses of the full model, but because it was not related to the outcome in all of the analyses, it was dropped from the final model.

REFERENCES

This research was supported in part by grants from the National Institute of Mental Health (MH43084) and the Carnegie Corporation (B4850) awarded to Edward Seidman, J. Lawrence Aber, LaRue Allen, and Christina Mitchell.

Aber, J. L., E. Seidman, L. Allen, and C. Mitchell. Poverty-related risks and the psychosocial adaptation of urban youth. Manuscript submitted for publication.

Achenbach, T. M., and C. Edelbrock. 1987. *Manual for the Youth Self-Report and Profile.* Burlington: University of Vermont Department of Psychiatry.

Achenbach, T. M., and S. H. McConaughy. 1992. Taxonomy of internalizing disorders of childhood and adolescence. In *Internalizing disorders of childhood and adolescence,* edited by W. M. Reynolds, 19–60. New York: John Wiley.

Allgood-Merten, B., P. Lewinsohn, and H. Hops. 1990. Sex differences and adolescent depression. *Journal of Abnormal Psychology* 99:55–63.

American Psychiatric Association. 1994. *Diagnostic and statistical manual of mental disorders.* 4th ed. Washington, D.C.: American Psychiatric Press.

Belle, D. 1982. *Lives in stress: Women and depression.* Beverly Hills, Calif.: Sage.

Burnam, M. A., R. L. Hough, M. Karno, J. I. Escobar, and C. A. Telles. 1987. Acculturation and lifetime prevalence of psychiatric disorders among Mexican Americans in Los Angeles. *Journal of Health and Social Behavior* 28:89–102.

Cauce, A., R. D. Felner, and J. Primavera. 1982. Social support in high-risk adolescents: Structural components and adaptive impact. *American Journal of Community Psychology* 10:417–28.

Children's Defense Fund. 1993. Child poverty hits record levels. *CDF Reports* 14 (12):11.

DuBois, D. L., R. D. Felner, S. Brand, A. M. Adan, and E. G. Evans. 1992. A prospective study of life stress, social support, and adaptation in early adolescence. *Child Development* 63:542–57.

Griffith, J. 1983. Relationship between acculturation and psychological impairment in adult Mexican Americans. *Hispanic Journal of Behavioral Sciences* 5:431–59.

Harter, S. 1987. *The perceived competence scale for adolescents.* Manuscript.

Harter, S. 1990. Causes, correlates, and the functional role of global self-worth: A lifespan perspective. In *Competence considered,* edited by R. J. Sternberg and J. Kolligian, 67–97. New Haven: Yale University Press.

Holzer, C., B. Shea, J. Swanson, P. Leaf, J. Myers, L. George, M. Weissman, and P. Bednarski. 1986. The increased risk for specific psychiatric disorders among persons of low socioeconomic status. *American Journal of Social Psychiatry* 6:259–71.

Kashani, J. H., and L. S. Schmid. 1992. Epidemiology and etiology of depressive disorders. In *Clinical guide to depression in children and adolescents,* edited by M. Shafii and S. L. Shafii, 43–64. Washington, D.C.: American Psychiatric Press.

Marín, G., S. Sabogal, B. V. Marín, R. Otero-Sabogal, E. J. Perez-Stable. 1986. Development of an acculturation scale for Hispanics. *Hispanic smoking cessation research project: Technical report no. 1.* San Francisco: University of California Department of Medicine.

McClelland, G. H., and C. M. Judd. 1993. Statistical difficulties of detecting interactions and moderator effects. *Psychological Bulletin* 114:376–89.

McGrath, E., G. P. Keita, B. R. Strickland, and N. F. Russo. 1990. *Women and depression: Risk factors and treatment issues. Final report of the American Psychological Association's National Task Force on Women and Depression.* Washington, D.C.: American Psychological Association.

McLoyd, V. C., and L. Wilson. 1990. Maternal behavior, social support, and economic conditions as predictors of distress in children. *New Directions for Child Development* 46:49–69.

Meswick, S. 1992. Migration, health, and social stress among Puerto Rican adolescents. In *Puerto Rican children on the mainland: Interdisciplinary perspectives,* edited by M. D. Alvarez and A. N. Ambert. New York: Garland.

Nolen-Hoeksema, S., and J. S. Girgus. 1994. The emergence of gender differences in depression during adolescence. *Psychological Bulletin* 115:424–43.

Petersen, A. C., B. E. Compas, J. Brooks-Gunn, M. Stemmler, S. Ey, and K. E. Grant. 1993. Depression in adolescence. *American Psychologist* 48:155–68.

Rogler, L. H., D. E. Cortes, and R. G. Malgady. 1991. Acculturation and mental health status among Hispanics. *American Psychologist* 46:585–97.

Sabogal, F., G. Marín, R. Otero-Sabogal, and B. C. Marín. 1987. Hispanic familism and acculturation: What changes and what doesn't? *Hispanic Journal of Behavioral Sciences* 9: 397–412.

Seidman, E., L. Allen, J. L. Aber, C. Mitchell, and J. Feinman. 1994. The impact of school transitions in early adolescence on the self-system and perceived social context of poor urban youth. *Child Development* 65:507–22.

Sodowsky, G. R., E. W. M. Lai, and B. S. Plake. 1991. Moderating effects of sociocultural variables on acculturation attitudes of Hispanics and Asian Americans. *Journal of Counseling and Development* 70:194–204.

Soto, E., and P. Shaver. 1982. Sex-role traditionalism, assertiveness, and symptoms of Puerto Rican women living in the United States. *Hispanic Journal of Behavioral Sciences* 4 (1):1–19.

Spurlock, J. 1973. Some consequences of racism for children. In *Racism and mental health,* edited by C. V. Willie, B. M. Kramer, and B. S. Brown, 147–64. Pittsburgh: University of Pittsburgh Press.

Szapocznik, J., and W. M. Kurtines. 1993. Family psychology and cultural diversity: Opportunities for theory, research and application. *American Psychologist* 48:400–407.

Taylor, R. D., R. Casten, and S. M. Flickinger. 1993. Influence of kinship social support on the parenting experiences and psychosocial adjustment of African-American adolescents. *Developmental Psychology* 29:382–88.

Taylor, V. L., E. C. Hurley, and M. T. Riley. 1986. The influence of acculturation upon the adjustment of preschool Mexican American children of single parent families. *Family Therapy* 13:249–56.

U.S. Congress, Office of Technology Assessment. 1991. *Adolescent health* OTA H-466, 467, 468. Washington, D.C.: U.S. Government Printing Office.

Valle, R., and G. Bensussen. 1985. Hispanic social networks, social support and mental health. In *Stress and Hispanic mental health: Relating research to service delivery,* edited by W. A. Vega and M. R. Miranda, 147–73. Rockville, Md.: National Institute of Mental Health.

Vazquez-Nuttall, E., and I. Romero-Garcia. 1989. From home to school: Puerto Rican girls learn to be students in the United States. In *The psychosocial development of Puerto Rican women,* edited by C. T. Garcia Coll and M. de Lourdes Mattei. New York: Praeger.

Vega, W. A., R. C. Hough, and M. R. Miranda. 1985. Modeling cross-cultural research in Hispanic mental health. In *Stress and Hispanic mental health: Relating research to service delivery,* edited by W. A. Vega and M. R. Miranda, 1–29. Rockville, Md.: National Institute of Mental Health.

Vega, W. A., and B. Kolody. 1985. The meaning of social support and the mediation of stress across cultures. In *Stress and Hispanic mental health: Relating research to service delivery,* edited by W. A. Vega and M. R. Miranda, 48–75. Rockville, Md.: National Institute of Mental Health.

Wagner, B. M., B. E. Compas, and D. C. Howell. 1988. Daily and major life events: A test of an integrative model of psychosocial stress. *American Journal of Community Psychology* 16:189–205.

Warheit, G. J., W. A. Vega, J. Auth, and K. Meinhardt. 1985. Psychiatric symptoms and dysfunctions among Anglos and Mexican Americans: An epidemiological study. In *Research in community and mental health,* edited by J. R. Greenley, 3–32. London: JAI Press.

Yoshikawa, H. 1994. Prevention as cumulative protection: Effects of early family support and education on chronic delinquency and its risks. *Psychological Bulletin* 115:28–54.

# VII

# Career Development

This final section focuses on how views of self and future opportunities are shaped by environmental influences. A majority (59%) of women with children under six were in the labor force in 1993 compared to 30% in 1970 (Children's Defense Fund 1994). Despite these changes in social expectations, young women's career development has not been the focus of much adolescent research. Many agree that enhanced life options for urban adolescent girls would help to deter early childbearing and reduce welfare dependency. But how do urban girls learn about career options, what different jobs pay, and how one trains for them? Little is known about these processes. More is known about the influences that propel them toward low paying career choices, including early educational tracking, lack of educational success, minimal family resources for college educations, depression, and lack of role models. Career counseling in middle schools is frequently absent or focused only on course choices to meet college entrance requirements, rather than on exposing girls to a range of possible career options. Indeed, college attendance is often considered to be the only route to adult work; American youths who do not attend appear to have been *forgotten* in school-based career development curricula (William T. Grant Foundation 1988).

McLoyd and Jozefowicz, in chapter 20, further the discussion of both the obstacles to girls' aspirations and the points of resistance that enhance their opportunities, by their research with seventh and eighth grade African American girls and their mothers. They find that the girls' perceptions of the degree of financial strain experienced by their mothers, their own and their mothers' perceptions of their academic ability, and more years of schooling achieved by the mothers are positively associated with the girls' future expectations of economic hardship or of a family life course marked by out-of-wedlock births, early marriage, and divorce. The processes by which family poverty and the strains of financial hardship are transformed into views of self and future opportunities are alarmingly evident in this analyses.

In chapter 21, De León reviews social and school contexts of career development for Hispanic urban adolescent girls. She argues that strong sex-role stereotypes that see Hispanic girls as passive, submissive under-achievers are reinforced by family, school, and media. Despite the growing numbers of female-headed households and poor socioeconomic conditions of many Hispanic families, career development of Latina adolescent girls has virtually been ignored. De León presents guidelines for career development that are sensitive to and build on Hispanic cultural experiences.

REFERENCES

Children's Defense Fund. 1994. *The state of America's children*. Washington, D.C.: Children's Defense Fund.
William T. Grant Foundation. 1988. *The forgotten half: Non-college youth in America*. Washington, D.C.: William T. Grant Commission on Work, Family, and Citizenship.

# 20

# Sizing Up the Future: Predictors of African American Adolescent Females' Expectancies about Their Economic Fortunes and Family Life Courses

Vonnie C. McLoyd and Debra M. Hernandez Jozefowicz

Single parenthood and its attendant socioeconomic disadvantages are salient features of the social ecology of many African American children. In 1991 54% of all African American children lived in mother-only families. Some 65% of these children were poor, compared to 19% of African American children who lived in two-parent families. During the same period 17% of white children lived in mother-only families; 46% of these children were poor, compared to 9.5% of white children who lived in two-parent families (U.S. Bureau of the Census 1992a, 1992b). The risk of poverty in mother-only families is high as a result of several factors, including low wages for women, unfavorable economic conditions, the low educational attainment of many single mothers, the large number of single mothers who are adolescents, and the large number of fathers who provide no financial support for their children (Ellwood 1988; Huston, McLoyd, and Garcia Coll 1994).

The high rate of mother-only families among African Americans raises questions about how children who live in this context formulate expectancies about their economic futures and their family life courses. The purpose of the present chapter is twofold: (1) to present a brief discussion of literature that helps illuminate socialization processes that may influence African American adolescents' expectations about their economic well-being and family life and (2) to present findings from a study of the effects of socioeconomic factors, beliefs, values, and expectations on the economic and family life course expectations of African American adolescent females living in economically disadvantaged, mother-headed families.

## Intergenerational Upward Mobility: The Disparity between Aspirations and Reality

American society is characterized by markedly less intergenerational income mobility than has been recognized. As a result of flawed and limited data (e.g., single-year measures of earnings) and unrepresentative, homogeneous samples, virtually all of which are limited to fathers and sons, studies of intergenerational income mobility published during the 1970s and 1980s appear to systematically underestimate the correlation between father and son income status. This, in effect, overestimates the frequency of intergenerational income mobility, that is, the likelihood that a child's income level will differ from his or her parent's income level. Whereas most past studies reported father-son correlations in earnings and family income of about .20 or less, recent research reports correlations of substantially higher magnitude (Solon 1992). Using intergenerational data from the Panel Study of Income Dynamics, a nationally representative, longitudinal survey of about five thousand families, conducted annually since 1968, Solon (1992) found father-son and mother-son correlations of about .40 or higher in long-run earnings, hourly wages, and family income. Based on this estimate, a son whose father is in the bottom 5% of earners has only a 1-in-20 chance of making it into the top 20% of families, a 1-in-4 chance of rising above the median income of American families, and a 2-in-5 chance of staying poor or near poor. Unfortunately, comparable data were not presented for father-daughter and mother-daughter dyads.

The American Dream of ever-increasing purchasing power and off-spring who do better economically than their parents, always less tenable for the poor than for the middle class, has become even less so in recent times. Loss of higher-paying manufacturing jobs as the economy shifts from good-producing to service-producing industries has forced substantial numbers of African American blue-collar workers into much lower-paying trade or service positions, if not into the ranks of the unemployed (James 1985; Simms 1987). In addition to contributing to downward mobility, structural changes in the economy have made it harder for noncollege youth to climb out of poverty and to do better economically than their parents. For example, the real mean earnings in 1986 of African American males between the ages of twenty and twenty-four with a high school education were 44% less than the earnings of the identical age group thirteen years earlier. For their white counterparts, the figure was 24% (William T. Grant Foundation Commission on Work, Family, and Citizenship 1988). The proportion of high school graduates likely to earn more than a poverty level income fell from 84% in the 1970s to 75% in the 1980s among African American men, and from 93% to 88% among white men (Nasar 1992).

This marked erosion in the economic well-being of working-class men in general, and African American men in particular, has been accompanied by a decline in marriage rates, an increase in divorce rates, an increase in the number of mother-only families, and an increase in rates of childhood poverty. For example, among African Americans, marriage rates for females fifteen years and older dropped from 54% in 1970 to 38% in 1991. During the same period divorce rates for this group increased from 4.4% to 11%, and the proportion of mother-only families of all African American families increased from 28% to 46% (U.S. Bureau of the Census 1992a). Between 1971 and 1990 the poverty rate for African American children under eighteen years of age increased from 40.7% to 44.2%, with the sharpest increases occurring during the 1980s. Wilson (1987) has argued cogently that a major cause of these trends is the deteriorating economic status of African American men.

Notwithstanding the rather limited intergenerational income mobility that appears to exist in American society, having offspring who do better economically than their parents is a strong aspiration of American parents from diverse racial, ethnic, and socioeconomic backgrounds. Intergenerational mobility as a goal among African Americans, rooted partly in their history of virulent, legalized racial oppression that functioned to severely restrict economic and educational opportunities, has been documented in several studies and accounts of African American family life (Dill 1980; Scanzoni 1971; Tatum 1987). In her qualitative study of African American mothers who worked as domestics, for example, Dill found that these women consistently and ardently expressed a determination to ensure that their children acquired skills and training to increase their prospects of upward mobility. One of them stated:

I never intended for my children to have to work for anybody in the capacity that I worked. Never. And I never allowed my children to do any babysitting or anything of the sort. I figured it's enough for the mother to do it and in this day and time you don't have to do that. . . . So they never knew anything about going out to work or anything. They went to school. (1980, 109)

In some families there is an explicit expectation that children whose parents have worked to facilitate the former's upward mobility will, as parents, do likewise for their own children, ensuring that mobility occurs across multiple generations. One African American middle-class father said, reflecting on the roots of his strong sense of parental responsibility:

When you see your parents work four and five jobs just to keep food on the table during their times and the economic situations and the racial problems that they incurred, that's the reason that I struggled so hard to make sure that when I had a family that I was going to try and . . . follow in the pattern of my grandparents, my father, to give them the necessities, even if I had to work as hard as they did. Like my grandfather and my father always told me, "We tried to do the best we could for you, and the only thing we ask of you is to do better by yours." And that's what I'm trying to do. (Tatum 1987, 47)

## Sizing Up the Future: The Importance and Determinants of Expectancies

Against this backdrop of economic decline juxtaposed with limited but highly valued intergenerational mobility in American society, we examine how African American adolescent girls living in financially strapped, mother-headed families perceive their economic futures and family life courses. What predictions do they make about the economic circumstances they will confront during adulthood and the courses of their marital and family lives? Do they expect to escape the web of economic hardship marked by low-wage jobs, checkered employment, welfare use, and single parenthood common to their mothers' lives? Do these adolescent girls comprehend the connection between economic hardship and a family life course marked by out-of-wedlock births, early marriage, and divorce?

The stereotypical view of African American adolescent children growing up in economically strapped mother-only families characteristically underplays psychological heterogeneity within this segment of the population, in part because the latter is often juxtaposed conceptually and empirically with white middle-class children living in two-parent families (Graham 1992). The work presented in this chapter is intended to demonstrate that even within an economically distressed sample of African American adolescent females, considerable variation exists in expectancies and, moreover, that a significant proportion of this variation can be accounted for by attitudinal and maternal socialization factors (Greene 1990).

Expectancies are important partly because of their potential to influence behavior. For example, longitudinal research indicates that adolescent females' expectancies of paid employment in the future predict their labor force participation as adults (Macke and Morgan 1978). Sociologists have long considered occupational and educational aspirations and expectations as critical intervening social-psychological variables in the occupational and educational attainment process (e.g., Sewell, Haller, and Ohlendorf 1970; Sewell, Haller, and Portes 1969).

Research that examines determinants of task performance and motivation also underscores the importance of expectancies for behavior. Numerous studies find that when asked to estimate their future performance on academic tasks, children who state higher expectancies of success show superior performance and persist longer on the academic tasks in question (Dweck 1978). Likewise, Coleman and colleagues' well-known national study (1966) of children's achievement found that indicators of children's expectancies of success were among the strongest predictors of school achievement. Such findings are in keeping with expectancy-value theory, which posits that behavior is a function of the individual's expectations of acquiring specific outcomes as a result of performing certain behaviors and the degree to which the individual values these outcomes (e.g., Eccles Parsons et al. 1983).

This chapter builds on and expands standard status attainment and expectancy-value theories by focusing on the predictors of two specific sets of expectations highly relevant to the sample being studied, namely, expectations of economic hardship (e.g., job loss, experiencing difficulty finding a good job, and having to go on welfare) and expectations of a family life course marked by transitions associated with lower economic security and socioeconomic status (i.e., out-of-wedlock birth, marriage immediately after high school, and divorce) (Garfinkel and McLanahan 1986; Rubin 1976). In particular, we assess the degree to which economic distress, socialization factors, attitudes, and beliefs account for variation in the expectancies of a sample of urban African American adolescent females living in mother-headed families and experiencing a relatively high level of economic hardship.

## The Influence of Economic Hardship on Adolescent Expectations

Research has found that white adolescents living in families experiencing transitory economic hardship brought on by income or job loss are more likely to reduce their occupational aspirations and expectations of job success (Galambos and Silbereisen 1987), are less likely to expect to go to a four-year college, and are more likely to expect to go into vocational training after high school, compared with those living in families whose economic circumstances are more favorable (Flanagan 1990). Evidence also exists that African American students' level of optimism about their chances for occupational attainment is related to the extent to which they perceive that the opportunity structure is open to them and that they can control what happens to them (Baly 1989). Socioeconomic disadvantage reduces the strength of these perceptions and restricts children's knowledge about various occupations and the nature of progression and training required to reach particular occupational goals (Baly 1989; Glasgow 1980; Parnes 1970).

In keeping with these findings, we expected that even within the economically disadvantaged sample we studied, socioeconomic factors would shape adolescent females' expectations. In particular, we predicted that adolescent females who live in families with fewer resources (i.e., per capita income and maternal education) and who perceive their families to be under more financial strain would expect more economic hardship during adulthood and have higher expectations of experiencing family life course transitions associated with economic hardship and lower socioeconomic status (e.g., out-of-wedlock birth).

### The Influence of Maternal Outlook on Adolescent Expectations

Previous research with white families indicates that parents experiencing economic hardship, compared with more economically advantaged parents, are more pessimistic about the future of their children, feel less confident about helping their children prepare for future work roles, and report more negative change in educational plans for their children (Flanagan 1990; Galambos and Silbereisen 1987; Larson 1984). These changes in parental outlook and behavior appear to be partly responsible for negative changes in children's aspirations and expectations following the onset of economic hardship (Galambos and Silbereisen 1987).

Likewise, mothers who perceive their families to be under greater financial strain and mothers who are more inclined to foresee economic difficulties in their daughters' future may tacitly or explicitly communicate to their daughters higher levels of pessimism about the future. Because children and adolescents often look to their parents to interpret the meanings and implications of economic events and circumstances, maternal pessimism may encourage daughters to perceive their own futures less positively. We hypothesized that mothers who perceive their families to be under greater financial strain would have daughters who perceive their economic futures less positively and who have higher expectations of family life courses associated with economic hardship. For similar reasons we hypothesized that mothers who expect more economic hardship in their daughters' future would have daughters who themselves perceive their economic futures less positively.

*The Influence of Perceptions of Ability, Educational Values, and Work
Socialization on Adolescent Expectations*

Another domain of maternal cognitions that may influence daughters'
projections about their futures is mothers' perceptions of their daughters'
abilities. Perceptions of ability represent the subjective assessment of an
individual's competence based on recollections of past performance and
beliefs about how others view one's competence (Eccles Parsons et al.
1983). Contrary to what might be expected, evidence suggests that ability
perceptions are more strongly related to the latter than to the former: in a
study of white parents and their children, Eccles Parsons, Adler, and
Kaczala (1982) found that parents' perceptions of their children's abilities
predicted children's perceptions of their own abilities more strongly than
children's previous performance did. Perceptions of ability, in turn, predict expectancies, values, and behaviors. For example, in a study of
African American public high school students, Taylor and his colleagues
(1994) found that students' perceptions of ability predicted both students'
grades and their reported engagement in school.

Also of particular interest here is evidence that American children and
adults evaluate ability as very important in accounting for school success
and, by implication, economic success (Stevenson, Chen, and Lee 1993;
Stevenson, Lee, and Stigler 1986). This orientation is compatible with
another strong predilection among Americans, the tendency to explain
poverty by reference to individual differences (e.g., lack of ability) rather
than social-structural or political factors (Feather 1974; Leahy 1990). In
the present study we hypothesized that the mother's and daughter's
ability perceptions would account for a significant portion of variance in
the daughter's expectancies, and more specifically, that the lower the
mother's and daughter's perceptions of the latter's ability, the greater
would be the daughter's expectancies of economic difficulties and family
life transitions associated with such difficulties.

Education has long been embraced by many African Americans as the
most viable means by which to mitigate the forces of oppression and to
improve the individual and collective fortunes of African Americans
(Ladner 1971; Scanzoni 1971). This emphasis on education stems, to a
major degree, from the fact that until the 1970s other avenues to upward
mobility, such as entrepreneurship, were either closed to African Americans, or African Americans' access to them was severely restricted. Moreover, education took on special meaning during the period of legalized
racial discrimination and economic exploitation, because it represented an
intangible that was not subject to the appropriation and rapacity of

Whites (Grier and Cobbs 1968; Scanzoni 1985). Children were implored to acquire as much education as possible because "that's something no one can take away from you" (Grier and Cobbs 1968, 116). This urging conveyed a message that was empowering but also threatening, for as Grier and Cobbs point out, it told African American children "a great deal about a vicious social order which rapes and exploits them and in which only a black man's ideas are safe from the white predator" (1968, 128).

While emphasizing the importance of preparing oneself educationally for opportunities that may arise, African American parents may simultaneously acknowledge to their children the possibility that they may not receive remuneration in accord with their educational achievement. For example, the female domestics in Dill's study, as they helped their children understand the barriers posed by racism, insisted that they not succumb to them, but rather equip themselves through education to take advantage of whatever opportunities might arise resulting from cracks in the barriers posed by racism. As one of them put it, "It's fine to prepare yourself so that when opportunity knocks, you'll be able to catch up" (1980, 112).

In view of the strong emphasis on education as a means toward upward mobility among African Americans, as well as evidence that parents' educational and occupational values influence children's educational and career aspirations, expectations, and achievements (Baly 1989; Seginer 1983), we expected that if adolescent females and their mothers perceived good grades as more important and regarded education as more useful in securing a good job (i.e., utility value of education), they would report lower expectancies of economic hardship. We also expected that the utility value of education would relate more strongly to expectations of economic hardship than the importance of grades, because the former is more directly relevant to the economic expectations under investigation.

Historically, African American mothers have been exempt from the role of economic provider with far less frequency than have white mothers (Collins 1987). Economic need (prompted in part by the relatively low and unstable wages garnered by African American men), role modeling, direct training (e.g., recurrent messages to daughters about the value of being economically independent and, conversely, the economic, psychological, and interpersonal hazards of being dependent on a man), and normative approval of maternal employment in African American culture have all contributed to African American women's increased tendency to assume wage-earning responsibilities in conjunction with their roles as mothers (McLoyd 1993). Like education, maternal employment has been emphasized as a means to upward mobility and indeed is largely responsible for narrowing the gap during the past two decades between the incomes of two-parent African American families and two-parent white families (Geschwender and Carroll-Seguin 1990).

It is unclear whether the socialization press toward labor force participation for African American adolescent females varies as a function of social class or family structure. Nonetheless, just as this factor partly accounts for race or ethnic differences in women's labor force participation (McLoyd 1993), it may partly explain within-race differences in the economic and family life course expectations of economically disadvantaged adolescent females. We expected that frequency of mothers' discussions with daughters about the personal qualities and skills needed for occupational success (i.e., work socialization) would predict lower expectancies of economic hardship and lower expectancies of family life transitions associated with economic hardship. Such discussions may render the future less threatening and the adolescent's outlook more positive or less pessimistic by enhancing both the adolescent's knowledge about the world of work and her belief in her ability to control what happens to her.

## Method

### Study Overview

Data used in this study were collected as part of a larger study, which began in the fall of 1989. The larger study was designed to examine the impact of economic hardship on single African American mothers and their adolescents (McLoyd et al. 1994). The sample was recruited from two predominantly African American junior high schools in a lower- to working-class urban community. For a more detailed description of the recruitment process, see McLoyd et al. (1994).

### Sample Recruitment

Personnel from a small research unit located in the community were trained extensively by project researchers and staff in order to ensure interviewer competency, consistency, and accuracy. Both mothers and adolescents were interviewed in their homes at two time points (wave one and wave two) approximately six months apart. All mothers were interviewed by an African American female interviewer. Adolescents were interviewed by both African American and white female interviewers. Data collected during the wave one interview are used in the present study.

## Sample

The adolescent sample consisted of 115 seventh and eighth grade African American female students from two junior high schools in an urban midwestern city. The mean age of the adolescents at the time of the interview was 14 years ($SD$ = 1). The adolescents had a mean grade point average (GPA) of 1.8 ($SD$ = .9) on a 4.0 scale.

The parent sample consisted of 115 single African American mothers. Forty-five percent of the mothers had never been married, 29% were divorced, 18% were separated, 6% were widowed, and 2% were not married but were living with someone. Mothers had a mean age of 37 ($SD$ = 7) and had 12 years of schooling on average ($SD$ = 2). Sixty-eight percent of the mothers were not working at the time of the interviews, 21% were working full time, and 11% were working part time. Sixty-five percent of the mothers were welfare recipients. The mean level of per capita income (calculated as reported annual family income divided by the total number of household members) was $3,096 ($SD$ = $2,555).

## Measures

Mothers and daughters responded to a number of Likert-scale type items designed to assess a broad range of economic, mental health, attitudinal, and behavioral constructs. Multiple-item scales were factor analyzed in order to determine which scale items loaded together on a single factor. Based on the results of the factor analyses and a priori conceptualizations about meaningful constructs, scales were constructed by adding individual items together and taking their mean. Alpha coefficients were obtained for these scales and are presented below.

*Expectancies.* (1) *Daughter's expectation of economic hardship* (6 items, alpha = .71) was assessed by asking the daughter how likely it would be that during her adult life she would experience difficulty finding a good job, experience difficulty supporting her family financially, experience difficulty finding a spouse who has a good job, lose her job or be laid off from her job, be unemployed, or have to go on welfare (1 = not very likely, 6 = very likely). *(2) Daughter's expectation about her family life course* (3 items, alpha = .56) was measured in the same way as economic hardship expectations; the daughter was questioned about the likelihood that she would have a child without being married, get married immediately after high school, or get divorced (1 = not very likely, 6 = very likely). Although these two expectation variables were related ($r$ = .42), there were both statistical and theoretical reasons for examining them as separate constructs. Statistically, the items that comprise the scales loaded separately on different factors. Conceptually, we were particularly interested in the potential differences in the predictors of economic versus family life course expectations. *(3) Mother's expectation of economic hardship for daughter* (3 items, alpha = .76) was measured by asking the mother how much she worried that her daughter, as an adult, would get stuck in a dead-end, low-paying job; not be able to find a steady job; or have to depend on welfare (1 = not at all, 5 = a great deal).

*Demographic Indicators.* (1) *Per capita income* was calculated by dividing the mother's report of the family's annual income by the number of dependents in the household. A log transformation was performed on this variable because of the skewed distribution (i.e., few mothers fell within the upper range of per capita income). *(2) Maternal education* was determined by a single item that asked mothers how many years of schooling they had attained.

*Subjective Economic Indicators.* Mothers' and daughters' subjective experiences of economic hardship were assessed. *(1) Mother's perception of financial strain* (3 items, alpha = .63) was measured by asking the mother to indicate on a four-point scale how often in the past two years, in order to make ends meet, she had borrowed money from friends or family to help pay bills and how often she had decided not to buy something she really needed for herself or her children because she could not afford it (1 = not at all, 4 = a lot). A third item in the scale asked the mother how difficult it had been to pay the family bills lately (1 = not difficult at all, 4 = very difficult). *(2) Daughter's perception of financial strain* is a single-item measure that asked, "How often does your family have problems paying for basic necessities like food, clothing, and rent?" (1 = never, 5 = almost always).

*Perceptions of Adolescent's Ability.* (1) *Mother's perception of daughter's academic ability* (3 items, alpha = .80) includes the mother's ratings of her daughter's ability in three academic domains: mathematics, science, and language arts.[1] (1 = poor, 4 = excellent). *(2) Daughter's perception of her academic ability* (3 items, alpha = .65) was assessed in the same manner as the mother's: the daughter was asked to rate her ability in mathematics, science, and language arts (1 = poor, 4 = excellent).

*Educational Values.* Two dimensions of educational values were assessed, perceived importance of good grades (attainment value) and perceived economic or occupational utility of education. *(1) Mother's perception of the importance of good grades* (6 items, alpha = .76) is a measure of the importance the mother attached to her daughter's getting good grades in mathematics, science, and language arts (1 = not at all important, 5 = very important), in addition to her ratings of how upset she would be if her daughter received low grades in these domains (1 = not at all upset, 4 = very upset). *(2) Daughter's perception of the importance of good grades* (6 items, alpha = .81) was measured in the same manner as the mother's. The daughter rated the importance of getting good grades in the three academic domains (1 = not at all important, 5 = very important). She also indicated how upset she would be if she received low grades in these domains (1 = not at all upset, 5 = very upset). *(3) Mother's perception of the utility of education* (3 items, alpha = .74) was assessed by asking the mother to indicate how true the following statement is for mathematics, science, and language arts: "Knowing (academic domain) will help my child find a good job as an adult" (1 = not at all true, 5 = very true). *(4) Daughter's perception of the utility of education* (9 items, .64) was assessed by asking the daughter how much she agreed that reading, writing, and mathematical skills would help her find a good job as an adult; that the skills taught in mathematics, science, and language arts would be useful for the type of work she wants to do as an adult; and that education leads to a better life and job (1 = strongly disagree, 6 = strongly agree). In addition, the daughter rated how useful to their jobs she thought adults found what they learned in mathematics, science, and language arts courses (1 = not useful at all, 4 = very useful).

*Work Socialization.* This variable is based on five items (alpha = .81), three of which asked the mother how often she talked to her daughter about the following issues: the education and training it takes to get into different types of jobs; the personal qualities (e.g., discipline, hard work, and skill) necessary to succeed in different kinds of occupations; and the importance of learning skills and good work habits while she is in school so that she can perform well in future jobs. The remaining two items asked the mother how often she told her daughter that she could be successful if she worked hard and that getting a good education is more important than ever because there are fewer high-paying factory jobs (1 = never, 5 very often).

## Results

Before presenting the findings from the tests of the multiple regression models predicting adolescent females' expectancies, we examine the bi-variate relations among all of the variables used in our analyses. This examination seems appropriate because so little empirical study has been devoted to the linkages among these variables in African American adolescent females and their mothers.

## Descriptive Analyses

The means, standard deviations, and correlations among variables are shown in table 20.1. Mothers and daughters reported very strong valuation of good grades and believed the economic or occupational utility of education to be very high. In addition, mothers reported talking very frequently with their daughters about job requirements and other work-related issues. However, means for the remaining variables indicate low to moderate levels of the characteristics named. For example, on average, both mothers and daughters reported experiencing moderate levels of financial strain, perceived the daughter to have average academic ability, and forecast a moderate likelihood that the daughter, as an adult, would experience various negative economic events and conditions (e.g., difficulty finding a good job or having to go on welfare).

*Economic Resources, Ability Perceptions, and Expectancies.* Among both mothers and daughters, perceptions of financial strain are related to expectations of economic hardship. Mothers who perceived more family financial strain expected their daughters to experience more economic hardship as adults. A parallel, but only marginally significant relation, was found among daughters. Per capita income and mothers' education are related to neither mothers' nor daughters' expectations of economic hardship. Turning to the second expectancy variable, daughters' expectations about their family life courses are unrelated to mothers' and daughters' perceptions of financial strain, per capita income, and mothers' education.

Per capita income and mothers' education, but not mothers' perceived financial strain, are significantly and positively related to mothers' perceptions of their daughters' ability. Although mothers' perceptions of their daughters' ability are highly correlated with daughters' self-perceptions of ability, mothers' expectation of economic hardship for daughters is unrelated to daughters' own expectations of economic hardship. For both mothers and daughters, the higher the daughters' perceived ability, the lower the expectancy of economic hardship. It is also interesting that mothers' perception of their daughters' ability is negatively related to daughters' expectations of hardship and that, likewise, daughters' self-perception of ability is negatively related to mothers' expectation of economic hardship for their daughters. Also noteworthy is that daughters

TABLE 20.1
Means, Standard Deviations, and Correlations of All Variables

| Variables | Mean (SD) | 1 | 2 | 3 | 4 | 5 | 6 | 7 | 8 | 9 | 10 | 11 | 12 | 13 |
|---|---|---|---|---|---|---|---|---|---|---|---|---|---|---|
| **Mother** | | | | | | | | | | | | | | |
| 1. Perceived financial strain | 2.34 (.79) | — | | | | | | | | | | | | |
| 2. Perceptions of daughter's ability | 2.63 (.71) | .16 | — | | | | | | | | | | | |
| 3. Perceived utility of education | 4.18 (.60) | .18 | .27$^d$ | — | | | | | | | | | | |
| 4. Perceived importance of good grades | .00$^a$ (.67) | .14 | −.12 | .39$^e$ | — | | | | | | | | | |
| 5. Work socialization | 4.51 (.48) | .05 | .16$^b$ | .34$^c$ | .08 | — | | | | | | | | |
| 6. Expectations of daughter's hardship | 2.45 (1.09) | .29$^d$ | −.26$^d$ | .12 | .13 | .17$^b$ | — | | | | | | | |
| **Daughter** | | | | | | | | | | | | | | |
| 7. Perceived financial strain | 2.26 (1.07) | .11 | .13 | −.02 | −.15 | −.03 | .14 | — | | | | | | |
| 8. Perceptions of ability | 2.88 (.65) | −.07 | .35$^e$ | .18 | .15 | −.00 | −.21$^c$ | −.06 | — | | | | | |
| 9. Perceived utility of education | .00$^a$ (.51) | .11 | .19$^c$ | .15 | .17 | .00 | −.18$^c$ | −.08 | .27$^d$ | — | | | | |
| 10. Perceived importance of good grades | 4.26 (.58) | .15 | .26$^d$ | .20$^c$ | .20$^c$ | −.06 | .02 | −.09 | .45$^e$ | .55$^e$ | — | | | |
| 11. Expectations of hardship | 2.40 (.88) | −.12 | −.21$^c$ | −.01 | −.29$^d$ | −.03 | .13 | .18$^b$ | −.28$^d$ | −.23$^c$ | −.21$^c$ | — | | |
| 12. Expectations about family life course | 2.44 (1.08) | .07 | −.14 | −.05 | −.05 | .06 | .07 | .14 | −.12 | −.11 | −.13 | .42$^e$ | — | |
| **Demographic** | | | | | | | | | | | | | | |
| 13. Per capita income | $3,096 (2,556) | .03 | .24$^d$ | .15 | .05 | .11 | −.07 | −.07 | .04 | .03 | .06 | −.04 | −.11 | — |
| 14. Mother's years of schooling | 12 (1.77) | .12 | .24$^d$ | .11 | −.01 | .10 | .05 | .22$^c$ | −.06 | −.06 | −.05 | .01 | −.11 | .29$^d$ |

NOTE: The number of cases for each value differs because of missing data.
[a] Because items in these scales were measured on different metrics, the items were standardized before combining them.
[b] $p < .10$;
[c] $p < .05$;
[d] $p < .01$;
[e] $p < .001$

who valued good grades more highly had mothers who thought their daughters were less likely to experience economic hardship as adults.

Daughters who perceived themselves to have more academic ability believed more strongly in the importance of good grades and the economic or occupational utility of education. The latter two variables are significantly related to daughters' expectations of hardship but unrelated to daughters' expectations about their family life courses. In particular, those who held less strong beliefs about the economic or occupational utility of education and the importance of good grades had higher expectancies of economic hardship. Finally, as noted previously, daughters who expected more economic hardship also expected to experience more family life transitions associated with economic distress.

*Educational Values, Work Socialization, and Perceptions.* Mothers' perceptions of the utility of education and the importance they attached to their daughters getting good grades are significantly correlated. Furthermore, mothers who perceived education to be more useful had daughters who valued good grades more highly. Work socialization is marginally related to mothers' perceptions of their daughters' ability and mothers' expectations that their daughters will experience economic hardship as adults. The marginally significant, positive correlations indicate that the more academically capable mothers perceived their daughters to be, and the greater the economic hardship mothers expected their daughters to encounter as adults, the more mothers tended to discuss with their daughters the importance of education, training, and skills for the purpose of gaining access to and succeeding in various occupations.

The only significant correlate of work socialization is mothers' perceptions of the utility of education. Mothers who engaged in more work socialization believed more strongly that education would confer economic and employment benefits to their daughters. Work socialization is unrelated to perceived or actual economic resources, mothers' educational level, mothers' perceptions of the importance of their daughters' getting good grades, daughters' educational values, and daughters' expectancies.

### A Multivariate Model of Adolescent Females' Expectations of Economic Hardship

Using ordinary least squares regression, we fitted a model describing the multivariate relation of the twelve hypothesized predictors to adolescent daughters' expectations of economic hardship. Our checks for violation of the assumptions of the regression model did not reveal any serious departures from these requirements. This first regression analysis was followed up by another regression analysis, in which adolescents' grades were introduced as a control variable. This was done because adolescents' grades were correlated with several variables in the model, the most notable being mothers' perceptions of daughters' ability and daughters' self-perceptions of ability. We were unable to obtain grades for a sizable proportion of girls ($N = 30$), so there was a smaller sample for the second analysis. Because of the resulting loss of statistical power, the regression analysis that includes adolescents' grades is less reliable. Examination of the two regression analyses revealed a similar pattern of results. Therefore, results based on the first regression analysis are presented here. Because individuals' missing data on any of the variables in the regression analyses were deleted, the final sample consisted of 101 mother-daughter pairs.

The regression coefficients for the predictors are presented in table 20.2. Together, the predictors in our model account for 18% of the variability in daughters' expectations of hardship after adjusting for degrees of freedom. As predicted, daughters' perceptions of financial strain, as well as their self-perceptions of ability, predicted their expectations of hardship. Specifically, daughters who perceived their families to be experiencing greater difficulties in paying for basic necessities and daughters who perceived themselves to have less academic ability expected to experience significantly more economic hardships as adults. Also in keep-

TABLE 20.2

*Standardized Regression Coefficients Predicting Adolescent Females' Expectations of Economic Hardship*

*($N = 101$)*

| Predictors | Coefficient | Standard error |
|---|---|---|
| Demographic indicators | | |
|   Family per capita income | .03 | .09 |
|   Mother's years of schooling | −.04 | .06 |
| Subjective economic indicators | | |
|   Mother's perceived financial strain | −.08 | .34 |
|   Daughter's perceived financial strain | .18[b] | .08 |
| Mother's expectation of hardship for daughter | .07 | .09 |
| Perception of adolescent's academic ability | | |
|   Mother's | −.20[a] | .15 |
|   Daughter's | −.25[c] | .15 |
| Educational values | | |
|   Mother's perceived utility of education | .17 | .15 |
|   Mother's perceived importance of good grades | −.30[d] | .20 |
|   Daughter's perceived utility of education | −.10 | .20 |
|   Daughter's perceived importance of good grades | .05 | .18 |
| Mother's work socialization | −.04 | .18 |
| $R^2$ (adjusted) | .18[d] | |

[a]$p < .10$;
[b]$p < .06$;
[c]$p < .02$;
[d]$p < .001$

ing with our predictions, mothers' valuation of good grades and mothers' perceptions of their daughters' academic ability predicted daughters' expectations, although the latter relation only approached statistical significance. Mothers who valued good grades more highly and perceived their daughters to have more academic ability had daughters who expected to experience less economic hardship during their adult lives.

Contrary to prediction, neither of the maternal indicators of economic well-being (perceptions of financial strain and maternal education) nor per capita income predicted daughters' expectations of economic hardship. Likewise, daughters' educational values, mothers' perceptions of the utility of education, mothers' expectations of economic hardship for daughters, and work socialization were not significant predictors of daughters' expectations of hardship, contrary to our hypotheses. Finally, our hypothesis that mothers' and daughters' perceptions of the utility value of education would be stronger predictors of daughters' expectations of economic hardship than mothers' and daughters' valuation of good grades, respectively, was not supported.

## A Multivariate Model of Adolescent Females' Expectations about Family Life Course

Similar statistical procedures were used to test our hypothesized model predicting adolescent females' expectations about their family life courses. As shown in table 20.3, the overall regression model only approached statistical significance and accounted for only 5% of the variability in daughters' family expectations. Two variables, daughters' perceptions of financial strain and mothers' education, significantly predicted daughters'

TABLE 20.3

*Standardized Regression Coefficients Predicting Adolescent Females' Expectations about Their Family Life Course*
$(N = 101)$

| Predictors | Coefficient | Standard error |
|---|---|---|
| Demographic indicators | | |
| Family per capita income | .01 | .11 |
| Mother's years of schooling | − .26[c] | .07 |
| Subjective economic indicators | | |
| Mother's perceived financial strain | .13 | .39 |
| Daughter's perceived financial strain | .21[b] | .10 |
| Perception of adolescent's academic ability | | |
| Mother's | − .07 | .16 |
| Daughter's | − .07 | .17 |
| Mother's work socialization | .08 | .21 |
| $R^2$ (adjusted) | .05[a] | |

[a] $p < .08$;
[b] $p < .05$;
[c] $p < .02$

expectations about their family life courses. Each of these relations was in the hypothesized direction. Specifically, adolescents who perceived their families to have more difficulty paying for basic necessities and adolescents whose mothers were less educated were more likely to anticipate that their family life courses would be marked by out-of-wedlock childbearing, marriage immediately after high school, and divorce.

## Discussion

For exploratory purposes we examined the bivariate relations among the variables used in our analyses. Nevertheless, our discussion focuses on findings yielded by the multiple regression analyses, as the latter analyses provide estimates of the unique variance explained by each of our predictor variables (i.e., economic distress, socialization factors, beliefs, and values) when controlling for all other predictor variables.

Previous studies of adults point to perceived financial strain as both a strong determinant of mental health and a robust mediator of the link between economic stress and mental health. For example, in Kessler, House, and Turner's sample (1987) of blue-collar workers, perception of insufficient money to cover basic bills each month and purchase adequate food, medical care, and clothing was the most potent mediator of the adverse effects of unemployment on psychological health. Likewise, financial strain was the strongest predictor of depression in Dressler's study (1985) of African American adults. The present study extends this research to a different stage of development (i.e., adolescence) and to new psychological constructs (i.e., expectancies). Adolescent females who perceived their families to have more difficulty paying for basic necessities were less sanguine about their futures. They projected themselves as more likely to experience economic hardship and its attendant family life circumstances, compared to adolescent females who perceived their families' economic situation more positively. These findings suggest that these adolescents' expectancies about their futures as adults are shaped by their appraisal of their current economic well-being within the family context. In this sense the adolescents in our study might be described as more realists than idealists.

Moreover, the significant correlation between the two dependent variables (i.e., the higher the expectations of hardship, the higher the expectations for future family transitions associated with hardship) suggests that these adolescent females in some way appreciated the connection between out-of-wedlock births, early marriage, and divorce and the economic well-being of women and their children. Whether and in what ways comprehension of the linkage between family life course and economic circumstances influences the future behavior and choices of these adolescent females are important questions deserving empirical study. Research also is needed to determine the short- and longer-term consequences of each of these expectancies in their own right. We believe that these expectancies may significantly influence adolescent girls' academic behavior, willingness to invest in occupational training and higher education, sexual behavior, and vulnerability to peer pressure, among other things. Tests of these hypothesized relations await future research.

Although adolescent females' expectations for economic hardship and family life course were positively related, the predictors of these variables were somewhat different. Both daughters' and mothers' perceptions of daughters' academic abilities predicted daughters' expectations about economic hardship, but neither predicted the daughters' expectations about their family life courses. Instead, mothers' level of schooling predicted daughters' life course expectancies, with daughters of more educated mothers expecting fewer family transitions associated with economic hardship. These findings may be indicative of a different process of expectancy formation for the domains of work and family life. More specifically, there are some conceptually compelling reasons to expect differential predictors of the two sets of future expectations. For example, as noted above, when both mothers and daughters rated the daughters' academic competence as high, daughters expected to encounter less economic difficulty during adulthood. This may reflect Americans' tendency to emphasize ability as an explanation for economic difficulties (e.g., Stevenson, Chen, and Lee 1993; Stevenson, Lee, and Stigler 1986) and the tendency of those living in conditions of economic hardship to blame themselves for their financial situation (e.g., Feather 1974; Leahy 1990). Perceptions of abilities may not relate to family life course expectations because folk theories about how academic competence affects marital and family transitions are less salient and prevalent in American society than theories about personal inadequacies as causes of poverty. The relation between mothers' level of schooling and daughters' family life course expectancies may represent mothers' implicit role modeling or explicit instruction about the importance of acquiring education before getting married or having children. That is, the single African American mothers in our study who had achieved a higher level of education may stress to their adolescent daughters both directly and indirectly the importance of delaying childbirth and marriage until they achieve their educational goals, regardless of their daughters' academic abilities.

Perceived financial strain, but not our "objective" measure of economic hardship (i.e., per capita income), predicted adolescent females' expectancies. The greater predictive power of subjective, compared to objective, indicators of economic hardship is in keeping with findings from a number of studies indicating that financial strain has greater explanatory power in analyses of psychological and family functioning than static indicators such as unemployment, job loss, income loss, or income (e.g., Elder, Conger, and Foster 1989; Lempers, Clark-Lempers, and Simons 1989). For example, in his investigation of how urban Anglo-Americans and African Americans coped with the high inflation and recession of the mid-1970s, Caplovitz (1979) found that the measure of subjective inflation crunch (i.e., respondents' perception of the degree of hardship caused by inflation) was even more strongly related to mental health than objective measures of inflation.

As important as it is to know that adolescent females' perceptions of their families' current economic circumstances are linked to their expectancies, it is equally important to understand the source of this perception. That is, what experiences inform adolescents' appraisal of their families' economic well-being, and how accurate are these appraisals? Unfortunately, our study casts no light on this issue and produced no evidence of the validity of adolescents' appraisal of the degree of economic hardship experienced by their families. Zero-order correlations indicated that adolescent females' perception of their families' economic well-being was related to neither per capita income nor mothers' perceived financial strain. In addition, its positive relation to mothers' education is counterintuitive and difficult to explain. One possible source of perceptions of familial economic hardship may be cutbacks or deprivations that directly affect individual patterns of consumption (e.g., clothing or recreation). The latter may be a more potent determinant of perceived financial strain than cutbacks that curtail the consumption of other family members or the family as a unit (e.g., utility use). The item about cutbacks included in our measure of maternal financial strain did not distinguish among these categories of cutbacks. This lack of differentiation may partly explain why neither mothers' nor daughters' reports of financial strain were related to per capita income, as well as why mothers' and daughters' reports of financial strain were unrelated.

The latter finding is only one of several that contribute to an overall picture of mother-daughter disparity, rather than congruence, in perception. For example, mothers' expectations of economic hardship for daughters was unrelated to daughters' own expectations of hardship. Research is needed to understand the source of these differences in mother vs. daughter perceptions, as well as the consequences of such differences for a range of outcomes including the quality of mother-daughter relations, daughters' achievement behavior, mothers' influence on daughters' academically related behaviors and choices, and the level of difficulty daughters experience in making the transition from school to work. We also need to determine whether the level of mother-daughter disparity in perception changes over time. Daughters' perceptions may become more similar to their mothers' as daughters approach adulthood, as a result of increased maternal influence, an increase in the number of adolescent experiences that validate the socialization messages that mothers impart, and greater cognitive maturity, among other factors. Alternatively, mothers' perceptions over time may shift closer to the perceptions of their adolescent daughters, although we believe that this is less likely because of the relative power of the maternal role.

The two areas of mother-daughter agreement in the present study were perceptions of daughters' ability and perceptions of the importance of good grades. Both of these perceptions may be shaped to a significant degree by daughters' grades, which constitute "objectified" information to which both mothers and daughters are privy. Convergence in the perceptions of mothers and daughters may be greater when such perceptions are based on discrete information available to both mothers and daughters. However, previous research has also shown that regardless of the availability of more objective measures of performance (e.g., grades), adolescents still base their perceptions of their academic abilities largely on the perceptions of significant others such as parents (e.g., Eccles Parsons, Adler, and Kaczala 1982) and teachers (e.g., Eccles Parsons, Kaczala, and Meece 1982). In the present study the potency of mothers' perceptions of their daughters' abilities is illustrated by the finding that when daughters' self-perceptions of abilities are controlled, mothers' perceptions still have an effect on daughters' expectancies of economic hardship. This finding may indicate that mothers who perceive their daughters as lacking academic skills are dampening their daughters' expectations of economic success, regardless of the daughters' own self-perceptions of abilities. Future research is needed to examine both parental and other influences (i.e., teachers, friends, etc.) on the perceptions of abilities of African American female students.

Contrary to our predictions, the strongest predictor of adolescent females' economic hardship expectations was mothers' endorsement of the importance of getting good grades. Mothers whose belief in the importance of getting good grades was less strong tended to have daughters who expected more economic hardship in their futures. This could reflect the mothers' influence on their daughters' feelings of control over their future economic prospects through educational achievement (i.e., getting good grades). That is, as a result of the mothers' strong emphasis on getting good grades, daughters may be more optimistic about attaining economic security. This is consistent with the strong press toward upward mobility through education espoused by African Americans, as reported in several studies (e.g., Dill 1980; Stevenson, Chen, and Uttal 1990). However, it is unclear why daughters' own educational values (both utility of education and perceived importance of getting good grades) and mothers' perceptions of the utility of education were unrelated to daughters' expectations of hardship. One explanation could be the lack of variation on these measures, which may derive in part from our failure to control for social desirability (i.e., most mothers and daughters rated these values very high). Another possibility is that the educational values that distinguish between those adolescent females who expect to do well economically and those who do not are more subtle than the ones tapped in our study.

Mothers in the present study reported very frequent transmission of information to their daughters about the prerequisites of occupational success; this suggests that these mothers were acutely aware of the need to prepare their daughters for the role of worker and economic provider. Furthermore, significant bivariate correlations indicated that mothers who engaged in more work socialization believed more strongly in the usefulness of education and had daughters who valued good grades more highly. However, maternal work socialization did not predict adolescent expectancies. The mean for the work socialization variable was 4.51 on a 5-point scale, with a standard deviation of .48, suggesting that our failure to find the hypothesized relations may be due to ceiling effects in work socialization as assessed in the present study. Notwithstanding our null findings, we believe that there are individual differences in the extent to which the population of mothers from which our sample was drawn socialize their daughters about work-related issues, as well as individual differences in the nature of that socialization. As is the case with educational values, advances in our understanding of these issues will require development of more sensitive and multidimensional measures of work socialization.

A notable limitation of the present study is its lack of attention to extrafamilial but proximal factors that influence the economic and life course expectations of African American adolescent females. Children's interactions with members of the extended family, peers, teachers, neighborhood characteristics (e.g., socioeconomic status, rate of adolescent childbearing and welfare use), and human interactional patterns within the spatial domains of neighborhoods are obvious areas for investigation in future efforts to understand the bases on which African American adolescent females forecast their economic well-being and family life courses. In addition, understanding the unique nature of the normative development of expectations among economically disadvantaged African

American adolescent females will likely be informed by comparisons of these processes to those found among their more affluent female counterparts and among African American males and adolescents from other ethnic groups experiencing economic hardship.

## NOTE

1. All items were collapsed across the academic domains of math, science, and language arts. Although there is evidence to suggest that expectancies and values may differ by domain, the moderate to high intercorrelation among items justified our decision to combine these items.

## REFERENCES

This research was supported by grant R01MH44662 from the National Institute of Mental Health and a Faculty Scholar Award in Child Mental Health from the William T. Grant Foundation, both awarded to Vonnie C. McLoyd. Appreciation is expressed to the families who participated in the study and to Steve Nikoloff, director of research and testing, Flint Community Schools, Flint, Michigan; Alice Hart; Jane Zehnder-Merrill; and the research staff at Project for Urban and Regional Affairs, University of Michigan, Flint, for their invaluable assistance and cooperation in recruiting and interviewing families. We also acknowledge with much gratitude Eve Trager, Lisa Duncan, and Heidi Schweingruber for their competent preparation and processing of the interview schedules and Kathryn Clabuesch, Robin Soler, Sudakshina Raar, and Katherine Weber for their assistance in data coding.

Baly, I. 1989. Career and vocational development of black youth. In *Black adolescents,* edited by R. Jones, 247–65. Berkeley, Calif.: Cobb and Henry.

Caplovitz, D. 1979. *Making ends meet: How families cope with inflation and recession.* Beverly Hills, Calif.: Sage.

Coleman, J. S., E. Q. Campbell, C. J. Hobson, J. McPartland, A. M. Mood, F. D. Weinfeld, and R. L. York, eds. 1966. *Equality of educational opportunity.* Washington, D.C.: U.S. Government Printing Office.

Collins, P. H. 1987. The meaning of motherhood in black culture and black mother/daughter relationships. *Sage* 4:3–10.

Dill, B. T. 1980. "The means to put my children through": Child-rearing goals and strategies among black female domestic servants. In *The black woman,* edited by L. Rodgers-Rose, 107–23. Beverly Hills, Calif.: Sage.

Dressler, W. 1985. Extended family relationships, social support, and mental health in a southern black community. *Journal of Health and Social Behavior* 26:39–48.

Dweck, C. S. 1978. Achievement. In *Social and personality development,* edited by M. Lamb, 114–30. New York: Holt, Rinehart and Winston.

Eccles, J. S. 1984. Sex differences in achievement patterns: A test of alternate theories. *Journal of Personality and Social Psychology* 46:26–43.

Eccles Parsons, J. S., T. F. Adler, R. Futterman, S. B. Goff, C. Kaczala, J. L. Meece, and C. Midgley. 1983. Expectancies, values, and academic behaviors. In *Achievement and achievement motives,* edited by J. T. Spence, 75–146. San Francisco: Freeman.

Eccles Parsons, J. S., T. F. Adler, and C. Kaczala. 1982. Socialization of achievement attitudes and beliefs: Parental influences. *Child Development* 53:310–21.

Eccles Parsons, J. S., C. Kaczala, and J. Meece. 1982. Socialization of achievement attitudes and beliefs: Teacher influences. *Child Development* 53:322–39.

Elder, G., R. Conger, and E. Foster. 1989. *Families under economic pressure.* Manuscript. University of North Carolina.

Ellwood, D. T. 1988. *Poor support: Poverty in the American family.* New York: Basic Books.

Feather, N. 1974. Explanations of poverty in Australian and American samples. *Australian Journal of Psychology* 26:199–216.

Flanagan, C. 1990. Families and schools in hard times. In *New directions for child development. Economic stress: Effects on family life and child development,* edited by V. C. McLoyd and C. Flanagan, 7–26. San Francisco: Jossey-Bass.

Galambos, N., and R. Silbereisen. 1987. Income change, parental life outlook, and adolescent expectations for job success. *Journal of Marriage and the Family* 49:141–49.

Garfinkel, I., and S. McLanahan. 1986. *Single mothers and their children: A new American dilemma.* Washington, D.C.: Urban Institute.

Geschwender, J. A., and R. Carroll-Seguin. 1990. Exploding the myth of African-American progress. *Signs* 15:285–99.

Glasgow, D. G. 1980. *The black underclass: Poverty, unemployment, and entrapment of ghetto youth.* New York: Vintage Books.

Graham, S. 1992. "Most of the subjects were white and middle class": Trends in published research on African Americans in selected APA journals, 1970–1989. *American Psychologist* 47:629–39.

Granrose, C. S., and E. A. Cunningham. 1988. Post partum work intentions among black and white college women. *Career Development Quarterly* 37:149–64.

Greene, B. 1990. Sturdy bridges: The role of African-American mothers in the socialization of African-American children. *Women and Therapy* 10:205–25.

Grier, W. M., and P. Cobbs. 1968. *Black rage.* New York: Bantam.

Huston, A., V. C. McLoyd, and C. Garcia Coll. 1994. Children and poverty: Issues in contemporary research. *Child Development* 65:275–82.

James, S. D. 1985. *The impact of cybernation technology on black automobile workers in the U.S.* Ann Arbor: UMI Research Press.

Kessler, R., J. House, and J. Turner. 1987. Unemployment and health in a community sample. *Journal of Health and Social Behavior* 28:51–59.

Ladner, J. 1971. *Tomorrow's tomorrow: The black woman.* Garden City, N.Y.: Doubleday.

Larson, J. 1984. The effect of husband's unemployment on marital and family relations in blue-collar families. *Family Relations* 33:503–11.

Leahy, R. L. 1990. The development of concepts of economic and social inequality. In *New directions for child development. Economic stress: Effects on family life and child development,* edited V. C. McLoyd and C. Flanagan, 107–20. San Francisco: Jossey-Bass.

Lempers, J., D. Clark-Lempers, and R. Simons. 1989. Economic hardship, parenting, and distress in adolescence. *Child Development* 60:25–49.

Macke, A. S., and W. R. Morgan. 1978. Maternal employment, race, and work orientation of high school girls. *Social Forces* 57:187–204.

McLoyd, V. C. 1993. Employment among African American mothers in dual-earner families: Antecedents and consequences for family life and child development. In *The employed mother and the family context,* edited by J. Frankel, 180–226. New York: Springer.

McLoyd, V. C., T. E. Jayaratne, R. Ceballo, and J. Borquez. 1994. Unemployment and work interruption among African American single mothers: Effects on parenting and adolescent socioemotional functioning. *Child Development* 65:562–89.

Nasar, S. 1992. Those born wealthy or poor usually stay so, studies say. *New York Times,* May 18, 1, C7.

Parnes, H. 1970. Knowledge of the world of work. In *Career thresholds: A longitudinal study of the educational and labor market experience of male youth,* Vol. 1, edited by H.

Parnes and R. Muljus, 119–38. Washington, D.C.: U.S. Department of Labor Manpower Administration.

Rubin, L. B. 1976. *Worlds of pain: Life in the working-class family*. New York: Basic Books.

Scanzoni, J. 1971. *The black family in modern society*. Boston: Allyn and Bacon.

———. 1985. Black parental values and expectations of children's occupational and educational success: Theoretical implications. In *Black children: Social, educational, and parental environments,* edited by H. P. McAdoo and J. L. McAdoo. Beverly Hills, Calif.: Sage.

Seginer, R. 1983. Parents' educational expectations and children's academic achievements: A literature review. *Merrill-Palmer Quarterly* 29:1–23.

Sewell, W. H., A. O. Haller, and G. W. Ohlendorf. 1970. The educational and early occupational status attainment process: Replication and revision. *American Sociological Review* 35:1014–27.

Sewell, W. H., A. O. Haller, and A. Portes. 1969. The educational and early occupational attainment process. *American Sociological Review* 34:82–92.

Simms, M. 1987. How loss of manufacturing jobs is affecting blacks. *Focus* 15:6–7.

Solon, G. 1992. Intergenerational income mobility in the United States. *American Economic Review* 82:393–408.

Stevenson, H. W., C. Chen, and S. Lee. 1993. Mathematics achievement of Chinese, Japanese, and American children: Ten years later. *Science* 259:53–58.

Stevenson, H. W., C. Chen, and D. Uttal. 1990. Beliefs and achievement: A study of Black, White, and Hispanic children. *Child Development* 61:508–23.

Stevenson, H. W., S. Lee, and J. Stigler. 1986. Mathematics achievement of Chinese, Japanese, and American children. *Science* 231:693–99.

Tatum, B. D. 1987. *Assimilation blues: Black families in a white community*. Northampton, Mass.: Hazel-Maxwell .

Taylor, R. D., R. Casten, S. M. Flickinger, D. Roberts, and C. D. Fulmore. 1994. Explaining the school performance of African-American adolescents. *Journal of Research on Adolescence* 4:21–44.

U.S. Bureau of the Census. 1991. The black population in the United States: March 1990 and 1989. *Current population reports,* Series P-20, No. 448. Washington, D.C.: U.S. Government Printing Office.

U.S. Bureau of the Census. 1992a. The black population in the United States: March 1991. *Current population reports.* Series P20, no. 464. Washington, D.C.: U.S. Government Printing Office.

———. 1992b. *Statistical abstract of the United States: 1992*. Washington, D.C.: U.S. Government Printing Office.

William T. Grant Foundation Commission on Work, Family, and Citizenship. 1988. *The forgotten half: Pathways to success for America's youth and young families*. Washington, D.C.: Author.

Wilson, W. J. 1987. *The truly disadvantaged: The inner city, the underclass, and public policy*. Chicago: University of Chicago Press.

# 21 Career Development of Hispanic Adolescent Girls

## Brunilda De León

Mayra is a ten-year-old Puerto Rican girl who lives with her paternal grandmother in a poor neighborhood in a midsize inner city in the Northeast. Mayra's parents were adolescents when she was born and never married. Soon after her birth she came to live with her father and her grandmother, and her grandmother was granted legal custody. Both parents left high school before graduation. Her father obtained his high school diploma while working part time and living with his mother and Mayra. Her mother has had only a couple of part-time jobs and is currently unemployed and living with relatives. Mayra's father is now married and lives nearby with his wife and her eleven-year-old daughter. After holding various low-paying jobs and being unemployed several times, Mayra's father now works as a handyman repairing small electric appliances, painting houses, cleaning rugs, and doing carpentry and home improvements. Mayra's parents visit her and her grandmother frequently and provide financial support. Mayra and her grandmother attend their neighborhood's Catholic church one night every week and on Sundays.

Mayra is a regular fifth grader in a school of approximately five hundred students. Almost all her fellow students come from low-income families. Mayra prefers to communicate in English, but she also speaks Spanish frequently. Both English and Spanish are used in her classroom. At home she speaks mostly Spanish. The school is racially and culturally diverse, with approximately 40% Hispanics (mostly Puerto Ricans), 35% African Americans, and 25% Whites. The principal, a Puerto Rican woman, is highly respected by teachers, parents, administrators, and members of the larger community. In this school the students' cultures and the Spanish language are integrated into school activities and are part of the learning experiences of these youngsters.

Mayra's teachers and other school personnel describe her as a bright, talented, friendly, and outgoing student with leadership skills who is admired by her peers. She is a member of the school council and writes for the school newsletter. Mayra enjoys interviewing teachers, administrators, and members of the community for her work on the newsletter. She enjoys reading, writing, math, science, and especially history. She is learning how to play the piano and enjoys acting and singing. Her favorite hobbies are reading and playing the piano.

When I asked Mayra about her educational and career aspirations, she said that she wanted to be either a teacher, a veterinarian, or a news reporter.

*What would you like to be when you grow up?*

I would like to be a teacher . . . because I like being around children, and I would like to teach them. At my house, I play a lot about teacher, and so my friend, my next door neighbor, she gives me compliments, she says that I would be a great teacher. I like being around kids, I love seeing them learn and having fun. My teacher sometimes take me up to the board (If I did my homework). I would write down what I did and I would show the class what I did on the board.

*What do you think you have to do to become a teacher?*

To be a teacher I would have to go to college for about four years, and work hard and never give up. It is important to be smart, never give up, just try to accomplish your dream any way possible. Try to do your best in school.

*What would stop you from getting there (becoming a teacher)?*

What would stop me? If I see another career I like better, because I have a lot of things I want to be, but mostly I want to be a teacher. Sometimes I think I rather be a veterinary . . . because I love animals and I like taking care of them. Then, I also think about being a piano player because I love playing the piano. But maybe I just be either a teacher or a veterinary and also play the piano and if I am good at it, I can record one or two CDs and give the money to homeless children. Also if I start failing in my classes, that would stop me. If I start getting lazy; if I drop out of school before I reach college.

*Where do you get information about different kinds of jobs, careers, and occupations?*

I get lots of information from my family. Like my uncle, he's a bus driver, and so, once, I wanted to be a bus driver like him. But then I said uh uh . . . , then my aunt—she's a nurse, then I wanted to be a nurse, but then I said uh uh, because taking out blood . . . I don't think so. I also get a lot of information in school, especially from the teachers, because for our radio show, well, I had to interview them, it's called "School Super Stars." And from my father because he owns his own company, and sometimes he takes me with him to his work, and I help him. He goes to houses and buildings to repair things and uses several different machines and I have learned a lot about repairing house, cleaning rugs and cleaning. And I'm still thinking about that, about my father, because he says that when I grow older, I'm going to start owning his job with my sister.

*Who is the person (or persons) you admire the most? Why?*

I admire my grandmother, my father, my mother, my cousin (she is 14), and my teachers because they care for me and they tell me that if I keep doing well in school, I can be anything I want to be when I grow up.

Mayra is one of the many Hispanic girls who, regardless of the many obstacles and barriers in their social environment, is highly motivated, optimistic, and hopeful about the future. As far as she knows, she is doing all that is expected of her in order to be successful in school, complete her education, and be able to choose a good career. She hopes that her hard work will someday pay off. According to her teacher, she is getting a lot of support from her family, the school, and other members of her extended family and her community. What she probably does not know is that the challenge is greater than she anticipates; there are many other factors that will be a constant threat to her success and life goals.

To understand the complexity of the career development of Mayra and other Hispanic adolescent girls living in inner cities, we must examine the sociocultural, educational, and environmental realities of their lives. The demographics of Hispanics in general, and especially of Hispanic women in the United States provide a clear picture of the conditions that continue to place Latina inner-city adolescents at risk for poor career outcomes. There is an urgent need to develop alternatives to address the educational, vocational, and psychological needs of inner-city Hispanic adolescent girls. The following sections present the demographic profile of Latinos in the United States, with an emphasis on Latina women and adolescents. This is followed by a brief overview of the most prominent theories and salient issues on career development as they apply to women in general, Hispanic females, and particularly to inner-city Hispanic girls. Some guidelines and recommendations for future research, interventions, and career program development are provided.

## Hispanics in the United States

According to the 1990 U.S. Census (U.S. Bureau of the Census 1990), the total Hispanic population in the United States is over twenty-two million, constituting approximately 36% of the U.S. minority population. This Hispanic population encompasses Mexicans (62.6%), Puerto Ricans (11.6%), Cubans (5.3%), and individuals from Central and South America and other countries (20.5%), including, among others, the

Dominican Republic, El Salvador, and Guatemala (Amaro and Russo 1987). Hispanics are the nation's fastest growing and second largest minority population, growing about five times faster than the total population (Banks 1991; National Council of La Raza 1992). An increase of approximately 53% occurred between 1980 and 1990 (National Council of La Raza 1992). Hispanics will become the largest ethnic minority group in the United States around the turn of the century (U.S Bureau of the Census 1990). This rapid growth is primarily due to high birth rates and to immigration patterns among Hispanics (Banks 1991; National Council of La Raza 1992). Population statistics show that Puerto Ricans (97.0%) and Mexican Americans (90.6%) are more likely to live in urban areas than are Anglos (74.6%) (U.S. Bureau of the Census 1990). Therefore, issues of inner cities are more likely to affect Hispanics than Anglos.

Hispanics have a long history of lower educational attainment and greater numbers living below the poverty level than black Americans and Anglos. According to the 1990 U. S. Census, only 51.3% of all Hispanics twenty-five years old or over have four years of high school or more, compared to 80.5% of non-Hispanics. The lowest percentages are among Mexican Americans (43.6%) and Puerto Ricans (58.0%), followed by Cubans (61.0%), Central and South Americans (60.4%), and other Hispanics (71.1%).

Despite their strong commitment to the labor force, as shown by some improvement in their active job-seeking behaviors, employment rate, and household income during 1990 (National Council of La Raza 1992), Hispanics continue to have significantly lower family incomes and higher unemployment rates than non-Hispanics. Because of their concentration in lower-income jobs, higher labor force participation rates of Hispanics do not improve their socioeconomic situation. In 1990 the average income for Hispanic families was only $23,431, compared to $36,915 for the total population. Puerto Rican ($18,932) and Mexican-American ($21,025) families have the lowest incomes among all Hispanic and non-Hispanic groups. Not surprisingly, an alarming percentage of Hispanic families (25.0%)—as well as Hispanic individuals (28.1%)—are living below the poverty level, compared with the general population (10.4%). Poverty rates are highest among Puerto Rican families (37.5%), compared with the rates for Mexican Americans (25.5%), Central and South Americans (22.2%), Cubans (13.8%) and non-Hispanics (9.5%).

## Hispanic Females in the United States

The circumstances of Hispanic females have been a concern to researchers, mental health professionals, and policymakers (Amaro and

Russo 1987; Comas-Díaz 1987; National Council of La Raza 1992). For example, Hispanic women are younger (median age = 25.9) than women in the general U.S. population (median age = 32.5) (U.S. Bureau of the Census 1990). Mexican American (23.6) and Puerto Rican (26.8) women are the youngest groups in the whole population (U.S. Bureau of the Census 1990). The steadily growing number of female-headed families, the large number of adolescents who are mothers, and the poor socioeconomic conditions of many Latina women have been long recognized as problematic (Amaro 1993; Amaro and Russo 1987; Zambrana 1982). Hispanic females also are at risk because of poor housing conditions and health care and psychological problems (Amaro and Russo 1987; Centers for Disease Control 1993; Canino 1987; Comas-Díaz 1987; Espin 1987).

Nevertheless, Latinas have made some progress and have achieved some success in the educational, occupational, and sociopolitical spheres (Acosta-Belén 1986; Amott and Matthaei 1991; Baca Zinn 1980). For a long time Latinas have participated in the labor force, and despite the many barriers they confront, they have shown determination and motivation to succeed (Arbona 1990; Christensen 1979; Gándara 1980). Yet, in spite of these successes, impoverished living conditions shape everyday realities for the great majority. Even those Hispanic females who are employed, for example, continue to work at low-paying jobs (National Council of La Raza 1992; National Puerto Rican Coalition 1991). Their low income and limited occupational and career opportunities are to a great extent a result of their limited educational attainment. These conditions perpetuate the cycle of poverty and their disadvantaged position. Many researchers, including myself, argue against using issues of culture to explain the disadvantaged position of Hispanic females in the United States (Amott and Matthaei 1991; Arbona 1990; Baca Zinn 1982; Comas-Díaz 1987; Vázquez 1982; Young 1992). Instead, lack of support, limited recruitment and retention efforts in institutions of higher education, poor secondary education, and lack of information about and access to career awareness programs and incentives are some of the reasons for the limited educational and vocational opportunities of Latina women that need to be examined (Arbona 1990; Baca Zinn 1980; Vázquez 1982).

## Hispanic Girls in Inner Cities

Hispanic families living in inner-city areas are increasingly isolated, not only from participation in the economy but also from mainstream American society. Latina girls are likely to be exposed to deteriorating educational facilities, inadequate medical care, poor recreational facilities, and other problems associated with inner cities.

Many Latina girls lack academic skills, career-related experiences, and perceived career opportunities. Their only realistic chance of ending the cycle of poverty rests in systematically designed and adequately funded educational, career awareness, and training programs and access to resources in the community.

Unfortunately, governmental policies and local funding resources have limited their support for such programs. Poor inner-city Hispanic girls remain excluded from adequate educational opportunities, fair participation in the labor force, and other benefits available to mainstream American citizens. These girls see that the majority of their relatives and neighbors are unemployed. They lack adequate role models and individuals from the community (preferably from the same ethnic background and similar experiences) who could serve as advocates, supporters, and mentors (D'Andrea and Daniels 1992). This increases their risk of not having strong career or vocational aspirations and of having unrealistic and immature career plans. In addition, Hispanic families and girls living in inner cities have different levels of familiarity with and willingness to utilize community resources and social agencies. Their help-seeking and community participation behaviors and attitudes are frequently mediated by levels of adaptation to mainstream American society, acculturation, language usage (English language proficiency), place of residence, and other sociocultural and personality variables (Marín and VanOss-Marín 1991).

Few social scientists have examined the career development of inner-city Hispanic girls. The remainder of this chapter reviews the most prominent theories of career development, as well as the literature on gender differences in career development, career development of ethnic minorities, and cross-cultural counseling. I conclude with suggestions for improving the cultural sensitivity of career counseling for Hispanic girls.

## The Career Development Process

One of the major tasks of adolescence is choosing and preparing for a career. In our society the choice of a career helps to develop and reinforce an adolescent's self-concept (Super 1980). Indeed, vocational identity is an important part of overall identity for those who have chosen a vocation (Conger 1991; Erikson 1968; Marcia 1980). Having a job that society values enhances self-esteem and helps in the development of a strong sense of identity, self-confidence, and feelings of self-worth. Conversely, individuals who feel that their skills are not needed and that employment opportunities are not available to them experience poor self-esteem, self-doubt, and a negative self-image and identity.

Developmental theories of career choice explain how the career-related attitudes and behaviors of young people emerge and how young people make decisions about their future careers. The developmental theories that grew out of the early work of Eli Ginzberg (1972) and Donald Super (1980, 1990) have exerted the most influence upon the ongoing discourse in career development, with the social system or situational theories gaining favor in recent years. Super and Ginzberg both focus on individuals and propose multistage theories of development. Ginzberg emphasizes the four stages of career development: fantasy, tentative choice, exploration, and crystallization. Super's research was innovative in several respects. He was among the first to point out that career development extends throughout the life span, rather than ending during young adulthood. Second, he linked career choice and self-concept. According to Super, an individual's self-concept is critical to the stages of career development and the ability to make mature career choices. Third, he emphasized that the process of change may be summed up in a series of life stages characterized by growth, exploration, establishment, maintenance, and decline.

In his recent work Super (1990) emphasizes procedures that permit the inclusion of interventions for ethnic minorities and women. He also acknowledges the influences of socioeconomic status. Super makes the suggestion that preparation for career development should begin in elementary school. During the elementary school years the emphasis should be upon cognitive awareness, that is, information. Exploration takes place during middle or junior high school and leads to "preparation" for career development beginning with the tenth grade.

Osipow (1983) advanced the view that the occupational and career development of young people are not only related to personality characteristics, but are directly affected by opportunities available in their environment. He also emphasized the effects of social class, race, ethnicity, gender, parents' occupation, marital status, income, and so forth, on career choice. Osipow's work is a useful balance to the individually oriented approaches taken by Ginzberg and Super. Together these researchers address the range of issues that must be accounted for in an adequate explanation of the career development process.

## Career Development of Women

For many years career development theories ignored or gave very little attention to the career choices of women. This indifference was partly a result of the devaluation of women's participation in the economy. By the end of the sixties, however, sociologists, in particular, became interested in the study of how employment opportunities were affected by gender. Many career experts also questioned the appropriateness of available theories to an understanding of the career choice of women (Brooks 1990; Farmer 1985; Fitzgerald and Crites 1980; Hackett and Betz 1981; Jenkins 1989; Krumboltz 1976).

Women's perceptions of appropriate female behaviors and their attitudes toward their own careers are important in shaping their career choices (Hawley 1971; Tyler 1964). Many researchers have argued that important elements in women's career development—for example, marriage, timing of children, and spouse's attitudes—need to be taken into account to explain the process of career development in females. In addition, theorists of women's career development are concerned with distinctions between women who combine marriage and income-producing work and those who engage in either homemaking or income-producing work as full-time activities (Osipow 1983).

Several studies have found that professional women do not surrender their vocational aspirations easily and, further, their career development involves more decision-making steps compared to that of men (Brooks 1990; Fitzgerald and Betz 1983; Hackett and Betz 1981; Osipow 1983; Zunker 1994). As a result several factors come into play. First, women's career development is a different constellation of historical, political, psychological, and cultural factors from men's. Second, women engage in many more social roles and responsibilities than men, including such roles as spouse, homemaker, primary parent, and career woman. Third, the sequence of career behaviors for women is more complex, because of their multiple role experiences, a different sequence of life roles, more interruptions in their educational and career development process, and other factors, such as gender discrimination and persistent sexual stereotypes. Lastly, women continue to increase their participation in the work force, and they are moving in large numbers into male-dominated areas and broadening the range of "acceptable" career options.

The literature on the career development of Hispanic females is practically nonexistent. Several researchers have cited the lack of research and theory in this area (Arbona 1990; Bingham and Ward 1994; Brooks 1990; Zunker 1994). From these reviews it is clear that the career development of Hispanics and other minorities is different from that of Anglos. The extent of these differences, however, is yet to be documented. Arbona (1990), for example, noted that the literature on Hispanics in general is characterized by a lack of theoretical foundations and by theoretical assumptions based on small samples of white middle-class males. Arbona found that the effects of race, ethnicity, and culture are rarely considered when examining individuals' career behaviors. Other researchers also have criticized the underlying assumptions and theoretical constructs of career development because of their irrelevance to racial and ethnic minorities, particularly individuals from lower socioeconomic backgrounds (Fouad 1993; Fouad and Keeley 1992; Smith 1983). Because of ethnic and cultural differences, the instruments and research on Anglos may not be appropriate. Career and vocational theories and counseling interventions are strongly influenced by the mainstream Anglo culture, which emphasizes a worldview that is different from that of many members of ethnic minority groups (Fouad 1993; Fouad and Keeley 1992).

Although most career experts recognize the importance of issues of race, ethnicity, and culture in the career behaviors of ethnic minorities, they emphasize the need to examine career theories and interventions from a sociocultural perspective that stresses the crucial role of structural influences on the career development and behaviors of ethnic minorities (Arbona 1990; Brooks 1990; Fouad 1993; Fouad and Keeley 1992; Hotchkiss and Borow 1990; Zunker 1994). For inner-city Hispanic female adolescents in particular, variables such as socioeconomic background; academic achievement; prevocational experiences; influence of parents, peers, and role models; and access to community resources will have a significant impact on their educational and career outcomes.

In terms of strategies for change, contemporary career theorists, educators, and counselors emphasize the need to (1) provide female role models for adolescent girls and for women in general; (2) provide support and mentoring activities to girls and adult women in order to increase their participation in educational and career awareness programs; (3) design programs and activities that will increase young women's awareness about the social structural barriers that limit their educational and career development and participation in society; (4) use models of intervention that enhance girls' sense of self-confidence, assertiveness, and achievement motivation; (5) help girls to acquire information about careers, improve their perceptions about their possibilities, and expand their range of career aspirations and options; and (6) help girls to develop effective ways to identify personal and external barriers to their educational attainment and career aspirations. In addition, because socialization into educational and vocational options begins early in life, interventions to help girls in their career development process should be implemented during the elementary school years.

### The Role of Socialization in the Career Development of Girls

Socialization refers to the processes through which children learn the behaviors, attitudes, and skills that will make them competent to survive in society (Rivers, Barnett, and Baruch 1990). There is a lively and ongoing debate about the extent of the differences in socialization between boys and girls. Most researchers now agree that although there may be underlying biological predispositions for the acquisition of some sex-typed behaviors, the roles of learning, social interactions, and parental influence are far more important in developing sex role identification. The classic review of the literature by Maccoby and Jacklin (1974) marked the reemergence of the debate. Their surprising conclusion that most of the developmental differences between boys and girls were myths generated a considerable amount of controversy and research. Their finding that boys excelled at spatial abilities and that girls were superior in verbal abilities created a debate between the constructivists and the essentialists regarding the explanation of these differences. The essentialists argue that differences in developmental patterns are due to biological differences. The constructivists emphasize the influence of context and the processes by which social institutions shape development. The constructivist approach is exemplified in the work of Gilligan (1982) and Kegan (1982), who emphasize the active agent making meaning of the world. Included here is a recognition of the developmental changes in gender definition, construction of self-other relationships, and changes in the orientations of girls toward decision making, caring, and responsibility.

Children develop gender schemas to help them organize their experiences around the issues of gender (Bem 1987). According to Bem (1987), a gender schema is a network of associations embodying the culture's conception of sex roles, which children use to guide their own behavior and which structures children's perceptions of their environment.

In American society boys and girls are socialized in very different ways. Girls, for example, are socialized to pay great attention to personal relations and to develop such traits as sensitivity, empathy, warmth, and concern about others (Huston 1983; Rivers, Barnett, and Baruch 1990; Williams 1983). In addition, they are encouraged to overemphasize physical appearance, dating, popularity, intimacy, emotionality, and other behaviors and qualities usually associated with their roles as wife, mother, and caretaker (Chodorow 1978; Rivers, Barnett, and Baruch 1990; Weiler 1988; Williams 1983). In other words, they are socialized to be feminine.

Although the career options for girls have greatly expanded over the past two decades, girls are still commonly socialized into occupations that have been traditionally reserved for women. Rivers and associates (1990) summarized findings from research on girls' career choices: (1) girls tend to choose a more restricted, less varied range of occupations; (2) occupational choices are highly stereotyped at an early age; (3) regardless of social class or race, about one-half to two-thirds of girls aspire to be either teachers, nurses, or secretaries; (4) girls not only stay with their early choices, but they tend to avoid high-prestige occupations.

The way gender stereotypes are fostered through the media, school, texbooks, and other educational materials has been well documented (Nieto 1983; Rivers, Barnett, and Baruch 1990; Vázquez-Nuttall and Romero-García 1989; Weiler 1988). The result of these socialization processes is that many girls and women are encouraged to become competent in activities that center around the home and family. Boys, on the other hand, are trained toward activity and achievement. They are socialized to become successful in their education and career development. These are common themes in the literature and development of women, and they are also echoed in the literature on Hispanic culture and the socialization of Latina females.

Hispanic children also learn their culture's schemas of themselves as boys and girls. These schemas are organized around a set of values that are passed on from one generation to another. Child-rearing practices and the socialization of Latina girls are congruent with the cultural patterns and values found among Hispanic families. It is important to emphasize that Hispanic families are not homogeneous. There are substantial differences between Hispanic subgroups and between members within each subgroup. Therefore, it is a mistake to overgeneralize about cultural values and child-rearing practices. Child-rearing practices and the socialization of Latina girls are shaped by their parents' socioeconomic backgrounds, generational (first vs. second or third generation) status, migration status, levels of acculturation, and degree of endorsement of their traditional cultural heritage. These factors will influence the degree of endorsement and acceptance of Anglo-dominant culture. Because of the recognition that Hispanic families are very heterogeneous, and because of the lack of updated information about cultural values and child-rearing practices of Hispanics, we must be cautious in supporting stereotypes about Hispanic families and the educational and career development of Latina females. Instead, the reader is encouraged to consider Hispanic families in specific contexts and to take note of their degrees of maintenance of traditional cultural values.

Sotomayor (1989), for example, argues that there are three salient cultural values and traditions common to all the Hispanic subgroups: a preference for close nuclear and extended family ties, a commitment to a sense of community, and strong religious affiliations. Regardless of nationality, length of residence in the United States, ethnic background, social class, or religion, the family remains the most important institution in the Hispanic culture, and loyalty to family is emphasized (Amott and Matthaei 1991; Fitzpatrick 1987; Inclán and Herron 1989; Ramirez 1989;

Sotomayor 1989). Hispanic families are characterized by a tradition of a close-knit nuclear and extended family and larger social and family networks. The extended family includes not only close relatives but often distant relatives, friends such as godparents, friends from church, human service providers, teachers, and other members of the community. For most Hispanics the family is viewed as an interactive intergenerational system that encourages interdependence and mutual obligations and responsibilities. The Puerto Rican culture, in particular, is transmitted through the specific family relationships, valuing familism *(familismo)*, respect *(respeto)*, personalism *(personalismo)*, and dignity *(dignidad)* (Sotomayor 1989; Fitzpatrick 1987).

Traditional Hispanic families also tend to be more hierarchical, and the authority of the elderly, the parents, and males is recognized and accepted. Children are expected to be obedient to parents, grandparents, and other adults in their extended family. Similarly, they are encouraged to be obedient and respectful to teachers, other school staff, and church and community members. Child-rearing practices among more traditional Hispanic families also involve a tendency to endorse and encourage more clearly defined sex-role differentiations for boys and girls. These parents also tend to limit discussions of sexual topics with children, particularly with females, and to restrict sexual behaviors of adolescent females. Girls in these families are closely watched, protected, and monitored in their social relationships by brothers, parents, and other responsible adults. Very strict curfews for girls are common, and girls are not allowed to move freely about the community without trusted supervision. It is commonplace for these young girls to become involved in chores around the home (i.e., cooking and cleaning), rearing young siblings, caring for others, and other adult responsibilities. These strictures upon Latina girls continue through adolescence, and they are most prevalent among families that are less assimilated and who favor traditional values.

The values, attitudes, and socialization practices of Hispanic families living in the United States are influenced by many contextual variables, and there is evidence that the cultural values of this population are undergoing some important changes. Some of the more salient changes documented in the literature are related to family roles, marital decision making, and sex roles (Andrade 1982; Comas-Díaz 1987; De León 1993; Zambrana 1982; Amaro and Russo 1987). There is evidence that gender roles are more flexible and contemporary than previously documented (Andrade 1982; Amaro and Russo 1987; Amott and Matthaei 1991; Baca Zinn 1982; De León 1993). Hispanic scholars have also begun to challenge prevailing stereotypes that portray Hispanic females as passive, submissive, and underachievers and males as totally authoritarian, aggressive, and dominant (Andrade 1982; Arbona 1990; De León 1993; Vázquez-Nuttall, Romero-García, and De León 1987). As a result, a more positive and culturally sensitive description of the socialization process of Hispanic females is emerging (Andrade 1982; De León 1993; Vázquez-Nuttall, Romero-García, and De León 1987).

Several researchers have noted the many benefits and the importance of the nuclear and extended family for Hispanics (Amott and Matthaei 1991; Baca Zinn 1982; Fitzpatrick 1987; Sotomayor 1989). The family is a valued resource that provides its members with material resources, emotional support, and advice in times of crisis or major decision making. During the elementary school years these values are absorbed easily into the gender schemas of Latina girls. Given the importance of the family for Latina girls, it is understandable that the family is influential in decision making with regard to education, personal development, and career aspirations. These young women see themselves in relationship to their families, and these families are very willing to contribute their limited resources to helping them achieve their goals. Therefore, Latinas easily identify with and turn to their families for support and direction.

In addition, the Spanish language plays a crucial role in the transmission of cultural values, because it links one generation to another as well as the island experience to the United States. Even Hispanic children who speak primarily English receive advice and guidance in Spanish and learn to communicate with their grandparents, elders, and often their parents in Spanish. These youngsters are absorbing the culture and its values through the language, and simultaneously they are encouraged to maintain that experience.

It is essential for those who work with Latina girls and their parents to explore the similarities and differences between the girls and their parents with regard to the value and importance they place upon their cultural heritage and mainstream Anglo culture.

## Mayra Revisited: Hispanic Culture and Its Implications for Career Development

As part of an ongoing career awareness curriculum project, Mayra and her classmates were asked to write about what they wanted to be in fifteen years. There were thirteen girls in the class, and all of them saw themselves pursuing careers that require further training after high school. Several of the girls were interested in multiple careers. This is the time for fantasy and exploration of career possibilities. Seven of the girls in Mayra's class were interested in nontraditional careers, including pianist, karate teacher, doctor, police officer, business person, and news reporter. The more traditional career choices were teacher, secretary, social worker, hair dresser, and model.

What would be the elements in an effective career development program that would help these girls achieve their goals and dreams? Based on a review of the literature, information from interviews with Mayra and her classmates, and my work with Latina girls, the following guidelines are suggested. These guidelines build upon the cultural experiences of these young women and provide more adequate support for program intervention. It should be noted that language and acculturation are cultural aspects that sharply differentiate Latina girls and their families from the larger mainstream community.

1. *The Spanish language continues to be an important element of the Hispanic culture.* Hispanic girls and their families are very heterogeneous in terms of their preference for Spanish usage; nevertheless, it is the language that is the special marker of the community. Many inner-city Hispanic girls communicate best in Spanish. In addition, even when children are English proficient, many of their parents are not. Communication with the girls and their parents will be facilitated if individuals working with Latina girls provide staff, activities, and materials in both English and Spanish.

2. *Hispanics in the United States vary in terms of levels of acculturation.* Their degrees of acculturation to American values will influence Hispanic parents' attitudes toward teachers, schools, community resources, and human service agencies. Levels of acculturation also influence gender roles, child-rearing practices, and acceptance of external, extrafamily forces participating in the decision-making process and arrangements for after school, nonacademic, or social activities for children. Also, for many immigrant Hispanic families the process of adaptation to mainstream society is potentially stressful and brings conflicts between parents and adolescents who disagree about cultural practices (Inclán and Herron 1989; Ramirez 1989). Therefore, awareness of the level of acculturation, the adaptation process, and the parenting style should be taken into consideration when working with Latina girls. Strategies to facilitate parent participation and to inform parents about activities for their daughters should be included in programs for Latina girls.

3. *The family is a major source of support and pride for most Latina girls (familism).* The inclusion of family is a necessary element in programs of

career development. Familism has been found to be one of the most important values in Hispanic cultures. This cultural value involves a strong identification with and attachment to the nuclear and extended families, strong feelings of loyalty, and mutual respect, support, and solidarity among members of the same family (Marín and VanOss-Marín 1991). Therefore, encouraging parents to be part of their daughters' educational and career development not only shows respect for their culture but also facilitates the process. In addition, this strategy will strengthen communication between girls and their parents and between parents and school. It is important to engage the family because it is the family that often "gives permission" for Latina girls to disengage from the family and to begin the process of upward mobility. During the process of giving permission the family also provides support for these young women as they explore the world of work and new careers.

4. *Latino families value the extended family and large social networks.* Because of their strong emphasis on collectivism and familism, any efforts to improve a Latina girl's educational and career development should include members of the extended family—such as uncles, aunts, grandparents, godparents, and neighbors—and other individuals who are important to the girl and the family. The sense of community and social network in Latino families will also facilitate the inclusion of social and community resources, interested parties, and potential supporters from the community (e.g., private industries, colleges, local business people, government agencies). Furthermore, this approach will help many of these families who are isolated from traditional support systems. This sense of community will provide opportunities to build new relationships among parents and other community resources and individuals. Networks offer options to young people, increase awareness, provide information about community resources, and validate young girls' career dreams.

5. *Hispanic families tend to be very religious (traditionally, Catholic).* Although research data in this area is limited, the literature continues to support the idea that the church is a very important influence in the lives of Hispanic families. Thus, the church is a potential supporter of programs designed to help Latina girls. There is a trend in the religious faith of low-income Hispanic families living in inner cities in United States to affiliate with community-based churches regardless of their denomination. These churches are a center of communal activities that give new immigrants to the city a sense of belonging and can meet many of their needs.

*6. Orientation toward group work and collaboration.* One of the most important values of Hispanic cultures, and a necessary program element, is a sense of collectivism (Marín and VanOss-Marín 1991). Because of this value Hispanics tend to emphasize interdependence, mutual respect, cooperation, and willingness to sacrifice for the welfare of the group. They prefer interpersonal relationships and participation in groups that are nurturing, friendly, and based on mutual trust and cooperation. Latina girls are especially responsive to group activities and collaboration with each other, because cooperation rather than individualistic competition is the preferred style for problem-solving situations and learning environments. Group counseling and group activities should be utilized as much as possible when working with Hispanic girls and their parents.

*7. Hispanic girls are socialized to perform many different social roles.* In the literature, Hispanic parents are frequently charged with maintaining a double standard of socialization that fosters sex-typed or traditional gender roles. From a more positive perspective one can argue that from a very early age Latina girls are being trained to perform the multiple roles that increasing numbers of woman must now confront. For example, they are socialized to be organized, responsible, good students; to take care of younger siblings; and to be responsible for many duties at home, in school, and in the community (e.g., at church). Data from the literature on Hispanic women as well as this writer's experience working with Latina girls indicates that these girls are finding assertive and culturally appropriate ways of coping with and negotiating these role demands.

*8. The individual's success and accomplishments are perceived as success for the family and the group.* Thus, the success of a Hispanic girl will be the success of each family member and the community. Because Hispanic culture emphasizes a collective rather than an individualistic sense of identity and pride, any attempt to help Latina girls must include some way of formally recognizing the support of parents, relatives, and other members of the extended family or social network. Many Latina girls who complete their high school education and have a chance to attend college are among the very few or even the first family member to have an opportunity to become highly educated and career oriented. Therefore, ensuring the support of family members is crucial in sustaining the motivation of these young women and minimizing any potential conflict or stress that might result from "being the first one."

*9. Programs should bring together institutions to form a community of support, advice, and mentoring for Latina girls.* Community programs should be based on the assumptions that Latina girls can be successful, that they will be good students, and that they will develop the skills to have successful careers.

REFERENCES

Acosta-Belén, E., ed. 1986. *The Puerto Rican woman: Perspectives on culture, history, and society.* 2d ed. New York: Praeger.

Amaro, H. 1993, August. *Women don't get AIDS, they just die from it.* Paper presented at the American Psychological Association Convention, August, Toronto.

Amaro, H., and N. F. Russo. 1987. Hispanic women and mental health: An overview of contemporary issues in research and practice. *Psychology of Women Quarterly* 11:393–407.

Amott, T. L., and J. A. Matthaei. 1991. *Race, gender, and work: A multicultural economic history of women in the United States.* Boston: South End Press.

Andrade, S. J. 1982. Family roles of Hispanic women: Stereotypes, empirical findings, and implications for research. In *Work, family, and health: Latina women in transition,* edited by R. E. Zambrana, 95–106. New York: Hispanic Research Center.

Arbona, C. 1990. Career counseling research and Hispanics: A review of the literature. *Counseling Psychologist* 18(2):300–323.

Baca Zinn, M. 1980. Employment and education of Mexican-American women: The interplay of modernity and ethnicity in eight families. *Harvard Educational Review* 50:47–62.

———. 1982. Fatalism among Chicanos: A theoretical review. *Humboldt Journal of Social Relations* 10:228–43.

Banks, J. A. 1991. *Teaching strategies for ethnic studies.* 5th ed. Boston: Allyn and Bacon.

Bem, S. L. 1987. Gender schema theory and its implications for child development: Raising gender-aschematic children in a gender-schematic society. In *The psychology of women: Ongoing debates,* edited by R. M. Walsh, 226–45. New Haven: Yale University Press.

Bingham, R. P., and C. M. Ward. 1994. Career counseling with ethnic minority women. In *Career counseling for women,* edited by W. B. Walsh and S. H. Osipow, 165–95. Hillsdale, N.J.: Erlbaum.

Brooks, L. 1990. Recent developments in theory building. In *Career choice and development,* edited by D. Brown and L. Brooks. 2d ed. San Francisco: Jossey-Bass.

Canino, G. 1987. The Hispanic woman: Sociocultural influences on diagnoses and treatment. In *Mental health and Hispanic Americans,* edited by R. Becerra, M. Karno, and J. Escobar, 117–38. New York: Grune and Stratton.

Centers for Disease Control (CDC). 1993. U.S. cases reported through June 1993. HIV/AIDS Surveillance Report: Second quarter edition, 5 (2). National Center for Infectious Diseases, Division of HIV/AIDS. Atlanta, Georgia.

Chodorow, N. 1978. *The reproduction of mothering: Psychoanalysis and the sociology of gender.* Berkeley: University of California Press.

Christensen, E. W. 1979. The Puerto Rican woman: A profile. In *The Puerto Rican woman: Perspectives on culture, history, and society,* edited by E. Acosta-Belén. New York: Praeger.

Comas-Díaz, L. 1987. Feminist therapy with mainland Puerto Rican women. *Psychology of Women Quarterly* 11 (4):461–74.

Conger, J. J. 1991. *Adolescence and youth: Psychological development in a changing world.* 4th ed. Denver: HarperCollins.

D'Andrea, M., and J. Daniels. 1992. A career development program for inner city black youth. *Career Development Quarterly* 40:272–80.

De León, B. 1993. Sex role identity among college students: A cross-cultural analysis. *Hispanic Journal of Behavioral Sciences* 15 (4):476–89.

Erikson, E. H. 1968. *Identity: Youth and crisis.* New York: Norton.

Espín, O. M. 1987. Psychological impact of migration on Latinas: Implications for psychotherapeutic practice. *Psychology of Women Quarterly* 11:489–503.

Farmer, H. S. 1985. Model of career motivation for women and men. *Journal of Counseling Psychology* 32(3):363–90.

Fitzgerald, L., and N. Betz. 1983. Issues in the vocational psychology of women. In *Handbook of vocational psychology,* edited by B. Walsh and S. Osipow, vol. 1, 83–51. Hillsdale, N.J.: Lawrence Erlbaum.

Fitzgerald, L. F., and J. O. Crites. 1980. Toward a career psychology of women: What do we know? What do we need to know? *Journal of Counseling Psychology* 27:44–62.

Fitzpatrick, J. P. 1987. *Puerto Rican Americans: The meaning of migration to the mainland.* 2d ed. Englewood Cliffs, N.J.: Prentice-Hall.

Fouad, N. A. 1993. Cross-cultural vocational assessment. *Career Development Quarterly* 42:4–13.

Fouad, N. A., and T. J. Keeley. 1992. The relationship between attitudinal and behavioral aspects of career maturity. *Career Development Quarterly* 40:257–71.

Gándara, P. 1980. Passing through the eye of the needle: High achieving Chicanas. *Hispanic Journal of Behavioral Sciences* 4:176–79.

Gilligan, C. 1982. *In a different voice: Psychological theory and women's development.* Cambridge: Harvard University Press.

Ginzberg, E. 1972. Toward a theory of occupational choice: A restatement. *Vocational Guidance Quarterly* 20:169–76.

Hackett, G., and N. E. Betz. 1981. A self-efficacy approach to the career development of women. *Journal of Vocational Behavior* 18:326–39.

Hawley, P. 1971. What women think men think: Does it affect their career choice? *Journal of Counseling Psychology* 18:193–99.

Hotchkiss, L., and H. Borow. 1990. Sociological perspectives on work and career development. In *Career choice and development,* edited by D. Brown and L. Brooks. 2d ed. San Francisco: Jossey-Bass.

Huston, A. C. 1983. Sex-typing. In *Handbook of child psychology,* vol. 4, *Socialization, personality, and social development,* edited by P. H. Mussen. 4th ed. New York: John Wiley and Sons.

Inclán, J. E., and D. G. Herron. 1989. Puerto Rican adolescents. In *Children of color: Psychological interventions with minority youth,* edited by J. T Gibbs and L. N. Huang, 251–77. San Francisco: Jossey-Bass.

Jenkins, S. R. 1989. Longitudinal prediction of women's careers: Psychological, behavioral, and social-structural influences. *Journal of Vocational Behavior* 34:204–35.

Kegan, R. 1982. *The evolving self: Problems and process in human development.* Cambridge: Harvard University Press.

Krumboltz, J. 1976. A social learning theory of career selection. *Counseling Psychologist* 6(1):71–81.

Maccoby, E., and C. N. Jacklin. 1974. *The psychology of sex differences.* Stanford, Calif.: Stanford University Press.

Marcia, J. E. 1980. Identity in adolescence. In *Handbook of adolescent psychology,* edited by J. Adelson, 159–87. New York: Wiley.

Marín, G., and B. VanOss-Marín. 1991. *Research with Hispanic populations.* Applied Social Research Methods Series, Monograph no. 23. Newbury Park, Calif.: Sage Publications.

National Council of La Raza. 1992. *State of Hispanic America: An overview.* Report no. 141, ERIC Document Reproduction Service no. ED 344 967. Washington, D.C.: National Council of La Raza.

National Puerto Rican Coalition. 1991. *A blueprint for change: A Puerto Rican agenda for the 1990s.* Position paper no. 120. ERIC Document Reproduction Service no. ED 334 321. Washington, D.C.: National Puerto Rican Coalition.

Nieto, S. 1983. Children's literature on Puerto Rican themes. Parts 1, 2. *Interracial Books for Children Bulletin* 14(1–2):6–16.

Osipow, S. H. 1983. *Theories of career development.* New York: Appleton-Century-Crofts.

Ramirez, O. 1989. Mexican American children and adolescents. In *Children of color: Psychological interventions with minority youth,* edited by J. T. Gibbs and L. N. Huang, 224–50. San Francisco: Jossey-Bass.

Rivers, C., R. Barnett, and G. Baruch. 1990. *How women grow, learn, thrive.* New York: Ballantine Books.

Smith, E. J. 1983. Issues in racial minorities' career behavior. In *Handbook of vocational psychology,* edited by W. B. Walsh and S. Osipow, vol. 1, 161–222. Hillsdale, N.J.: Erlbaum.

Sotomayor, M. 1989. *The Hispanic elderly and the intergenerational family.* New York: Haworth Press.

Super, D. E. 1967. *The psychology of careers.* New York: Harper and Row.

———. 1980. A life-span life-space approach to career development. *Journal of Vocational Behavior* 16:282–98.

———. 1990. A life-span, life-space approach to career development. In *Career choice and development: Applying contemporary theories to practice,* edited by D. Brown and L. Brooks, 197–261. 2d ed. San Francisco: Jossey-Bass.

Tyler, L. E. 1964. The development of career interests of girls. *Genetic Psychology Monographs* 70:303–12.

U.S. Bureau of the Census. 1990. Current population survey. Washington, D.C.: U.S. Government Printing Office.

Vázquez, M. T. 1982. Confronting barriers to the participation of Mexican American women in higher education. *Hispanic Journal of Behavioral Sciences* 4:147–65.

Vázquez-Nuttall, E., and I. Romero-García. 1989. In *The psychological development of Puerto Rican women,* edited by C. T. García Coll and L. M. Mattei. New York: Praeger.

Vázquez-Nuttall, E., I. Romero-García, and B. De León. 1987. Sex roles and perceptions of femininity and masculinity of Hispanic women: A review of the literature. *Psychology of Women Quarterly* 11 (4):409–25.

Weiler, K. 1988. *Women teaching for change: Gender, class, and power.* New York: Bergin and Garvey.

Williams, J. H. 1983. *Psychology of women: Behavior in a biosocial context.* 2d ed. New York: W. W. Norton.

Young, G. 1992. Chicana college students on the Texas-Mexico border: Tradition and transformation. *Hispanic Journal of Behavioral Sciences* 14 (3):341–52.

Zambrana, R. E. 1982. Introduction to *Work, family, and health: Latina women in transition,* edited by R. E. Zambrana. New York: Hispanic Research Center.

Zunker, V. G., ed. 1994. *Career counseling applied concepts in life planning.* 4th ed. Pacific Grove, Calif.: Brooks/Cole.

# Index

# Index

# Index

# Index

# Index

# Index